1995517

The Peruvian Experiment

Written under the auspices of the
Center for Inter-American Relations.

A list of other Center publications
appears at the back of this book.

The Peruvian Experiment

Continuity and Change under Military Rule

edited by Abraham F. Lowenthal

Princeton University Press
Princeton, New Jersey

Copyright © 1975 by Princeton University Press
Published by Princeton University Press
Princeton and London

All Rights Reserved

Library of Congress Cataloging in Publication Data will
be found on the last printed page of this book

Publication of the paperback edition of this book has been
aided by a grant from the Center for Inter-American Relations

This book has been composed in Linotype Baskerville

Printed in the United States of America
by Princeton University Press, Princeton, New Jersey

Contents

List of Tables

List of Figures

Preface

This book is the first systematic and comprehensive treatment
published in any language of Peru's current process of military-
directed change, of Peru's "revolution." It draws on the individual and collective expertise of twelve social scientists, two of
them Peruvian nationals, all with recent and extensive field research in Peru. It aims to provide previously inaccessible data
about central aspects of contemporary Peru, particularly by
analyzing the evolution of changing public policies against their
national background. It seeks to discuss enough of the major issues of recent Peruvian history to permit an interim general assessment of the nature and significance of Peru's military regime,
the subject of considerable international attention but very little
social science analysis. And it is intended to contribute in several
more general ways: to the evaluation of shifting patterns of Latin
American politics; to the comparative analysis of military
regimes; to the study of the policy consequences of regime
changes; and to the general literature on social, economic, and
political development in the Third World.

The volume results from the multidisciplinary Seminar on
Continuity and Change in Contemporary Peru held at and sponsored by the Center for Inter-American Relations in New York
during the first half of 1973. Our seminar brought together for
sustained discussions a group of persons interested in and knowledgeable about Peru from a variety of professional, political, and
disciplinary perspectives: Peruvians and North Americans, economists, historians, sociologists, political scientists, anthropologists, businessmen, and journalists. We neither assumed nor
sought a consensus about the ultimate meaning and value of what
is happening in Peru. Several of us would differ sharply on the
context and criteria for such judgments, and we do not even
agree, as will be evident, on what to call Peru's current government. What we do have in common is an interest in exploring

some of the major ways in which Peru is said to be changing under the military regime and a desire to analyze the extents, limits, significance, and sources of these changes. And we agreed that we could probably advance our understanding most, not by broad-ranging discussions on the "Peruvian process" (though we did permit ourselves one full day of free-for-all discussion at our June session), but rather by focusing on a somewhat more specific set of topics.

We decided to concentrate on analyzing how the military regime differs from its predecessors (or does not) in its handling of major problem areas long central in Peruvian discourse: land tenure, income distribution, economic organization, economic policy generally, education, urbanization, the incorporation of peasants into the political system, and the treatment of foreign investment. By writing papers on the substance, evolution, and impact of Peruvian governmental policies in the specific issue area each author knew best, we felt we would coax out substantial previously unavailable data, particularly on the background of the various reforms and on the translation of declarations into decisions, actions, and consequences. We expected that by focusing on how the military regime compares with its predecessors in handling major problems, we might highlight differences apparently associated with the 1968 regime change, or else continuities over time, and might be able to help explain these differences or similarities. We made no attempt to cover all possible or even all important topics, but cast our net widely to facilitate eventual general statements about the nature and effects of the military regime's approach.

I should make clear what will soon become evident to readers: this book was completed (corrected page proofs and all) before the removal of President Juan Velasco Alvarado from the Peruvian presidency on August 29, 1975, and his replacement that day by General Francisco Morales Bermudez, the top-ranking cabinet member (and therefore the institutionally designated successor). My own essay, Chapter 1, was revised for the final time early in 1975; most of the other chapters in the volume were finished by late 1974. Delays between research, writing, and publication are a well-known and probably inevitable hazard, which we hope will be understood and forgiven.

Only a week has passed since General Velasco's tenure ended; any instant punditry I allow myself to record now is almost certain to be overtaken by events before this volume is printed. Still, some observations should be offered.

First, initial indications from Lima suggest that the military regime is still well ensconced and that the basic outlines of its avowedly "revolutionary" policies remain unchanged. General Morales Bermudez, a member of the Cabinet since 1969 except for a brief interlude as Army Chief of Staff, emphasized in his first major statement as president (to the closing session of the Conference of Non-Aligned Nations, meeting in Lima) that "The Revolution which today says goodbye to you is the very same one which received you with a fraternal embrace a few days ago." Two days later, in an informal chat with Peruvian journalists, Morales Bermudez stressed that under his direction the government would not deviate "a single millimeter from the basic lines of doctrine and policy" outlined in the Revolutionary Government's major public documents issued from 1968 on. "The government is the same; only its leadership has changed," the new president affirmed. Granted that leadership makes a difference, and that the regime's basic documents are subject to various interpretations, the emphasis on continuity is bound to be significant nonetheless.

Second, the new president's first moves clearly were aimed at responding to the unpopularity the regime was experiencing by 1974-1975, as pointed out in several of this volume's chapters and highlighted in Chapter 1. Among the new leadership's efforts to win public approval were the decision to invite a civilian technocrat to enter the cabinet for the first time since the military takeover, its reversal of a series of political deportations and measures closing opposition journals, and even the new president's gesture of chatting informally with reporters on his way home from Sunday mass (the president being dressed in civilian clothes). Whether such gestures portend any more serious effort to engage public participation in decision-making, or whether—as seems more likely—the change of leadership will not solve the regime's participation dilemma remains to be seen.

Third, the speculation about the timing of a presidential succession found on pages 41-42 of Chapter 1 may well be relevant. General Morales Bermudez's first cabinet shifts removed three members of the original COAP group from the cabinet, while the senior active officers (who still outrank the 1968 colonels of the first COAP) seem to have gained increased power during the new regime's first few days. Clearly it is too early to tell, but one suspects that some of the dynamic radicalizing thrust of the Peruvian "revolution," stressed in Chapter 1, may be at least temporarily slowed or even arrested. The immediate warmth with which the *New York Times* editorially greeted the new regime suggests that some observers, at least, think the Morales regime will eschew radical nationalist economic policies.

Finally, perhaps the most noteworthy aspect of General Morales Bermudez's accession to the presidency and the attendant shifts in the cabinet and in the Army hierarchy is precisely how smoothly they appear to have occurred. The military regime seems to have survived its first succession crisis intact. Its top leadership has changed, but the regime's central feature—a comprehensive reform program under the institutional auspices of the Peruvian armed forces—continues. The Peruvian experiment continues to warrant close examination.

Let me add an introductory word on each of the chapters before leaving readers to find their way through this symposium.

Chapter 1 represents my own attempt, drawing on the other essays and on my own research, to provide an interim assessment of the Peruvian military regime as of early 1975. It is intended both to state my general interpretation of Peru's "ambiguous revolution" and to highlight themes which will be encountered in subsequent chapters.

Chapter 2, contributed by Julio Cotler, provides an alternative overview of Peru's current government and its place in national and regional history. Although my own view differs in interpretation and emphasis from Cotler's, I wish to record here the special debt I owe to his writings and to our many conversations.

Chapters 3 through 10 take up individually the various policy areas previously mentioned: economic and political, rural and urban, national and international.

The first several chapters deal with selected aspects of the vast inequalities in power and resources which characterize Peruvian society. Richard Webb analyzes income distribution in Peru and government policies affecting (or failing to affect) the very uneven pattern; he specifically compares the programs of the military regime and the predecessor Belaúnde government. David Collier considers how Peruvian regimes since World War II have dealt with rapid urbanization; he focuses particularly on government policy toward Lima's mushrooming squatter settlements. Susan Bourque and Scott Palmer discuss how Peruvian governments and other political actors have handled the problem of expanding peasant participation in a country where peasants were effectively nonparticipant until political and social mobilization began to occur in the 1960s. Colin Harding focuses more specifically on the problem of land tenure and the emergence of agrarian reform as a policy response; he emphasizes particularly the reform's evolution and partial radicalization during the military government's tenure. And Robert Drysdale and Robert Myers take up national education policy, attempting to assess the significance of the military regime's educational reform in a society where education has long been a means of preserving class structures and divisions.

A second group of chapters deals with selected aspects of national economic policy and the military regime's impact thereon. Shane Hunt's chapter discusses how Peruvian regimes have handled the always vexing problem of foreign investment, an issue of central economic and political importance in Peru for several decades. Peter Knight concentrates on the evolution of the military regime's ideas about the proper form and content of economic organization; he stresses particularly the debate on "social property" which the Peruvian government conducted during 1973–1974 and shows how this debate illuminates the nature of the military regime. Finally, Jane Jaquette compares the rhetoric and reality of general national development policy under Belaúnde and under the military regime; she traces elements of ideological and political continuity and change.

Acknowledgments are, of course, in order. First I express here the appreciation of all the seminar members to our gracious host, the Center for Inter-American Relations, and especially to its director of public affairs, Ronald G. Hellman, whose professional and personal interest in the seminar and its members exceeded the call of organizational duty. Anthony Ginsberg, the seminar's rapporteur, contributed substantively to the group with his prompt and excellently drafted notes; Sari August provided very efficient administrative assistance. Martin Domb and Alexis Anderson, Princeton undergraduates, provided invaluable help as well. All the authors of this volume join me in expressing our special thanks to Mr. Donald K. Moore for his meticulous editorial assistance and to Mr. Sanford Thatcher and Mrs. Gail

Filion of Princeton University Press for their encouragement and advice.

My deep personal appreciation is owed to those Peruvians and other friends who encouraged me to interest myself in Peru and who have helped me learn something about that country, especially during the three years I worked in Lima for the Ford Foundation. I am also grateful to the Council on Foreign Relations and Princeton's Center of International Studies for the support and hospitality which enabled me to organize this symposium. Most of all, I thank the other members of our seminar for the spirited interest they took in what I think we all regard as a genuinely collaborative enterprise and as only one step in a continuing exchange of views.

Abraham F. Lowenthal

Princeton, New Jersey
September 5, 1975

Contributors

Susan C. Bourque (Ph.D. Cornell 1971) teaches Latin American politics at Smith College. She conducted research in Peru during 1965–1966, 1968–1969, and 1970. Her publications include *Cholification and the Campesino* (Cornell Latin American Dissertation Series) and "Organizaciones Campesinas y el sistema política del Perú," Estudios Andinos, Dec. 1971.

David Collier (Ph.D. Chicago 1971) is an Associate Professor of Political Science at Indiana University. In addition to his work on Lima squatter settlements, he is engaged in comparative research on the timing and sequence of different aspects of development.

Julio Cotler (Ph.D. University of Burdeos 1960) is currently at the Universidad Nacional Autónoma de México. He is a research sociologist at the Instituto de Estudios Peruanos in Lima and has been a member of the Joint Committee on Latin American Studies of the Social Science Research Council. He has published several articles, in Spanish and English, on Peruvian society and politics.

Robert Drysdale (Ed.D. Harvard 1971) is currently a fellow at Harvard University Center for International Affairs. He worked in Peru from 1970 to 1974 as a Ford Foundation official. Previous publications include several articles on education in Peru and Latin America.

Colin Harding (B. Phil. Oxford 1969) is currently on the staff of *Latin America*, London. He carried out research in Peru in 1971 and 1973 while a member of the Centre of Latin American Studies of the University of Cambridge and has written a paper on *Agrarian Reform and Agrarian Struggles in Peru* in the Centre's Working Papers series.

Shane Hunt (Ph.D. Yale 1963) is a Professor of Economics at Boston University. He worked in Peru during 1963–1964 and 1969 and has written on Peruvian economic history, economic statistics, and public finance.

Jane S. Jaquette (Ph.D. Cornell 1971) is currently teaching Political Science at Occidental College in Los Angeles. In addition to a dissertation ("The Politics of Development in Peru," Latin American Program Series No. 33) and articles on ideology and economic policy in Peru, she has done work on women in Latin America and is editor of *Women in Politics* (John Wiley, 1974).

Peter T. Knight (Ph.D. Stanford 1970) is currently a visiting fellow at Cornell University. From 1967 through 1974 he was Program Adviser in Economics and Agriculture with the Ford Foundation's Lima office; previously he had been at the Brookings Institution. Previous publications include *Brazilian Agricultural Technology and Trade* (Praeger Publishers, 1971).

Abraham F. Lowenthal (Ph.D. Harvard 1971) is Acting Director of Studies at the Council on Foreign Relations and Lecturer at Princeton University's Woodrow Wilson School of Public and International Affairs. He worked in Peru from 1969 to 1972 as a Ford Foundation official. Previous publications include *The Dominican Intervention* (Harvard University Press, 1972) and various articles on Latin American politics and inter-American relations.

Robert G. Myers (Ph.D. University of Chicago 1967) is presently a program officer with the Latin American office of the Ford Foundation in New York and was formerly an assistant professor in the Comparative Education Center, the University of Chicago. His publications include *Education and Emigration* (David McKay and Co., 1972), a study based on extensive field research in Peru.

David Scott Palmer (Ph.D. Cornell 1973) is Assistant Professor of Government at Bowdoin College. He served as Peace Corps Volunteer Leader in Ayacucho, Peru (1962–1964) and as Visiting Professor at Catholic University in Lima (1971–1972). Publications on Peru include articles in several readers and the *Peruvian Times*.

Richard Webb (Ph.D. Harvard 1974) is currently a research economist with The International Bank for Reconstruction and Development in Washington. He worked in the Central Reserve Bank of Peru from 1963 to 1969 and subsequently taught at the Catholic University of Peru and at Princeton University.

The Peruvian Experiment

Peru's Ambiguous Revolution

Abraham F. Lowenthal

Peru's "Revolutionary Government of the Armed Forces" has now completed its first six years in power, the equivalent of a presidential term under the country's constitution. Headed by General Juan Velasco Alvarado, the army's top-ranking officer when he led the October 1968 coup which toppled President Fernando Belaúnde Terry, the Peruvian regime has already attracted considerable attention. Military officers and civilian politicians in countries as different as Argentina and Ecuador, Bolivia and Brazil, Cuba and the Dominican Republic, Uruguay and Colombia, have expressed their interest in (and usually their admiration for) the Peruvian experiment. Fidel Castro has acclaimed the Peruvian undertaking; Juan Perón extolled it. *Peruanista* factions have been identified, and have sometimes identified themselves, in the armed forces of several South American countries.

The Peruvian regime is generally seen not as the typical Latin American *caudillo* government but rather as an essentially institutional effort. Although a government of force, it is widely regarded as relatively unrepressive. Although led by staunchly anti-Communist officers, many with considerable training in the United States, the Peruvian government has established friendly relations with several Communist nations as part of its campaign

An earlier version of this essay was presented at the 1973 Annual Conference of the Inter-University Seminar on Armed Forces and Society held at Chicago October 11-13, 1973, and the first written draft was circulated to members of the Peru Seminar and selected friends in Peru. Valuable suggestions from all three sources are gratefully acknowledged, as is financial support for this research from the Council on Foreign Relations and from the Center of International Studies, Princeton University. Portions of the essay appeared in *Foreign Affairs* (July 1974) and are reprinted here with the permission of that journal.

to escape external "domination," particularly by the United States.

Most important, although it is the nation's force for order, the Peruvian military has promoted substantial change. Through a burst of laws and decrees unprecedented in Peru, the military regime has set out to transform many basic areas of national life. Major structural reforms have affected land tenure and water rights, labor-management relations, the educational system, the state's role in the economy and in the communications media, the role of foreign enterprise in Peru's economy, and even fundamental concepts of economic and political relationships. Particularly noteworthy has been the regime's announced determination to move steadily away from capitalist principles by creating a new "social property" economic sector (based on collective ownership of the means of production), destined to become the "predominant" mode of economic organization.[1] And the Peruvian regime has emphasized its aim to promote a drastic change in national values, to create a "new Peruvian man," one dedicated to "solidarity, not individualism."[2]

Peru's military regime has unquestionably put the country on the world political map. Host of the "Seventy-seven," active participant in the Algiers conference of nonaligned nations, frequent spokesman for Latin America in the World Bank, chief proponent of reform in the Organization of American States and in the inter-American military system, host and leading supporter of the Andean pact, current member of the UN Security Council, Peru has projected itself into the international arena. Washington, Moscow, Peking, and Havana have all expressed special interest in Peru's affairs. The Lima embassies of the latter three are now probably their biggest in South America, and the U. S. embassy has argued (with limited success) that Washington's policy toward Peru should be sympathetic, despite the political and legal difficulties posed for the U. S. government by Peru's treatment of certain American investments.

[1] The social-property sector is extensively discussed in Peter T. Knight, "New Forms of Economic Organization in Peru: Toward Workers' Self-Management," Chapter 9 of this volume.

[2] Perhaps the best source for the Peruvian regime's approach to changing values is the *Informe general: reforma de la educación peruana*, Lima, Comisión de Reforma de la Educación, Ministerio de la Educación, 1970. See also Juan Velasco Alvarado, *Velasco: la voz de la revolución*, Lima, Ed. Participación, 1972, passim. There are twenty-one references to "solidarity" in this official collection of President Velasco's speeches.

From several foreign perspectives, Peru's current process of military-directed change is regarded with hope. For many on the international Left, Peru seems especially significant, particularly now that the "Chilean way" has been so abruptly closed. From this vantage point, Peru is contrasted with Brazil. In Brazil, leftist intellectuals have lost their jobs and rights, and some have suffered torture; many of their counterparts in Peru are advising the regime or are at least sympathetic to it (though a few have been interfered with, and some even deported). Bishops in Brazil condemn their regime; Peruvian bishops generally support theirs. The Brazilian regime promotes capitalist expansion, national and foreign, but the Peruvian government announces its aim to move away from capitalism. And while Brazil has tied itself ever more closely to the United States, Peru has acted to reduce its dependence on Washington.

Paradoxically, many international lenders and even some investors also regard Peru's experiment favorably. The military regime has earned plaudits for its prudent fiscal management and for its pragmatism in dealing with foreign companies. From this standpoint, Peru's regime is contrasted with Chile's under Allende and with Castro's. Whatever the short-term nuisance of renegotiating contracts and absorbing nationalist rhetorical attacks, some foreign investors think the military regime is making Peru safe for them, now and for some time to come.[3]

Within Peru, however, the military regime's program is not so widely acclaimed. Articulate observers from both sides of the political spectrum assail the government. Though the traditional (Moscow-line) Communist party openly supports the military regime, many on the Left regard it as far from "revolutionary," but rather as an ally of international capitalism, exploiting the Peruvian masses for the sake of dominant minorities.[4] From the Right, the military government's program is also viewed with deepening distrust. Even those businessmen who had adjusted themselves

[3] See, for example, Esteban Ferrer, "Peru: The General as Revolutionary," *Columbia Journal of World Business* 5 (Nov.–Dec. 1970), pp. 37–45, and John Utley, "Doing Business with Latin Nationalists," *Harvard Business Review* 51 (Jan.–Feb. 1973), pp. 77–86. Cf. Shane Hunt, "Direct Foreign Investment in Peru: New Rules for an Old Game," Chapter 8 of this volume.

[4] See Ricardo Letts, *Perú: mito de la revolución militar*, Caracas, Ed. Barbara, 1970; Aníbal Quijano Obregón, *Nacionalismo, neoimperialismo, y militarismo en el Perú*, Buenos Aires, Ed. Periferia, 1971; and the first four issues of *Sociedad y Política*, a journal published in Lima during 1972 and 1973 but closed down by the military regime in September 1973.

to the agrarian reform, a greatly extended state role in the economy, enforced profit-sharing and worker-management schemes, and countless other changes they might have resisted under other circumstances, found themselves alarmed by the sudden nationalization in 1973 of the entire fishmeal industry (Peru's main earner of foreign exchange) and by the repeated, escalating stress on social property.[5]

Despite its international stature, the Peruvian regime finds itself almost bereft of conspicuous support at home. No group is likely soon to displace or even seriously challenge the military, but the government encounters concerted opposition within several important sectors: labor, business, peasants, students, and professionals. One politically meaningful election after another reflects antiregime sentiment; opposition candidates have won the recent polls held by sugar workers' and teachers' cooperatives as well as the laywers', doctors', and engineers' associations, and militantly antiregime student groups hold sway in practically all Peruvian universities. Some backing, particularly among the urban poor and among highland peasants who have benefited from the agrarian reform, is demonstrated from time to time, especially through mass meetings, but contrary evidence is even more striking. General strikes in several provincial areas, including Arequipa, Cuzco, and Puno, forced the regime to suspend constitutional guarantees temporarily in mid-1973 and again later that year, and major antigovernment demonstrations have occurred on several other occasions.

The National System to Support Social Mobilization (SINAMOS) established in 1971 partly to organize support for the government, has instead been the object of intensifying attack from all sides, and even of some backbiting from within the regime. And though the army is surely Peru's preeminent middle-class institution, middle-class distress is increasingly perceptible. Housewives, bureaucrats, teachers, taxi drivers, secretaries: all are grumbling.

[5] This and many similar general statements throughout this essay are based on the Peruvian press accounts and on extensive personal interviews I conducted in Peru from 1969 through 1973. In this case, for example, the pages of *El Comercio* and *La Prensa* for May 1973 are filled with communiqués and letters protesting the fishmeal nationalization.

I have limited the footnotes to references, in this volume or elsewhere, where important specific points are more extensively discussed or to clarification and exemplification of points made in the text.

How should the Peruvian process be characterized? What accounts for its international reputation, and for its trouble at home? What has the regime accomplished? Where is the regime heading, or likely to head? For that matter, where did the Peruvian process come from? What explains the adoption by Peru's armed forces of its comprehensive program?

These questions cannot all be discussed, let alone answered, in a brief essay: readers will find illumination in each of the following chapters. It is appropriate here, however, to highlight some of the main points and to attempt an overall, if interim, assessment as of early 1975.

CHARACTERIZING THE PERUVIAN REGIME

The current Peruvian process cannot yet be easily labeled. Many of the regime's key activities remain ambiguous or apparently contradictory. In other areas, gaps have developed between rhetoric and practice, and it is hard to tell which, if either, will eventually be modified.

In the economic sphere, the regime's most obvious accomplishment has been to expand and fortify what had been one of South America's weakest states.[6] The government has announced its intent to control all industries it defines as basic. It has already taken over, in addition to the fishmeal industry, a major share of mining and metal refining; all petroleum refining, most petroleum marketing, and some oil exploration; the railroad, telephone, and cable companies, and Peru's international air carrier; cement companies and a steadily increasing share of the electric utilities; 51 percent of every television station and at least 25 percent of each radio station; cotton, sugar, tobacco, and mineral exporting; importing and distributing of several key commodities; considerable food marketing; a majority of the banking system and of the insurance business; all reinsurance; even the operation of the airport's duty-free store and of a small chinchilla farm. Incipient government participation in pharmaceutical man-

[6] For a discussion of Peru's relatively undeveloped state apparatus, see Shane Hunt, "Distribution, Growth, and Government Economic Behavior in Peru," in Gustav Ranis (ed.), *Government and Economic Development*, New Haven, Yale University Press, 1971, pp. 375–428. Cf., however, Carl Herbold, Jr., "Development in the Peruvian Administrative System, 1919–1939: Modern and Traditional Qualities of Government under Authoritarian Regimes," unpublished doctoral dissertation, Yale University, 1973.

ufacturing and distribution may portend further expansion in this and other areas. All told, the state's share of national investment has jumped to almost 50 percent from 13 percent in 1965 (though this change reflects some decline in private capital formation as well as the expansion of government spending).[7]

The Peruvian government's increasing strength has been evident in many other ways as well. All sorts of previously flouted regulations are now being taken more seriously, as Peruvians experience, in some ways for the first time, a government that governs. Strict regulation of credit, of the use of foreign exchange, and of other major aspects of national economic life is increasingly a fact; collection of taxes already on the books has risen substantially.[8] The public sector's capacity is strengthening rapidly as professionals from business and the universities take government jobs.

But while the Peruvian state grows, the military regime repeatedly asserts it does not mean to end major private economic activity. When the fishmeal nationalization shocked the private sector (the official 1971–1975 national plan had assured that the fishmeal industry would remain private), no fewer than seven cabinet ministers stressed within a week that the measure was exceptional and that complete abandonment of private enterprise was by no means contemplated. Reassurances to private business have not been limited to verbal expressions; generous tax incentives, tariff breaks, efforts to reorganize Lima's stock exchange, and other measures to stimulate private investment and reinvestment have accompanied the regime's moves in some sectors toward state ownership. Repeated government statements advocate "economic pluralism" and talk of four types of enterprise (state, social property, reformed private, and unreformed private for small-scale firms). No one explains convincingly, however,

[7] The figure for 1965 may be found in Banco Central de Reserva del Perú, *Cuentas nacionales del Perú: 1950–1965*, Lima, 1966, p. 11. Data for 1971 and projections to 1975 may be found in Instituto Nacional de Planificación, *Plan del Perú: 1971–1975*, Lima, 1971, p. 19. Extensive data on the growth of Peru's public sector may be found in Peter S. Cleaves and Martin J. Scurrah, "State-Society Relations and Bureaucratic Behavior in Peru," unpublished manuscript, Lima, August 1974, especially in Table 4, p. 39.

[8] My judgment on tax collection is based on analysis of *Cuentas nacionales del Perú* (1968–1973), published by the Banco Central de Reserva, supplemented by personal interviews and correspondence with authorities on Peru's fiscal and tax system.

how such very different modes of economic organization can effectively coexist. Some Peruvians believe the private sector is doomed to extinction, therefore, and cite the measures taken against Empresas Eléctricas (universally considered a model firm) as further evidence that the regime means to finish off private enterprise. Others regard the social-property sector as an elaborate facade and point to cases like Bayer's acrylic fiber plant (accorded especially favorable treatment as a "strategic" industry) or the deal, highly favorable to the company, by which ITT transformed its assets in the telephone company into a hotel investment, as indicative of what is really happening.[9] Not only Peruvian industrialists, but even the regime's own former minister of economy and finance, have had to call for clarification of the "rules of the game" under which Peru's economy is to operate.

In the political arena, the regime has been similarly active, but again with ambiguous results. The government has vowed to destroy the traditional political system dominated by special interests and to replace it with one open equally to the influence of all citizens, a "social democracy of full participation." The task of destruction is being rapidly accomplished, but the second task is still far from realization.

The military regime has systematically undercut almost all organizations politically influential in Peru before 1968 except the church and, of course, the armed forces. Established parties have been severely hampered. Economic interest groups have been crippled; the once-powerful National Agrarian Society has been dissolved, and the National Industries Society has been stripped of its formal standing and has been forbidden to represent itself as national; its president has been deported. The government has weakened the labor unions by playing rivals (the CGTP and the CTP) off against each other and against a regime-blessed alternative (CTRP), and there are signs it expects to move eventually toward a government-sponsored and controlled united labor federation.[10]

Lima's newspapers, once influential, were first cowed into al-

[9] See César Germaná, "¿Si es Bayer . . . es bueno?" *Sociedad y Política* 2 (Oct. 1972), 31ff.

[10] CGTP is the Confederación General de Trabajadores del Perú, the Communist party labor organization. CTP is the APRA-affiliated Confederación de Trabajadores Peruanos. The regime-sponsored CTRP is the Confederación de Trabajadores de la Revolución Peruana.

most total blandness by a skillful combination of legislation, intimidation, and incentives, and then taken over by the regime and entrusted, under conditions that amount to probation, to diverse political and social groups. The judicial system, perceived by the regime as a restraint, has been "reorganized" and is being made much more responsive (to say the least) to government desires. Private universities, until 1969 governed individually, have had their autonomy curtailed by the creation of a central national university system. Autonomous peasant federations, which gained some strength in the 1960s, were first pushed toward atrophy and then effectively banned under a law establishing the National Agrarian Confederation.[11] Individuals and families who only five years ago were among Peru's most powerful— Pedro Beltrán, the Prados, the Pardos, the Gildemeisters, and the Ayulos, to name just a few—have had their influence, if not their wealth, very sharply reduced.

What is not clear, however, is whether the new political order is really to be anything different from a particularly efficient version of a traditional dictatorship, governed this time by a military-technocrat coalition. Despite all the regime's talk about full participation, very few Peruvians have a prescribed role in influencing government decisions, and few feel that the regime is responsive to their claims. It is no wonder that the regime lacks public support: citizens, particularly those whose views used to find expression through established political channels, resent an autocratic regime, completely military at the cabinet level, which can act arbitrarily without restraint.

The government's dealings with labor and peasant unions, professional and student organizations, business lobbies, and other groups suggest that the regime distrusts any autonomous organizations and wishes to deal only with units established or legitimized by the regime. The implicit—and sometimes explicit— concept for political organization is corporatist. The regime is steadily building up the apparatus by which one group after another is to be tied directly to the executive, which will attempt to harmonize all interests perceived by the regime as legitimate and expressed through channels considered appropriate. Political

[11] The history of peasant federations and the impact of Law 19400, establishing the National Agrarian Federation, are extensively discussed in Susan C. Bourque and David Scott Palmer, "Transforming the Rural Sector: Government Policy and Peasant Response," Chapter 5 of this volume.

parties are not so regarded; persons with recent party responsibilities are specifically prohibited from becoming officials of various newly-created participatory mechanisms: in the shantytowns, in educational units, in agricultural cooperatives, etc. Although repeatedly proclaiming its desire for participation and dialogue, the government evinces increasing impatience with those who question any of a number of central ideas.[12] In short, the regime is authoritarian, and increasingly so.

Stable government without severe repression does set Peru apart from its immediate neighbors. (Brazil's regime is impressively stable but surely repressive, Chile's under Allende was unrepressive but unstable, and Chile's current junta is so brutally repressive as probably ultimately to be unstable. Ecuador's government is neither stable nor repressive, but Bolivia suffers a regime that is both unstable and repressive.) Yet a closer look at contemporary Peru provides a somewhat murkier view. Protesting miners and peasants have been gunned down on occasion, as so often before in Peru's history. The press has been muzzled. Vague standards of "counterrevolutionary activities" have been intimated and sometimes applied—expressing opposition to the agrarian reform is prohibited, for instance. Leading antiregime personalities have been harassed, and over a score have been deported. The regime has repeatedly shown—in dealing with students or with striking teachers, miners, and doctors, for example—that it prefers to quiet opposition by accommodation rather than by force. But when push comes to shove, the regime acts without regard for the niceties of constitutional doctrine. Several jailings and deportations within the past year, and some blatant instances of censorship, suggest that the limits within which free discussion is permitted in Peru may be narrowing as time goes on and problems mount.[13]

[12] The following quote from President Velasco, complaining about the critical tone of the comments the regime had elicited from the public on the social-property draft legislation, conveys something of the government's approach: "We have not opened up the dialogue so that they can make us lose time by alleging the inconvenience of adopting this new sector. That decision has been taken and will not be revised. That was taken a year ago. We want patriotic and constructive opinions about the outlines of the project, the institutions to be created, and so on. Not on whether or not to create the sector." *El Comercio*, Sept. 27, 1973.

[13] Among the examples of this trend have been the jailing of leaders of teachers' unions, the deportation of several union leaders, politicians, busi-

But one cannot dismiss the Peruvian military's talk of "full participation" as mere rhetoric. The regime's spokesmen may well be right in asserting that only harsh treatment of the previous power structure could facilitate eventual political participation by the Peruvian masses. Now that the preliminary job is mostly done, some efforts have been initiated, especially through SINAMOS and through the educational and industrial community mechanisms, to decentralize decision making and transfer it to the local level. At least a few of the top government leaders, especially in SINAMOS, and many of its operating personnel, seem sincerely committed to helping peasants, shantytown dwellers, parents of schoolchildren, and industrial workers organize to achieve effective power. While much of the regime's activity seems aimed (successfully so) at demobilizing previously influential Peruvian groups, SINAMOS appears to be politicizing and "raising consciousness" among several sectors which will eventually be in a position to pressure the army itself. It would appear that the regime is taking at least some first steps to redeem its promise to provide for new forms of participation, even by those mostly unrepresented in Peru. Whether these steps will eventually influence the regime's course substantially, or whether they will signify but a minor or temporary countercurrent, remains to be seen.[14]

In foreign policy, the Peruvian regime is widely acknowledged to be inventive and imaginative. Diplomatic relations have been established with the Soviet Union, China, and Cuba, and each of these ties has opened up significant possibilities for trade diversification and eventual expansion. The USSR bought over 15 percent of Peru's sugar exports in 1973, China bought over 10 percent of Peru's copper, and both Cuba and China were important purchasers of Peru's fishmeal in 1972 (when Peru last had extra fishmeal to sell and badly needed a market). Substantial Eastern

---

nessmen, and social scientists, and the closing of *Caretas, Oiga, Peruvian Times, Sociedad y Política*, and other journals.

[14] Discussion of SINAMOS is difficult because evidence of its programs and impact are inherently hard to obtain. The stated objectives and organizational outlines of SINAMOS are discussed by James Malloy in "Authoritarianism, Corporatism, and Mobilization in Peru," *Review of Politics* 36 (Jan. 1974), pp. 52–84, but one suspects Malloy takes the official rhetoric too seriously. A much more skeptical analysis is provided by Julio Cotler in "The New Mode of Political Domination in Peru," Chapter 2 of this volume.

European investment and technical cooperation have been obtained. Major Japanese loans and investments have begun to come in, both for infrastructure and for industrial facilities.

All these steps, together with Peru's role in the Andean pact and other international organizations and its spirited championing of the two hundred-mile territorial sea limit, have been portrayed as reducing Peru's dependence, principally on the United States. Government spokesmen repeatedly claim—with considerable credibility in a country previously pushed around by Washington in connection with the International Petroleum Company (IPC) case, the refusal to sell supersonic military aircraft, and other issues—that Peru has now regained its dignity. And they suggest that important economic decisions affecting Peru, once made in New York and Washington, are now made in Lima.

The major growth sectors of the Peruvian economy—petroleum and mining—are still mostly premised on major foreign private investment, however.[15] The military regime has signed no fewer than eighteen contracts with foreign oil companies; and though the terms of these contracts are probably more favorable to Peru than those of previous contracts, they appear to be at least as generous to the foreign firms as are comparable arrangements made by other countries (like Indonesia) not noted for their revolutionary credentials. In the industrial area, even Brazil's avowedly pro-foreign-investment regime gets better terms, at least in some sectors, than Peru can command. It is hard to say, therefore, whether Peru's new foreign policy amounts to much more than a particularly flamboyant adjustment to the shifting realities of international power and to new fashions in international rhetoric. Making that adjustment intelligently is no negligible accomplishment, but it is not so fundamental a change as Peru's spokesmen herald.

The Peruvian military bases its claim to be revolutionary primarily on the structural reforms it has designed, promulgated, and begun to administer. Here, again, no easy label is appropriate.

[15] This fact is made very clear in the National Plan and especially in the Sectoral Plan for the Ministry of Energy and Mines. See *Plan del Perú*, pp. 137–160, and Ministerio de Energía y Minas, "Plan sectorial de desarrollo: exposición del Ministerio de Energía y Minas," Lima, 1973. See also Janet Ballantyne, "The Political Economy of Peruvian *Gran Minería*," unpublished doctoral dissertation, Cornell University Business School, 1974.

The agrarian reform of 1969 has brought a substantial redistribution of land in a country where the ownership of land has long been exceptionally concentrated.[16] Within less than five years the regime has taken over virtually all Peru's large estates, beginning with the vast sugar plantations (which were not to be affected at all under the previous Peruvian agrarian reform legislation) and moving next to the highland areas. Land has been expropriated and title redistributed at a pace faster than that of any recent Latin American reform but Cuba's, and perhaps Chile's under Allende. Legislation affecting access to water, without which land ownership may be useless, has also been sharply revised.

The industrial or enterprise reform provides workers a share not only in profits but also in management.[17] Workers within each firm employing six or more workers receive a fixed percentage of their company's profits, some distributed immediately in cash but more retained as commonly owned shares in the firm, which is eventually to be half-owned by the "labor community"—the collectivity of a firm's workers. The community's representatives have the right to participate in management decisions, to audit company books and records, and generally to assure that the workers' actual and prospective interests are being protected. Similar mechanisms exist in the mining, fishing, and telecommunications sectors.

The educational system is being extensively reorganized.[18] Among the reform's features are a stress on preschool and extrascholastic (including adult) education, on common and terminal secondary education with a vocational focus, on bilingual educa-

[16] Peru's Gini index of land distribution was the worst reported in the *World Handbook of Political and Social Indicators*. See Charles L. Taylor and Michael C. Hudson, *World Handbook*, New Haven, Yale University Press, 1972, p. 267. See also Colin Harding's essay, "Land Reform and Social Conflict in Peru," Chapter 6 of this volume.

[17] Knight discusses the industrial reform in Chapter 9 of this volume. See also Jane Jaquette, "Belaúnde and Velasco: On the Limits of Ideological Politics," Chapter 10 of this volume and the items mentioned in the Appendix, section B2, "Industrial Reform."

[18] Robert S. Drysdale and Robert G. Myers deal with the educational reform in "Continuity and Change: Peruvian Education," Chapter 7 of this volume. Useful background is provided by Rolland Paulston, *Society, Schools and Progress in Peru*, New York, Pergamon Press, 1971.

tion for Peru's Quechua- and Aymara-speaking indigenous groups, and on the values of nationalism and solidarity.

The social security system, built up piece by piece over a fifty-year period, has been reorganized and rationalized.[19] For those already covered it provides generous retirement, accident, and health benefits more equitable than before, and it extends coverage to a few new groups, including domestic servants and even artists. And labor legislation has been revised to assure increased job security to the employed.

Each of these reforms transfers resources—present and especially future—from more to less privileged Peruvians. All represent considerable advances over the measures that previous Peruvian regimes had been willing or able to undertake. Substantial numbers of Peruvians, surely a majority of those groups whose members have voted in Peru's past national elections, are obtaining more, some significantly more, from the national system than they did prior to the military regime.

Viewed from another perspective, however, the current reforms are at least as noteworthy for their limits as for their advance. The military regime's measures are carried out, if somewhat self-consciously, under the banner of Tupac Amaru, the *mestizo* leader who headed Peru's main Indian uprising against the Spanish conquerors. But the reforms seem unlikely to affect significantly the fundamental distribution of power and rewards in Peruvian society—i.e., between those already participant in Peru's economy and politics and those (the Indians, generally speaking) still largely excluded from the system's benefits. As Richard Webb and Adolfo Figueroa have shown, the income distribution resulting from the laws decreed so far—even if they are fully implemented—will occur almost exclusively within the top quarter of Peru's income recipients; three-quarters of Peru's population is unlikely to be much affected.[20] The great majority of Peruvians will not obtain land, because there is not enough to go

[19] The history of Peru's social security system is well discussed in Carmelo Mesa-Lago, "Social Security Stratification and Inequality in Latin America: The Case of Peru," unpublished paper, University of Pittsburgh, 1973.

[20] Webb's analysis is presented in Chapter 3, "Government Policy and the Distribution of Income in Peru, 1963–1973." See also Adolfo Figueroa, "El impacto de los reformas actuales sobre la distribución de ingresos en el Perú," Serie Documentos de Trabajo no. 8, CISEPA, Catholic University of Peru, 1973.

around.[21] They will not become members of industrial communities, because they are not among the aristocracy of Peruvian laborers working in industrial firms of the requisite size. They will not get improved social security benefits, because they are not among the privileged minority covered by the "national" scheme, nor will they enjoy job security, because they have no steady job to begin with. And the benefits their children get from the educational reform will probably be strictly limited, for, on the past record, their children are likely to be among the majority of school attenders who drop out before the sixth grade.

The coastal sugar estates, the seizure of which (in 1969) provided the most dramatic earnest of the regime's intent, poignantly illustrate the limits of the reforms.[22] Profits which formerly went to the land-owning families—or to the Grace Company—are now largely being distributed among the permanent workers at each plantation. These workers were already mostly unionized, politicized, and relatively prosperous before 1968; now they are even better off. But seasonal workers on the same estates, not made members of the new cooperatives, are about as badly off as they were before. And they, in turn, are better off than the legion of still landless peasants of the highlands, who will not be among the beneficiaries of the agrarian reform.

In short, the military regime is distributing resources and rewards in a more equitable way to those Peruvians already able to make their own demands heard and felt—by strikes, land invasions, votes, or other forms of organized expression. In this sense, the military government is carrying on the process of "segmentary incorporation" that Peru's elites have managed for generations: to admit claimants with voice and power into the political and economic system, but on terms that will protect its boundaries and prevent the minority within from being overwhelmed by a coalition of the majority without. The identity and relative influence of those on top has changed somewhat, and that is im-

[21] See Hylke Van de Wetering, "The Current State of Land Reform in Peru," *L.T.C. Newsletter* no. 40 (Apr.–June 1973), Land Tenure Center, University of Wisconsin, pp. 5–9.

[22] See Giorgio Alberti and Julio Cotler, "La reforma agraria en las haciendas azucareras del Perú," unpublished paper, Instituto de Estudios Peruanos, Lima, 1971.

portant. But the process of internal domination continues, and those on the bottom are pretty much the same as before.[23]

Moreover, the regime is not doing things which a revolutionary government might be expected to do, or which Castro's, for example, has done. The regime has not undertaken major tax reforms, which would significantly increase the burdens on Peru's middle class. (Income tax exemptions in Peru remain among the highest in South America, and gasoline taxes the lowest; at last report a gallon of gasoline in Lima cost but twenty cents.) It has not undertaken an "urban reform," restructuring urban real property holdings, and has announced repeatedly that it will not.[24] A commercial reform, promised in 1970, has so far been avoided. Foreign interests in Peruvian banks have been strictly limited, but Peru's major private bank, the Banco de Crédito, is still flourishing. Although the regime hampered and intimidated the press from the beginning, it did not until 1974 close down or take over the major opposition newspapers perceived as reactionary obstacles, nor has it monopolized the media. In reforming education, the regime has left Lima's elite private schools largely unrestricted. Proposals threatening to privileged groups—such as the measure, included in the draft law, which would have barred instruction in foreign languages until the end of primary school—were dropped or severely altered.

From all these comments, a reasonably clear characterization of the regime might seem to emerge: a government carrying out the kind of limited changes—within established class and sectoral limits—which the previous Belaúnde regime and earlier groups, including Alianza Popular Revolucionaria (APRA), had often promised but generally failed to deliver.

That interpretation would neatly fit the stereotype that many if not most observers of Peru were inclined to see from the very first days of the military regime. The military government's ambitious declarations of revolutionary intent drew skeptical responses from almost all sides at first. The Peruvian Communist

[23] The phrase "segmentary incorporation" and much of the analysis presented here come from Julio Cotler, "The Mechanics of Internal Domination and Social Change in Peru," *Studies in Comparative International Development* 3, no. 12 (1968), pp. 227–246.

[24] David Collier deals with the nonoccurrence of "urban reform" in Chapter 4 of this volume, "Squatter Settlements and Policy Innovation in Peru."

party weekly, *Unidad,* for example, denounced the coup immediately, alleging that it had been cooked up in Washington to protect established U.S. interests.[25] The quick take-over of IPC's installations surprised the most doctrinaire observers but seemed to others just an easily explainable exception to the general rule that a military regime will maintain the status quo. Two sociologists noted early in 1969, for instance, that it was "too early to tell whether this beginning [the IPC expropriation] will be followed by a series of coherent measures and become the basis of a thoroughgoing developmental policy or will remain as an isolated event" but added that "up to now, the few indications we have point in the direction of the latter."[26] A general book on Peruvian politics, published in mid-1969, took note of the regime's first few months and concluded that "the Peruvian political system should be able to survive the present coup without going through a redistribution of power or of societal rewards."[27] And a *New York Times* article in January 1970 asked "How Genuine the 'Revolution' in Peru?" and answered that there was "nothing very new" about it.[28]

Even after the agrarian and industrial reforms have suggested that something, at least, is new, periodic reports on Peru have indicated that "the 'revolution' has run its course," that the military regime has "run out of steam," that it has turned from "advance to consolidation" or some such phrase. At every sign of indecision or delay on the regime's part, many have been ready to conclude that whatever the reasons for the Peruvian military's course to date, it was now turning to a consistent, conservative role, more in keeping with the observers' expectations. The regime's recurrent attempts to improve its relations with business

[25] *Unidad*'s skepticism was registered in its edition of October 4, 1968. The regime's first statement, the manifesto of October 2, 1968, promised the new government would "transform Peru's social, economic, and cultural structures." See "Manifiesto del gobierno revolucionario" (Oct. 3, 1968), *La política del gobierno revolucionario* (Lima, 1969).

[26] Arlene Bergman and Magali Sarfatti Larson, *Social Stratification in Peru,* Berkeley, Institute of International Studies, University of California, 1969, p. viii.

[27] Carlos Astiz, *Pressure Groups and Power Elites in Peruvian Politics,* Ithaca, N.Y., Cornell University Press, 1969, p. 275.

[28] Graham Hovey, "How Genuine the 'Revolution' in Peru?" *New York Times,* Jan. 26, 1970.

leaders have lent themselves well to this interpretation, for it has seemed often that the military's alliance with the national bourgeoisie was being cemented, presumably at the expense of further reform.[29]

Reports of the "revolution's" death have proved premature each time, however. On the contrary, the evidence this book presents suggests that despite the limits of what has so far been done in Peru, the trend has been toward more profound reform. The thrust of the regime's action has been, and continues to be, not to pull back or even to consolidate, but to go further—or at least to leave open the possibility of further advance.

Consider the reforms so far neglected: although tax reform measures have so far been limited mostly to rationalizing and improving the enforcement of existing regulations, income tax rates for middle and upper brackets were raised considerably in 1971. Moreover, there are indications—the creation and staffing of a special tax research office, for example—that the regime may be working on eventual, more thorough, tax reforms. Although the regime has repeatedly denied it will undertake an urban reform or nationalize private banks, rumors persist that these steps are under consideration (against a background of previous denials that pension plans would be changed, that the fishmeal sector would be nationalized, and so on). Although some opposition newspapers were allowed to persist during the regime's first five years, others were taken over earlier, and there is considerable reason to believe that only strenuous objection by the navy and some army officers prevented *El Comercio* from being closed down or taken over by its workers in August 1973. By July 1974, those objections had been overcome (at the expense of evident disunity within the armed forces) and the major remaining private newspapers were all expropriated.

The reforms already decreed have in several cases been carried further than at first seemed likely. The scope of the agrarian reform has been expanded by eliminating "private reforms," by excusing small farmers from certain payments, and especially by strongly emphasizing collective and cooperative forms of ownership as well as regional planning. Though seasonal workers have so far been denied equal access to the reform's benefits, the re-

[29] See, for example, James Petras and Robert Laporte, *Perú: ¿transformación revolucionaria o modernización?* Buenos Aires, 1971, esp. pp. 191–194.

gime has served notice that it will also act to improve their lot.

Likewise, the industrial reform of 1970 is now described by the regime as only a partial (some say transitional) measure to transform that part of the economy still to be organized along capitalist lines. The principle of a "compensation fund" to make income distribution somewhat more equitable within each sector has now been extended to the fishing and mining sectors and is apparently to be pushed still further. The establishment of the social property sector reflects the same intent to redistribute property, at least future property, even more widely.

And so it goes all along the line. Initially largely technical and managerial, the educational reform has become more concerned with basic substantive and structural changes. Increasing emphasis is being given to bilingual education, which, if seriously implemented over a sustained period, could perhaps do more than any other single measure to undermine Peru's class and caste divisions. Significant talk of facilitating mass participation did not begin until 1971, but since then there have been important first steps to make it possible. Each move to establish improved rapport with businessmen has given way to a new cycle of hostility, confounding those who perceived or predicted a military-bourgeois alliance. And while observers have been debating the regime's attitude toward foreign investment, the government has expropriated, nationalized, or bought out one foreign interest after another.

In sum, the measures adopted within this six-year period seem generally to have become more "radical"; they are more statist, somewhat more redistributive, clearly less tied to traditional capitalism, more concerned with participation—at least at the rhetorical level—and seemingly more oriented to a profound restructuring of Peru's social, economic, and political relations. Though current class and sector limits are obvious, there are indications that these may be at least partially transcended. Some even contend that the regime has chosen consciously and wisely to wait before curtailing middle-class prerogatives, that the only way to achieve change in Peru was to enlist middle-class support for an attack on oligarchic privilege, and only later to affect the middle class. Such an interpretation is, up to now, still compatible with the regime's conduct.

BACKGROUND AND CONTEXT

How can one account for the adoption by Peru's military rulers of a genuinely reformist program, an occurrence so unexpected that, as Fidel Castro remarked, it is as if the "fire had started at the firehouse?"[30] Why did the Peruvian army do the unexpected, or why were we not prepared to understand what they were doing?

There can be little doubt that most foreign (and even some Peruvian) assessments of the military regime have regarded it mainly in terms derived from the experiences of other countries, rather than from Peru's own past. Those who think primarily of other Latin American military regimes have understandably discounted the Peruvian government's professions of reform; they have consequently either been perplexed by what the regime seems actually to be doing or else quick to emphasize any evidence that it is doing less than it seems. Even those who, recognizing that armies vary substantially in their political roles, frame their approach to different military regimes within a broader (often class-based) analysis, find themselves puzzled by the Peruvian case, for the army's program unquestionably outruns what most middle-class Peruvians support.

Established conceptual boxes have not served well to characterize or explain the Peruvian process. Rather, familiar categories have led analysts astray, causing them to be so surprised at Peru's apparent nonconformity to their expectations that they have tended either to try to salvage their schemes by grasping at fragmentary evidence and ignoring contradictions, or to relax their critical scrutiny of the regime's ambiguities in deference to what seems to be a puzzling exception.

In seeking to explain the Peruvian military's policies, one may profitably concentrate on understanding Peru before 1968, analyzing changes both within the Peruvian armed forces and in the larger society within which it operates.

Víctor Villanueva and Luigi Einaudi have focused on the Peruvian military's evolution.[31] They advance several explanations for

---

[30] The Castro quotation may be found in Elizabeth Hyman, "Military Power and Political Changes in Latin America," *Survival* 15, no. 2 (Mar.–Apr. 1973), p. 65.

[31] See Luigi Einaudi, "The Military and Government in Peru" in Clarence E. Thurber and Lawrence Graham (eds.), *Development Administration in*

the army's recent course: the effects of recruiting and promoting middle-class officers, primarily of provincial origin; the impact of the army's extensive training program, particularly the course at the Centro de Altos Estudios Militares (CAEM), Peru's equivalent of the National War College, and the instruction at U.S. installations; the legacy of the army's past traumas and the officers' consequent distrust of civilians; and especially the experiences top-ranking officers suffered in putting down guerrilla uprisings in the mid-1960s. All these factors help account for the army's approach since 1968, clarifying in part why Peruvian officers reject the landed elite, favor planning and an expanded state role generally, oppose politics and politicians, and see reforms as essential for national security.

Comparative data suggest, however, that none of these factors by itself, nor even all together, can provide a sufficient explanation for the military's comprehensive reform program.[32] Almost all officer corps in Latin American armies come predominantly from the provincial middle class, but few (if any) parallel the Peruvian army's current stance. The CAEM program is unusual among Latin American countries, but it is by no means unique. Most officers who have graduated from nearly equivalent institutions in Argentina and Brazil, for instance, have emerged with attitudes and policy preferences very different from those their Peruvian counterparts declare. Besides, not even the most ardent believers in the efficacy of education would claim that a ninemonth course—or even shorter exposure to foreign training— could fundamentally affect the values and behavior of mature professionals. And other armies in Latin America and elsewhere have emerged from battles with guerrillas determined to repress them, not eager to foster structural change.

When one considers the civilian context in which Peru's armed

Latin America, Durham, N.C., Duke University Press, 1973, and the several other essays by Einaudi noted in the Appendix. See also Víctor Villanueva's many books, especially *100 años del ejército peruano: frustraciones y cambios*, Lima, Ed. Mejía Baca, 1971, and *El CAEM y la revolución de la fuerza armada*, Lima, Instituto de Estudios Peruanos, 1970. Villaneuva's extensive writings, listed in the Appendix, are critically discussed in James Malloy, "Dissecting the Peruvian Military: A Review Essay," *Journal of Inter-American Studies and World Affairs* 15, no. 3 (Aug. 1973), pp. 375–382.

32 Cf., for example, John S. Fitch III, "Toward a Model of the Coup d'Etat as a Political Process in Latin America—Ecuador, 1948–1968," unpublished doctoral dissertation, Yale University, 1973.

forces has acted, however, the fact that Peru's officers came to power in 1968 with a reform program is much less surprising. What is remarkable, indeed, is that the goals and means the current military regime espouses took so long in Peru to become an implemented government program.

In 1968 Peru was poor—probably the least developed of the larger Latin American countries, not just in *per capita* income but in urbanization, literacy, mass media exposure, and other aspects of social development. (A composite measure of "social mobilization indicators" prepared by David Scott Palmer ranks Peru sixteenth among the twenty Latin American countries considered, followed only by the Dominican Republic, Guatemala, Honduras, and Haiti.)[33]

Property and income distribution were exceptionally unequal. Less than 2 percent of Peru's agricultural estates (many of them owned by the same individuals or families) accounted for some 85 percent of the country's land, while 95 percent of properties took up but 10 percent of the land.[34] One percent of Peru's population received about 31 percent of the nation's income; the top 10 percent obtained half the national total, and the bottom quarter got only 3 percent.[35] This last group corresponded roughly to the residents of Peru's "*mancha india*," the provinces of Ancash, Apurímac, Ayacucho, Huancavelica, Cuzco, and Puno. Eighty-seven percent of the persons over five years old in these six provinces spoke Quechua or Aymara at the time of the 1961 census, and more than half did not speak Spanish.[36]

Industry, exports, and credit—like land—were controlled by small groups, members of a reduced number of Peruvian families or else foreigners, tied in with international firms.[37] And national

[33] David Scott Palmer, "Revolution from Above: Military Government and Popular Participation in Peru, 1968–1972," Dissertation Series, Latin American Studies Program, Cornell Unversity, 1973, pp. 7–9.

[34] Comité InterAmericano de Desarrollo Agrícola (CIDA), *Tenencia de la tierra y desarrollo socio-económico del sector agrícola: Perú*. Washington, D.C., Pan American Union, 1966, p. 35.

[35] See Richard Webb, "The Distribution of Income in Peru," Discussion Paper no. 26, Woodrow Wilson School, Princeton University (Sept. 1972), p. 3.

[36] Cotler, "Mechanics of Internal Domination," p. 232.

[37] See Carlos Malpica, *Los dueños del Perú*, Lima, Ed. Ensayos Sociales, 1968, for data—inaccurate in some details but useful as a general guide—on the holdings of Peru's major families and firms. Cf. François Bourricaud, *Power and Society in Contemporary Peru*, New York, Praeger, 1970; the following paragraphs owe much to Bourricaud's analysis.

policies systematically protected the interests of Peru's dominant elites, domestic and international. Free currency exchange, protection for infant industries, incentives for foreign investments, tax regulations of various sorts, irrigation projects and water rights: all helped the rich and powerful retain their place.

Peru as it was before 1968 had not escaped challenge, of course. Beginning with Manuel González Prada in the late nineteenth century, writers had assailed the injustice of a society based on exploitation of the many by the few.[38] National and foreign observers alike had characterized Peru as a "beggar sitting on a throne of gold" and had argued that prosperity could only be achieved by a just and rational social reorganization. Standard remedies for Peru's acknowledged ills had been advocated for years by church and lay thinkers, by Marxists and anti-Communists, by Apristas and by military men. All agreed that Peru needed to educate and incorporate its Indian masses, to redistribute property and its rewards more equitably, to expand production and markets, and to exploit its resources to benefit the entire population rather than just a few families or foreigners. José Carlos Mariátegui and Víctor Rául Haya de la Torre, Peru's internationally influential writers, agreed in their emphasis on these points, however much they disagreed on others.

Creating a stronger state and undertaking planning; establishing controls to assure that foreign investment serves Peru; ending, or at least reducing, dependence; reforming land tenure and general property distribution; extending and transforming education: these were all points of consensus among professionals, intellectuals, *técnicos*, and even some industrialists, indeed among virtually all politically aware Peruvians not themselves directly dependent on perpetuating a preindustrial, land-based system of nearly feudal characteristics. Many differences remained among these sectors in 1968, but few, if any, opposed in principle the kinds of reforms the military regime announced it would undertake. It is instructive to note, for instance, that even Acción Popular's right wing (as reflected in the Ulloa-dominated cabinet of 1968) had pressed foward with measures designed to subordi-

---

[38] See Manuel González Prada, *Horas de lucha*, Callao, Tip. "Lux," 1924. For an excellent discussion of the history of Peruvian social thought, see John Plank, "Peru: A Study in the Problems of Nation-Forming," unpublished doctoral dissertation, Harvard University, 1958.

nate private interests to a strengthened state.[39] The 1962 and 1963 campaigns had included pro-reform appeals not only by Belaúnde's Acción Popular but also by APRA, the Democristianos, and the Socialprogresistas, and the prospective 1969 campaign promised more of the same.[40]

By 1968 structural reforms of the type the Economic Commission for Latin America (ECLA, CEPAL in Spanish) had been proposing for years were, in Peru, an idea whose time had come. The concepts and rhetoric had been around a long time, attaining widespread legitimacy, and they were made more compelling by the facts of social and economic change, which had begun to accelerate in Peru after World War II.

From 1945 on, Peru experienced striking economic growth, urbanization, and general social mobilization. National economic production grew at an annual rate of close to 6 percent, fueled by a major expansion of copper mining and by the explosion of what quickly became the world's largest fishmeal industry. Peru's population rose by more than 3 percent a year, and the impact of this rapid growth was made even more dramatic by migration to Peru's cities, mainly to Lima. Thirty-eight percent of Peru's population lived in cities in 1940; by 1967 the figure was 51 percent and still climbing fast.[41] Lima-Callao swelled to about three million, sprawling out over the city's vital agricultural land as well as over miles of flat desert. School enrollment, at the primary and secondary levels especially, climbed sharply during the 1950s and 1960s, pushing literacy rates up from 43.4 percent in 1940 to 81 percent in 1970, and feeding pressures to expand university facilities.[42] (This expansion, like that of income, was very unevenly distributed; few rural Indian children obtained more than two or three years of schooling, even in the 1960s.) Communications intensified and extended its ambit; by 1965 transistor radios dotted the Peruvian highlands, and television antennas

[39] See Jane Jaquette, "The Politics of Development in Peru," Dissertation Series, Latin American Studies Program, Cornell University, 1971.

[40] See, for instance, the party statements contained in S. Martinez, *Ideario y plan de gobierno de los partidos políticos, 1962,* Lima, Ed. Industrial Gráfica, 1962.

[41] Bergman and Larson, *Social Stratification in Peru,* p. 137.

[42] See Drysdale and Myers, "Continuity and Change: Peruvian Education," Chapter 7 of this volume.

were beginning to sprout in the shantytowns of Lima and other cities.

Pressures on Peru's elites began to mount from an increasingly urbanized and literate population that was insistently seeking a larger share of the nation's resources. Rural and urban land invasions, guerrilla outbursts, student demonstrations, strikes, and increasing electoral support for reformist candidates reflected their demands.

No revolutionary coalition of the aggrieved had developed in Peru by 1968. No doubt this was in part due to repression, as Lima's elites managed to suppress individual challenges and to prevent the organization of concerted efforts among dissident groups. In part, however, Peru's revolution could be postponed, or avoided, because individual demands were more or less being satisfied.[43] The booming export-led economy permitted Peruvian governments to yield to specific pressures after World War II. Land invasions produced results: the acceptance and even the promotion of squatter settlements in the cities and the beginnings of land reform in the rural areas. Wages were raised in industry after industry, and social security benefits were increased. Universities multiplied at a dizzying pace, from six in 1955 to at least thirty in 1968. Tens of thousands of housing units were constructed during the Belaúnde period alone; the number of hospital beds was doubled, electric power production multiplied, and service was extended.[44] Each pressure was responded to on its own terms, however; little effort was made to devise comprehensive policies or to undertake structural changes. On the contrary, some concessions were granted with obvious disregard for their wider effects; Law 15215, providing an unrealistically rapid increase in teachers' salaries beyond the country's financial capacity, exemplified this problem.

While Peru's society began to change, its political system did not keep pace. The landholding oligarchy continued to exercise predominant political influence into the 1960s. Its power was clearly beginning to wane. For example, only about two-thirds of Belaúnde's cabinet officers were from landed families; under pre-

[43] Cf. David Chaplin, "Peru's Postponed Revolution," *World Politics* 20 (Apr. 1968), pp. 393–420.

[44] Guillermo Hoyos Osores, "Crisis de la democracia en el Perú: causas de su quebranto y condiciones para su recuperación," *Cuadernos Americanos* 7, no. 31 (Jan.–Feb. 1969), especially pp. 14–15.

ceding governments almost all were.[45] But the oligarchy still dominated Congress, particularly by controlling the politics of the rural provinces, which accounted for 29 percent of the population and 27 percent of the seats but only 14 percent of the votes.[46] (Highland Peru was almost totally ignored, except in rhetoric, by Peru's politicians until candidate Belaúnde's extensive travels in the 1956 and 1962–1963 campaigns. And even in 1963, residents of the densely-populated Sierra were prevented by literacy requirements from becoming a major electoral force.) The significance of the oligarchy's entrenched hold on Congress was reinforced by the unusual importance of Peru's legislature in national politics; the Congress retained and exercised a system, unique in Latin America, permitting not only interpellation but even the censure of individual ministers.[47] With their control of Congress, plus their influence on the press, on access to credit, and on the interest associations, Peru's landed families assured themselves that comprehensive reforms would not advance.

The history of agrarian reform in Peru illustrates both how the consensus on structural reforms emerged and how actual reform efforts prior to 1968 were thwarted.[48] Although the idea of land reform had been espoused for years by various intellectuals, landed interests successfully prevented it from becoming a matter for serious governmental consideration or even for significant public debate until the late 1950s. When domestic pressures and

[45] See Richard Stephens, *Wealth and Power in Peru*, Metuchen, N.J., Scarecrow Press, 1971. For an interesting interpretation of the 1962 military coup and the subsequent accession of Belaúnde as the occasion when Peru's middle class began to displace the landed families in political power, see Arnold Payne, *The Peruvian Coup d'Etat of 1962: The Overthrow of Manuel Prado*, Washington, D.C., Institute for the Comparative Study of Political Systems, 1968.

[46] Cotler, "Mechanics of Internal Domination," p. 236.

[47] See Terry McCoy, "Congress, the President and Political Instability in Peru," in Weston Agor (ed.), *Latin American Legislatures: Their Role and Influence*, New York, Praeger, 1971.

[48] In addition to Harding's essay in Chapter 6 of this volume, the following paragraphs draw extensively from: Bourricaud, *Power and Society*; Petras and Laporte, *Perú: ¿transformación revolucionaria o modernización?*; Thomas Carroll, "Land Reform in Peru," *AID Spring Review of Land Reform*, Washington, D.C., Agency for International Development, 1970; and John Strasma, "The United States and Agrarian Reform in Peru," in Daniel Sharp (ed.), *U.S. Foreign Policy and Peru*, Austin, University of Texas Press, 1973, pp. 156–205.

international trends made it impossible any longer to avoid considering the land tenure problem, however, the Prado regime in 1956 established a National Commission on Agrarian Reform and Housing. But the commission's chairman was Pedro Beltrán, editor of *La Prensa* and Peru's leading apostle of classical economic liberalism, and five of eight members were either large landowners or their direct agents. The commission's report was predictable; the recommendations consisted primarily of opening unused jungle lands for colonization and extending coastal irrigation projects.

When the peasant invasions of La Convención and Hugo Blanco's successes there convinced Peruvian army officers and others that land reform was needed to dampen a perceived threat to national security, the measure eventually decreed was limited to the geographic area actually suffering acute unrest. When the Belaúnde regime won election on a platform promising (among other items) a major agrarian reform, APRA opposition and the resulting congressional bargaining substantially watered down the initial proposal. The eventual law, passed in 1964, circumscribed the potentially affected areas severely; subsequent provisions regarding financing and implementation assured that not even a limited reform could be rapidly effected. By 1968, therefore, the aim of substantial agrarian reform was no longer debated among Peruvian *técnicos*; their concern, rather, was to obtain a government with sufficient strength and commitment to put such a reform into practice despite the opposition of Peru's landed families.

Proposals to strengthen the state and to assure that foreign investment would serve national needs had also been advanced but were even slower to become Peruvian public policy. Almost every writer on Peruvian problems in this century has emphasized the need to strengthen the public sphere, but Peru in the early 1960s was still a nation where taxes could be collected by a private banking firm which actually charged the government for the use of its own revenue. Peru's Central Bank in the early 1960s was still directly responsive to the private sector. The Peruvian state's share of national investment in 1960 was probably lower than that in any comparable South American nation.[49] And those with a stake in Peru's land-based economic and political

[49] See Hunt, "Distribution, Growth, and Government Economic Behavior," pp. 391–92.

system did what they could to keep the state weak. Planning as a concept was discredited in Peru, thanks largely to *La Prensa*'s influence, long after it had been accepted elsewhere, and other terms of national debate on economic and social policy were similarly shaped by Lima's oligarchy at least until 1960.[50]

Things were changing in Peru by the late 1960s, but ever so slowly. The National Planning Institute was established in 1962 (by the caretaker military regime) but remained weak during the Belaúnde years. The Central Bank was somewhat restructured but stayed closely tied to dominant private interests. Public investment began to climb, but Peru's public sector was still weaker than that of any of Peru's neighbors, except perhaps Ecuador.

As for toughening the terms on which foreign investment entered Peru, which Haya de la Torre had advocated since at least 1928, Peruvian governments after 1950 actually bucked the general Latin American nationalist trend.[51] One concession or incentive after another was granted by Peru to foreign investors in mining, petroleum, and manufacturing. By the 1960s, Mexico, Brazil, and Argentina had long since nationalized their petroleum companies. In Peru, however, IPC was not only private and foreign but even enjoyed subsoil rights unique (and questionable) under Peruvian law. Special tax advantages were also exercised by Conchán (itself half owned by a U.S. company), the other main oil refining and distribution enterprise in Peru. The Peruvian mining code of 1950 was universally considered one of Latin America's most generous to foreign investors, as was the 1952 Petroleum Law, and the special provisions of the Toquepala copper contract were particularly favorable to the foreign investor, Southern Peru Copper Corporation. Industrial incentive laws were similar; the automobile assembly industry, for instance, drew thirteen companies to Peru in the 1960s for a total market of less than twenty thousand vehicles a year. Here again, change began to occur in the 1960s as Peru gradually imposed stricter reinvestment obligations, higher taxes, and other requirements. More sweeping reforms, however, were always frustrated

50 See Bourricaud, *Power and Society*, for an extensive discussion of the Peruvian oligarchy's remarkable success at controlling the agenda for public discussion. Shane Hunt notes that the "chronic gap between what is widely desired and what is politically feasible is the power of the elite"; see Hunt, "Distribution, Growth, and Government Behavior," p. 381.

51 This paragraph draws considerably on Hunt's "Direct Foreign Investment in Peru: New Rules for an Old Game," Chapter 8 of this volume.

by the hold the landed elite continued to exert on the political system.

By 1968 Peru was considerably behind most of its neighbors with regard to various economic and political reforms. Ready consensus existed among *técnicos*, civilian and military, regarding what needed to be done. A considerable and obvious policy vacuum was waiting to be filled.

It should not have been surprising that the military regime eventually occupied that space. Already in their short-term takeover of 1962–1963, top army officers had shown their disposition toward reform, a disposition underlined by the armed forces' widely understood support for the Belaúnde platform. Army officers shared with their civilian brethren in the middle class a desire to break the oligarchy's hold, a desire which underlay the birth of Belaúnde's Acción Popular, of the Democristianos, and of the Movimiento Socialprogresista. All took essentially the same approach; the army officers taught at CAEM by civilians from these groups were by no means alone.

Nor should it have been surprising that Peru's armed forces in 1968 had both the sense of legitimacy and the power to proceed at once with a reform program. Throughout the 1950s and 1960s, while civilian political institutions were proving increasingly anachronistic and were being questioned by Peruvian critics of several political persuasions, the armed forces were growing in size, strength, capacity, and coherence. Imbued—at CAEM and other military schools, in the intelligence service, and through their military journals—with a "new professionalism," Peru's officers looked to the problems of national development as a legitimate and high priority battleground.[52] Their sense of competence often reinforced by success in university studies and other civilian spheres, Peru's officers felt confident they could tackle long-deferred problems.

Their way was relatively unimpeded at the start. Peru's still relatively low level of prior social mobilization and participation, the weak and dependent nature of Lima's industrial bourgeoisie, the dwindling economic base of Peru's rural elite, and especially the general disrepute which civilian politicians had achieved: all

[52] See Alfred C. Stepan III, "The New Professionalism of Internal Warfare and Military Role Participation" in Stepan (ed.), *Authoritarian Brazil*, New Haven, Yale University Press, 1973, pp. 47–65.

left Peru's officers virtually unchallenged as they took over. The army was vociferously opposed only by APRA, its traditional antagonist. And APRA—by 1968 mainly a party of old men and their memories—could easily be outflanked, especially by the immediate nationalization of IPC, so long an issue in Peruvian politics, and then by the agrarian reform.[53]

That Peru's armed forces came to power talking about structural reforms, that they really intended to undertake them, and that they were able to begin doing so with relative ease are much more easily understandable, therefore, when one considers the national background and context of the military take-over. Personal leadership, contingent circumstances, the international environment—these and other factors undoubtedly influenced the Peruvian regime's initial approach and its subsequent evolution. But the fundamental fact, which this essay seeks to underline and which is documented repeatedly in the chapters to come, is that Peru's military rulers entered power prepared institutionally to try to overcome the evident gap between Peru's socioeconomic reality and its political institutions and public policies. Whatever the final outcome of this attempt, there can be no doubt that the attempt is being made.

EVOLUTION OF THE "REVOLUTION"

It is not so difficult, then, to conclude that the Peruvian military regime is a genuinely reformist one and to explain why this should be so. But why have Peru's officers gone beyond their original program, as they seem to have done? Why have they deepened and extended the process of reform?

Available interpretations of the Peruvian military regime fit generally into two categories. The first and larger group takes the regime's decree laws and the speeches of key government officers as its primary, almost exclusive data. The analytical tasks adopted are principally to organize and explicate the regime's aims and assumptions, not always clearly stated, to deduce and define its "ideology," and then to relate these to already familiar

[53] For a discussion of the effects of the military government's measures on APRA, see Edward C. Epstein, "The Effect of the 1968 Coup d'Etat upon the Apra: A Motivational Analysis," unpublished paper presented at the Southwest Political Science Association Meeting, San Antonio, Tex., 1972.

cases. The Peruvian approach has been characterized variously as reformist, revolutionary, corporatist, populist, modernizing, authoritarian, Nasserist, Bismarckian, or something cf the sort. Finally, speculation about the regime's future is derived from its supposed nature.

The second approach draws on a much richer data base: not only normative laws but implementing regulations and administrative practice, not just set speeches but press conference remarks and other informal expressions, not just government acts and statements but failures to act or to comment. Here too, however, the tendency is often to assume that behind the many actions and omissions is a coherent model, the nature of which can be deduced from the regime's record, and which can be used to predict the character of subsequent measures. Analysts of Peru, even the best informed, have tended so far to treat the military regime as if it were a continuous and highly cohesive government implementing a coherent, perhaps preexisting, plan; this tendency has been reinforced, no doubt, by General Velasco's claim that his government's major actions were outlined in a "secret plan" prepared before October 1968 and released by Velasco on July 28, 1974.

A closer look, however, suggests that the supposed plan (even assuming, despite evidence to the contrary, that it existed in 1968 in the form in which it was eventually released), did not amount to much more than a list of objectives; it did not bind the Peruvian armed forces to a detailed course of action. There is, indeed, reason to question the presumed unitary, cohesive, and institutional nature of the Peruvian regime. Much of the reason both for the regime's contradictions and for its "radicalizing" trend may derive, in fact, precisely from discontinuities and divisions within the government, from shifts in its composition, and from its successive reactions to external constraints.

The Peruvian regime proclaims itself and is generally accepted as an eminently institutional "government of the armed forces." Undoubtedly part of its strength, durability, and relative success does owe to its harnessing of military discipline and solidarity for political and administrative tasks. But it is important to note that the 1968 coup apparently resulted not from institutional deliberation and agreement among the services, but rather from a decision by selected army officials. When the new government was established on October 3, the ranking navy officer was not named minister but was retired instead.[54] Both the top- and the second-ranking air force generals also resigned immediately, and five air force generals retired prematurely within the regime's first eight months. The ranking army generals with command of troops in the country's various geographic regions were made cabinet ministers, though there are indications that at least some of them knew nothing of the coup until it had occurred. Several of the army's senior generals were excluded from the government from the start or were pushed aside in a series of internal changes during the regime's first year.

Of all the original cabinet members, only President Velasco himself retains the post he held at first. Most of the first cabinet members have long since retired: several prematurely, and at least some over policy or political differences. Their places and other key political and military posts have been taken by officers who were colonels in 1968. Of special importance is a group of men, most of whom have considerable background in army intelligence, whose alliance with General Velasco has catapulted them to predominant national influence: Fernández Maldonado, Rodríguez Figueroa, Gallegos Venero, Segura Gutiérrez, Hoyos, Meza Cuadra, Richter Prada, and Graham Hurtado being key figures. Many of these officers reportedly worked on preparing the 1968 coup and the outlines of the eventual government program ("Plan Inca"). Most became members immediately after the coup of the Comité de Asesoramiento de la Presidencia (COAP), a specially created, all-military presidential staff, charged primarily with developing and coordinating legislation.

Not only has the cabinet's membership altered substantially; many ministries have had a complete turnover in their chief civilian and military officials. Several key figures of the regime's first two years have been eased out of influential positions. Traditional political advisers (like Alfonso Montesinos or Alfonso Benavides Correa) and *pensador*-type economists (such as Jorge Bravo Bresani or Virgilio Roel) have seen their prestige and power decline. Other civilian advisers, many of them at least uncommitted or even unsympathetic to the regime, have joined the government in important posts. A new class of civilian *técnicos*—most between twenty-five and forty years old, many educated

---

[54] The discussion in this paragraph draws substantially from José García, "Dissent, Consolidation, and Reform: The First Year of the Velasco Regime," unpublished paper, California State University at Chico, 1973.

abroad, several prominent student leaders in Lima's universities ten to fifteen years ago, all committed to planning and to an expanded state role, most of them disillusioned about the failures of earlier promised reforms under civilian auspices—has increased in number, self-consciousness, and influence.[55]

The civilian advisers, though increasingly important, are far from homogeneous. They tend to cluster in distinct constellations, each one providing a special flavor to actions emanating from its respective sector. Apolitical technocrats, many of them upper middle class in origin and trained in the United States, predominate in the Ministry of Industry. The National Planning Institute reflects the predominance of a cadre of ECLA-trained, mostly U.S.-polished, politically astute technicians. The Ministry of Economy and Finance, in turn, draws largely on a somewhat earlier generation of technicians, several of them former Planning Institute and Central Bank officials. Christian Democratic and Marxist activists (even some former guerrilla leaders), ranged in the 1960s on opposite sides of political mobilization efforts, now work together, especially in SINAMOS and in local implementation of the agrarian reform. Augusto Salazar Bondy, a philosopher of the Socialprogresista tradition, had been the Education Ministry's top adviser from 1970 until his death in 1974, though his influence and that of other intellectual reformers has been diluted by military intelligence officers, career bureaucrats, and thousands of teachers and their representatives. Other Socialprogresista figures have played a significant part in the agrarian reform process, in the control of mass communications, in foreign policy formulation, and—particularly at an early stage —in helping to devise national mining and petroleum policies. There is even an ex-Aprista cluster in the Ministry of Fisheries, not to mention the several cases of individual ex-Apristas, Carlos Delgado foremost among them, participating in key roles.[56]

These and other civilians affect sectoral policies importantly. None, however, is called upon to assist the cabinet, COAP, and

[55] Peter Cleaves and Martin Scurrah provide valuable data showing that the percentage of upper-level posts in Peru's public administration occupied by civilian or military *técnicos* climbed from 55.7 percent in 1963 to 74.9 percent in 1974. See Cleaves and Scurrah, "State-Society Relations," Table 1.

[56] Delgado, once Haya de la Torre's personal secretary, became President Velasco's chief speech writer early in 1969 and has participated extensively in the elaboration of the educational reform and in the establishment and implementation of the regime's political agency, SINAMOS.

President Velasco with overall policy coordination. Delgado (and perhaps to a lesser extent, top Planning Institute personnel) seems to be exceptional among civilians for having been consulted on a broad range of issues, and even his role appears to be more important in the articulation of announced policy and ideology than in the resolution of conflicting priorities or claims.

Sectoral policy responsibilities are assigned to the various ministries, each with its particular nucleus of civilian advisers and each responsive to a different clientele. The situation is complicated, and policy contradictions made more likely, by the fact that each ministry is assigned permanently to one of the armed services. For example, the navy, traditionally conservative in Peru as almost everywhere, retains the Industry and the Housing portfolios (in addition to the Navy Ministry itself), and policy in these sectors is undoubtedly influenced by the preferences of the navy's officer corps. (Ministers from the air force and the navy apparently consider the stance of brother officers, and/or the institutional preference of their respective services, as relevant but not binding in their own positions.) Reported presidential attempts to designate individual officers from within services other than the army to serve in cabinet posts have been thwarted. Efforts to achieve uniform or even consistent national policies across sectoral lines, therefore, must be left to the cabinet, where bargaining and compromise among the services no doubt abound, and/or to the COAP.

The Peruvian regime, then, reflects the predominant influence of a minority army faction within the considerable constraints imposed by the perceived need to preserve the unity of the armed forces, that is, to secure acceptance of government policies by other army officers and by officials of the air force and navy. Policies are shaped, as well, by the conflicting advice of civilian officials, some of them with great influence in particular sectors.

Moreover, external pressure should by no means be discounted as an influence on the regime's evolving policies, however much the government denies that it can be moved from its course by unsanctioned protests or displays. Regime policy making has been characterized by an iterative process in which general goals are announced, a normative law is decreed, implementing regulations taking into account initial reactions to the law are released, and eventually the law is modified. In several fields the regime has amended its own laws in response to pressures and on the basis of experience; this was true regarding student participation in university governance, worker participation in the management of the sugar cooperatives, and the terms under which agricultural land is distributed or urban settlements authorized. Strikes and demonstrations on the sugar estates and at the Huando hacienda, the protests of small and medium landholders, the Pamplona urban land invasion: each produced a government response.[57]

It should not be surprising, therefore, that actions taken by one ministry may not always be consistent with those taken by another, nor that decisions taken recently differ significantly from related choices in 1968 or 1969. Although some degree of consensus must have existed within the military hierarchy on the general aim of structural reform and perhaps on the main specific measures to be adopted (about which considerable accord existed outside the armed forces as well), the limits of that prior accord were undoubtedly reached early in the regime's tenure. Peruvian officers may have agreed, by and large, that improved national security would depend on growth and development, more equitable distribution, expanded education, greater participation in the national community by "marginal" populations, more nearly national control of economic and political decisions, and so on, but there was probably no clear agreement on how and with what relative priority to pursue these goals. From the beginning the Peruvian regime has been devising policies within a very broad framework, one which allows much scope for changing priorities and for reversals and contradictions.

Although the Peruvian military's course has been considerably less clearly defined than is generally recognized, the regime *has* tended to move beyond its originally announced program toward more extensive and fundamental reforms. The "revolution" has become radicalized, albeit within limits. Why?

One important cause has undoubtedly been the leadership of President Velasco. His skill in holding the military coalition together and assuring that discrepancies and divisions are kept internal is increasingly recognized, particularly after his sudden

[57] These instances are discussed in several chapters of this volume, especially those by Bourque and Palmer, Collier, Drysdale and Myers, and Harding.

and severe illness early in 1973 removed him from the palace temporarily. What is not so generally perceived is Velasco's own tendency to push for more extensive reform. Velasco's commitment to sweeping agrarian reform has been demonstrated, for instance, by his unswerving support for officials (especially Benjamín Samanez Concha, the agrarian reform's director) whose handling of specific issues has drawn criticism—even from within the government—for being too extreme or rapid. Velasco's own desire to establish improved rapport with students (and to have something dramatic to say on the four hundredth anniversary of San Marcos University) is said to have precipitated the commitment to expanded student participation in university governance. Members of the Educational Reform Commission report that Velasco's personally expressed concern about the rural areas and about reaching the Quechua- and Aymara-speaking populations led to a revision of their draft proposal in order to give greater emphasis to bilingual education. Changes in the final draft of the social-property legislation, particularly those providing greater redistribution of benefits, are attributable to the president's initiatives. And at least some of the thrust in Peru's foreign policy may derive from the sense of indignation President Velasco himself has felt on account of foreign domination of Peru. Separating out General Velasco's personal impact on these or other questions is probably impossible on the basis of accessible information, but it seems likely that he has consciously led the armed forces toward policies most officers would have rejected in 1968 as too extreme.

A second important influence has been the COAP. COAP has clearly been central to the regime's development, though data about COAP's functions, its impact, and even its composition are hard to obtain. Enough has been learned, primarily from interviews with current or former COAP officers and other Peruvian government officials, to suggest that COAP furnishes important elements of policy coherence and continuity that might otherwise be lacking. COAP's role in initiating and staffing out reform measures, in helping to prepare presidential speeches, and especially in commenting on legislative drafts emanating from the various ministries provides a process by which differences among services or sectors may often be reconciled.

But if COAP provides more consistency to government policy than would otherwise occur, it does so on terms considerably more radical than many army officers, practically all top navy and air force officers, and probably several cabinet ministers would choose for themselves. COAP's impact was evident already early in the regime, when its staff worked, with help from two civilian holdovers from Belaúnde's National Planning Institute, to draft Premier Montagne's major speech of December 5, 1968, outlining the regime's long-term economic and social policies. Since then, COAP has played a major role in undertaking or revising several of the key reforms, often apparently against the opposition, or at least without the active participation, of the relative ministries. COAP officers reportedly drafted the 1969 Agrarian Reform Law and presented it to Agriculture Minister José Benavides, whose refusal to accept some provisions forced his removal from the cabinet. The "enterprise reform" was under consideration in COAP for some weeks in 1970, but was kept secret from the select nongovernment civilians asked to review and comment on "the" draft law, and perhaps even, at least for a time, from some cabinet officials. COAP initiatives sharply altered part of the regime's first University Reform Law, originally drafted by military intelligence officers in the Education Ministry with the advice of a small group of civilians, in order to restore and expand student rights. The SINAMOS mechanism, and more recently the social-property legislation, have been developed by COAP task forces, each one involving civilian and military participants from ministries and from outside the government, but all under the direction of a general from COAP.

COAP's effect has been to shift the government's center of policy-making gravity somewhat to the left: this may be because of its membership (first it was a haven for some of the colonels active in the coup who were too junior to take cabinet posts in this institutionally-organized regime, and more recently it has been an assignment for the most politically oriented officers), because it operates as the president's own staff and responds to his inclinations, or because its functions dispose or require COAP officers to see connections among problems that lead them to propose structural solutions—or for a combination of these and perhaps other reasons. (Experience in COAP seems to have had a similar effect on individual officers as well; officers like Ramón Meneses Arata, for instance, are said to have become much more radical during their tenure at COAP.) Part of the regime's general trend may be attributed to the unrivaled influence of COAP, together with that of Delgado, in formulating general strategy. COAP's influence on policy might well have been even greater had not COAP itself been subject to the military practice of rotating almost all officers; most COAP officials were transferred to other assignments in 1971 and 1973, and this led to a temporary decrease of the organization's effectiveness and influence.

Closely related, no doubt, has been the increasing influence of the first COAP's members, most of whom have been steadily ascending in military rank and seniority and have occupied key posts in the cabinet, in regular army duties, and in SINAMOS. An illuminating reflection of the link between General Velasco and the younger officers here identified as the first COAP occurred in March 1973 when it appeared that Velasco was seriously ill, perhaps mortally so. No group was as vociferous and insistent as this cadre in its view that Velasco personally and promptly must resume the regime's leadership. COAP's chief, General José Graham Hurtado, apparently engineered a move by which the temporary assignment of certain powers from the ill chief executive to Premier Edgardo Mercado Jarrín (a step previously authorized by the three-man junta, representative of the services, in which national sovereignty formally vests) was amended to limit the transfer to one month. Had General Velasco been unable to return to office, this military group—most influential in regime policy making but still not at the top of the army hierarchy—might well have found its position vulnerable.

A third reason for the regime's evolution has surely been the officers' diminished confidence, based on experience, that the initial measures could by themselves produce the desired effects. At first, the military government seemed genuinely to believe that "prerevolutionary mentalities" would change and that conflict among Peruvians could consequently be avoided. That faith has been shaken. The various means used by businessmen to minimize or avoid the effects of the 1970 Industrial Law, for instance, apparently shocked those in the government who had expected rapid, if somewhat grudging, acceptance of the new arrangements. Reluctance by labor unions to have their prerogatives curtailed, even in cases where labor has in effect become owner, has also been revealing to the Peruvian leadership. The military's distrust of those whose interests are seen as obscuring or biasing their perceptions has been reinforced, so that critical response from affected sectors has largely been screened out. The exaggerated reaction of many businessmen to the regime's initiatives, on the other hand, has dampened the chances for improving the dialogue between business and government. The possibility that the military government might alter some policies in ways acceptable to the private sector has on several occasions been minimized by the private sector's own intransigence.

The influence of technocrats, not so easily understood as having interests of their own, has consequently increased. And the best-trained and most self-confident *técnicos* have tended to recommend that the reforms be carried further. The Planning Institute's impact, especially, has been to define the regime's approach in more comprehensive terms, to push fcr eliminating policy inconsistencies by generalizing the more radical of conflicting approaches. The regime has found itself both pushed and pulled to *profundizar la revolución*.

The international context—the early efforts by Washington to force Peru to back down on the IPC expropriation and later U.S. attempts to accommodate Peru, Cuba's extraordinary gestures of support, the advent of radical governments in Bolivia and Chile, the Andean Group's decision to adopt Peru's approach toward foreign investment—also probably affected the Peruvian regime's tendency to go beyond its original thrust. Whereas U.S. pressures had intimidated and constrained Peru in earlier periods, the bluster of a Vietnam-mired America in 1968–1969 served mainly to strengthen the more radical and nationalist of Peruvian officers and advisers. Until recently, Peru found its approach becoming increasingly accepted within the Andean region. Measures which might earlier have been unacceptably radical could be portrayed as consistent with, or even less extreme than, the approaches Peru's neighbors were taking.

The unanticipated consequences of its own decisions have also affected the regime's program, as the fishmeal nationalization illustrates. Peruvian officials were probably quite candid in asserting that the take-over was intended to be an isolated measure, practically forced upon the government by circumstances beyond its control. A natural disaster, the virtual disappearance of the anchovy, had brought most of the industry close to bankruptcy. Only the more efficient, better-financed firms, which were American owned, seemed likely to survive the year. The industry was nationalized simply to prevent a foreign take-over of Peru's major earner of foreign exchange. But Peruvian businessmen generally responded as if the nationalization implied or signaled a larger decision to abandon private enterprise. As private investment declined further, the regime found itself forced to expand the public sector's role even more.

Little has occurred so far, on the other hand, to cause the Peruvian government's leaders to consider abandoning their course. The reasonably good performance of Peru's economy (satisfactory growth with somewhat improved distribution and without startling inflation), plus the international reputation Peru has attained, have no doubt reinforced the convictions of Peru's officers that they are on the right track. That domestic support is clearly lacking has been understood by most government officials. But the absence of public enthusiasm is attributed largely to the continuing power of vested interests and to the regime's inability so far to provide many tangible benefits, or even a sense of genuine participation, to large numbers of Peruvians. Peru's rulers appear to believe sincerely that popular support will eventually be forthcoming, when the impacts of the reforms are more widely felt and when the structure for facilitating mass participation has been better established. Until then, apparently, opposition is to be conciliated whenever possible, but suppressed when necessary. So far, repression has not been required often enough to prompt the self-questioning that more systematic measures might eventually induce within the armed forces.

THE FUTURE OF PERU'S EXPERIMENT

Notwithstanding its tendency toward more radical measures, the military regime in Peru has, as noted earlier, left a number of central issues unresolved in its first six years. The extent and form of popular participation, the eventual role of the private economy and of foreign investment, whether and how to extend the benefits of reform substantially beyond Peru's modern and advantaged quarter, and above all what, if anything, will be done to institutionalize the "revolution"—all these remain largely open. They raise a final set of questions: Will the regime continue to radicalize? What problems may it encounter, and how will these affect its course?

A presidential succession, if it occurred soon, would not only eliminate President Velasco's own influence but would probably weaken the impact of the original COAP's officers, the military group most disposed to further and more fundamental reforms. A succession occurring in 1977 or later, however, would probably find precisely these officers fully in charge of the Peruvian army, with all the leverage that hierarchical superiority would afford.

Continuing relative success in economic management would presumably reinforce the self-confidence of both civilian *técnicos* and their military peers. On the other hand, a strong economic downturn, perhaps as a consequence of international events beyond Peru's control, might bring the regime's current policies into question. Again, timing is crucial. If the Peruvian government can weather the storms immediately ahead until the expected major expansion of copper and, if all goes well, petroleum exports scheduled for 1976 and ensuing years, its course may well proceed unchallenged. But weathering the storms means, among other things, controlling strong inflationary pressures and restraining labor's demands, not easy tasks.

Changes in the international context can also affect Peru. The fall of Torres and Allende in Bolivia and Chile, Perón's return to Argentina and his break with the extreme Left, and the election of an Acción Democrática president in Venezuela have made Peru's leaders feel considerably more isolated than at any previous point. This may produce greater caution in Peruvian domestic and foreign policies.

One major problem arises precisely from the trend this essay underlines. The faster the regime's policies advance toward a more fundamental realignment of Peruvian society, the more likely they are to provoke tensions between the military's political and institutional roles and responsibilities.[58] Signs of distress within the officer corps are already evident on issues like the role of SINAMOS, the campaign against *El Comercio* and the eventual expropriation of all the major newspapers, and there are indications that officers' opinions may well have constrained the educational reform. It will require extraordinary political skill by Peru's military rulers to maintain the unity of the armed forces as policies continue to evolve. The dramatic resignation of the navy minister and the housing minister (also a ranking navy officer) in June 1974 emphasized this point.

A second, related, problem concerns the viability of an economy based more every month on the public sector. Satisfactory growth has been achieved since 1970 by constantly increasing the

[58] Cf. Alfred C. Stepan III, *The Military in Politics: Changing Patterns in Brazil*, Princeton, N.J., Princeton University Press, 1971, esp. pp. 253–267.

scope and intensity of the state's economic activities. The private sector's earlier dynamism has never recovered and shows few signs of doing so. Whether public enterprises are capable of efficiently developing Peru's resources is by no means certain, however. Telltale signs that Peru's bureaucracies are already overloaded have begun to accumulate. The Peruvian regime's legislative feats, however impressive, are largely accomplished; the current and future period of implementation will call upon talents and energies not yet fully tested.

Probably the toughest challenge the Peruvian regime faces is the issue of popular participation. If the great majority of Peruvians continue to feel left out of the "revolution," the regime's capacity to deal with opposition without harsh repression may end, and the vicious circle of violence so far mostly avoided may begin. Expanded participation would also have its costs. Precisely those Peruvians who are most mobilized and best able to participate are those who have pushed the regime hardest, seeking additional gains for themselves. Those who stand to benefit from the government's program, apart from the military-bureaucratic elites which obviously gain the most, are either out to secure an even greater share or, up to now, have been glad to receive what is offered. But they have felt few ties to a government which concedes them benefits but grants them little or no say in deciding how these benefits will be achieved or distributed. The advantages of organizing a political apparatus are obvious to many of the regime's civilian and military strategists, but so are the dangers of strengthening organizations which may acquire interests, aims, and power of their own.

An important experiment is under way in Peru. It tests whether soldiers as rulers can use their power to implement major structural changes sufficient to open the way to equitable and integrated national development without turning to repression, closing off participation, or merely replacing a civilian oligarchy with one in uniform—and without undermining the military institution itself. Several years of intense activity have already stamped this regime's impact on Peru.

In Julio Cotler's phrase, the military government "has unquestionably closed one chapter of Peru's history and opened another." How this new chapter will conclude and what will succeed it are not yet known. But enough has already occurred to suggest that this transitional phase in Peru's development deserves the careful analysis the following essays provide.

The New Mode of Political Domination in Peru

Julio Cotler

The Revolutionary Government of the Armed Forces, which came to power on October 3, 1968, has unquestionably closed one chapter of Peru's history and opened another. It has brought profound transformations to the economic, political, and social life of Peru. Perhaps the central feature of these transformations has been the elimination of what had been in the twentieth century the most important center of economic and political power in Peruvian society—the export oligarchy and the foreign economic interests with which this sector of the oligarchy had been closely associated. In place of this dependent-oligarchic mode of economic organization, the military government is moving toward the full development of modern capitalism in Peru in the form of a type of state capitalism which is closely linked to multinational firms. In place of earlier forms of political domination, the military government is implementing a corporative model of political control through which it seeks to structure popular participation in the economic development of the country. The linkages between state and society which form the basis of this system of control are characterized by their carefully structured vertical ordering and the technocratic orientation that guides their design.

OVERVIEW OF THE GOVERNMENT'S PROGRAM

The program of this government may be seen as having three major components: the antioligarchic reforms, the expanded role

This chapter is a substantially revised version of two articles previously published in Spanish: "Las bases del corporatismo en el Perú" and "Concentración del ingreso y autoritarismo político en el Perú," which appeared in *Sociedad y Política*, numbers 2 and 4, October 1972 and September 1973. I would like to thank David Collier and Abraham F. Lowenthal for their valuable substantive comments on this chapter and their generous assistance in preparing the translation of the state in the economy, and the corporative ordering of political relationships.

The antioligarchic orientation of the government has been clearly reflected in a series of dramatic reforms: the agrarian reform, the reorganization of industry and mining, the nationalization of fishing, the partial nationalization of banking and commerce, and a new, nationalistic foreign policy. Together, these policies constitute a carefully coordinated strategy, virtually a "military strategy," though certain contradictions and internal tensions among these policies must be recognized. Basically, the strategy has been to eradicate Peru's semicolonial export economy in its traditional form; to end the high concentration of resources in foreign enclaves and in the hands of a small fringe of native capitalists, a concentration which has severely limited the country's internal capitalization; and to end Peru's extreme social and economic heterogeneity—to end the phase of Peruvian history in which the most advanced forms of modern capitalism and the "semifeudal," traditional agriculture of the highlands were incongruously juxtaposed within the same nation.

The elimination of the oligarchic-dependent structure goes hand in hand with expanding and strengthening the state, which, as a result of expropriations of national and foreign capital, has assumed a central role as an entrepreneur and promoter of economic activity. Peru's government has thus acquired an unprecedented capacity to accumulate capital and reach new agreements with international capitalism (in the form of multinational corporations), agreements which form the basis for the joint economic exploitation of the country. The attempt to homogenize Peruvian society likewise plays a central role in the government's attempt to form a modern, integrated nation-state.

The state, led by the military and by *técnicos*, is thus carrying out the developmental tasks which in many earlier-developing countries of Latin America and Europe were performed by the bourgeoisie. In Peru, the bourgeoisie was, by contrast, too weak to carry out these tasks. Among the most important of the reasons for this weakness was the preponderant role of foreign capital in Peruvian economic growth, which severely limited the development of the national bourgeoisie.

With regard to the question of political control, the government is forced to limit demands for mass political participation and economic redistribution in order to achieve its economic objectives. This is necessary, in the first place, because the intensity of popular pressure exceeds the redistributive potential of the system and because redistribution would conflict with much-needed capital accumulation. In the second place, the government does not wish to allow other organizations to share or compete with the armed forces in the formulation and implementation of the state's policy. For this reason, a basic feature of the political orientation of the government is its attempt to exercise corporative control not only over those organizations which promoted the interests of the oligarchy, but also over lower- and middle-class organization. The government is seeking fundamental restructuring of society along authoritarian and technocratic lines, with the purpose of depoliticizing the lower and middle classes.

THE BACKGROUND OF CHANGE IN PERU

The political and economic strategy of the present government, which has evolved over the last two decades among certain groups within the Peruvian Army, is a response to growing pressures from various sectors of society which have been seeking a substantial redistribution of wealth and political power in Peru. These pressures produced the political and social crisis of the 1960s. The strategy of the military government is, in the last analysis, a response to the much-proclaimed need to readjust the functioning of the Peruvian system, due to the threat posed by the political radicalization of the more organized sectors within the dominated classes.

During the past two decades, Peru's economy and society have undergone a process of expansion and diversification. This modernization of Peruvian capitalism was led by a new type of foreign investment which came into conflict with the previous mode of investment in agricultural and mining enclaves. Because of the emergence of these contradictory forms of economic development and of the new social sectors which they produced, Peruvian society entered into a social and political crisis which affected both the church and the army. This crisis manifested itself through increasingly acute pressures from the new urban and popular sectors, as well as from widespread peasant revolts which culminated in the establishment of a rural guerrilla movement in the mid-1960s.

This political crisis involved a multifaceted conflict among various factions of the native bourgeoisie, linked in differing ways with the old and new forms of foreign investment, and among different sectors of the petite bourgeoisie, who led the reformist-populist parties which directed their appeal toward the lower classes.

The irreversible character of these changes in social structure, along with the weakness of reformist political parties and the inability of the revolutionary Left to pose a viable political alternative, stimulated other societal groups—the church and especially the army—to abandon their traditional role of cooperation with the ruling oligarchy. In this situation, the military was able to assume power and to implement, in a decisive way, the reforms which the bourgeoisie and the petite bourgeoisie had been unable to carry out.

THE OLIGARCHIC CRISIS

Characterizing more broadly the situation that led to the rise of the present military government, it is fair to describe it as a fundamental crisis of the traditional oligarchy. The traditional oligarchic structure was based on an economy oriented toward the export of raw materials and toward the importation of capital goods, primarily for the export sector, and of goods and services destined primarily for the propertied classes. Though the export oligarchy was in many ways distinct from the sector which owned the semifeudal haciendas of the highlands, these two sectors had, over many years, been in a close political alliance. This particular juxtaposition of divergent social and economic forms was the basis for the designation of Peruvian society as "feudal-bourgeois" or "dualistic." It was because of the remarkable persistence of these contradictory forms that the analyses of Peruvian society carried out by Haya de la Torre and Mariátegui in the 1920s continued to pertain in the 1960s.[1]

The open, semicolonial character of the Peruvian economy, linked with the precapitalist sector, resulted in a high degree of concentration of economic, social, and political power, oriented around the institutional network controlled by primarily foreign

[1] On this subject see Víctor Raúl Haya de la Torre, El antimperialismo y el Apra (Santiago: Ediciones Ercilla, 1936), and José Carlos Mariátegui, Ideologia y Política, in Obras Completas, vol. 13 (Lima: Editora Amauta, 1959).

capital (principally North American) and secondarily by local capitalists. This latter group maintained the peasant population at the margin of political participation through the *gamonal* system.[2] Within this system of linkages with foreign capital, the native bourgeoisie had to content itself with whatever spoils were left them by North American enterprises. These spoils allowed the native bourgeoisie to perpetuate the system of political domination. Yet under this system, the potential for internal capitalization was very limited, and the capacity for distributing resources to the middle and lower classes was relatively small. The dominant class was therefore never able to achieve hegemony, to legitimate its position, or become the political-economic core of the country. As a result, over the past forty years, the native bourgeoisie had to turn to the army whenever it was faced with a situation of major political conflict or crisis, producing a pattern of frequent military intervention in Peruvian politics.

Beginning in the 1950s, however, this traditional structure began to crack. Changes in international trading patterns following the Second World War brought a substantial increase and diversification in Peruvian exports of primary products, which increased the capacity of the state and the native bourgeoisie to accumulate capital. The newly acquired resources served to satisfy, although in a limited and segmentary manner, the demands of the urban middle and lower class, which led to the growth of the urban economy. As a result, the rural bourgeoisie and foreign capitalists involved in the agricultural and mining enclaves began to diversify their investments to include the construction industry and the production of consumer goods, and to encourage private saving through the formation of credit institutions, particularly savings and loan associations. At the same time, however, they maintained their investments in agriculture and mining.[3]

This shift in investment helped to encourage substantial economic growth in the urban sector. The industrial sector, for example, had an annual growth rate of 10 percent during the 1950s and by the end of the decade represented a larger proportion of

[2] Julio Cotler, "The Mechanics of Internal Domination and Social Change in Peru," in Irving Louis Horowitz (ed.), *Masses in Latin America* (New York: Oxford University Press, 1970).

[3] J. Marrou, "Peru's Landed Oligarchy and Its Economic Power" (mimeo, Berkeley, Calif., 1967).

the gross national product than the agricultural and livestock sectors combined. Thus, within the semicolonial and precapitalist structure, a new form of capitalist accumulation and reproduction developed which began to break the traditional modes of production, *but without eliminating the political presence of oligarchic, dependent institutions.*

In this context, in which the traditional system of domination was breaking down and modern capitalism was emerging but had not yet established its political supremacy, other important social and political transformations began to occur as well: the massive migration to the cities of peasants who hoped to escape the traditional domination of the rural areas and to enter centers of the newly flourishing capitalism; peasant invasions and uprisings stimulated by the desire to destroy precapitalist modes of ownership and to join the newly expanding market economy; and the increasing frequency of strikes by workers seeking to improve their economic conditions and to take advantage of new opportunities for employment and consumption. This period also saw the spectacular growth and diversification, in terms of social class composition, of educational enrollment; the growing importance of education as a channel of mobility for middle- and lower-class migrants to the cities; and the mobilization of university students seeking to democratize student and faculty recruitment, the orientation of curriculum, and the administration of centers of higher learning.

This situation of change and crisis helped to stimulate important ideological changes in the church and in the army. There was a recognition in both institutions that the survival of the oligarchic regime was likely to strengthen the position of "anti-Christian" and revolutionary forces. A strong concern with internal security developed in the Center of Higher Military Studies (CAEM), and especially within the army's Intelligence Service. This concern led not only to a considerable emphasis on preparing the Peruvian armed forces to use the military techniques of counterinsurgency, but also to an interest in reform as an alternative to insurgency. This new emphasis on reform brought the thinking of many important military leaders surprisingly close to the position of Peru's reformist political parties and of the country's most noted intellectuals.

In summary, the oligarchic crisis of the 1960s resulted from contradictions which arose in the heart of Peruvian society. The military government which came to power in 1968 would try to resolve this crisis by suppressing all mass-based movements while at the same time seeking to eliminate the traditional structures from the Peruvian economy and society.

THE ANTIOLIGARCHIC, NATIONALIST ORIENTATION OF THE MILITARY GOVERNMENT

The military government of Peru is carrying out by means of administrative fiat from above the antioligarchic and nationalistic reforms which various other Latin American countries have achieved through the intervention of the masses—led by sectors of the petite bourgeoisie—as active protagonists. Obvious examples include the Bolivian and Mexican revolutions, the abortive revolution in Guatemala, and the initial stages of the Cuban Revolution. However, these other revolutions took place under circumstances in which the more advanced forms of imperialist domination and the "new dependency" had not yet entered the scene. The corresponding rigidity of the traditional system of domination prevalent in those countries required the direct revolutionary intervention of the popular masses and the radicalized petite bourgeoisie.

In the case of Peru, on the other hand, antioligarchic reforms can be achieved bureaucratically, without recourse to large-scale intervention by the popular masses, but rather in the context of the exclusion of most forms of popular political participation. Indeed, this is one of the distinctive features of the Peruvian case. This "peculiar revolution," which rejects meaningful mass political participation, can be carried out without popular participation precisely for the reasons already mentioned: because the traditional political-economic power was in a state of collapse at the same time that the popular movements and the revolutionary Left were crippled following the failure of the guerrilla movement in the mid-1960s.

One of the major goals of antioligarchic and nationalist revolutions is the homogenization of the social structure, which facilitates the expansion of capitalist forms of production. They seek to integrate the various sectors of productive activity under a dominant mode, with the consequent elimination of internal colonialism in class relations; and to widen and unify the internal market through a state policy of redistribution, which further promotes national integration. These factors should lead, according to the ideology, to the establishment of a representative state which, by controlling and directing the economy as well as by generating capital, will encourage the development of an autonomous bourgeoisie that will unify the country's society and economy.

We may therefore consider the antioligarchic and nationalistic revolutions in Latin America as, in a sense, equivalent to the bourgeois revolutions of Europe. In light of the traditionally conservative role of the military in Peru, it is ironic that the present military government should have the same goals which were pursued by numerous civilian political leaders and political parties in Peru who essentially wanted to achieve a bourgeois revolution in their own country. These leaders and parties would include Manuel Pardo in the last century, and in the present century Francisco García Calderón, Haya de la Torre, the Social Progressive Movement, Acción Popular, and Christian Democracy. These individuals and parties all shared the goal of creating a state which could shape and represent the nation and of creating a unified country in which class differences would be erased or buried under the concept of nationhood.

These are precisely the goals that the present military government wishes to achieve. The heterogeneity of the sources from which the government has drawn its program is clearly reflected in the remarkable variety of backgrounds of the civilian technocrats, administrators, ideologists, and propagandists who are working for the government. Former Apristas, Acción Populistas, Christian Democrats, Socialprogresistas, Communists, and Trotskyites may be found occupying high positions within government bureaucracies. Yet they remain under the jurisdiction and close surveillance of the military—the same military which, until recently, was considered to be the backbone of the oligarchic regime. Under this new regime, political debate and political decisions are made within the bureaucracies, and political conflict within the government centers around the evolution of contending civil-military coalitions in the bureaucracies. The conflicts which arise, however, are never disclosed. They are the carefully guarded secrets of the state.

THE MAJOR REFORMS

The series of reforms which has been carried out by the military government over the past six years may usefully be understood in terms of the antioligarchic, nationalistic framework which has just been presented. The aim of these reforms is to promote capitalist production in association with foreign capital, the predominant source of capital at this stage of Peruvian development.

Agrarian Reform

The government is attempting through the agrarian reform to eradicate not only the most traditional, semifeudal sector of the economy and the *gamonal* political system, but also one of the principal footholds of oligarchic power, the foreign enclaves. Agrarian reform is supposed to encourage the expansion of agriculture and livestock raising, thereby creating an important and cheap source of food for the urban population. This should lead to a reduced reliance on imported food, which now represents about one-third of total imports, thereby saving foreign exchange, which can be used instead for internal investment. The expansion of agricultural productivity is also supposed to increase the demand for manufactured goods, thereby increasing the income of the state, of foreign enterprise, and of the industrial bourgeoisie, and also thereby increasing the economic integration of the agricultural workers with the industrial market.

In addition, the agrarian reform is intended to encourage a transfer to the industrial and mining sectors of capital previously accumulated in agriculture. Under the Agrarian Reform Law, the agrarian reform bonds which are issued in compensation for the expropriation of rural landholdings may be redeemed if the bondholder engages in specified types of investment in industry or mining. In this way, the government seeks to encourage the rural elite to transfer its wealth to these other sectors. The agricultural sector will thus be left in the hands of various types of agricultural cooperatives and of smaller-scale landholders whose holdings fall below the minimum size required for expropriation.

Industrialization

In addition to decolonizing the export sector of the economy, the government also seeks to create industries for the production and transformation of raw materials coming from agriculture, mining, and fishing. In addition to achieving import substitution, these developing industries would promote employment and convert the country into an exporter of manufactured goods, with all the corresponding advantages in terms of international trade.

The Andean Pact plays an important role in the plans for industrialization, since it offers a greatly expanded market, nominally of 60 million people (although, given the present income structure of the Andean countries, it in effect involves about one-fifth of that total). The government is committed to creating a bourgeoisie which is regionally, rather than nationally, oriented.

In order to carry out this act of displacing the export sector, the government has redefined the role traditionally assigned to the state, to the native bourgeoisie, and to foreign capital. The state, according to the new formula, not only becomes the leader of this new dynamic economy, but it also intervenes directly as the principal investor and contractor in many areas of economic activity, especially those considered strategic for the development of the national economy, such as cement, electricity, iron and steel, transport, petrochemicals, banking, and finance. Each of the ministries has formed several public enterprises, in accordance with this plan, designed to develop a specific sector. These include the Corporación Financiera de Desarrollo (COFIDE), Industrias del Perú, Petróleos del Perú, Minero Perú, Aerolíneas del Perú, Electricidad del Perú, Empresa Pública de Servicios Agrícolas, Empresa Nacional de Commercialización Industrial, and Empresa de Turismo del Perú. The result of all of these innovations is to move Peru clearly toward state capitalism. Indeed, approximately 40 percent of the gross national product is now generated by the state.

The national bourgeoisie has unquestionably benefited from these innovations in that, by itself or in association with the state, it may now become involved in the areas of economic activity which, until 1968, were monopolized by foreign capital. At the same time, the native bourgeoisie is required to modify its earlier, dependent, orientation by making use of domestically manufactured parts in the production process, moving toward import substitution, and producing manufactured goods for export. The bourgeoisie is encouraged to participate actively in the Andean Group. Yet this supposed reorganization of the bourgeoisie may prevent it from achieving autonomy; indeed, it encourages its collaboration with multinational corporations. As is well known, the development of these new linkages with international capitalism will result in the continuation of heavy foreign influence in the Peruvian economy and the continued transfer of a major proportion of the benefits of economic growth to foreign capitalists. The most important areas of foreign involvement in the economy, in addition to large-scale and highly profitable mining investments such as Toquepala, Marcona, and—soon—Cuajone, will include participation, in association with the government, in industrial development and petroleum extraction.

Wherever foreign capital enters into partnership with the national bourgeoisie, it is committed (according to Decision Number 24 of the Andean common market agreement) to automatic "progressive nationalization" through the transfer of up to 51 percent of its stock to its domestic business partner. The national bourgeoisie is thus encouraged to develop a close relationship with foreign capital. It should be emphasized, however, that this association was not established spontaneously, nor is it developing with great ease. It requires, in fact, long and difficult negotiations between the government and the foreign enterprise.

It is also important to note that though it is now increasingly evident that the government is enjoying good relations with international capitalism, the initial foreign reaction to the anti-oligarchic reforms was negative. The expropriation of the International Petroleum Company and the firm defense of the two-hundred-mile fishing limit resulted in powerful international pressure against the Peruvian government. This pressure continued in adverse reaction to the reforms which limit the role of foreign capital in certain productive sectors, culminating in the previously mentioned Decision Number 24, which provided criteria for the participation of foreign capital for the entire Andean region.

However, the virtual embargo imposed on Peru by the Inter-American Development Bank, the World Bank, private international banks, and industrial suppliers was lifted after timely negotiations in 1971 created new opportunities for the entry of foreign capital in the areas of petroleum, mining, and industry. Beginning in 1973, Peru has received major loans from international credit institutions and international financial sources, in addition to the unanimous support of the government's economic policies by the International Monetary Fund, the World Bank, and the Interamerican Committee for the Alliance for Progress.

The execution of these actions, designed to integrate the national economy and displace the export sector, involves a major task of internal financing, which requires obtaining foreign investments, credit from suppliers, and government loans. Thus the Development Plan: 1971–1975 urged that the country must invest over this period the sum of 270 billion soles, or about $6 billion, of which close to a third must come from abroad, including the total foreign debt which the country has contracted. If these recommendations were followed, Peru would considerably raise its rate of investment and the state, by 1975, would be making 56 percent of all investments.

It was soon realized that these estimates were, in fact, too low. At the 1972 meeting of the "Paris Club," the Peruvian minister of economics presented a $3 billion package of industrial projects to be financed internationally, $1.9 billion of which were approved by the club. It has thus quickly become evident that this antioligarchic, nationalistic government actively encourages the expansion of foreign financing of economic growth.

Control of Financial Institutions

In order to achieve control of finance and carry out its plans for investment and for the integration of the economy, the government has nationalized a major portion of financial institutions and has compelled foreign capital to transfer to the national bourgeoisie a significant part of its control over credit. It has nationalized the Central Reserve Bank and has expanded the role of the Banco de la Nación, making it the most important bank in the country. In addition, it has nationalized the fishmeal industry and important mining centers (and before that the marketing of these products), thereby gaining control of nearly 70 percent of Peru's total exports; it controls the movement of foreign exchange, which provides the government with an important reserve of capital, thereby allowing it to control speculation; and it regulates both public and private importation in order to make international commerce more efficient. Finally, the state seeks through COFIDE to attract both private and public savings, as well as to channel international loans with which to finance state, mixed, and private enterprise.[4]

Assessment of These Reforms

These are some of the concrete steps through which the present government seeks to achieve the modernization of capitalism in Peru and the elimination of oligarchic and semicolonial features of the economy which were already in the process of decomposition. This process involves the discarding of anachronistic elements in the Peruvian economy and the encouragement of new modes of capitalism and imperialism which had already begun to establish their supremacy and required only political consolidation.

It is noteworthy that the timing of these reforms has important implications for whether they increase or decrease Peru's economic autonomy. If these same reforms had been carried out in the 1930s in the form of an "Aprista" revolution, it would have involved the elimination of what were then the dominant economic institutions in the country and the dominant form of linkage with the international economy. In the 1970s, by contrast, these reforms do not contribute to national economic autonomy. Rather, they have hastened the adaptation of the Peruvian economy to a more advanced form of capitalism and to new forms of imperialism, thus increasing the degree of Peru's integration in the new international economic system. As opposed to forty years ago, the imperialism of today not only does not oppose industrialization within its dependent countries, but, due to changes in international capitalism, allows and even encourages industrialization on its periphery.[5]

Collaboration with a national bourgeoisie, a regional bourgeoisie (as in the case of the Andean Group), or a national state is in no way incompatible with the interests of international capitalism. On the contrary, these national and regional groups may become partners—subordinate, but nonetheless important partners—that facilitate the accumulation and reproduction of private capital on an international scale. This kind of association can

[4] República Peruana, Presidencia de la República. *Plan Nacional de Desarrollo para 1971–1975* (Lima, 1971).

[5] Consejo Económico para América Latina, *Estudio Económico de América Latina, 1970*, pp. 301–348.

serve to protect international enterprises from accusations of "imperialism" and from nationalistic sentiment, as has been recognized by executives of these enterprises. This relative lack of opposition on the part of international capitalist centers to reforms which aim at modernizing the social system and integrating Peru in the world market, as well as the weakness of popular political organizations and of the labor movement in particular, explain how the revolutionary government can carry out its reformist strategy in a technocratic way and in an atmosphere ruled by secrecy without having to resort to mass political mobilization.

The relationship with international capitalism enjoyed by the present Peruvian government contrasts strikingly with the experience of the Mexican, Guatemalan, Bolivian, and Cuban revolutions. The powerful economic and political-military opposition experienced by these revolutions could only be countered by massive popular political participation in the revolutionary process. Due to the specific situation in Peru, however, the civil-military and technical apparatus was able to function until 1972 in the midst of relative political calm with neither violent opposition from the displaced, traditional sectors nor spontaneous and fervent support from the popular masses. The downfall of the once powerful oligarchy and the timidness of its protests closely paralleled the passive response of the popular masses to the new measures which would supposedly benefit them. Whenever the masses showed signs of taking some kind of initiative, the army undertook to demobilize them and in several cases to repress them, as in Huanta, Cobriza, Chimbote, and Arequipa.

The bureaucratic nature of the Peruvian reform program might be attributed to the fact that it is carried out under strict military control. However, to consider this as the determining factor would be to neglect the historical circumstances under which this government was formed. For example, there is no doubt that had "El Zorro" Jiménez or General Rodríguez successfully unleashed an antioligarchic revolution in the 1930s, it would have led to a process in which the popular masses in urban and rural areas would have been the protagonists of the transformation.[6] Hence, the present pattern cannot simply be explained by the fact that the reforms are being introduced by the military.

[6] Jiménez and Rodríguez unsuccessfully attempted to link army groups with Aprista elements.

It could also be argued that in the 1930s, the military figures who might have led such a revolution would have been isolated individuals, whereas today it is the "institution" as a whole which is in charge of carrying out the transformation of the country. As a general in a high position in the present government is reported to have said: "Sánchez Cerro [a populist military president of the early 1930s] was alone, but there are forty of us." However, we must not forget the high degree of Apra penetration of the military during the 1930s, which suggests that would-be military reformers in that period might not have been as isolated as some might imagine. In addition, in 1968, the military "institution" was, in fact, divided over the October 3 coup. It was only eight officers, strategically situated, who made the decision to take over the government and to carry out a plan which had been developing within the military. Hence, it is misleading to make a contrast between hypothetical "isolated" reformers in the 1930s and a unified, reformist military in the 1970s.

The crucial factor in the present situation is not that the reforms are being carried out by the military or that the military is unified as an institution. It is essential to underscore instead the structural conditions which led to the formation of this type of government, rather than merely circumstantial conditions. These structural conditions involve the underlying transformation in Peruvian society which we have discussed at length and the particular response of the military to these transformations—specifically, the emergence of the internal security ideology discussed above and the resulting conclusions which were reached within certain sectors of the military concerning the need for reform in Peruvian society.

THE NEW SOCIETY: NEITHER COMMUNIST NOR CAPITALIST

The inadequacy of the reforms with regard to national autonomy and redistributive potential (as will be shown later), as well as the way in which these reforms are carried out—by restricting the development of democratic structures for popular participation—have led government spokesmen to shield themselves behind the idea that the military revolution is still only in the process of achieving its goals. The revolution is thus a *process* in which reforms are aimed at the achievement of "a pluralistic and humanistic society, neither capitalist nor communist, based on social democracy of full participation." This definition, which overlooks the class structure of Peruvian society and favors unification of groups, as is characteristic of this kind of regime, seeks a state of compromise and conciliation among different social classes. The military feels comfortable with this system, since, as was indicated by one of the ministers, it is "undesirable" to view a society in terms of a perspective of antagonistic groups.

In order to create a pluralistic and humanistic society, neither capitalist nor communist, social mechanisms must be created to integrate different classes and eliminate the conflicts among them. General Graham, head of the COAP, has made this intention clear in a very graphic way.[7] In his many speeches, he has described Peruvian society before 1968 as an expanse divided by a barbed-wire fence. The objective of the government is to eliminate this division. In order to do so, it has created the labor communities, and in September 1973 it made public its plan to establish an area of social property, which the military had been considering for two years.

Throughout the sixties, reformist parties pushed for an entrepreneurial reform which would grant workers administrative rights as well as a share of the profits. It was their intention to create communal enterprises in which community spirit would replace the individualistic, selfish, and profit-oriented spirit of capitalistic enterprises. The Christian Democratic party formally proposed the formation of these communities in 1968 as a means of reconciling the two basic interest groups in modern society: capital and labor. Reformist parties and the military, influenced by Christian doctrine, were both convinced that the capitalist system was at the root of the country's ills. The task was to search for a way to create a system of participation which would de-emphasize the existence of classes and the conflicts which they bring about.

At the same time, the traditional anti-Communist and anti-Stalinist positions of the military and the bureaucracy further increased the appeal of a mode of industrial organization which would ease class conflict. Another important consideration was the desire to improve the government's image in the international political and financial community by carrying out innovative reforms.

[7] COAP's role is discussed in Abraham F. Lowenthal, "Peru's Ambiguous Revolution," Chapter 1 of this volume.

According to the pluralistic, humanistic, noncapitalist and non-Communist model which has been adopted, the country's economy will be divided into four sectors: the state sector, the social-property sector (which in time should become the predominant sector); the reformed private sector, in the form of labor communities; and the private sector, composed of crafts, small-scale commerce, and small-scale agriculture. Workers in businesses with more than six employees and capitalized for more than 6 million soles (about $150,000) will organize into labor communities in industry, mining, or fishing. Through profit sharing, workers may acquire up to 50 percent of the property. As they acquire a share of the ownership, workers are entitled to participate in management in proportion to their share of ownership. In the case of state enterprises and enterprises which the state and foreign investors own jointly, workers receive certificates of profit shares, but they may not purchase any property or participate in the management of the enterprises, except nominally, in an advisory capacity.

A major aim of this organizational arrangement is to reduce the influence of labor unions. As several government spokesmen have made clear, workers should think twice before going on strike or making salary demands, since it is against "their own interests" to do so. During work stoppages, government officials have repeatedly used this argument and have maintained that since workers could not be "irrational," strikes could only be the result of infiltration and agitation by activists intent on destroying the military's revolutionary program.

If labor communities function according to the government's plan, they will forge a communitarian model which will blur class differences and class consciousness. The system would also provide a mechanism for reinvestment, since 10 percent of the communities' annual profits must be reinvested in the firm. It encourages investment in another way as well, since, if the original owners wish to retain majority control of the enterprise, they merely have to accelerate their own schedule of investments so as to keep the total size of their investment greater than that of the workers. Inflation would also be contained because of the workers' identification with their communities, since it would make them less likely to demand salary increases.

The program for communal ownership has not been entirely successful, however. Labor has discovered that businesses falsify financial statements and deceive the workers, creating a situation which leads to polarization and antagonism. In terms of real benefits, most workers have not perceived a real change for the better. According to official data, the average community presently owns approximately a 5-percent share of the enterprise with which it is associated, and several recent studies have shown that even under the most favorable circumstances, it will take twenty years for a community to acquire 50 percent of the stock.

Similarly, the distributive potential of labor communities remains limited, as will be seen later. As to employment, labor communities are notorious for favoring capital-intensive technology. In some cases, workers themselves have opposed expansion of employment so as to avoid having to share the annual profits among a larger number of people. This is why some generals have pointed to signs of "selfishness" among community workers.

A second aspect of the strategy to erode class differences and class consciousness is the proposal to form a new sphere of "social property." According to the projected plans, this form of property will involve the creation of enterprises (not their expropriation, as in Chile) to be owned by the workers who will be employed by the enterprises. It thus involves group property. The formation of such a group would begin with a feasibility proposal which would evaluate the benefits anticipated from a concentrated income structure of this type. This proposal would be examined by six different government agencies, which would then look for ways to finance the venture. As in the case of the labor communities, however, the head of the commission that drafted this project has pointed to the danger of workers' seeking to maximize their benefits to the detriment of the rest of the population.

To what extent do these new forms of property in fact contribute to the achievement of a noncapitalist, non-Communist, "communitarian" society? It may be argued that a crucial aspect of the distribution of economic power in society is whether the accumulation and investment of capital takes place in the private or public sphere, and not the relative predominance of state, private, or self-managing enterprises. Just as capitalist countries may have precapitalist remnants or advanced types of cooperatives, so China and Cuba, for example, may have remnants of private property. But the dominant forms of accumulation at the societal level are clearly private in the former case, and therefore class oriented, and public, and therefore socialist, in the latter case.

The formation of a sphere of social property, if it is to be distinct from private property in any important sense, requires in addition the socialization of accumulation and its counterpart, socialization of consumption. Accordingly, either Chacarilla del Estanque or El Agustino (an elegant suburb and a slum, respectively) could be eliminated on this score. At the same time, members of labor communities or social-property groups involved in private models of production are likely to exhibit the "selfish" tendencies about which the military is presently concerned.

In short, as long as the dominant form of capital accumulation remains private, and therefore class oriented, the state will continue, directly or indirectly, to subsidize the national and international bourgeoisie (as is typical of cases in which the state assumes a central role in the economy) and the area of social property will play only a complementary role.

The transition from capitalist modes of production to noncapitalist, non-Communist modes should involve the control of the distribution of resources according to the requirements of the dominated class. Yet this is clearly what we call socialism, and it is clearly not present in the Peruvian case.

RELATIVE DEMOCRATIZATION, "WELFARISM,"
AND CLASS CONCILIATION

As was stated at the outset, the military government has ended the oligarchic phase of Peru's history. Even given the limitations already mentioned, the antioligarchic and nationalistic reforms clearly represent a partial response to interests and demands for which the popular and middle sectors have fought historically. This partial response to popular demands has involved *segmentary* distribution of the benefits which have resulted from the reforms undertaken by the government, segmentary in the sense that the benefits have been directed selectively at the best-organized or potentially most politically troublesome groups within any given social sector. It should be noted that earlier governments employed a similar segmentary approach among the most-organized urban sectors, especially during periods of crisis, in order to satisfy their demands, neutralize their political participation, and isolate them from the rebellious peasantry.[8] This segmentary distribution involved offering both jobs and political patronage. Today, by contrast, it is accomplished through structural reforms which, regardless of the intentions of the government, in fact reach but a small portion of society. Because the reforms are antioligarchic but not anticapitalist, they have not succeeded in producing a comprehensive redistribution of resources, but rather a limited and fragmentary one. For example, the agrarian reform enables sugar workers, who represent 2 percent of the economically active rural population, to receive approximately one-third of the total resources which are available for redistribution in rural areas. With regard to the labor communities in the industrial, mining, and fishing sectors, the redistribution will take place only within these sectors, that is to say, among the 250,000 workers who constitute only 12 percent of the economically active urban population. In the industrial sector, the redistribution in fact takes place only within each unit of production. This means that enterprises of greater economic profitability, such as mining, are capable of granting greater benefits to members of the labor community than those of less economic profitability. Hence, those sectors of the working class which have previously had the highest incomes continue to have the highest incomes.

Other quantitative analyses of the most important reforms also show that their impact is limited. This is due to the fact that, as we have suggested, many of the reforms which have been carried out affect the capitalist-dependent structure only marginally. They are directed in considerable measure at the semifeudal agriculture of the highlands.

Two studies support these claims.[9] An examination of income-distribution data allowed Webb to point out that, in general, inequality and income concentration in 1961 were more pronounced in Peru than in many other underdeveloped countries. According to Webb's computations, 10 percent of the population with the highest income received 50 percent of the national income, whereas the poorest 10 percent received only 1 percent of

---

[8] Cotler, "Mechanics of Internal Domination."

[9] See Richard Webb, "Government Policy and the Distribution of Income in Peru, 1963–1973," Chapter 3 of this volume, and Adolfo Figueroa, "El impacto de las reformas actuales sobre la distribución de los ingresos en el Perú" (mimeo, Lima: CISEPA, 1973).

the national income. The average income among the top 10 percent was thus fifty times as great as in the bottom 10 percent.

TABLE 2.1
Income Distribution in Peru, 1961

	Annual per Capita Income	Percent of Population	Percent of National Income
Less than	2,000- 5,000 soles (about $47 to $116)	37	6
	5,001–10,000 soles (about $117 to $232)	25	12
	10,001-20,000 soles (about $233 to $463)	22	20
Over	20,000 soles (about $464)	16	62

Source: Derived from Richard Webb's data (see Chapter 3 of this volume). (Dollar estimates calculated at the rate of 43 soles to the dollar.)

Table 2.1 presents additional data on Peru's very unequal pattern of income distribution. If we assume that these patterns did not change significantly until 1969, we may ask how the agrarian, industrial, mining, and fishing reforms—the most radical of the government's measures—have affected this pattern of income distribution.

In the first place, these measures favor income distribution *internally* within each productive sector. Areas of greatest productivity, mining for example, do not transfer benefits to those of least productivity, like agriculture. Redistribution within each sector, with the exception of mining and fishing, is, in turn, carried out within each unit of production, thus further restricting the scope of redistribution.

As for the agrarian reform, Adolfo Figueroa suggests that, "strictly speaking, the redistribution of income generated by redistribution of land touches only the economic surplus which was previously appropriated by the landlord: the implicit rent on the property and its net utility. . . . The transfer of income thus involves 14 percent of the total income generated in the agricultural sector, or 14 percent of 7,859 million soles (about $180 million), which is close to 1,200 million soles (about $28 million), or almost 1 percent of the national income in 1966. This is what the agrarian reform redistributes. . . . If this percentage were redistributed in an equal manner, the agrarian reform would raise the income of those peasants who constitute the poorest 25 percent of the population by 0.5 percent. However, given the way in which the agrarian reform has been implemented thus far, not even this effect is likely."

This is due to the fact that "the agrarian reform does not simply distribute income within each subsector. For at least a quarter, and perhaps half, of the rural population, the redistributive process is doubly stacked against them: redistribution takes place in the sector of lowest productivity and in the most backward subsector within that division." From this Figueroa concludes that "the agrarian sector has been segmented by the strategy of income redistribution."

If we accept the idea that "the main problem with income distribution in Peru is that the agrarian sector determines the overall distributive profile," we then reach the conclusion that the effect of the agrarian reform on the country's income structure is very limited.

In addition, a study by H. van de Wetering has shown that, on the basis of the present distribution of land, about one-fifth of the country's rural population will receive three-fourths of the land.[10] This leaves little land for the vast majority of the rural population.[11] The same author points out that most of the limited income which is received by the peasants will be transferred to the commercial and industrial sectors, representing the nucleus of modern capitalism.

Using official statistics, Aníbal Quijano has pointed out that the peasants who benefit from the agrarian reform will have to pay to the state, over the next twenty-five years, a total of 40 billion soles (about $930 million), which the state will, in turn, pay to the expropriated landowners. This amount is three times as great as the total private investment in the industrial sector.[12]

[10] Hylke van de Wetering, "Agrarian Reform: An Approach toward Measuring Its Impact on the Provincial Economy" (mimeo, Lima, 1970).

[11] As a way of dealing with these limitations, the government is planning the Programas Integrales de Asentamiento Rural. The success of this program is hard to assess, however, as is often the case with government programs, since the details of their implementation are kept secret by the government.

[12] "Die Agrarreform in Peru," in Ernest Feder (ed.), *Gewalt und Ausbeutung* (Hoffman und Campe, Hamburg, 1973), pp. 421–436.

This decapitalization of the countryside means that the peasantry will be unable to increase the value of agriculture, to create employment, to increase productivity and income, or to be in a position to increase industrial demand.[13] This will clearly undermine the intended "strategy" of rural modernization. Instead, it transfers the benefits to the new urban bourgeoisie, which, due to the easy convertibility of agrarian debt bonds to industrial credit, is investing increasingly in manufacturing.

The General Industrial Law follows the same pattern as the agrarian reform. Figueroa has argued that "the law applies to the manufacturing sector, which generates approximately 15 percent of the national income and comprises 5 percent of the labor force. However, the application of the law is based ˜n an estimate of the net profits of the enterprises that are involved, which represents roughly 30 percent of the industrial sector's income. The law therefore affects 4.5 percent of the national income. It transfers 10 percent of this sum (about 0.5 percent of the national income) directly to the workers and 15 percent to property accumulated for the workers" (roughly an additional 0.5 percent of the national income). But again, the distribution turns out to be unequal, since, "of the 10 percent to be dispensed directly among workers, only 5 percent is distributed equally among them, and the remaining 5 percent is distributed in proportion to individual salaries."

Business executives, who also belong to the industrial community, have an average salary seven times greater than that of laborers. As a result, "it is estimated that in 1971, participation in 10 percent of the net income meant an increase in the average annual income of 2,611 soles (about $61) per worker, or an increase of 4 percent." However, because of the provisions of the law, this average obviously conceals a great inequality between the benefits received by workers and managers.

---

[13] Some clarification is needed in order to avoid misunderstandings. Neither I nor any of the authors referred to have developed these arguments in order to deny the importance of the agrarian reform. Rather, they are meant to stress its limitations. Agrarian reform is a necessary but not a sufficient condition for raising the peasants' standards of living. The success of agrarian reform depends on its specific nature and, more broadly, on the relationship between the countryside and the rest of the economy. For example, Figueroa and Webb show how agricultural pricing policies and the importation of foodstuffs considerably reduce the benefits otherwise available to peasants on the fringes of export agriculture.

Finally, Figueroa is emphatic as to the limited redistributive impact of the mining and fishing reforms. "The mining and fishing laws affect 2 percent and 8 percent of national income, respectively. If we assume that net income is 50 percent of these percentages . . . and that out of this 1 percent and 4 percent, 8 percent and 4 percent are distributed as income to workers, then we see that the total amount to be distributed is negligible." Hence fishermen received an average of 2,500 soles (about $59) in 1972 from the fishing communities.

It should also be recalled that the industrial, mining, and fishing reforms favor a small fraction of the working population which does not amount to 10 percent of the country's labor force. The urban unemployed and underemployed—between 40 percent and 50 percent of the economically active population, according to official figures—do not benefit from those reforms.

If we add to all these considerations the unofficial estimate that the rate of inflation in 1973 will be about 30 percent, we may conclude that the real benefits received by the lower class as a result of the reform programs are very limited. The income pyramid which existed previously has not been affected substantially. The conclusion to Webb's chapter of this volume is clear on this point: "The necessary changes appear to be so large, and so far from current policies, that they would amount, indeed, to a revolution."

The limited distribution of income may be explained by the class nature of the measures enacted; they affect only marginally the hegemonic nucleus of capital controlled by the state and international enterprises in association with the native bourgeoisie. For purposes of illustration, we may note that if the industrial communities were to receive half of the value of the enterprises, the increase in their income would not be 4 percent but 25 percent, according to Webb's calculations. It is precisely the lack of depth in social and economic reforms that limits the redistributive impact. By aiming these antioligarchic reforms in considerable measure at the decaying traditional sectors and not at the hegemonic structures, the amount of redistribution among the popular classes remains very small.

It is for this reason that the class struggles since 1969 are of a different kind. Until then, popular pressures were directed at eliminating the traditional oligarchic forms. Today, as a result of the reforms which have been carried out, popular pressure has shifted to capitalism in its modern versions, thus uncovering with increasing clarity its fundamental class orientation.

An awareness, even though only partial and segmentary, of popular demands, implies a relative democratization of society, within the limits imposed by a system of class domination. But this process is not related to the democratization of the state, which, on the contrary, is increasingly under the authoritarian control of the civil-military bureaucracy. There are also limits to this social democratization in the sense that, despite formal acceptance of the legitimacy of popular demands for such things as employment, income, land, housing, education, health, and recreation, the social system is incapable of offering a growing and equitable participation in the social product. The state is therefore obliged to develop a policy of selective "welfarism" as a substitute for effective and permanent social redistribution. In order to compensate for its failings, this policy is complemented by populist ideology and propaganda on the one hand, and by organizational forms of corporative control and political repression on the other.

Similarly, due to the weakness of the native bourgeoisie, the state has assumed a major role in entrepreneurial functions and had achieved, especially until 1972, a relative margin of autonomy with respect to society as a whole. Given these circumstances, the government has insisted on broadening its role in society, and, since the wave of strikes beginning in late 1972, has actively expanded its intervention in the political realm. In his speech of July 28, 1973, General Velasco mentioned the need to "strengthen the political flank of the revolution." Because of growing popular pressure, the regime has moved toward police repression in addition to its attempts to control popular political participation through organizations like SINAMOS.

Yet the state's relative autonomy, achieved through the reforms of the first few years and its policy of welfarism, allow it to play the role of arbiter among classes, though it does not permit it to challenge the basic class structure of society. Even its role as arbiter, however, has been increasingly challenged by pressures in all areas and from all popular sectors in the country throughout 1973.

For example, the government has guaranteed salary increases to certain working sectors, has recognized several hundred unions in the last five years, and has responded to important demands from industrial communities. At the same time, it has banned strikes, jailed union leaders, and continues to deport labor leaders and other political figures. On the other hand, the government also deports representatives of the petite and middle bourgeoisie who criticize, from an oligarchic perspective, the decrees in the area of social property. In this way it tries to balance the social tensions among classes and to develop an ideology which presents the military regime as a "pluralist" government.

The new political system is concerned with the conciliation and harmonization of the various classes and various economic sectors. Having eliminated the oligarchic centers of power, it attempts to integrate all classes in the name of a higher cause: national development. More than once the members of the Executive have summoned "all" Peruvians to "don the two-colored jersey," without any distinctions, since "all Peruvians" should form part of a total, harmonious unit, like a good soccer team. Social antagonisms would thus be put aside in favor of national and political integration, which is the final objective of the military strategy of the present government.[14]

[14] In two articles published in *Oiga* (nos. 487 and 488), Carlos Delgado tried to refute my conclusion regarding the conciliatory nature of the military regime. Delgado's argument centers around the fact that participation of workers in the means of production through labor communities should eliminate the existence of classes by reducing the antagonistic polarization between bourgeoisie and proletariat. "The constant opposition between the 'bourgeoisie' and the traditional 'proletariat' would cease to exist"—says Delgado—"not because the interests of both classes would have been 'reconciled,' but because the absolute polarization between total property on one side and total lack of property on the other would have disappeared. In short, both proletariat and bourgeoisie would vanish as social classes." Delgado goes on to suggest that "if workers owned 50 percent of the means of production, the proletariat—in Marxist terms—would no longer exist. Neither would the bourgeoisie."

The argument is older than Apra; it is nourished by the most reactionary sources of social thought (which does not make it any less ridiculous). Capitalism has doubtless changed substantially since the nineteenth century, yet we cannot seriously maintain that capitalism and class conflicts have disappeared. One of the many changes in capitalism is that it now frequently offers workers a share of profits derived from their own labor, leading them to believe that they receive the entire product of their work. It also grants them participation on boards of directors and convinces them that their decisions play an important role in determining the direction taken by their company and their society. Such is the case in many of the advanced capitalist countries. But this is simply and clearly "participationism."

In spite of what he says, the implications of Delgado's claim are clear: his

THE CORPORATIVE DESIGN OF THE PERUVIAN STATE

This military strategy aims at the depoliticization of the dominated classes, in order to ensure that they do not develop class consciousness and thereby to prevent their organization along class lines. Organizations which tend to achieve concrete and immediate objectives are supported, such as those operating in places of residence, work, or study. Organizations and programs which tend to transform politics into "a problem of everyday life" are encouraged.

The conciliation and harmonization of classes pursued by the military government and the resulting depoliticization of the dominated classes is based on the creation of institutional mechanisms designed to incorporate those sectors which oppose, or threaten to oppose, the government. This may reduce pressures (which overflow the capitalist and technocratic boundaries placed on the country by the military government) from sources such as the strikes by teachers, miners, and sugar workers; the popular uprisings of Cuzco, Arequipa, and Puno in 1972 and 1973; and the continued pressures from other labor sectors as well. In the same manner, these institutional mechanisms seek to undermine the weak foundations of the labor unions and union-based parties which the government controls, but pretends to grant a relatively large degree of autonomy, as in the case of Apra and the Communist party, the Confederation of Peruvian Workers (CTP), and the General Confederation of Workers in Peru (CGTP). Finally, these mechanisms aid in the proper channeling of popular demands for assistance and welfare in such a way as to win the loyalties of the dominated classes and insure that these demands do not endanger the investment requirements of the state.

The government anticipates that it will take until 1990 to carry out its program. In order to attain its objectives, large-scale capital formation will be required, which must not be interrupted by popular consumer demands that might endanger the state's investment plans. Hence, it is necessary to organize popular groups in order to limit welfare spending and to encourage workers to

---

argument points to the political demobilization of the working classes, which is accomplished by making them believe that they have no separate interests, but rather that they are merged with the interests of the nation as a whole.

meet their own immediate needs in spite of their reduced opportunities for employment and savings.

The institutional mechanisms designed to accomplish this task began to evolve over the first two years of military rule, but without adhering to a definite plan. However, beginning in June 1971 with the creation of SINAMOS—the National System for the Support of Social Mobilization—this situation has changed substantially. The nation-wide teachers' strike and the unrest among the miners and sugar workers which occurred in 1971 indicated the need to create organizations which would act as mediators between the state and the masses. These would serve both as channel for welfare programs and political control, on the one hand, and as a means of channeling popular demands, on the other. SINAMOS has become the government agency in charge of organizing, or reorganizing, the popular masses in order to ensure that they conform to the aims of the revolutionary government and in order to achieve what is referred to as a "social democracy of full participation." The limited organization of the popular masses and their political weakness, due to the lack of autonomy of unions and political parties, constitute, together with the antioligarchic and nationalistic reforms, important factors in aiding the state—through SINAMOS—in achieving the above-mentioned objectives.

One of the most important sectors of society which have been organized by SINAMOS involves the peasants who have benefited from the agrarian reform. This part of the rural population has joined a series of organizations, such as cooperatives, agricultural societies, and reorganized indigenous communities. Until 1972, these institutions were loosely connected to the regional offices of various public agencies. Beginning in May of 1972, however, in accordance with Decree Law 19400, the National Agrarian Society, which was closely identified with the export oligarchy, was abolished, along with all peasant organizations which had been established in the previous fifteen years. This law specifies the organizational characteristics to which the newly formed agrarian organization must conform, as well as the hierarchical structure of which they must be a part. It defines the objectives they must pursue: "to support the policies adopted by public agencies for the rural area and to cooperate with government programs which deal with the economic, social, and cultural development of the rural area." It also restricts their involvement in party politics and requires that they register with SINAMOS in order to be granted juridical personality—which is a prerequisite for having basic legal rights. The law also establishes the power of SINAMOS to dissolve these organizations "when they do not conform to their stated goals or to the law." Finally, it creates the National Agrarian Confederation at the top of a complex hierarchy of rural organizations.

The regime's authoritarian and technocratic character is manifest in this law, which clearly contradicts the rhetoric of "social democracy of full participation." While it pretends to promote "social mobilization" it serves in fact as a means of controlling mass political participation.

There have been attempts to control other sectors of society as well, including the urban-industrial working class and the petite and middle bourgeoisie. This latter group, but *not* the upper bourgeoisie, is opposed to the government's new policy toward industrial communities, among other measures, because the policy severely limits its income. With regard to the industrial working class, the government's attempts to control the interest groups representing this sector have been particularly significant. In 1972, the Ministry of Industries convened the Congress of Industrial Communities. This assembly was of crucial importance, since it could have created a strong organization which might have given important support to the government's program to develop the industrial communities. At the same time, the Ministry of Industries and the intelligence agencies were concerned about the possible outcome of such a meeting and feared that it could result in an organization which would try to radicalize the industrial community program. Nevertheless, due to pressures from some important industrial communities, from the organizational commission, and from radicals within the government who were trying to "move it to the left," the Ministry of Industries was forced to go through with the congress.

In order to protect it from any kind of radical "infiltration," the meeting was held at a military high school where the delegates and government officials were kept in seclusion throughout the proceedings. Outsiders were not allowed to enter the school, except by special permission of the sponsoring organization.

Despite these precautions, the delegates severely criticized the ministry's Department of Industrial Communities and ultimately forced the director of this department to resign. The criticisms were aimed at the failure of the ministry to respond to the numerous complaints made by industrial communities against businesses, which had found numerous ways to evade the provisions of the Industrial Community Law.

While supporting the government's basic program, the assembly moved to grant veto powers to community delegates vis-à-vis business management and later demanded that the government immediately transfer 50 percent of the ownership of industrial enterprises to the industrial communities. These proposals were severely criticized in the official press, which presented only very partisan reports of the meeting. Subsequently, the government decided to relegate to a minor role the Confederation of Industrial Communities (CONACI)—which resulted from the above-mentioned congress—and its declarations now have only symbolic importance. Given this attempted opposition of the CONACI to the government, labor organizations, rather than opposing CONACI, have sought its support in presenting their redistributive demands to the government. The whole affair turned out to be a fiasco for the government, as the workers demonstrated that they understood the class nature of the regime's reforms and would refuse to be co-opted by them.

The years 1972 and 1973 witnessed a marked upsurge in labor unrest, in which the Communist Labor Confederation (CGTP) played an ambivalent role. This is illustrated by the fact that it tried to mediate disputes and to discourage strikes, while at the same time it attempted to maintain its independence from the government. During this period, SINAMOS attempted to win over union leaders in order to form its own labor confederation which would be free from party interference (especially from the Communist party and Apra). At the same time, the Intelligence Service, through the Ministry of Interior, also organized and staffed its own labor group: the Confederation of Workers of the Peruvian Revolution (CTRP). The government thus tried to compensate for important failures in the SINAMOS program. However, this confederation has failed to attract the support of any major workers' organization. In 1973, a year marked by labor unrest in every major city as well as by growing opposition to the government among peasant organizations, the government declared a state of siege and imprisoned many union leaders, replacing them with government sympathizers or establishing its own substitute unions. For example, as a result of the teachers' strike, which paralyzed the south of Peru, the government declared the teachers' union to be illegal, jailed hundreds of teachers, and deported the national and regional leaders of the union. It did this in spite of the fact that in the government-sponsored cooperative elections, the syndicalist slate had captured 75 to 80 percent of the votes. In a famous press conference General Velasco announced that, if necessary, half the teachers would be fired. Shortly thereafter, the government announced the formation of an official union, the Sindicato de Educadores de la Revolución Peruana (SERP) and withdrew recognition from the established Sindicato Unico de Trabajadores de la Educación Peruana (SUTEP).

Recently, several ministers have emphasized the need to combine the different factions of the labor movement into one organization in order that the labor movement might have a single representative. The implications of this proposition are obvious. The "integration" of the labor movement into a single organization, which could be implemented through a special law which has been ready for over a year, would insure the political-military control of labor, which today, more than ever, is clearly moving toward autonomy from the government.

The middle bourgeoisie, which is organized in the Society of Industries (SNI), has, like the workers, also expressed opposition to the regime's industrial policies, in this case because the introduction of the industrial communities has significantly reduced its profits. The Ministry of Industries has therefore reorganized the SNI. The restructuring of the institution involved changing its name (it is no longer called "national") and required that it accept delegates from the industrial communities, appointed by the ministry. This could represent the first step—dictated from above—toward bringing together capitalist and working-class sectors in a single interest group and may be a sign of what will happen in other areas of the economy as well.

The position of the middle bourgeoisie, as reflected in the fate of the SNI, contrasts strikingly with the position of the upper bourgeoisie, which strongly supports the government's policy of expanding and rationalizing industry in collaboration with foreign capital. This sector of the bourgeoisie is represented by the Association of Exporters (ADEX). This organization actively supports the government's policy of promoting large-scale industry which is competitive at the regional and world level and of making active use of foreign investment and technical assistance.

The divergence between SNI and ADEX was made clear when SNI held a public meeting in which SNI's president harshly attacked the government's policies and the minister of industries. That same day, the minister of industries left for Caracas, accompanied by several hundred ADEX businessmen, in search of new markets. Later, while Raymundo Duharte, president of the SNI, was abroad, the government in effect deported him by preventing him from returning to Peru.

Another area in which the government has moved decisively in its attempt to preempt potential opposition is in urban squatter settlements. These have been officially renamed "new towns" (*pueblos jóvenes*). When the present government first came to power, administrative responsibility for squatter settlements was given to the National Office of New Towns. The program of this office was carried out in close collaboration with the military garrisons which are located in each area where there are squatter settlements. The squatter settlements of Lima, for example, were divided into four zones, each under the direction of a military garrison. These garrisons have become actively involved in the squatter settlements, devoting themselves particularly to leveling and building streets and to cleaning and beautifying the communities.

After the founding of SINAMOS in 1971, this office was incorporated into SINAMOS as the "New Town Sector." In this later period, it actively continued a program developed earlier of organizing the settlements down to the block level and helping to organize the election of neighborhood leaders. As in the case of the sugar cooperatives, SINAMOS imposed certain prerequisites which local leaders were required to meet. These included holding a steady job (eliminating the underemployed); a formally legalized marriage, rather than the common-law marriages common in squatter settlements; and, finally, having neither a penal nor political background—that is, having been neither a common criminal nor an active member of a political party. Working through the community organizations in squatter settlements, SINAMOS has encouraged the development of water and sewage systems and the formation of savings associations which accumulate capital to pay for various kinds of community improvement. In this way, the immediate needs of the squatter settlements are being actively attended to by the revolutionary government.

There is an unprecedented emphasis on "community development" and local "self-help." The government hopes that this program will play an important role in depoliticizing the squatter settlement population, at least temporarily.

In addition to the program in squatter settlements, the responsibility for welfare programs more generally has been centralized in SINAMOS, having previously been administered by a variety of different public agencies. The vertical, authoritarian nature of the state's relations with the popular masses has thus been institutionalized. According to the law which created it, SINAMOS is supposed to organize the population both functionally and territorially—that is, in terms of class groupings and geographic areas. SINAMOS has six priority areas: squatter settlements and inner city slums; rural organizations; youth; labor organizations (unions and labor communities); cultural and professional groups; and social-property organizations (cooperatives, agricultural societies, and self-managing enterprises). SINAMOS's organizational structure is itself revealing. As a "system" (this is the first word of the official title), it consists of a carefully ordered hierarchy involving central, regional, zonal, and local offices, as well as offices representing sectoral, as opposed to territorial, groupings.

The geographic organization of SINAMOS corresponds to that of the military, and the generals in charge of the principal military regions of Peru, with a few exceptions, are also in charge of the corresponding regions of SINAMOS. On the basis of advice from technocrats who work for SINAMOS, these generals are responsible for developing the program for all areas of SINAMOS activity.

The organizations sponsored by the government with the purpose of achieving the "full participation" of the population are, in fact, designed to encourage the segmentary incorporation of the lower class through the establishment of strong vertical, hierarchical linkages. This results in the depoliticization of the dominated population at the same time that the antioligarchic reforms are eroding the widely divergent modes of life within the dominated population. Taken together, these programs seek to institutionalize the integration of the masses with the dominant class, inhibit the development of class interests among the dominated groups, and increase harmony among social classes.

These tactics of fragmenting the popular classes by means of vertical, hierarchical organizational linkages and through co-opting the leading groups within the dominated sectors corresponds to typical corporative political strategy. Corporatism is the political-organizational scheme through which social classes are segmented through their vertical, authoritarian integration into multiclass, functional organizations which represent the principal economic sectors in society. The state imposes on these organizations an authoritarian control and an ideology of conciliation of interests. If in these circumstances the bourgeoisie joins the state, the dominated classes will lose their autonomy and ability to develop their own organizations and thereby will also lose their capacity to develop class consciousness. This situation has not yet been consolidated in Peru, but the tendency suggests the government seeks that end.

It must be emphasized that the implementation of the authoritarian, corporative system adopted by the revolutionary government does not depend on systematic repression. This may be explained by two factors which have already been mentioned. First, the antioligarchic, nationalistic character of the regime's policies give it an important basis of legitimacy. Second, popular political and syndicalist organizations are relatively weak. Both of these factors reduce the need for the use of systematic repression in support of the implementation of corporatism.

Nevertheless, the government's efforts at distribution and democratization may create a force which will work against the government's long-term objectives, in that groups within the dominated classes may increasingly demand their share of national resources. In addition, as opportunities for new antioligarchic reforms begin to exhaust themselves, popular pressure favoring an attack on the new economic and social structure of Peru's modern capitalism may intensify. It is in this new situation that the corporative political organization should play a fundamentally important role by impeding the development of these pressures in an organized and class-conscious manner. Even today, when SINAMOS has not yet entirely taken over the workers' organizations, whenever popular demands arise which seek to push for the attainment of further revolutionary goals, SINAMOS takes charge of appeasing, channeling, and persuading the newly mobilized groups as a means of attempting to control them.

The official press plays a decisive role in this process. While it does not always oppose isolated strikes to gain incremental benefits, it systematically attacks any popular movement which has clear class content and potential. The press argues (without in any way considering the position of workers) that popular movements threaten the national economy and suggests that they are directed by the CIA and by Apra and political "extremists," which are somehow blessed with the ability of being everywhere at once.

In spite of the efforts of the government through SINAMOS, through the official press, and through many other channels, however, the level of political tension and violence remains high. Because of the pressures to which the dominated classes are subjected due to inflation and the requirements of capital accumulation, the social peace which the government seeks to achieve through its corporative design will inevitably be threatened. Under these circumstances, a major component of violence must be added to the corporative program, as has occurred throughout 1973. It is clear that the popular revolt which is presently developing will ultimately lead to a direct confrontation with the government, something that did not happen in the Latin American countries in which antioligarchic reforms were carried out by populist movements. This makes clear a basic irony of the Peruvian case: that the government which has carried out the antioligarchic reforms is facing a confrontation with the working-class and middle-class sectors who are the presumed beneficiaries of the reforms. The basic problem—which has been emphasized throughout this essay—is that given the present level of development of capitalism in Peru, these reforms are insufficient to provide the basis for a fundamental redistribution of resources that will include the dominated class in its entirety. In addition, the refusal to rely on popular mobilization as a means of supporting the reforms increases the need to rely on corporative tactics in order to maintain the present program of reform.

From this perspective, it appears that the most likely outcome will be the eventual development of a *popular, mass-based* revolutionary movement which will confront the so-called Revolutionary Government of the Armed Forces. The constant state of crisis in many SINAMOS programs during 1973-74 would appear to be a prelude to this confrontation.

3

Government Policy and the Distribution of Income in Peru, 1963–1973

Richard Webb

Es tradición nacional que todo presidente se figure venir como un
ser providencial que pega un tajo decisivo entre el hoy y el ayer.
Manuel González Prada, *Horas de Lucha*, 1903[1]

The inevitability of gradualness.
Sidney Webb, presidential address to the annual conference
of the Labor party, 1920[2]

This essay attempts to measure the impact of government policy
on the distribution of income in Peru since 1963. The governments of Belaúnde (1963–1968) and Velasco (since 1968) have
both professed a deep concern with economic injustice, and both
have been held up as models of peaceful progress toward social
justice. During the last decade the Peruvian state has sharply
expanded its size and its control over the economy. Both regimes can point to important redistributive measures. Belaúnde
stressed schooling and rural development, for instance. Velasco
decreed a land reform, an industrial reform, and other property
transfers. The objective of this paper is to quantify the distributive impact of those measures and to relate them to the size of
initial inequalities. This comparison will include the effects of
policies not primarily aimed at redistribution, and it will relate
distributive changes to the changes that result from trends in the
market distribution of incomes. How much of a dent have recent
Peruvian governments made on income inequality? Has the military regime under General Velasco approached this problem in

[1] "It is a national tradition that every president sees himself making a decisive break between the past and the present."

[2] An interesting, if dubious, attempt to reconcile this outlook with the
official "revolutionary" image was made recently by the minister for industry
and commerce, Admiral A. Jimenez de Lucio. Jimenez described current policy as both *gradualista* and *revolucionaria*: "El gradualismo . . . da pasos
claros. . . . Cada paso significa un nuevo avance revolucionario" (speech,
July 1972).

ways that are similar to, or substantially different from, the approach of the Belaúnde regime?

To answer these questions I will first describe the distribution of income—Who are the rich and the poor, how unequal are their incomes, and what are the long-run trends concerning Peruvian income distribution? Next I will sketch a model that explains the principal features of that distribution and provides a conceptual framework for analyzing distributive policies. Third, I will discuss the incidence of specific policies and programs of the Belaúnde and Velasco governments. Finally, I will draw some conclusions regarding the alternatives available to redistributive policy.

Before I review the evidence, however, it would be useful to restate several generally held views on these questions. The past is seen by all in more or less the same terms: an exceedingly unequal distribution of income caused principally by the concentration of property ownership, and a trend toward growing inequality as the benefits of growth were entirely bottled up for the benefit of a small, powerful minority. The "domination theory" attributes this growing concentration to exploitation made possible by political power. Though some domination theorists speak of a "modern sector" and of "labor elites," the bulk of the labor force is pictured as exploited, impoverished, and, often, as suffering a fall in real incomes.

Assessments of the current situation are less unanimous. The Velasco regime sees its many reforms and policy changes as a radical attack on social injustice, at some cost perhaps, to economic growth. Leftist critics, however, see the survival of a large capitalist sector as evidence that there is no fundamental change.[3] And there is a growing awareness of the limited reach of many recent redistributive measures.[4] Though data is rarely cited, most observers (Peruvian and foreign) seem to regard current policies as a significant break with the past; the pattern and amount of redistribution are thought to have been altered substantially, chiefly through measures which have nationalized or redistributed private wealth.

[3] Aníbal Quijano Obregón, "Nationalism and Capitalism in Peru: A Study in Neo-Imperialism," *Monthly Review*, vol. 23, no. 3 (July–Aug. 1971), pp. 1–22.

[4] See, for instance, Adolfo Figueroa, *El Impacto de las Reformas Actuales sobre la Distribución del Ingreso en el Perú* (Lima: CISEPA, Universidad Católica, 1973).

THE DISTRIBUTION OF INCOME

Principal Features

Table 3.1 reveals an extreme degree of overall inequality. The top decile share of personal income, 49 percent, is higher than that found in most less-developed countries, though comparable to that in Colombia, Brazil, and Mexico, three countries that share with Peru a similar stage of early industrialization, a colonial heritage of highly structured social and class relations, and markedly contrasting modern and traditional sectors. Also, the poor get slightly less in Peru; the bottom two deciles receive 2.5 percent, and the lower six deciles only 18.2 percent, well below the 30 percent that Kuznets cites as characteristic of both developed and underdeveloped countries.[5]

A wide range of incomes is associated with such dualism. The ratio between top and bottom decile shares is 49:1. It is more significant perhaps that inequality runs much deeper than is apparent from the high share received by a handful of very wealthy proprietors. If we deduct dividends, cash rents, and interest from the top decile share, the spread between first and last deciles is still 32:1.

Wage and salary incomes of top decile recipients start at U.S. $970 a year;[6] the median labor income in the group is $1,270 a year. This may be "middle class" or even modest by the standards of more-industrialized countries, but over a third of the population receives incomes under $186 a year.

Enormous vertical distances characterize more than Peru's geography. Almost any subdivision of the population is a sample with a high degree of income dispersion. "Social classes," such as the city wage earner or the Sierra peasant, turn out to be extremely heterogeneous with regard to income, as may be seen in Tables 3.2 and 3.3. City wages, for instance, range from about $190 a year to $1,500 a year, spanning three quartiles. As may be expected, the city self-employed are even more spread out: 14 percent are in the bottom quartile, and 26 percent in the upper quartile; 11 percent reach into the top decile.

[5] Simon Kuznets, *Modern Economic Growth* (New Haven, Conn.: Yale University Press, 1969), p. 424.

[6] In 1961 dollars.

TABLE 3.1
Percentile Shares of Income,
Selected Less-Developed Countries

	Bottom 20%	Lower 60%	Top 10%
Peru (1961)[a]	2.5	18.2	49.2
Brazil (1970)[b]	4.2	22.0	49.0
Colombia (1964)[c]	2.5	26.0	48.0
Mexico (1960)[d]	4.2	20.9	49.9
Average for 44 less-developed countries[e]	5.6	26.0	44.0

Sources:

[a] Table 3.2.

[b] Albert Fishlow, "Brazilian Size Distribution of Income," *AER*, vol. 62, no. 2 (May 1972), pp. 392, 399.

[c] Miguel Urrutia and Clara Elsa de Sandoval, "La Distribución de Ingresos entre los Perceptores de Renta en Colombia—1964," *Revista del Banco de la República* no. 513 (July 1970), p. 992.

[d] Ifigenia M. de Navarette, "La Distribución del Ingreso en México. Tendencias y Perspectivas," in *El Perfil de México en 1980* (Mexico City: Siglo Veintiuno Editores S.A., 1970), vol. 1, p. 37.

[e] From a recent compilation in Irma Adelman and Cynthia Taft Morris, *An Anatomy of Income Distribution Patterns in Developing Nations*, International Bank for Reconstruction and Development, economic staff working paper no. 116 (Washington, D.C., 1971), which reports percentile shares of national income for forty-four countries. Average shares for the top five and top twenty percentiles were 30 percent and 56 percent respectively, implying a top decile share in national income of 44 percent and a share in personal income of around 40 percent.

The geographical poles of the income distribution are perhaps best represented by the city of Lima and by the Mancha India, five contiguous departments in the southern Sierra which concentrate much of the Indian population.[7] Average incomes differ

[7] Apurímac, Ayacucho, Cuzco, Huancavelica, and Puno. See Julio Cotler, "La mecánica de la dominación interna y del cambio social en la sociedad rural," Instituto de Estudios Peruanos, *Peru Problema: 5 Ensayos* (Lima: Francisco Moncloa Editores S.A., 1968). Cotler includes the department of Ancash, where average income is 60 percent higher; this increases income dispersion within the region as he defines it.

TABLE 3.2

Labor Force and Income in Peru by Type and Income Level, 1961

Annual Income (1961 U.S. $)	Labor Force (In thousands)						Income (Millions of Dollars)		
	Sierra Rural (1)	Coast or Jungle Farmers (2)	Wage Earners (3)	White-Collar Employees (4)	Urban Self-Employed (5)	All Labor (6)	Labor (7)	Property (8)	All Income (9)
$ 0–75	349	0.7	17.0	1	30.0	400	23	1	24
76–112	229	5.0	21.0	3	29.0	289	27	1	28
113–186	253	14.0	83.0	8	63.0	429	63	3	66
187–280	128	16.0	201.0	15	84.0	459	106	5	111
281–373	72	25.0	107.0	19	80.0	312	102	6	108
374–466	52	23.0	86.0	20	45.0	233	98	6	104
467–559	34	17.0	72.0	28	26.0	183	90	5	95
560–746	26	28.0	82.0	59	37.0	240	156	9	165
747–119	40	49.0	51.0	91	46.0	280	255	16	271
1,120–1,865	13	17.0	23.0	64	26.0	149	208	19	227
1,866–2,610	—	0.6	3.0	18	7.0	30	66	13	79
2,611–3,730	—	—	0.8	12	3.0	17	52	11	68
3,731–18,650	—	—	0.2	11	0.3	13	80	43	123
18,659+	—	—	—	—	—	—	—	369	369
Total	1,196	196.0	747.0	350	476.0	3,034	1,326	512	1,838

Source:

Richard Webb, "The Distribution of Income in Peru," discussion paper no. 26, Research Program in Economic Development, mimeographed, Princeton University, Sept. 1972, p. 7. Incomes include imputed rents, subsistence food production, and payment in kind to domestic servants. The principal sources were the 1961 population census, urban household surveys, official provincial farm output statistics, Central Reserve Bank national accounts data on property incomes, and family income surveys of selected rural areas by the Ministry of Agriculture.

TABLE 3.3

Distribution of Labor Force Groups in Peru by Percentiles of National Distribution, 1961 (in thousands)

	Quartiles (Income range in 1961 U.S.$)				Highest Percentiles (Income range in 1961 U.S.$)			Total Labor Force[a]	Average Annual Labor Income (In U.S.$)[b]
	Poorest ($40-120)	II ($120-260)	III ($260-540)	Top (540+)	10% ($970+)	5% ($1,270+)	1% ($2,600+)		
All Peru	758	758	758	758	303	152	30	3,034	433
1. Sierra rural[c]	610	335	167	84	24	12	–	1,196	200
2. Coast or jungle farmers	8	25	65	98	35	14	–	196	605
3. Wage earners[d]	52	254	254	187	45	15	–	747	414
4. White-collar employees	–	25	67	259	137	88	25	350	1,126
5. Urban self-employed[e]	67	129	157	124	52	29	5	476	470
6. Rural	659	538	330	208	69	35	–	1,735	272
7. Urban	78	247	429	546	234	143	26	1,299	727
8. Lima	25	80	180	334	130	62	22	619	858
9. Mancha India[f]	383	158	105	105	45	17	4	750	276
10. Urban-traditional sector[b]	–	23	153	411	158	70	29	587	1,126
11. Urban-traditional sector[h]	83	236	312	160	47	19	–	792	407
12. Rural-traditional sector	637	347	222	186	64	36	–	1,392	264

Source: Webb, "Distribution of Income in Peru," p. 8.

a The discrepancies between labor force totals for different classifications are caused by the different numbers of workers classed as "unspecified" with respect to different categories: income, occupation, or industrial sector.

b The average incomes for Lima (line 8), urban (line 7), and modern sector (line 10) exclude corporate profits. The 1961 current soles data was converted at the 1961 exchange rate of 26.81 soles.

c Line 1 excludes rural white-collar employees and rural miners but includes "urban" farm workers. The census definition of *urban* includes all district capitals and other towns with a population greater than that of the respective district capital.

d Line 3 excludes *colonos* (wage earners on Sierra farms).

e Line 5 includes domestic servants.

f Line 9 covers departments of Apurímac, Ayacucho, Cuzco, Huancavelica, and Puno; all are in the Sierra.

g Line 10 covers all government urban establishments with five or more persons, sugar farms, miners, and self-employed professionals.

h Line 11 covers all urban workers in the modern sector but excludes "urban" farm forces in the Sierra.

sharply: $280 a year in the Mancha India, $870 in Lima. Yet variance within these regions is equally significant. In both areas, incomes span the four quartiles (Table 3.3). The spread is greater in the Mancha India, where half are in the lowest quartile, 14 percent in the top quartile, and 6 percent in the top decile.

This marked degree of income dispersion, both within and between groups, may be studied by examining the composition of different strata within the national distribution. Who are the rich? The poor? The middle groups?

The Rich

A major share of property income accrues to a few hundred families. Profits, including retained earnings of incorporated enterprises, net interest income, and cash rental income, made up 25 percent of national income in 1961. Given the restricted nature of corporate stock ownership and general knowledge regarding the concentration of wealth ownership in Peru, it is likely that almost all is received within the top 1 percent of recipients and that the greater part, estimated here at 19 percent of national income, goes to some one or two hundred wealth holders with annual incomes over $40,000.[8]

The next rung on the income ladder—under $40,000 (1 million soles) a year—corresponds to what is usually described as the "middle class." The handiest criterion for middle-class status in Peru is car ownership: in 1961, between 30,000 and 50,000 cars were owned for private use, so that the "middle class" corresponded roughly with the top 1 percent (30,000 persons).[9] Incomes of the top 1 percent started at $2,600 a year.

This middle class receives 11.4 percent of national income; of that amount, two-thirds is high white-collar salaries and the earnings of self-employed individuals, mainly professionals. The one-third received as property income has very diverse origins: some is entrepreneurial, being the profits of small and medium-sized

[8] See Carlos Malpica, *Los dueños del Perú* (Lima: Edición Ensayos Populares, 1968) for a list of corporations giving net worth and the names of directors.

[9] By this criterion, the middle class has been expanding rapidly as a proportion of the population: in 1970, about 4 to 5 percent of all families were car owners. Note that the word *middle class* is often used with a less restrictive economic sense, including, for instance, teachers, lower government clerks, and highly skilled workers.

businesses, and some is rent from urban real estate and from farms. Much of the net income generated on haciendas was spread out over multiple owners; large families had taken their toll on wealth concentration in the farm sector. Many middle class families in Lima enjoyed an income supplement from their inherited share of some large hacienda.

There has been a great deal of vertical mobility, in both directions, between the top wealth holders and the middle class. Upward mobility has been aided by rapid economic growth since 1950; probably a minority of the largest fortunes today are more than two generations old, a fact made plain by the large number of recent immigrant names among the very rich. And, as was said above, much landed wealth has diluted into middle-class rentier incomes. The two groups are essentially the same social class, sharing, for instance, the same race, families, schools, high degree of education, and residence (about three-quarters live in Lima).

Lower percentiles are more heterogeneous. The top 5 percent starts at $1,270; half are white-collar employees, and the other half are a mixture of highly skilled wage earners, merchants, artisans, prosperous medium farmers (20–50 hectares), and other self-employed persons. Only about a third reside in Lima. Aside from profits and rents going to middle-class families, property income within this and lower income groups is either imputed rental income or is an indistinguishable component of small business net income. The next 5 percent reaches down to $970 a year and has a similarly diverse occupational and geographical mix, but with a larger representation (26 percent) of farmers. This segment of the top decile is represented in many small towns, as by the wealthier businessmen in the Sierra town of Sicuani (population 10,000),[10] and the local "elite" of the town of Moyobamba (population 8,400).[11]

Finally, the upper quartile consists of all incomes over $540. It has a strong, though not exclusive, identification with Lima: 44 percent are in that city, and just over half of Lima's labor force is in the top quartile. All other economic or regional groups, how-

[10] According to a household budget survey carried out by the Instituto Boliviano de Estudios Andinos (IBEAS) in 1968; published in IBEAS, *Sicuani* (1969).

[11] CISM, *Aspectos Sociales y Económicos de la Ciudad de Moyobamba* (Lima: Servicio del Empleo y Recursos Humanos, 1968), p. 25.

ever, are also represented. Thus 14 percent live in the Mancha India, and about 16 percent are in some forty-five cities with populations over 10,000 (excluding Lima).[12] In terms of occupations, one-third are white-collar employees, most of whom (73 percent) are in this quartile. Another 21 percent are wage earners, mostly in modern establishments. There is an approximately equal number of farmers from the Sierra (10 percent of the group) and from the Coast and Jungle (12 percent).

The Poor

Workers in the poorest quartile, whose incomes range from about $40 to $120 a year, are mostly subsistence farmers living in Sierra provinces.[13] Of these, 80 percent are subsistence farmers, and 63 percent live in the Mancha India. Another 13 percent are nonfarm wage earners and independents in Sierra towns.

Many of the characteristics of these farmers are well known: they are mostly Indian (speaking Quechua or Aymara), and about 70 percent are illiterate.[14] Their principal source of livelihood is, on average, about 0.9 hectares of Sierra cropland, three head of cattle, and some other livestock.[15] Most earn some cash income by seasonal labor on larger farms or occasional sales of livestock products.

The preceding description, however, conveys a misleading impression of group cohesion based on geographical concentration, shared culture, source of income, and poverty. From the point of view of redistributive policy, a crucial characteristic of the

[12] Based on unpublished data from surveys conducted by the Junta Nacional de Vivienda in 1963 in forty-one cities.

[13] The 1961 census data on which these figures are based missed much of the Indian population in the Jungle, estimated by the census office at about 5 percent of the national population, most of whom live at subsistence income levels.

[14] Peru, Dirección Nacional de Estadística y Censos, Censo 1961, vol. 3, table 60A (Lima, 1965).

[15] Peru, Dirección Nacional de Estadística y Censos, Primer Censo Nacional Agropecuario (Lima, 1965). The figures assume that farmers in the bottom quartile correspond to those with farms under five hectares. A more exact estimate of the farm-size cutoff point for the lowest quartile would have been four hectares, implying smaller farms and fewer livestock.

rural poor as a social group is precisely the opposite: their fragmentation.[16] They are divided first into wage earners tied to
haciendas, and independent small farmers. But a more important
division is that produced by social and income stratification at
the level of every village and rural community. The uniform mass
of poor, flattened out along a subsistence income level, is a statistical abstraction. Instead, rural society is a myriad of small and
independent social pyramids, each with a different mix of rich
and poor.

TABLE 3.4
Sierra Provinces According to Proportion of Rural Poor, 1961

Proportion of Provincial Rural Workers Earning Less than $120 (In percent)	Number of Sierra Provinces
0–20	9
21–40	20
41–60	32
61–80	30
81–100	2
Total	93

Source: Webb, "Distribution of Income in Peru," p. 12.

One measure of this fragmentation is shown in Table 3.4: all
Sierra provinces contain some rural poor, but in almost all provinces there is also a substantial proportion of middle-income
farmers and other rural self-employed.

The bottom quartile also contains some urban poor, mostly
self-employed workers in smaller cities and towns; they are a
small fraction of the quartile (10 percent) and likewise a small
proportion of all urban workers (3 percent). Though cost of living differences inflate the apparent real incomes of urban residents, most urban incomes surpass the limiting income for the
bottom quartile—$120—by a margin much larger than any plau-
sible correction.[17] The common assertion that urban workers (ex-

[16] For Cotler, "La mecánica," this fragmentation is not accidental but a
method of domination.

[17] Adjustment for cost of living differences would be exceedingly complex
since consumption baskets differ by region, food prices vary by size of town,

cept for a lucky few placed in modern establishments) are no better off than the rural poor is an erroneous generalization derived from the case of the urban fringe, the poorest (and most visible) 5 or 10 percent.

A much broader measure of the poor—the lower 50 percent of income recipients, whose incomes range between $40 and $260 a year—does reach into the bottom quarter of the urban labor force: chiefly wage earners in small establishments and the self-employed. Of these urban poor, about 20 percent are in Lima, and 80 percent in smaller cities and towns. It also reaches into the lower levels of Coast and Jungle farmers, though most (81 percent) of this group have higher incomes. The lower half of the national income distribution, however, leaves out almost all white-collar workers and almost all of the modern sector.

Income Trends

Estimates of income growth are summarized in Table 3.5. They point up some expected and other less familiar aspects of the evolution of Peru's income distribution between 1950 and 1966.

The most evident conclusion is that labor incomes have become less equal. Though high growth rates are not fully correlated with high incomes, families in the upper half of the 1950 income distribution have by and large enjoyed faster rates of income growth. Most of the rural population, particularly that of the Sierra, and some groups of self-employed workers such as artisans and domestics, have become relatively poorer over the period.

The share of capital income in the national income has not grown, despite the evident growth of the more capital-intensive modern sector over the period. Corporate profits and net interest totaled 22.1 percent of national income in 1950, and 22.5 percent in 1966. Though the poor statistics on these components of value added may conceal some trend toward a growing share, the possible error is not likely to alter the above result to a significant degree. If net rental income is included, the share of capital in-

---

and prices of manufactures are higher *outside* the cities. An extreme correction would raise rural incomes by valuing farm output at Lima prices, which, in the case of Sierra products, were about 30 percent higher than farm-gate prices.

TABLE 3.5

Income Growth Rates in Peru, 1950–1966

	Size of Labor Force, 1950 (In thousands)	Annual Income Growth (In percent)
Modern Sector	*402*	*4.1*
Wage earners	196	4.9
Government employees	104	3.6
White-collar employees	102	3.3
Urban-Traditional Sector	*736*	*2.1*
Wage earners	145	3.3
Self-employed	361	1.9
Nonmanual employees	94	1.9
Domestic servants	136	1.6
Rural-Traditional Sector	*1,443*	*1.3*
Coastal wage earners	163	4.1
Sierra wage earners	240	1.5
Small farmers	1,040	0.8
(a) Coast and hinterland	(240)	(2.0)
(b) Other regions		
5–50 hectares	(120)	(2.7)
under 5 hectares	(680)	(0.0)

Source:

Richard Webb, "Trends in Real Income in Peru, 1950–1966," discussion paper no. 41, Research Program in Economic Development, Princeton University, 1973. The concept of "modern" sector used to prepare this table is that of "reporting" establishments—firms that provided statistical information to the Central Reserve Bank. In practice this coverage differs slightly from that of establishments with five or more employees—the criterion for "modern" used in the rest of this study. Growth rates given here and in other parts of this study refer to real income.

come declines from 29.9 to 28.0 percent between 1950 and 1966.[18]

The highest growth rates occurred in the modern sector—defined as covering all reporting business plus government employees and professionals—which expanded from 19 percent of

[18] Since house ownership is so widespread, however, it is not appropriate to sum net rental income with profits and interest as a measure of capital income accruing to the very rich.

the labor force in 1950 to 21 percent in 1966. Their earnings increased at an average of 4.1 percent a year during that period.

It is interesting to note that modern-sector white-collar employees in the private sector fared less well than modern-sector wage earners, tending to equalize incomes within the modern sector. The average rate of increase of reported salaries was 3.3 percent a year versus 4.9 percent for reported wages. One cause of this differential may be the fact that unions bargain hardest on behalf of their lowest-paid (and most numerous) members, though most firms have separate "white-collar unions." But a more likely cause may be found in the large proportion of unskilled and nonunionized white-collar workers (shop attendants and employees in service establishments are classed as "white-collar"). Many are also female and/or young. The small size of tertiary establishments and the high turnover of most employees limit unionization. Moreover, the supply of workers with formal schooling—the most relevant qualification for such jobs—has been growing exceptionally rapidly.

Less expected are the positive trends found within the urban-traditional sector, the employees in small, nonreporting establishments, domestic servants, and self-employed workers in a variety of occupations. As a group, they have grown more rapidly than the modern sector, from 24 percent to almost 32 percent during the period 1950–1966. And though the evidence on their incomes is weak—particularly for the self-employed—there is sufficient data to indicate the existence of positive, if moderate, trends in income. These range from the 1.6 percent a year of domestic servants to 3.3 percent a year in the case of unreported nonfarm wage earners.

These results conflict with the common extension of the marginality thesis to the urban-traditional sector of Peru. Quijano, for instance, writes that "the greatest part of people shown to be involved in tertiary activities are people who have neither employment nor income of any sort, and these people make up the great 'marginal' masses of the principal cities."[19] No data are cited to support this assertion; the frequent assumptions that incomes in the urban-traditional sector are close to rural incomes

19 Aníbal Quijano Obregón, "Tendencies in Peruvian Development and in the Class Structure," in *Latin American Reform or Revolution*, James Petras and Maurice Zeitlin, eds. (New York: Fawcett Publications, 1968), p. 300.

and that they are stagnant or falling is evidently a product of the easy (for middle-class observers) perceptual confusion between stagnation and changes at a very low absolute level of income, and of a generalization from the most visible cases of the urban poor (such as the street vendors and shoeshine boys) that make up the tail of the urban income distribution. Our data does not allow a comparison over time of the incomes of the lower 10 or 20 percent of the city income distribution, and it could be maintained that their income has not risen. But the evidence suggests that stagnation could only have been the case for a minority of the urban-traditional labor force.

It is difficult to explain growing incomes in the urban-traditional sector. The probable sources of growth can be identified: improvements and cheapening of the small-scale technology used by artisans and many small service establishments, capital accumulation, growing education and skills, and demand generated by the very rapid growth of modern-sector incomes. However, the rate of income change is the resultant of a balance between such factors and the rate of growth of labor supply to this sector. A slowing in the rate of expansion of the modern sector, or an acceleration in the rate of migration could possibly reverse the trend in incomes of this group. The period studied, 1950–1966, was one of exceptionally dynamic growth in the modern sector and of a lower rate of population growth than is now the case.

My conclusion regarding small-farmer incomes must be considered highly tentative. The estimate that the average income of all small farmers grew at about 0.8 percent a year is based mainly on statistics that show some growth in Sierra farm output per farmer and on the evidence of considerable commercial and urban expansion within the Sierra. It can be argued that such expansion, consisting of a growing expenditure on nonagricultural goods and services, necessarily implied increasing income levels. Also, some improvement in living standards was much more apparent in provinces of the central Sierra, located close to Lima and to the central Coast.

The data is inadequate to support any further statement regarding income trends *within* the very large class of small farmers. The question is of such significance however, that it warrants speculation. Thus, it seems reasonable to hypothesize that outside the central Sierra most income growth has been concentrated in the upper layer of small farmers, a class of relatively better-off peasants who account for between 10 and 15 percent of all small farmers but own a much larger portion of the land and livestock held outside haciendas. The relative economic success of this group parallels the more frequently cited emergence of a small-town class of traders, artisans, and bureaucrats.

This hypothesis has two implications regarding income trends that are relevant to the policies aimed at redistribution in favor of peasant farmers. First, there is a growing inequality within the class of small farmers. Second, for a large proportion of the population, which could plausibly range between 15 and 25 percent, there has been no absolute improvement in living standards. The extreme poverty of the latter group gives this statistical result an even greater significance than the fact of growing inequality in the national distribution of income.

Though the overall distribution of income has worsened, there are two characteristics of the pattern of income growth that are less consistent with most expectations. Firstly, there is no sharp break between trends in the modern sector and those in the rest of the economy: the growth rates of different income recipients are continuous. Secondly, and as a corollary to the above, income growth has been more widespread than is generally implied in statements regarding income trends in Peru. Thus, Thorp states that despite rapid per capita growth, "large portions of the country and of the population appear to have been left untouched, if not worse off than they were before."[20] Quijano is a more forceful proponent of the "dominant versus marginal" view. From data on the 1961 distribution of income,[21] he concludes that there is a "process of 'marginalization' and pauperization of the large mass of the active population"[22] and that "the working masses in general have been unable to prevent the constant reduction of their real wages and standard of living."[23] These statements are not consistent with the evidence presented in this chapter. On the basis of the above data one could plausibly sustain that many peasant farmers and other self-employed workers suffered a fall in real income, but this does not appear to be true for any large

20 Rosemary Thorp, "A Note on Food Supplies: The Distribution of Income and National Income Accounting in Peru," *Bulletin of the Oxford University Institute of Economics and Statistics*, vol. 31, no. 4 (Nov. 1969), pp. 229–241.

21 Quijano, "Tendencies in Peruvian Development," p. 325. The income distribution is that of the Instituto Nacional de Planificación.

22 *Ibid.*, p. 326.   23 *Ibid.*, p. 327.

category of workers, much less for "the working masses in general." The picture that emerges here is less dramatic and, perhaps, more ambiguous: there has been some absolute improvement for most of the population: for about 50 percent of the labor force, real earnings have grown at 2 percent or more a year, and for 75 to 80 percent, earnings have grown at over 1 percent a year. But, at the same time, there has been a growing degree of inequality, and those most in need of improvement have benefited the least.

The Model

The following model is designed to explain the principal features of the distribution of income described above and to provide a conceptual framework for the study of the distributive impact of government measures. The basic premise of the model is technological dualism, the coexistence of a modern sector of large-scale, capital-intensive firms with a traditional sector of labor-intensive haciendas, small-scale firms, and small farmers.[24] An important distinction is also drawn between the urban and rural components of the traditional sector.

The model is built on the distinctions between modern-traditional and urban-rural activities because these sectors define the boundaries of what seem to be the major discontinuities both in access to political power and in the coverage or reach of the key distributive policy instruments. There are discrete changes in power associated with (1) urban and (2) modern (or high-productivity) sector status. Likewise, some distributive mechanisms, such as wage policies, taxes, and the allocation of bureaucratic favors, have a differential impact on modern-sector and traditional-sector firms, while the coverage or impact of other policy instruments, such as public expenditures and price policies, differs sharply in the urban and rural sectors. These sectoral distinctions also coincide with key breakdowns in the market distribution of incomes of a dual economy. The three-sector model that is described below thus provides a convenient framework for examining how incomes are determined jointly by market forces and by political power working through specific instru-

[24] My definition of *modern sector* cuts across industrial sectors; except for electricity and banking, which are all modern, there are modern and traditional components in all activities.

ments, each with a specific coverage or ability to discriminate among the population.

The Value-Added Curve

A dual economy is characterized by a highly skewed distribution of productivity levels. The use of machinery, equipment, mineral deposits, and rich agricultural land is concentrated in a small segment of the population whose value added per worker is

FIGURE 3.1

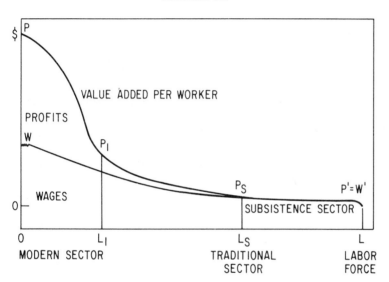

much higher than that of the rest of the economy. Such a distribution is described by the curve PP' in Figure 3.1, where the labor force is arrayed along the horizontal axis in descending order of value added per man, measured on the vertical axis. OL is the employed labor force; and the area under PP' measures national income. Since value added in each producing unit is determined by both physical productivity and prices, the shape of PP' will also depend on the relative prices: price distortions that favor firms with high physical productivity (e.g., tariffs on manufactures) will increase the skewness of PP'.

The point L_1 can be used to separate modern and traditional sectors, where L_1P_1 is an arbitrarily chosen level of productivity.[25] In our discussion the relevant feature of modern and traditional sectors is output per man, not the historical dating of the technology involved. Both sectors may include urban and rural components.

The shares of property and labor income in total value added are also shown in Figure 3.1. WW' measures the level of labor incomes in each producing unit: it is shown rising with productivity, but with no sharp break between the modern and traditional sectors. The area between PP' and WW', therefore, represents nonlabor incomes. At some point along the PP' curve, productivity will decline to a subsistence income level. In Figure 3.1 this point is marked P_s.

The growth path of the modern sector in Peru, as in many less-developed countries, has become characterized by more "capital deepening" than "capital widening": i.e., employment is growing slowly, as a proportion of the labor force, while investment and value added per worker are rising more rapidly than in the traditional sector.[26] In terms of the value-added curve, modern-sector growth can be described as largely vertical, contrary to the horizontal, labor-absorbing growth path predicted by the familiar labor-surplus models of economic development. The value-added curve is becoming increasingly skewed, as shown by P_1P' in Figure 3.2; a labor-absorbing path is described by PP_2. Migration into towns is thus transferring workers from the rural to the urban component of the traditional sector.

Labor incomes are also becoming increasingly skewed: there is a growing differential between modern- and traditional-sector earnings.[27] Within the traditional sector, wages are constrained

[25] Productivity declines gradually, but the modern and traditional sectors are sufficiently different in their nature to make the distinction—using some arbitrary dividing line—a useful one for purposes of analysis (cf. the distinction between urban and rural). To derive the statistics given in this study, I have used size of firm as a proxy for productivity: urban establishments with five or more employees were classed as modern; in agriculture, only sugar farms were defined as modern, since value added per man in cotton and other commercial crops is close to that of very small scale urban establishments.

[26] Modern-sector employment grew rapidly between 1950 and 1961, rising from 19.0 to 21.1 percent of the labor force; but it remained almost constant between 1961 and 1970, rising to only 21.6 percent in the latter year. (See Table 3.6.)

[27] See Table 3.5. Similar trends appear in data for Mexico, Colombia, and several countries in Africa: see Ifigenia M. de Navarette, "La Distribución del Ingreso en México. Tendencias y Perspectivas," in *El Perfil de México en 1980*

FIGURE 3.2

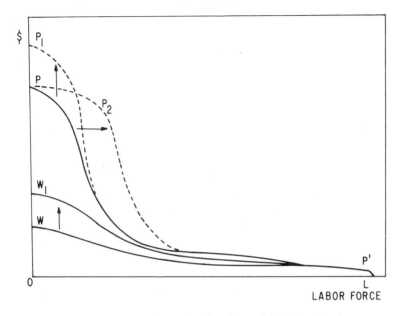

principally by low absolute levels of productivity in the sense that even if a worker received his total average product, his income would remain very low. In the modern sector, however, the value-added "ceiling" is not a significant constraint on the earnings of labor. Instead, wage levels are more sensitive to the institutional rules that decide the functional distribution of income—that is, the income accruing to each factor of production. In the classical labor-surplus economy with a competitive labor market, modern-sector wage levels will be close to those in the traditional sector, perhaps exceeding the latter by a small differential that compensates cost-of-living differences and the costs of migration. This assumption is reflected in the wage curve WW' of Figure 3.1. In socialist economies, direct controls produce a similar, relatively even curve. In most less-developed countries, however,

(Mexico City: Siglo Veintiuno Editores S.A., 1970), vol. 1, p. 38; Albert Berry, "Some Determinants of Changing Income Distribution in Colombia: 1930–1970," Economic Growth Center, Yale University discussion paper no. 137, mimeographed, 1972, p. 12; and Charles Frank, "The Problem of Urban Unemployment in Africa," Research Program in Economic Development, Princeton University, discussion paper no. 16, 1970, mimeographed, pp. 13–15.

modern-sector wages have risen significantly above their traditional-sector levels, resulting in a highly skewed wage curve.

The striking relationship observed between average productivity and wages is the point of departure for the discussion of modern-sector incomes below.

The Modern Sector

Why are modern-sector labor incomes rising in the face of large reserves of surplus labor in the traditional economy? Two economic explanations are (1) rising skill levels and (2) unionization. Others refer to the political power of modern-sector working groups. It will be argued below that each of these factors—"high" skill levels, strong unions, and direct political power—is a by-product of features that are inherent to modern-sector firms. The most relevant of those characteristics are capital intensity and urban presence.

One effect of capital intensity is to make the demand for labor in the modern sector more inelastic. Elasticity of labor demand varies directly with the share of labor in total cost. Also, capital intensity usually implies a large rent or quasi-rent component in the return to property, partly because large-scale capital assets tend to be long-lived, and partly because modern-sector assets in less-developed countries are often complementary with natural resources. Quasi-rent also arises from the monopoly element that is present in less-developed countries in much manufacturing and other activities as a result of tariffs, licenses, and other such privileges.[28]

Capital-intensive techniques generate "high wage" jobs for reasons that are often explained as the "high skill" requirements of modern technologies. Such firms, for instance, seem to have a greater demand for schooling and white-collar skills. But capital-intensive firms will pay higher wages whether or not they demand skills that are scarce in the long run—those that require long apprenticeships or scarce natural talents. Wage premiums will be paid in any case, first, to acquire "responsibility," and second, to reduce turnover.[29] Errors or irresponsibility by people

[28] Cf. Robert Slighton, "Perspectives on Economic Policymaking," in Luigi Einaudi, ed., *Latin America in the 1970's*, Rand R-1067—DOS (Santa Monica, Calif.: Rand Corporation, Dec. 1972), pp. 121–122.

[29] This argument was suggested by Charles Frank.

who work with expensive machinery are extremely costly. Firms therefore offer high wages—partly to seek persons who rank high in personal characteristics associated with carefulness and dependability, and partly to elicit responsibility through good will. High wages are also justified to reduce turnover. Turnover in such jobs is expensive: first, because skills are largely acquired on the job and thus represent a substantial investment by the firm, and second, because even a brief interruption in the availability of trained workers will be costly to firms with large fixed assets. Though some machine-complementary skills may not be difficult to learn, they are usually highly specific, perhaps to one or a few firms in any less-developed country, and therefore in short supply in the short run.

The link between capital intensity and wages also works through the supply side of the labor market: unions in less-developed countries usually originate in, and are often limited to, modern-sector establishments. Such firms tend to hire more-experienced and better-schooled workers, concentrate them geographically—in a small number of establishments and in one or a few cities—and provide them with an external environment of discipline and organization. Modern-sector firms, in short, are natural breeding grounds for unions.

But the power of the modern-sector labor force does not derive solely from unionization, nor does it work only through the collective-bargaining process.[30] Much of that power is directly political, with origins in the same features of modern-sector activity that favor unionization: urban presence, susceptibility to organization, and disruptive potential. Unionization and direct political power also reinforce each other. Political power can be used to raise incomes in two ways: directly, through minimum-wage and social security laws, for instance, and indirectly, either by reinforcing labor in the collective-bargaining process with legislation that is helpful to union activity, or by providing more sympathetic arbitration of wage disputes. It is direct political power, derived from some degree of control over modern-

[30] Some discussions of wage differentials in urban markets distinguish principally between the "organized" and "unorganized" sectors, thereby imputing most wage differences to unionization and political power. A contrary view, stressing the role of skills, is argued by Joseph Ramos in *Labor and Development in Latin America* (New York: Columbia University Press, 1970); see especially pp. 174–178.

sector sources of income, that best explains incomes in the bureaucracy.[31]

In short, there are elements inherent to modern, capital-intensive technology that tend to generate high wage levels. Some wage increase represents a distributive gain made possible by the introduction of capital-intensive techniques or activities into a low-wage traditional economy. Additional wage increases are made possible by *rising* capital intensity, caused in turn by the labor-saving nature of imported technological change. Finally, wage gains that do not result directly from shifting marginal-productivity curves tend to reinforce themselves by inducing further increases in capital intensity.[32]

How fast and how far wages adjust to exogenous sources of increased capital intensity will depend largely on the extent to which property incomes are rents or quasi-rents, and also on politics. The process of income redistribution in the modern sector— from capital to labor—has gone very far in some countries but has scarcely begun in others. These differences are surely related to varying political stages or systems in different countries: the process seems more advanced in Latin America than in Asia, for instance. Also, discrete changes in the balance of power may accelerate the process, as in Peru and Chile recently, or retract previous gains, as appears to have occurred in Brazil. These variations, however, should be seen in the context of the broader forces that are continually pressing modern-sector wages upwards.

This redistributive process can be contained by a strong property-owning class. But, more commonly today, the wage share is being constrained by middle-class elites whose interests have shifted from support for redistributive policies to a concern with economic growth, as they have moved up the power ladder.[33]

[31] Though government employees are here classed as part of the modern sector, it would be more correct to exclude them from the analysis of the relationship between value-added and income levels, since their wages and productivity levels cannot be distinguished.

[32] The link between productivity and wage increases is also reinforced by the setting of "noninflationary" wage guidelines based on productivity changes.

[33] Cf. Samuel Huntington, *Political Order in Changing Societies* (New Haven: Yale University Press, 1968) on military governments: "Their historical role is to open the door to the middle class and to close it on the lower class" (p. 222).

Growth is seen as an assurance of longer-run political stability; and growth requires that modern-sector surplus be invested rather than used to increase wage earners' consumption. Also, a strong middle-class government can afford some concern for the broader constituency in the traditional sector, whose claim on resources also conflicts with further gains by modern-sector labor.

The Urban-Traditional Sector

The best point of departure for a study of urban-traditional sector incomes is the close relationship between this sector and the modern sector. First, the urban-traditional sector has a high degree of trade dependency on the modern sector: budget studies show that urban-traditional sector families in Peru spend about half their income on food and about a quarter on factory goods or "modern" services such as medical and transport services. About three-quarters of their expenditure is therefore spent on "imports" into the sector.[34] Though some urban-traditional sector output is exported to the rural sector—chiefly in smaller towns—the bulk is sold to the modern sector. Assuming that any net capital inflow into the urban-traditional sector is minor, and therefore that sectoral "exports" approximate "imports," it follows that close to three-quarters of urban-traditional sector income is derived from sales to the modern sector and that the sector consumes only one-quarter of its own output. Both the modern and the rural-traditional sectors are much more self-sufficient.

Second, the relationship between the urban-traditional and modern sectors is more complementary than competitive: most urban-traditional sector producers do not compete with the modern sector. Competition is probably greatest in the case of small-scale manufacturing, where modern-sector efficiency has overwhelmed many lines of craft production. The continued existence of artisans is partly a competitive phenomenon, since higher modern-sector wages offset some of the competitive advantage created by more efficient technologies, but in part it reflects dif-

[34] This estimate is based on data on low-income family expenditure patterns in Lima obtained from unpublished tabulations of the Lima household budget survey by CISEPA, Catholic University of Peru.

ferentiation—carpenters and tailors who do custom work, whose output is valued as "hand-made," or who produce highly differentiated types of products. Further, two-thirds of the urban-traditional sector labor force in Peru consists of people in service activities who compete only marginally with the modern sector.[35] The two major service activities in the urban-traditional sector— commerce and domestic services—are affected more by technological developments, such as private cars (which make supermarkets possible), refrigerators, and washing machines, than by direct price competition.

The relationship between the size (total income) of the urban-traditional and modern sectors is therefore strongly dependent on the income elasticities of demand for urban-traditional sector output. In terms of the value-added curve, the urban-traditional sector can be pictured as a foothill to the modern-sector mountain (areas B and A in Figure 3.3). In Peru, this foothill has been growing at about the same rate as the modern economy: the ratio of total value added in these two sectors (B $\div$ A) was 31.5 percent in 1961 and 34.6 percent in 1970. At the same time, however, their shapes were changing. The modern sector grew vertically, with almost no increase in its share of total employment (21.1 percent in 1961 versus 21.6 percent in 1970). The urban-traditional sector grew in both directions: in that period, average income in this sector rose 28 percent while employment grew from 28.6 to 33.1 percent of the total labor force.

If modern-sector income is the chief determinant of total urban-traditional sector income, what explains the breakdown of that total into (1) average urban-traditional sector income and (2) urban-traditional sector employment? If providers of urban-traditional sector goods and services were not differentiated, migration would presumably equalize incomes within that sector, as well as between it and the rural sector. Any growth in the urban-traditional sector economy would then take the form of increased employment only. But there is in fact a great deal of

[35] This argument is in contrast with the stress placed on manufacturing, and thus on competition between sectors, by Richard R. Nelson, T. Paul Schultz, and Robert L. Slighton in *Structural Change in a Developing Economy: Colombia's Problems and Prospects* (Princeton, N.J.: Princeton University Press, 1971), chap. 5, "Urban Income Distribution in a Dual Economy." Yet, by their own figures (pp. 134–136), craft manufacturing accounts for only 0.4 million workers or 25 percent of the traditional nonfarm labor force.

FIGURE 3.3

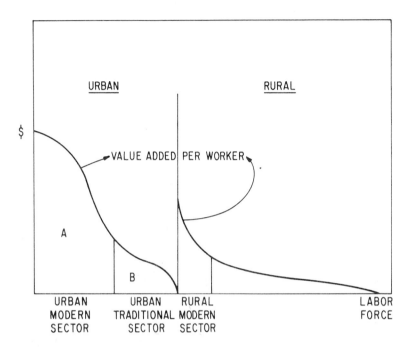

differentiation. First, physical productivity differs because skills differ and because, over time, producers accumulate capital and acquire market knowledge. But, more importantly, there is a strong quality aspect to much urban-traditional sector output, in both service and artisan activities. Quality differentiation creates a link between the income distribution of the modern and that of the urban-traditional sector. Domestic servants for instance, may earn twice as much in a rich residential district as in a *pueblo joven*. And the wage of an established "family" servant often rises over time.

Many benefit from rising modern-sector incomes because of the strength of client attachment, or preference for established or better-ranked providers, despite a growing number of competitors. The demand for a proven and trusted tailor, maid, or mechanic, for instance, is likely to have a low price elasticity and a positive income elasticity. Lower-ranked providers are less protected against new entrants; their incomes may rise or fall according to the strength of acquired market advantages relative to that of competition from entrants. Differentiation thus makes it possible for some urban-traditional sector incomes to rise above their rural-traditional sector opportunity cost level and at the same time reduces migration by protecting earlier or better-ranked producers from entrants.

The Rural-Traditional Sector

In Peru, as in most less-developed countries, the rural sector is still the largest and the poorest component of the traditional economy. A small part of the agricultural population works on highly capitalized farms—such as the sugar estates in Peru—which qualify as "modern" on the criterion of value added per worker. But value added per worker is generally low even in export and other commercial plantations. The extraction of large absolute property incomes requires large units of production and institutional mechanisms which keep wages at minimum levels.[36] A large segment of the rural population is dedicated principally to subsistence farming, where value added per worker, and earnings, are lowest.

The rural population thus appears to be locked into relative poverty by its size and low productivity. The demand effect from the growing urban economy is weak, because of Engel's law and because the trickle-down effects are spread over a very large segment of the population. The large numbers involved also dilute the impact of redistributive transfers from the urban population, while the low value-added ceiling limits the improvement possible by redistribution of income within the sector.

But the picture is not quite so gloomy, for several reasons. First, the impact of urban demand is a function of the relative sizes of the urban and rural economies. The rapid relative growth of the urban economy implies an acceleration of the demand effect that is not easily perceived at present, but which can become significant over time.[37] Second, government has more

[36] For a model and historical discussion of hacienda wages, see Shane Hunt, "The Economics of Haciendas and Plantations in Latin America," discussion paper no. 29, Research Program in Economic Development, mimeographed, Princeton University, 1972. The political instruments used to keep down rural wages in Peru are analyzed by Julio Cotler in "La Mecánica."

[37] Imagine, for instance, an economy where 40 percent of the population is urban and mean urban income is 50 percent higher than mean rural income: total rural and urban incomes will be equal. Assume that over a period of two

policy tools available for raising rural incomes than it has for raising incomes in the urban-traditional sector. Total urban-traditional sector income is largely constrained by modern-sector demand. But autonomous growth in rural-traditional sector output and income is possible, because the sector consumes much of its own output and because foreign trade creates opportunities for export and for import substitution. Policies directed at expanding productive capacity can thus be used to expand rural income.[38]

Income Redistribution

The value-added curve (PP') can be used to make the following distinction with regard to redistributive policy: income transfers can be considered *vertical* when they redistribute *within* a productive sector, or *horizontal* when the transfer takes place *between* productive sectors. The more dualistic the structure of production is, the greater the need for horizontal income transfers will be. Unfortunately, as will be seen, horizontal transfers are the more difficult to implement, for political, administrative, and psychological reasons. As a result, income tends to remain bottled up within the modern sector.

The principal form of vertical redistribution is wage policy.[39]

---

decades migration raises the urban population share to 6o percent while economic growth concentrated in the modern sector raises the mean urban income to a level that is twice the rural average. Total urban income will now be *three times larger* than total rural income. Even with low income elasticities of demand for farm products, there will be a large proportional increase in urban spending on the rural sector.

[38] It has been argued that this is not the case in Mexico, where foreign trade opportunities do not provide an outlet for the staple grain crops of small farmers. Programs that expand productive capacity therefore face an inelastic domestic demand for staples and consequently add little to small farmer incomes. See Roger Norton, *A Model of the Agricultural Sector in Mexico* (Washington, D.C.: Industrial Bank for Reconstruction and Development, 1972). Peru, however, is not constrained by a lack of import substitution possibilities available to small farmers: food imports now account for about a quarter of domestic food consumption.

[39] Wage policies also have secondary horizontal effects: higher modern-sector wages may lower traditional-sector wages through a supply effect, and seasonal migration creates a modern-sector source of wage income for traditional-sector labor. Indeed, most policies probably have both horizontal or vertical effects

Wage levels are influenced by numerous policy instruments, including minimum-wage laws, direct pricing (in the case of government employees), and legislation regarding union activity. Related forms of vertical transfer consist of social security laws and legislation regarding company benefits to employees. Finally, land reform and other "structural reforms" that transfer property ownership to workers are radical forms of vertical redistribution.

Horizontal transfers are brought about chiefly through fiscal and price policies. Thus the net tax burden (taxes less public expenditures) may differ significantly for modern and traditional sectors, causing net flows of income and wealth between those sectors. Price policies also redistribute income by raising or lowering the value-added curve in the modern and traditional sectors. The most powerful influence on relative prices is usually the combination of exchange rate and tariff policies, though most taxes have some relative price effects. The financial system can also cause income transfers, partly because of the frequent existence of price distortions in the savings market, and partly because most forms of investment yield external economies that accrue to the borrowing sector.

The most obvious impediment to horizontal redistribution is the association between political power and various inherent characteristics of modern sectors, chiefly income, wealth, education, and urban status. The urban-traditional sector enjoys some of these sources of power, with a corresponding advantage over the rural-traditional sector in its ability to press for horizontal transfers. But the traditional sector as a whole is weakened by the split into urban and rural components, since each is seeking different horizontal transfers: the urban-traditional sector wants hospitals, secondary schools, urban infrastructure, and low food prices; the rural-traditional sector benefits from preventive public health systems, farm-related basic schooling, rural infrastructure, and high food prices.

A related political liability of the traditional sector is that horizontal transfers cannot be taken by force; they must be obtained by voice: that is, by petition, persuasion, or political bargaining within government. Workers who can strike, or seize a factory,

---

through their impact on factor and commodity markets. It is useful, nevertheless, to distinguish between the direct and generally much larger primary impact of a measure and its secondary effects through markets.

or demonstrate for higher wages enjoy both a tactical and a psychological advantage over peasants seeking schools or roads for their communities. The availability of a visible and accessible target both facilitates mobilization and makes it possible to bargain with an immediate advantage in hand. A demand for a larger budget allocation for rural workers is not a banner that will mobilize peasant movements, nor are there accessible targets that could be seized by a dispersed rural population as bargaining counters relevant to that petition. The only available procedure is the exercise of voice within government. The effect of this procedure is to channel the petition into a single pool of competing claims where distributive decisions are more directly perceived as a zero-sum business. Peasants are in a stronger position to mobilize and press for land reform; but in the typical dual economy, where most income now originates in the modern sector, substantial equalization requires much more than a redistribution of land.

Vertical transfers are not only easier to implement, they also enjoy a moral support that is not associated with horizontal redistribution. This moral support is expressed, for instance, in the labor theory of value. It is rooted in those notions of justice that link rights to the creation of something of value, rather than to its use; in "historical" as against "pattern" or "end-state" conceptions of justice.[40] When Marxists and conservatives dispute the right to property income, the argument centers on the question of who really produced that income. Both parties are implicitly accepting the distributive claim arising out of the act of production. Catholic social doctrine has also defended the historical notions of justice; its appeal for a sharing of consumption has been based on the claims of charity rather than justice.

By contrast, the ideal of income equality, which is required to sustain policies of horizontal redistribution and, more generally, to separate distribution from production, is a weaker moral precept. Horizontal transfers are more commonly supported by feelings of charity than of justice, and charity is much the weaker of those sentiments. The communist precept—to each according to his needs—remains an ideal for a society of "new men," not a banner for political action today. Most of the indignation pro-

[40] See Robert Nozick, "Distributive Justice," *Philosophy and Public Affairs*, vol. 3, no. 1 (Fall 1973), pp. 45–126.

voked by "inequality" is satisfied by removing the extremes in income levels. In poor countries, that indignation amounts to a feeling of scandal at the existence of a few rich amongst the many poor; levelling down those extremes of wealth can be achieved without horizontal redistribution. These moral feelings, along with administrative costs, reinforce the natural political difficulties of achieving horizontal redistribution.

There are, however, two important exceptions to the rule that horizontal transfers are rare. First, there are many instances of redistribution from high productivity farmers to urban groups: through marketing boards in Africa, and through exchange-rate and tariff policies in Latin America. Second, horizontal transfers have favored the urban-traditional population. Some of the transfer is an accidental spillover of indivisible urban services, but much is clearly a political response.

Both types of horizontal transfers have occurred in Peru, but they do not substantially qualify the argument that horizontal redistribution is more difficult and more rare and that, in consequence, redistributive policies have done little to correct the concentration of income associated with a dual economy.

GOVERNMENT POLICIES AND THE DISTRIBUTION OF INCOMES

What follows is a discussion of how policies of the Belaúnde and Velasco regimes have affected income distribution. The principal questions that guide this discussion are: to what extent has progressive redistribution been stepped up under Velasco? What is being done for the very poor? The answer that emerges below to both questions is—very little.

The analysis that follows is built chiefly on the sectoral framework developed in the previous section and on an aggregate statistical picture of the sectoral distribution of income that relates income transfers to the levels and changes in market incomes. Those figures are contained in Table 3.6. Lines 1 through 4 of Table 3.6 amount to a statistical version of the shape and composition of the value-added curve in 1961 and 1970; they provide a perspective for judging the significance of income transfers that result from government policies. The principal forms of transfers are estimated in lines 5 through 11. The following sections will discuss these figures in more detail from the point of view of each of the three sectors.

The Modern Sector

Over the period under study most income redistribution in Peru has taken place within the modern sector. The net result has been some gain for labor at the expense of capital, though some measures transfer in the reverse direction. The sector as a whole appears to benefit at the expense of commercial agriculture and to lose to both the urban-traditional and the rural-subsistence sectors. As may be seen in Table 3.6, however, any such horizontal transfers are small in proportion to the size of the modern sector.

The modern sector transfers income to other sectors through the budget; it had a net budgetary loss equal to 15 percent of value added in 1970, versus small gains in the other sectors. The modern sector has the highest tax burden: in 1970, 23 percent of modern-sector value added was paid in taxes versus 20 percent in the urban- and 9 percent in the rural-traditional sectors. The modern sector paid three-quarters of all taxes. However, the tax ratio has been rising faster in other sectors, particularly in the urban-traditional, thereby lessening the degree of progressivity that existed in 1961.

Government expenditures are also far higher in the modern sector, though not sufficiently to offset the greater tax burden. Of the three components of government expenditure whose benefits could be allocated by sector (accounting for about half the total budget), the 1970 per capita benefits were all significantly higher in the modern sector: $260 per worker versus $170 in the urban- and $80 in the rural-traditional sectors. In contrast to tax policy, the incidence of expenditures improved over the period: their absolute growth between 1961 and 1970 was about equal in each sector, implying a faster proportional growth in the poorer sectors.

On the other hand, it could be argued that most of the non-allocated expenditures (chiefly defense, police, and some basic infrastructure) provide services that are more relevant to the modern sector than to the rest or, to some extent, consist of subsidized wages that accrue to modern-sector employees. More clearly, price policy works in favor of the modern sector; though it is both conceptually and statistically difficult to measure the amount of transfer involved, the estimates shown in Table 3.6 indicate the direction and changing size of that transfer, both

TABLE 3.6
Market Incomes and Income Transfers per Worker by Sector, 1961 and 1970
(All values in 1970 U.S. $ per worker)

	1961 Modern	1961 Traditional Urban	1961 Traditional Rural	1970 Modern	1970 Traditional Urban	1970 Traditional Rural
1. Percentage of labor force [a]	21.1	28.6	50.3	21.6	33.1	45.3
2. Value added [b]	2,690	630	530	3,590	810	600
3. Property income [c]	940	60	120	1,070	80	90
4. Wage [c]	1,750	570	410	2,520	730	510
5. Net budget transfer [d]	-300	60	20	-540	10	30
6. Taxes [e]	-530	-70	-30	-800	-160	-50
7. Education [f]	60	50	20	100	100	50
8. Health [g]	100	50	10	100	50	10
9. Public investment [h]	70	30	20	60	20	20
10. Price effect [i]	40	10	-30	80	30	-70
11. Property transfer [j]						
a. Wage	—	—	—	140	0	[60]
b. Profits	—	—	—	-120	—	[-60]

Notes:

[a] Sectoral definitions and 1961 data from Webb, *The Distribution of Income in Peru*, especially table 4. The 1970 data are estimated from (1) Central Reserve Bank worksheets, (2) *Informe Laboral*, Ministry of Labor, 1970, and (3) *Boletin de Estadística de Industria y Comercio* no. 1 (1970), p. 18.

[b] The 1961 data are from Webb, *Distribution*, table 4; 1970 from Webb, *Tax Policy*, table 4.6, which estimates national income by sector for 1969, plus extrapolations to 1970 based on national accounts data of Central Reserve Bank.

[c] The 1961 data are from Webb, *Distribution*, table 3 and worksheets. The 1970 data are from (1) national accounts wage and profits series for establishments in modern-sector and commercial agriculture, checked against Ministry of Labor wage series, (2) urban-traditional sector wage and profit breakdown approximated by multiplying ratio of employees to total urban-traditional sector labor force by 1961 modern-sector wage and profit shares.

[d] Sum of lines 6 through 9.

[e] 1961 data from Webb, *Tax Policy*, table 4.6. The 1970 data are extrapolated from 1969 tax ratios in table 4.6.

[f] From Ministry of Education provincial enrollment figures, by public and private schools, for 1961–1968. Enrollment was broken down into primary, secondary, and university. Average cost per student, by level, from *Plan Sectorial de Educación*, 1971–1975, p. 168. Breakdown of school attendance for modern and urban-traditional sectors based on CISM (Ministry of Labor) eight-city labor force survey, 1970.

g Ministry of Health budgets and *Plan Sectorial de Salud 1971-75*, p. 19, for total expenditure. Breakdown based on (1) per capita health expenditures by province, estimated from 1964 census of health sector by Ministry of Health, (2) Thomas Hall, *Health Manpower in Peru* (Baltimore: Johns Hopkins Press, 1969), (3) assumption that all social security, police, and military health services benefit modern sector only.

h The 1961 and 1970 government budgets, and *Plan Nacional 1971-1975* used for breakdown by type of investment expenditure. Allocations are approximations based on the assumption that housing went to modern-sector families, irrigation and other agricultural infrastructure to the rural sector, and that trunk roads were shared in proportion to income.

i Very crude estimates of order of magnitude based on (1) share of modern and urban-traditional sector income spent on foods affected by price controls or by tariff and exchange rate policies (chiefly meats, dairy products, wheat, and oils), (2) conservative estimates of price distortion: 20 percent in 1961 and 40 percent in 1970 (increase reflects doubling of tariff level on nonfood imports, increased price controls, recent rationing of meat, and trend in relative domestic to imported goods price levels).

j From national accounts data on 1969-1970 profits in reformed sectors. Bracketed rural-sector figures measure total *eventual* transfer on completion of agrarian reform; i.e., they assume that land has been fully and instantaneously redistributed. The figures for the modern sector reflect redistribution out of one year's profits. The wage gain (140) exceeds the profits loss (-120) because part of the transfer comes out of taxes.

favorable to the modern sector. The overall impact of government measures—the net budget transfer (—$540), plus price effect (+$80), plus unallocated expenditures (+$120 or more)[41]— may therefore be judged neutral or mildly negative for the modern sector.

The final shares of income accruing to capital and to labor *within* the modern sector are affected by wage policies, tax incidence, the allocation of public expenditures, and financial policy affecting the price and allocation of savings. Pricing policies also affect the outcome: some tariffs create monopoly profits; some price controls subsidize consumers. Finally, profit sharing and wealth transfers have become additional instruments of vertical transfers. The modern sector, in short, is a busy distributive marketplace (or battlefield?); with so much trading going on, less significance should be attached to the progressive or regressive nature of any specific measure except as a means to understand the final outcome.

Between 1961 and 1970, modern-sector wage levels rose at 4.1 percent a year, exceeding the growth of productivity. In the private sector, the average wage rose even faster, at 5 percent a year, while employment lagged; in government the growth in employment contributed more than that in average wage. The overall result was that the share of wages in modern-sector value added rose from 65 to 70 percent. It was argued above that this gain should be attributed to closely related technological and political characteristics of the modern sector. The political and union power of the modern-sector labor force was well established by 1963. Indirect evidence of union power is reflected in the strong relationship between wage levels and productivity in different sectors and size firms shown in Figure 3.2. Union power surely increased under the Belaúnde government. One index of political support is the number of unions granted official recognition: between 1962 and 1967 an average of 223 unions were recognized each year versus only 38 between 1950 and 1961. The

[41] A minimum share of unallocated expenditures could be estimated by allocating on a per capita basis; this yields the figure of $120; an allocation proportional to income raises modern-sector budget receipts per worker instead to $280, while a higher figure would result from assuming, as suggested above, that the most nonallocated expenditures are primarily of benefit to the modern sector.

exercise of working-class power was, if anything, reinforced during the first years of the Velasco government, which allowed wages to rise at over 5 percent a year in large mining and manufacturing establishments between 1969 and 1971.

The budget also appears to redistribute from capital to labor. Tax rates are progressive within the modern sector, and health and education expenditures are probably pro-labor in their incidence, largely as a result of the use of private schooling and health care by the upper and middle classes. Thus the more easily allocated budget items are progressive in their net incidence. Many public investments, such as roads and ports, are complementary to private-sector investment, but investments in housing, schools, irrigation of new lands, hospitals, etc., benefit middle- or lower-income groups more directly. There appears to have been little change in the mix of public investment, though more emphasis is now being given to "productive" and less to welfare-related investments. Also, tax changes have slightly reduced the progressivity of the fiscal system within the modern sector.

The principal change in distributive policy introduced by the Velasco government consists of the redistribution of profits and property within modern firms. The effect is to reinforce the vertical redistribution that has already been taking place through wage and fiscal policies.

The gross transfer involved is very large for a few workers, but for the modern sector as a whole it currently amounts to about 6 percent of labor income.[42] If the gradual transfer of share capital that will take place under the new industrial law (up to 50 percent of each firm's net worth) were instead done overnight, the redistribution would increase modern-sector labor income by between 20 and 25 percent.[43] The planned redistribution is therefore relatively large, but the gross transfer may prove larger than the net because wages may now rise less than otherwise. There are indications that the government is at present seeking to restrain modern-sector wage gains, but it will require a considerable change in political attitudes and behavior vis-à-vis organ-

[42] Table 3.6.

[43] Table 3.6. Based on percentage transfers allowed for each sector and on total 1970 property income, though much is not subject to transfer (e.g., rents, interest, state enterprises, etc.).

ized labor to prevent workers from reaping the benefits that will grow out of the *comunidades laborales* created by the Industrial Law.

The Urban-Traditional Sector

Since about two-thirds of the urban-traditional sector in Peru is self-employed and the rest are employees in small businesses, where profits per worker are low, vertical redistribution in this sector is largely irrelevant. Furthermore, minimum wages or similar legislation would be hard to enforce in small firms and households, and high price elasticities of demand for labor in this sector would cause a large employment effect.

These constraints are reflected in the little stress that governments have placed on any form of vertical redistribution within the sector. Minimum-wage laws were first introduced in 1962, by the military junta, and generalized across the country by Belaúnde, but there has never been a serious effort to police them at the level of small firms. Union legislation deliberately excludes small firms (under twenty employees). The Velasco government requires employers to pay social security contributions for domestic servants, but in an unregulated competitive market of this kind legislation requiring the payment of supplementary benefits to employees is undoubtedly largely nullified by eventual readjustments in the market wage. Finally, the sectoral property transfers decreed by Velasco so far completely exclude the urban-traditional sector.

What can be done for the poor in this group must therefore be done at the expense of other sectors. The major horizontal transfers received by the urban-traditional sector are public services and low food prices: both become available to all urban residents, though with varying degrees of discrimination.

Neither of the last two governments has a good record of transfers deliberately aimed at the urban poor. Both have given greatest publicity and money to housing, though it is the least effective way of reaching the very poor: costs per beneficiary are high, and, in the best of cases, few benefit. In practice, subsidized housing has gone almost entirely to middle-income employees. Recent government-subsidized housing is on the average reaching poorer groups than under Belaúnde, though prices still exclude the poorest, while creditworthiness standards still imply a bias against the self-employed.[44] Public expenditures on *barriada* roads, water, sewage, etc., have been minimal over the whole period.[45] Between 1964 and 1970, the Paseo de la Republica (an expressway linking downtown Lima to the richest residential areas) absorbed half of the total investment by the municipal government of Lima: from 1970 to 1972 the extension of this expressway to the beaches continued to be the largest municipal project.

Urban health services are far better than rural: in 1964 per capita health expenditures in fifteen cities were $15, versus $1 for the rest of the country. Urban health expenditures have risen since 1961, but neither government has seriously attacked the discrimination built into the three-tiered health system: the military, police, and white-collar workers have better services than modern-sector blue-collar workers, who in turn get more attention— from the social security system—than the self-employed or unregistered *obreros* of small-scale businesses, who must resort to ministry or charity hospitals. The Velasco government has made some moves in the right direction: it incorporated domestic servants into the social security system and has recently made some moves toward the unification of the white-collar and blue-collar social security systems. More than any other urban public service, the health system neatly discriminates between the modern and urban-traditional sectors.

The nature of the urban-traditional sector economy makes it difficult to raise incomes in that sector by raising productivity. The single greatest public expenditure in the urban-traditional sector is education, which is clearly of value as a current transfer. Whether it raises money incomes is less clear: would the

[44] See Alfredo Tapia, *Acción de las Instituciones de Credito Especializadas en el Financiamiento de Vivienda en el Perú* (Lima: Imprenta del Hogar de la Clinica San Juan de Dios, 1971), for statistics on housing prices and urban income levels.

[45] A 1967 survey of *barriada* residents by CISM revealed that 58 percent of the homes had no piped water, 61 percent had no sewers, and 87 percent were located on unpaved streets. On the other hand, only 2 percent of the families had children who were not attending primary school, and—what is more surprising—only 11 percent had children aged 13–21 who were not attending secondary school. Peru, Ministerio de Trabajo y Comunidades, *Barriadas de Lima* (Lima, 1967).

modern sector spend less on urban-traditional sector services and goods if workers in the latter sector were less educated? My feeling is that total expenditure would be similar, but more persons would be employed in the urban-traditional sector, thus increasing wage differentials between the modern and urban-traditional sectors but reducing them between the urban- and rural-traditional sectors. In any case, governments since 1961 have been heavily committed to providing education to the urban population, with no significant discrimination against the poor. The only apparent change in emphasis between the two governments has been the reduction in the university budget under Velasco, though projected improvements in the quality of education are potentially much more significant.

On the debit side, the urban-traditional sector has not fared well as a taxpayer. Its 1970 tax burden of 19.7 percent was almost as high as that of the modern sector (23 percent). Belaúnde's tax policy was particularly regressive with regard to this sector: its tax burden rose from 10.2 percent in 1961 to 20.5 percent in 1969. Though the overall tax burden is unlikely to rise as fast under Velasco, current tax changes also appear to discriminate against this sector: recent tax reductions largely benefit the modern sector, whereas excise tax increases and the conversion of the sales into a value-added tax hit low-income consumers most. The net burden worsened for the urban-traditional sector under Belaúnde, despite a doubling of educational expenditure per capita; since 1969 it has probably changed little.

To summarize: the nature of the urban-traditional sector economy makes it hard to help this sector; vertical redistribution is ruled out, and productivity-raising horizontal transfers in the form of education and productive infrastructure probably change the distribution of incomes and employment within this sector more than its total income. The urban-traditional sector does receive substantially more welfare transfers than the rural population, though less than the modern sector. Also, income is transferred from the rural population through food price policies. Most of the fiscal transfer is paid for through taxes, but the sector is clearly a net recipient of income from other sectors, once the effects of price policies and of unallocated public expenditures are counted. Finally, on all major aspects of distributive policy toward this sector, there has been considerable continuity between the Belaúnde and Velasco governments.

The Rural-Traditional Sector

The impact of distributive policies on the rural-traditional sector is easier to assess if the sector is separated into its commercial and subsistence components.

The *subsistence sector* can only benefit: further, if we classify all haciendas and their *colonos* as commercial, the remaining subsistence *minifundistas* (about 20 percent of Peru's population) can only benefit via horizontal, chiefly fiscal, transfers. Since most sell at least a small proportion of output and purchase some taxed items, they are affected to a minor extent—in both cases negatively—by price policies and taxes. The tax burden is very low, but price policy is discriminatory: food imports continue to be exempted from tariffs while the average duty on all other goods has risen from about 30 percent in 1961 to over 70 percent in 1970. Cheap beef imports compete with what is often the principal source of cash income for small farmers; in 1961, over 70 percent of beef cattle were owned on farms under five hectares. Meat imports grew so fast during the last ten years that rationing has now been imposed to reduce demand. Yet most meat is consumed by middle-class families. Tariff-exempt wheat imports favor the consumption of bread; a nondiscriminatory general tariff, or a reverse discrimination in favor of domestic foods, would raise Sierra income from potatoes and other substitutes for bread. Potatoes in particular are thought to be in relatively elastic supply, so that a potential exists for import substitution with large benefits to small farmers.

On the other hand, government expenditures do benefit the subsistence economy. The largest direct transfer is education. Belaúnde extended primary schooling to most of the rural sector, where enrollment rates now reach 70 to 80 percent.

Much more, however, could be spent on education in backward rural areas, where school materials are scarce, teachers are poorly prepared, secondary schooling is unavailable, and illiteracy remains high. The 1971–1975 development plan recognizes all these needs, but its projections do not add up to a large financial effort. There is no indication, for instance, of funding for a massive literacy program. Additional financial effort, however, may be less important than improvements in the quality of rural education, which at present probably adds little to the welfare or future income of the *campesino* who does not emigrate. Since the administrative self-improvement required to make significant changes in the quality of rural education will surely be a long and uncertain endeavor, it seems unlikely that education will be a vehicle for a substantial additional transfer to the subsistence sector during the next few years.[46]

Less money is spent on two more fruitful types of fiscal transfer to the small farmer: rural infrastructure and agricultural extension plus credit. Small roads and small irrigation projects in the Sierra were minor components of Belaúnde's investment program, and there has been no major change in the priority given to those programs. On the other hand, there is a larger allocation for trunk roads and other major routes through or into the Sierra, and these also favor small farmers; about one-third of 1971–1975 projected road expenditures will be in the Sierra. Most of the national road program is a continuation of projects that were initiated or planned under Belaúnde. Though the Sierra gets much less in per capita terms, road construction may well be the single most productive transfer to the poorer rural population. By contrast, potential small irrigation projects in the Sierra have been, and continue to be, almost entirely ignored.

The record of agricultural extension and credit to small farmers in the Sierra is one of extreme neglect. The extension service claimed a total of 117,000 assisted families in 1969, but about two-thirds were on the coast or in the Montaña; thus only 40,000 families, or about 4 percent of Sierra small farmers, received direct assistance. The distribution of farm credit was similar. It is difficult to judge how much more the present regime will do. The obvious fear is that the plan's preoccupation with land tenure changes and with large irrigation and colonization schemes will direct most effort and money to the 10 to 20 percent of the small farmer population who will receive land, including many on the coast. The 1971–1975 Agricultural Development Plan says very little about what is sure to be its principal constraint: the limited number of field workers who know more about Sierra farm techniques than the *campesinos* themselves and who are also able to communicate with and persuade the *campesinos* to change. The official programs do not plan for a substantial increase in the size and quality of technical assistance to small farmers.

The *commercial* part of the rural-traditional sector is defined

[46] This view is supported by the essay by Robert Drysdale and Robert Myers, Chapter 7 of this volume.

to include most Coast and Jungle farms (excluding sugar, here classified as modern sector), Sierra haciendas, and most small farmers in the central Sierra. Market participation is a mixed blessing for these farmers, since it opens them to large negative transfers via price and tax policies. Political weakness plus vulnerability to tax and price policies have combined to make this the most victimized sector in Peru, as it is in many less-developed countries.

Since 1963 there has been a great deal of income redistribution, both *within* commercialized agriculture and *from* this sector to the urban economy. Large landowners were clear losers. In the case of small farmers and wage earners, it is harder to determine the net incidence of better wages and public services on the one hand, and higher taxes and worsening terms of trade on the other. The sector as a whole was penalized by overvaluation, which reduced cotton and coffee earnings and cheapened competing food imports, and by the combination of food price controls and low tariffs on foods. Furthermore, some of the growing burden of indirect taxation spilled over to this group, while public investments complementary to *existing* commercial agriculture (e.g., improvement of existing irrigation systems and silos) received low priority.

Small farmers and wage earners, however, receive some compensation in the form of improved welfare services, chiefly education. And wage earners, including Sierra *colonos*, benefited from a favorable wage policy. During the late fifties and sixties, most Coast farm unions received official recognition and sympathetic official arbitration. As a result, Coast farm wages grew more rapidly than those of modern-sector workers.[47] Parallel gains were made during the period by Sierra *colonos* despite the discriminatory treatment of Sierra farm unions: of the 279 farm unions given official recognition between 1961 and 1967, only 5 were in the Sierra. Nevertheless, though the evidence is partial and scattered, there appears to be general agreement that peasant mobilization and union activities in the Sierra resulted in a

[47] Coast farm wages grew at about 5 percent a year between 1950 and 1966. Sugar farms account for only 10 percent of this labor force; the rapid rise in wages in other Coast farms, here classified as "traditional," was possible partly because wages were very low in 1950 and partly because productivity on these farms is relatively high within agriculture—they are on the margin of the modern sector.

better deal vis-à-vis the *hacendado* during the late fifties and early sixties; bargaining for better wage rates was helped by the minimum-wage legislation of the mid-sixties, but gains were also made in work conditions (days worked on the hacienda, provision of schools, etc.), and in the recovery of some communal lands.[48]

There has been a remarkable continuity in the pattern of redistributive policy toward the rural sector, characterized by negative horizontal transfers and a vertical redistribution of income and property from landowners to wage earners and some small farmers. Under the agrarian reform law, the vertical transfer has become radical. On the other hand, the negative incidence of both price and tax policies appears to have been heightened with the growth in excise and sales taxation, and a more rigid and extensive application of food price controls.[49] Also, positive fiscal transfers to the sector of both the productive and welfare type continue to be of a relatively minor order of priority.

Conclusions

The two main findings of the preceding description of distributive measures since 1963 are that their effects have been mildly progressive on balance and that the pattern of redistribution under Belaúnde and Velasco has been similar, characterized by redistribution downwards within sectors.

The progressive incidence of policy is most evident in the mod-

[48] An interesting witness to the retreat of the *hacendado* in one part of the Sierra during this period was the ex-guerrilla leader Héctor Béjar: "Hecho incontrovertible: el latifundio decae en todas partes, cada dia es mas dificil mantenerlo . . . los gamonales venden sus tierras o se alejan abandonando a sus siervos la posesión de los cultivos." *Peru 1965: Una Experiencia Guerrillera* (Lima, Campodonico, 1969), p. 93.

[49] Estimates of the redistribution caused by price policy are very tentative, but the estimates in Table 3.6 (line 10) indicate the order of magnitude of nonneutral tariffs and price controls on foods. To estimate the potential for raising rural incomes through price policy with a deliberate rural bias, one could assume, for instance, prohibitive tariffs on most imported foods, no food price controls, and possibly a higher exchange rate favoring agricultural exports. Rough calculations of the value of import-competing and exported farm products and of the domestic price elasticity of demand for goods suggest that such policies could raise incomes of individual farmers in the order of 10 to 50 percent, depending on the fraction of output that is marketed, and by over 20 percent for the sector as a whole.

ern sector, where the budget transfers income both downwards and across to the traditional sector, and where the market share of labor has been pushed up by wage policies and profit sharing. The urban-traditional sector is a net recipient of income transfers, partly at the expense of modern-sector taxpayers, but also partly from farmers as a result of food price policies. In the rural sector, the poorest families consist of subsistence farmers, who have received a positive and growing net budget transfer; their reduced market participation limits the negative impact of price policies and indirect taxation. Wage earners in commercial agriculture have benefited instead through vertical redistribution: they appear to break even with the budget; but they were favored by wage policies under Belaúnde and are now the principal beneficiaries of the agrarian reform. On the other hand, small and medium farmers producing for the market lose heavily from price policies, and do not gain from the budget: this "middle income" group is perhaps the major exception to the overall progressivity of government policy.

Though policy has worked in the "right" direction, the amounts transferred remain very small in relation to the large and growing market income disparities shown in Table 3.6. Also, the allocation of benefits has been unfair. The largest transfers have gone to urban, and particularly to modern-sector, employees, most of whom belong in the upper two or three deciles of the income distribution. Even within the modern sector, the cumulative impact of wage and profit-sharing measures had an unequal incidence, heavily favoring workers in capital-intensive firms. The rural sector has gained much less, and again the distribution of benefits has favored the better-off wage earners within the sector. The most radical redistributive measures to date—the sectoral reforms—actually worsen the distribution of labor income. In per capita terms, the overall pattern of *redistribution* may be considered grossly unjust.

The basic feature of that pattern of redistribution has been the propensity towards vertical transfers. Policy has tended to parallel, rather than offset, the dualistic structure of market incomes. In fact, market spillover has probably done more for the traditional sector than has distributive policy. Horizontal transfers do exist; the budget appears to favor most of the traditional sector. In the case of the rural-traditional sector, however, the budget transfer is more than offset by the reverse effect of price policies.

The net horizontal transfer to the traditional sector as a whole is insignificant in relation to either traditional- or modern-sector income. This is in contrast to the large per capita vertical transfers received by modern-sector employees. The continuity of this pattern under the Velasco government suggests that the underlying political, administrative, and psychological biases against horizontal transfers remain substantially unchanged. On balance, although there may have been some acceleration in the degree of redistribution, as there was under the Belaúnde government, the evidence does not point to any major change in either the amount or the direction of redistribution under the Velasco regime. Some very positive and dramatic measures must be set against several less visible, negative changes in tax, social-expenditure, and price policies. Although some recent redistributive measures have been favorable, the effects of other policies which are shaping the economic and political structure of the country are inauspicious for the poor. Those policies are increasing the dualism of the economy and diminishing the political power of the poorer groups.

The dualism of the productive structure is being reinforced in several ways, of which the most important is the change in the projected composition of sectoral output, with much more priority being given to the highly capital-intensive heavy industries and to mining. The race to establish a foothold in several branches of the metal-working, petrochemical, and chemical industries, in advance of the complementarity agreements that are to be worked out under the Andean Pact, is giving an extra edge to the high degree of priority already enjoyed by those industries. The Andean Pact will also discourage efforts to sacrifice industrial efficiency in the interests of labor intensity. In other activities, the government plan is strongly oriented toward large-scale investments that will be part of, or complementary to, the modern sector.

Dualism is also being reinforced by factor-price policies, which are not only maintaining but probably increasing the previous distortions favoring capital-intensive techniques. Wages have been allowed to rise substantially in high productivity establishments, but numerous incentives built into the Industrial Law and other sector laws tend to cheapen the cost of capital. Finally, the newly created workers' communities in most of the private modern-business sector will tend to resist employment expansion;

they will seek to maximize dividends per worker by maximizing capital per worker. Greater dualism will increase the concentration of value added in the modern sector and the consequent need for horizontal transfers.

Corporativist elements in the military government's approach to organization, such as the deliberate weakening of class associations and the stress on productive sectors as prime social units, appear to parallel the bias toward vertical redistribution.[50] Sharing of effort and rewards within each productive sector is to be the antidote to class conflict, but it will also reinforce the bottling-up of income within the rich sectors. The agrarian reform has removed the most effective instrument for peasant mobilization; the reform itself is a sizable transfer to some peasants, but for most peasants it will now be more difficult to press for a share in modern-sector productivity.[51] At present for instance, farmers seem powerless even to defend themselves from the worsening rural-urban terms of trade that have resulted from the price and import policies of the government. Much attention is also being given to dampen any potential for mobilization in the urban-traditional sector by the closely supervised vertical organization of separate *barriada* communities and, as in the countryside, by granting land titles to remove the major potential instrument for mobilization.[52]

The Velasco government has shown some awareness of the negative redistributive implications of its economic and political model. The gross unfairness of redistribution under the Industrial Law was not repeated in subsequent legislation which introduced sharing arrangements between firms in the mining and fishing laws. The early rejection of the "family farm" concept and the shift to ever-larger units of farm organization are, in part, motivated by a desire to spread benefits. The most visible, and embarrassing, case of exclusion—that of the sugar farm seasonal workers—has been publicly discussed by government officials. These concerns underlie the new Social-Property Law, which will socialize at least some of the rights to the control of, and in-

50 See the essays in this volume by Julio Cotler (Chapter 2) and Jane Jaquette (Chapter 10).

51 Susan Bourque and Scott Palmer (Chapter 5 of this volume) make this point forcefully in discussing government policy towards the rural sector.

52 See the essay in this volume by David Collier (Chapter 4) on government policy toward squatter settlements.

come from, private property. If this law is implemented in a vigorous and radical fashion—with rapid creation of social-property firms and a stress on very small scale, labor-intensive firms—it would eventually channel large amounts of capital to the traditional sector.[53]

Thus far, however, there is little to indicate that the government is willing to undergo and impose the political, administrative, and psychological changes that would be necessary for a substantial and prompt alteration in the degree and direction of income redistribution. The necessary changes appear to be so large, and so far from current policies, that they would amount, indeed, to a revolution.

Some Implications for Redistributive Policy

A focus on recent history and on the very poor tends to highlight the inequity of the economic system and the insufficiency of redistributive policy. One in four Peruvians today survives on less than $100 a year, a standard of living that has scarcely been touched by the expansion of the economy or by government measures over the last two decades. Despite greater government control and an evident distributive concern, the policies of the current regime, including the agrarian reform, are doing little for the very poor; those policies appear to reinforce, rather than reduce, the major income cleavages of the society. "Radical" redistributive measures are giving large dividends to workers whose wages are already between five and ten times the average income of subsistence farmers, whereas less visible tax and price changes since 1969 have been regressive, and no major initiatives have been made in expenditure programs for the rural poor.

Yet a longer view of the economy as a whole provides grounds for a less somber evaluation. In particular, the breadth of income

---

[53] The law seems designed more for change *within* the modern sector than for transfer of resources *out of* the sector. It is hard, for instance, to envision small (two- or three-person) traditional-sector establishments qualifying for social-property sector financing or meeting the complex operative and accounting requirements of the law. Also, the draft makes no reference whatsoever to its relationship with the existing cooperative and "social"-type agricultural organizations; agriculture is not even represented on the proposed Supervisory National Commission of Social Property.

See the essay in this volume by Peter Knight (Chapter 9) for a detailed discussion of the proposed social-property sector.

growth throughout the economy conflicts with the "domination" view, which pictures growth as being entirely bottled up for the benefit of a small, powerful modern sector which, like the divinity, fathers, inherits, and is the very spirit of growth. That view is premised on weaker linkages, fewer sources of autonomous productivity growth within the traditional sector, and a greater concentration of power (and of the benefits of government policy) than seem to be the case. Instead, there is evidence that demand has spilled over from a dynamic modern sector, benefiting many small farmers and workers absorbed into the construction, commercial, and service establishments of the urban-traditional sector, that less-publicized forms of modern technology have raised productivity directly in the traditional sector, and that government policy has worked to raise incomes of many groups of workers outside the modern sector.[54] Coast farm workers, for instance, even in smaller, nonreporting farms, now tend to be paid the minimum wage. The same is true of employees in many small enterprises in Lima. Road construction connected Sierra communities to city markets. The shift from automatic support of landowners to a more neutral position and even, during the early sixties, to open sympathy for peasant organizations and their claims helped many Sierra communities to recover land and to obtain higher wages and reduced obligations. More recently, the agrarian reform has added a further transfer to the rural sector.

These gradual developments over the last two decades follow the pattern of the long-run drift in distributive policy towards ever-larger groups which has been documented by Hunt.[55] No claim is being made that government policy was strongly redistributive; most of this study tends to demonstrate the contrary. But the data does not support the extreme view that, until recently, government policy and the economic system worked almost exclusively for the benefit of a narrow minority, preempting any economic improvement for a majority of the population. A more accurate picture is one of trickle-down, through both

[54] See Richard Webb, "Trends in Real Income," Discussion Paper no. 11, Research Program in Economic Development, Princeton University, Feb. 1974, for evidence of economic change in much of the traditional sector.

[55] Shane Hunt, "Distribution, Growth and Government Economic Behavior in Peru," in Gustav Ranis, ed., *Government and Economic Development* (New Haven: Yale University Press, 1971). Hunt examines budgetary policies since 1900.

the market and government measures; growing inequality has been accompanied by some improvement in the living standards of the majority and by social and cultural changes that have mobilized and spread power to larger groups. If this trend continues, the present slow rate of change for the very poor will accelerate.

But must the poor wait for this gradual spread of income? In the best of cases, trickle-down—even in its current "revolutionary" version—will mean a long period of persistent poverty and growing inequality. Certainly the economic potential already exists to achieve a dramatic improvement in the living standards of the very poor: a selective transfer of 5 percent of the national income, taken from the richest 1 percent of the population and given to the poorest quartile, would reduce absolute income at the top by only 16 percent and would *double* incomes at the bottom. By contrast, a highly successful development effort consisting of sustained 3 percent annual growth in all incomes would require over twenty years to achieve the same improvement for the bottom quartile, and an even longer period if one discounts for the waiting involved.

What would be involved in a program of substantial redistribution aimed at the very poor? The main implication of this essay is that in a dual economy, equalization will not go far without large horizontal transfers. Distributive policy in Peru has been biased towards vertical redistribution. Most social policy during the last decade—both the "reformist" measures of Belaúnde and the more radical wealth transfers of the Velasco regime—has redistributed income within the richer productive sectors, bypassing the poorest groups. To redistribute income in a dual economy, it is necessary not only to destroy systems of exploitation but to create systems for extracting from the richer sector and for channeling that income to the very poor. Yet both governments have regressed with respect to horizontal transfers: the net transfers to the traditional sector fell and were reversed between 1961 and 1970.[56] Further, they have both followed industrial, pricing, and other policies that tend to reinforce income inequality by increasing the dual structure of the economy. That Peru is now well advanced in terms of vertical redistribution is likely to make it politically more difficult to develop horizontal transfers, partly because more of the transfers must now come out of modern-

[56] See Table 3.6. The net budget transfer plus price effect to the traditional sector (weighted average of urban- and rural-traditional sectors) was 19 in 1961 and —7 in 1970.

sector wages rather than property income, and partly because land reform is demobilizing.

There is some awakening in Peru to the limited impact of the past and recent distributive measures; mostly this takes the form of a growing concern with "the employment problem." Employment policies can make an impact on income inequalities by reducing dualism. But equalization through a change in the structure of employment is not an alternative to substantial current redistribution for two reasons. First, to reach the poor quickly, stress must be placed on raising traditional-sector productivity, rather than on fostering labor-absorbing growth in the modern sector; otherwise, the last to benefit are likely to be the very poor. But rapid changes in the traditional sector require large transfers of current and/or capital resources from the modern sector. Bootstrap effort will do little in the short run; substantial redistribution of current resources is therefore a *precondition* for an increase in traditional-sector productivity. Second, dualism will at best be reduced slowly; aside from the weight of existing capital, this strategy must probably swim against a capital-intensive current of technological changes.[57]

If substantial redistribution is to occur in the context of dualism, the political system must develop in such a way as to overcome the many forces that tend to retain income in the richer productive sectors. Political change would need to be paralleled by new approaches to distributive planning, stressing horizontal transfers (fiscal and price policies) and targeting for the very poor. Economic planning should start with income-growth targets for specific groups and work back to the allocative, pricing, and transfer implications. Such planning would reduce the reinforcement that now occurs between production, distribution, and the consumption patterns of the rich, and it would reduce the leakages that result, through political pressures and bureaucratic biases, when distributive policy is aimed at proxy targets, such as employment or regional development. Finally, substantial redistribution seems to require changes in attitude; the elimination of poverty must precede a concern for equity per se, and the needs of the very poor must acquire the status of rights rather than a claim to compassion.

[57] Albert Hirschman, *The Strategy of Economic Development* (New Haven: Yale University Press, 1958), pp. 125–132, on reasons for the persistence of dualism in less-developed countries.

4

Squatter Settlements and Policy Innovation in Peru

David Collier

The reformist military government which has ruled Peru since 1968 has introduced important innovations in policy toward squatter settlements. Taken together, these innovations constitute a coherent policy which appears to be one of the more successful aspects of the government's effort to transform Peruvian society. At the same time, however, the program in the settlements is a curious blend of policies from earlier periods—drawing not only on policies of a previous reform government, but also on policies proposed and carried out by the Peruvian Right.

This chapter analyzes the steps through which the current programs in squatter settlements have evolved, focusing primarily on policy toward the settlements of Lima. It begins with a description of the growth of settlements in Lima and a characterization of government policy in earlier periods. Two phases of the evolution of policy under the present government are then examined: the definition of priorities up to the Pamplona invasion of May 1971 and the consolidation of the policy since that invasion. A concluding section places current policy in perspective by contrasting it with policy in other countries and under earlier governments in Peru.

SQUATTER SETTLEMENTS IN LIMA

The expression *squatter settlement* is used here to refer to residential communities formed by low-income families in which the

This is a revised version of a paper presented to the Seminar on Continuity and Change in Contemporary Peru of the Center for Inter-American Relations on April 13, 1973. I would like to acknowledge the valuable suggestions of Abraham F. Lowenthal, Alfred C. Stepan, Patricia H. Marks, Ruth B. Collier, Henry A. Dietz, Marcia Koth de Paredes, and members of the Peru Seminar. Alfred Stepan assisted with several important points of fact and interpretation, which are acknowledged in the notes, and also called my attention to useful documentary sources.

houses are constructed in large measure by the residents themselves and which are generally, but not exclusively, formed illegally.[1] The growth of settlements in Lima has occurred in the context of a massive increase in the city's population. As can be seen in Table 4.1, the population of the Lima metropolitan area increased by a factor of more than 20 from 1908 to 1972, growing by nearly 240 percent in the thirty-two-year period from 1908 to 1940 and by nearly 540 percent in the thirty-two years from 1940 to 1972. The growth of the settlement population has occurred primarily during the second of these two periods. Starting from a negligible level in 1940, it rose to over three hundred thousand by 1961, representing 20 percent of the metropolitan population, and over nine hundred thousand by 1972, representing 27 percent of the metropolitan population. There has been substantial additional growth since 1972.

This growth of the settlement population must be seen as stemming both from the problems and from the opportunities posed by rapid urban growth. The problems posed by urban growth for city dwellers and development planners are well known. In the context of rapid growth, major efforts are required merely to maintain previous levels of welfare in such areas as housing, employment, and health facilities. The widely held goal of increasing welfare is often unobtainable.

The growth of squatter settlements in Lima has helped to ease one of the major problems associated with rapid urban growth— the shortage of low-income housing. This shortage was first noted at least as early as 1922 with the publication of Alberto Alexander's *Estudio sobre la Crisis de la Habitación en Lima*,[2] and the problem has received wide attention since that time. Settlements help ease the shortage by providing rent-free housing for well over a hundred thousand low-income families[3] and offering opportunities for improvement of housing by the residents and for commu-

---

[1] The requirement of illegality has been loosened in this definition to permit the inclusion of government-sponsored settlements which are similar to other settlements in most regards except for the fact of government sponsorship. The definition thus follows roughly the current use of the term *pueblo joven* in Peru.

[2] Lima: Imprenta Torres Aguirre, 1922.

[3] This estimate is based on the population figure in Table 4.1 and on two assumptions: that there are roughly five individuals per family, and that a significant proportion, but substantially less than a majority, of families in settlements are subletting. If settlement growth since 1972 were included in this calculation, this estimate would be even higher.

TABLE 4.1
Selected Data on the Growth of Lima

	Lima Population (Metropolitan) (1)	Lima Settlement Population (Metropolitan) (2)	Settlement Population/ Metropolitan Population (3)	Lima Population/ National Population (4)	Lima Presidential Vote (Department) (5)	Lima Vote/ National Vote (6)
1908	154,615	—	—	3.9%	—	—
1919	199,200	—	—	4.2%	19,810	9.7%
1931	341,720	—	—	6.2%	34,747	28.2%
1940	520,528	Probably < 5,000	< 1.0%	8.4%	—	—
1961	1,578,298	318,262	20.2%	17.0%	757,403 (1963)	41.7% (1963)
1972	3,317,000	903,394	27.2%	24.2%	—	—

Sources:

The data in columns 1, 4, 5, and 6 were adapted from tables kindly supplied by Carl Herbold. The sources for columns 1 and 4 are Dirección de Salubridad Pública, *Censo de la Provincia de Lima de 1908* (Lima, 1915); Dirección de Estadística, *Resumenes del Censo de las Provincias de Lima y Callao de 1920* (Lima, 1927); Junta Departmental Pro-desocupados, *Censo de las Provincias de Lima y Callao en 1931* (Lima, 1931), p. 46; Dirección Nacional de Estadística, *Censo Nacional de Población y Ocupación de 1940*, vol. 5 (Lima, 1944), p. 5; A. Arca Parró, "La ciudad capital de la República y el Censo Nacional de 1940," *Estadística Peruana*, 1, no. 1 (1945), pp. 24–29; and Dirección Nacional de Estadística y Censos, *Centros Poblados*, 3 (Lima, 1966). The figure for 1972 is a preliminary estimate of the results of the 1972 census released by the Oficina Nacional de Estadística y Censos as reported in *La Prensa*, Sept. 23, 1972, p. 1. The national population figure for 1908 is from Arthur S. Banks, *Cross-Polity Time-Series Data* (Cambridge: M.I.T. Press, 1971). Interpolations were carried out by Carl Herbold in a few cases to provide data for comparable years.

The election data are from *Diario de Debates de la Asamblea Nacional*, 1, pp. 166–170: *Extracto Estadístico del Perú: 1931–1932–1933*, pp. 265–266; Jorge Basadre, *Historia de la República del Perú*, 14, p. 168; Rudolph Gómez, *The Peruvian Administrative System* (Boulder: University of Colorado Bureau of Government Research, 1969), p. 27; Richard W. Patch, "The Peruvian Elections of 1963," pp. 498–513 in Robert D. Tomasek, ed., *Latin American Politics* (Garden City: Doubleday, 1966), p. 509; and Carlos A. Astiz, *Pressure Groups and Power Elites in Peruvian Politics* (Ithaca, N.Y.: Cornell University Press, 1969), p. 50.

The estimate of the settlement population in 1940 is based on data compiled by the author. The figure for 1961 is from the national census of that year, cited above. The figure for 1972 is based on the estimate published in the *Informe Preliminar del Censo, 1970* (Lima: Oficina Nacional de Desarrollo de Pueblos Jóvenes, 1971), with the following modifications; (1) 217,050 was added to the figure as an estimate of the population of the settlements formed in 1971 and 1972; (2) a number of settlements were removed from the calculation because they were originally formed by renting, having been included in official definitions for political reasons; and (3) a few others were added which are not included in official definitions, but which were clearly settlements in their pattern of formation. The figure thus arrived at may be a low estimate, since the main source used is two years out of date. However, it seems likely that a great many of the residents of the settlements formed during these two years came from the older settlements—hence reducing the size of this error.

nity development projects based on cooperation among neighbors.[4] By providing a setting in which residents can invest their own labor in building homes and in community development—and often in raising a few chickens or pigs as well—settlements permit the development of what may be called an urban subsistence economy,[5] which not only eases the housing shortage, but also makes it easier for poor families to manage on low incomes.

The advantages of settlements in Lima are especially pronounced because Lima offers a highly favorable geographical and climatic setting for settlement formation. Because of the mild winters and the virtual absence of rain on the Peruvian coast, the minimal straw houses that first appear when settlements form are far more adequate than they would be in a less favorable climate. The absence of rain also simplifies drainage problems in these communities and eliminates the danger—common in other areas of Latin America—that settlements may be washed down hillsides in heavy rains. Finally, much of Lima is surrounded by unused desert land, which increases the opportunities for the formation of new settlements.

At the same time that the growth of settlements in Lima has served to help meet the problem of rapid urban growth, the appearance of settlements must also be understood as a response to

[4] See José Matos Mar, "Migration and Urbanization—The 'Barriadas' of Lima: An Example of Integration into Urban Life," pp. 170–190 in Philip M. Hauser (ed.), *Urbanization in Latin America* (New York: Columbia University Press, International Documents Service, 1961); Daniel Goldrich, et al., "The Political Integration of Lower-Class Urban Settlements in Chile and Peru," *Studies in Comparative International Development* 3, no. 1 (1967–68), pp. 1–22; William Mangin, "Latin American Squatter Settlements: A Problem and a Solution," *Latin American Research Review* 2, no. 3 (1967), pp. 65–98; and Mangin, "Squatter Settlements," *Scientific American* 217, no. 4 (Oct. 1967), pp. 21–29; John F. C. Turner, "Barriers and Channels for Housing Development in Modernizing Countries," *Journal of the American Institute of Planners* 32, no. 3 (May 1967), pp. 167–181; and Turner, "Uncontrolled Urban Settlement: Problems and Policies," *International Social Development Review* no. 1 (United Nations, 1968), pp. 107–130; Sandra Powell, "Political Participation in the Barriadas: A Case Study," *Comparative Political Studies* 2, no. 2 (July 1969), pp. 195–215; Henry A. Dietz, "Urban Squatter Settlements in Peru: A Case History and Analysis," *Journal of Inter-American Studies* 11, no. 3 (July 1969), pp. 353–370; and Frank M. Andrews and George W. Phillips, "The Squatters of Lima: Who They Are and What They Want," *Journal of Developing Areas* 4, no. 2 (Jan. 1970), pp. 211–224.

[5] This expression was suggested by Valmar Faria.

the political opportunities which arise from urban growth. Because of the growing demographic importance of Lima relative to the rest of the country, any party or program which can successfully reach a major portion of Lima's population thereby reaches a substantial proportion of the nation's population. The growth of the relative importance of Lima is clearly shown in columns four through six in Table 4.1. The population of the Lima metropolitan area as a proportion of the national total rose from 3.9 percent in 1908 to 8.4 percent in 1940 and 24.2 percent in 1972. The growing political importance of Lima is reflected in the rising proportion of the vote in national presidential elections which is concentrated in the Lima area—in this case in the department of Lima. It increased from 9.7 percent in 1919 to 41.7 percent in 1963. Though national elections are not being held in the present period of military rule, Lima's electoral importance continues to be of great political relevance because major political rivals of the government are parties whose power has been based in electoral strength. In light of the growing importance of the population of Lima, it is hardly surprising that all governments have been intensely concerned with programs which aid the growing population of the city.

It is only recently, however, that there has been full recognition of the degree to which settlement formation has occurred in response to opportunities for gaining political support.[6] It appears that through tolerating squatter invasions, and in many cases through encouraging the occupation of unused land on the periphery of Lima, both governments and political parties have worked actively to gain support from this increasingly important sector of the Lima population. This political involvement in settlement formation is an important part of the background of present policy and therefore requires some attention in the present analysis.

GOVERNMENT AND PARTY INVOLVEMENT
IN SETTLEMENT FORMATION

The first major period of government support for settlement formation occurred under the government of General Manuel Odría

[6] See my "Politics of Squatter Settlement Formation in Peru," in David Chaplin (ed.), *Peruvian Nationalism: A Corporatist Revolution* (New Brunswick, N.J.: Transaction Books, Inc., 1975).

from 1948 to 1956.[7] It is fair to say that Odría's involvement in settlements was so extensive that it was an important factor in causing settlement formation to become a large-scale movement in Lima.

The involvement of Odría in settlement formation must be understood against the background of the unsuccessful attempt to bring Apra into the Peruvian political system in the mid-1940s. Apra, a middle-class, reformist party with a strong base in the labor movement, had been outlawed during the 1930s and early 1940s. In 1945, Apra was allowed to enter the national elections of that year. As part of the National Democratic Front, Apra won the presidency for the non-Apra presidential candidate of the coalition, as well as a majority in Congress. The following three years were a period of vigorous efforts by Apra to build its party and union base, of a disastrous impasse between Apra's congressional majority and the president, and of widespread political violence, much of which appeared to be attributable to Apra. This violence was climaxed by an attempt by one faction of Apra to carry out a military coup in early October 1948. General Manuel Odría had already been building an anti-Apra coalition for many months, and in the face of Apra's attempted coup, and with the strong support of the Peruvian oligarchy, Odría carried out his own coup, thereby initiating nearly eight years of military rule.

Apra had already been outlawed before the coup, and Odría moved quickly to destroy its power and the union and party groups which it had formed. Large numbers of Apra members were arrested, others went into exile, and unions linked to Apra were destroyed or were taken over by leaders sympathetic to Odría. However, Odría's campaign against Apra was not based solely on repression, but equally on a strong appeal to the lower class in which he tried to offer an alternative to the kind of popular mobilization that Apra was promoting. Odría attempted to establish a more paternalistic relationship between government

[7] This brief history of government involvement in settlement formation in Lima is based on extensive interviews with individuals who were involved in the formation of settlements, as well as newspaper accounts and other published sources. For a discussion of these interviews and documentary sources, see my "Politics of Squatter-Settlement Formation." This article includes the tabulations which form the basis for the conclusions regarding the relative importance of the different periods and the different types of formation.

and the lower class by placing heavy emphasis on charity and gifts. It would appear that a major purpose in doing this was to provide an alternative to the political arrangement which Apra had been trying to promote in which benefits from the government came in response to mobilization and articulation of political interests.

One of the most important aspects of Odría's effort to reestablish paternalistic politics was his extensive promotion of the formation of squatter settlements. At times through covert suggesttions that the government would not interfere if a particular piece of land were occupied, at times through public authorizations, Odría actively promoted the formation of new settlements. He also made extensive use of settlements as a source of political support. Some settlements were named after people or dates associated with his government, and settlement residents were periodically marched to the main plaza in front of the presidential palace for demonstrations in support of the government. The largest and most important settlement formed during this period was named "the Twenty-Seventh of October," after the date of Odría's coup. To move to this settlement, one had to apply to an association run by close associates of Odría's. Particularly toward the end of his term of office, when he was considering running for president again in 1956, those who moved to the settlement were required to become members of his party. Evidence of association with Apra made it difficult to get a lot. Through these organizational ties, and through frequent personal visits, Odría and his wife developed a particularly close identification with the Twenty-Seventh of October.

It may thus be argued that in addition to serving as an important kind of aid for the urban poor and as a source of political support, Odría's activities in the settlements had another important purpose as well. This was the purpose of undermining a particular type of political relationship, one in which forceful political demand making was carried out by groups organized to a considerable degree along class lines in parties and unions. This feature of settlement policy would appear again under the military government which came to power in 1968.

Since the period of Odría, the government role in settlement formation has varied greatly. There was a less active role in the authorization of new settlements during Prado's second presidency from 1956 to 1962, a period of rigid prohibition of invasions in the early sixties, and a 1961 squatter settlement law that set up a procedure through which the government could legally be involved in the formation of new settlements. However, because numerous problems arose in applying the law, the government housing agency empowered to carry out the law had returned by the mid-1960s to a relatively informal pattern of authorization that differed little from what had occurred before the law.

The national government has by no means been the only source of support for settlement formation. Toward the end of Odría's term of office, a group of conservative leaders who wanted to be sure that Odría did not stay on as president after 1956 began to make preparations for the 1956 presidential elections. Most Peruvians who have had long experience with settlements believe that one of the leaders of this group, Pedro Beltrán, was involved in sponsoring one of the largest squatter invasions ever to take place in Peru, that of the Ciudad de Dios (City of God) settlement, on Christmas Eve 1954. It would appear that these leaders believed that if they were to compete politically with Odría, they needed to have their settlement as well. Beltrán was the owner of the newspaper *La Prensa*, and he became widely known in the 1950s for his energetic campaign for innovations in housing policy. His newspaper made frequent editorial reference to the Ciudad de Dios invasion as evidence of the seriousness of the housing shortage, and this settlement was used as a site for trying out certain of the housing innovations which Beltrán was promoting.[8]

Support for settlement that did not involve the national government has taken other forms as well. The second Prado government, from 1956 to 1962, was the hey-day of the *traficante*, who made a living working as an invasion leader and an adviser to settlements on legal and other problems. Though these leaders made use of party and government linkages, they were usually quite ready to shift their political loyalties when the situation required. In the Belaúnde period, from 1963 to 1968, there were at least four cases of sponsorship of settlements by opposition parties, principally Apra, which controlled municipal governments. Various types of formation occurred as well, including a spectacular case in 1968 in which Apra arranged an

[8] See, for instance, the editorial page of *La Prensa*, Dec. 29, 1954; Jan. 4 and 7, 1955; Jan. 1, Mar. 29, and Oct. 10, 1956; and Dec. 7 and 26, 1957.

invasion of land which was thought to belong to a prominent political opponent of Apra, Enrique León Velarde. León Velarde was the wealthy mayor of the settlement district formerly known as the Twenty-Seventh of October, which had been a major center of support for Odría. The purpose of the invasion was to force the mayor to call the police and evict the invaders, thereby discrediting him as a friend of the poor. Squatter invasions were clearly part of the political game in Lima.

HOUSING POLICY AND LEGAL STATUS BEFORE 1968

Apart from noting the role of the government and parties in supporting settlement formation, it is useful to introduce two other aspects of settlement policy before turning to an examination of policy under the present government: the role of settlements in general housing policy, and policy regarding the legal status of settlements.

Housing Policy

Though settlements have long contributed to easing the housing shortage in Lima, it was only in the mid-1950s that a recognition of their contribution began to influence discussions of housing policy. The long delay in this recognition is hardly surprising in light of the depth of the prejudice against settlements among the middle and upper classes of Lima. These prejudices are reflected in some of the labels which have been applied to settlements, such as *cinturón de miseria* (belt of misery), *urbanización clandestina* (clandestine housing development), *aberración social* (social aberration), and *cancer social* (social cancer).[9]

Early attempts to deal with the housing shortage focused on the construction of houses by public or semipublic agencies. Examples of this approach may be found at least as early as a 1918 law which authorized the state to build housing for public employees, and numerous laws have been passed since then which directly authorize the construction of housing projects or estab-

[9] These are just some of the various terms used in the Lima press, particularly in the 1950s. See also Pablo Berckholtz Salinas, *Barrios Marginales: Aberración Social* (Lima: 1963).

lish semiautonomous agencies concerned with the construction of housing.[10] The Ministry of Development has played a major role in housing projects, and the three semiautonomous agencies founded before the mid-1950s which were most actively involved in housing construction in metropolitan Lima were the Corporación Nacional de la Vivienda, the Junta de Obras Públicas del Callao, and the Fondo Nacional de Salud y Bienestar Social.[11] These three agencies had built over ten thousand housing units by the late 1950s, and thousands of other units had been built by other public or semipublic organizations.[12]

Other early measures dealing with the housing crisis included rent control and regulations intended to prevent the construction of substandard housing.[13] However, it appears that rent control may have inhibited investment in new housing, thereby worsening the shortage. Zoning requirements were so unrealistically strict that they could not be enforced and in fact gave the government less control over new housing developments than it might have had with more realistic standards. The construction of an important type of low-cost housing was banned, in spite of the fact that it was superior to many slum areas in which poor families lived.

One of the individuals who did most to change these approaches to housing problems in Peru was Pedro Beltrán, the conservative leader and newspaper editor referred to earlier. Beltrán's newspaper campaign of the mid-1950s dealing with housing and Prado's Supreme Decree No. 1 (August 10, 1956), which created a Commission for Agrarian Reform and Housing with Beltrán as president, did much to initiate the debate on

[10] See Peru, Corporación Nacional de la Vivienda, *Experiencias Relativas de La Vivienda de Interés Social en el Perú* (Lima, 1958) and Luis Dongo Denegri, *Vivienda y Urbanismo* (Arequipa: 1962).

[11] Corporación Nacional de la Vivienda, *Experiencias Relativas*, pp. 9–48.

[12] This is the author's calculation based on the report of the number of units in each of a large number of different projects reported in Corporación Nacional de la Vivienda, *Experiencias Relativas*.

[13] See Peru, Comisión para la Reforma Agraria y la Vivienda, *Report on Housing in Peru* (Mexico City: International Cooperation Administration, 1959), pp. 24–25; Luis Dorich T., "Urbanization and Physical Planning in Peru," in Philip M. Hauser, *Urbanization in Latin America*, pp. 283–285; Walter D. Harris, Hans A. Hossé, et al., *Housing in Peru* (Washington, D.C.: Pan American Union, 1963), pp. 405–406 and 408; and Dietz, "Squatter Settlements," p. 354.

housing in Peru.[14] Through his newspaper, through the *Report on Housing in Peru*, the report of his commission which was published in Spanish and English, and through the National Housing Institute, which he founded in 1960 when he was prime minister, Beltrán brought fundamental changes in housing policy.

Beltrán's program was based on the supposition that it was unrealistic to expect that the state would, by itself, have sufficient resources to solve the housing problem.[15] The solution was to stimulate self-help housing developments and to increase the role of the private sector in solving the housing shortage. Beltrán devoted particular attention to the potential for self-help which existed in the squatter settlements.[16] Another widely publicized aspect of Beltrán's self-help approach was the inexpensive housing unit called *la casa barata que crece*, the inexpensive house that grows.[17] This was a low-cost nuclear house to which additions could be made by the residents. One of the best-known examples of a project which used this type of dwelling was constructed in the Ciudad de Dios settlement,[18] whose formation had been aided by Beltrán. The activity of the private sector would be stimulated by the elimination of rent-control laws and a variety of other provisions that would stimulate investment in housing, including the introduction of mutual savings and loan associations, with which Beltrán was closely identified.[19]

Another center of innovative thinking about housing in the late 1950s was the Corporación Nacional de la Vivienda, founded in 1946,[20] which was referred to above. Though this agency had earlier been associated with conventional public housing projects, a number of people in the agency had come to recognize the great potential for community development which existed in the settlements. It was through a combination of the efforts of people in this agency and of leading legislators such as Dr. Arca Parró

[14] The editorials referred to in note 8 are a very small sample of the massive attention given to this topic in *La Prensa*. Supreme Decree No. 1 is included in the *Report on Housing in Peru*, app. 1.

[15] *Report on Housing in Peru*, p. 77.

[16] Ibid., chap. 5.

[17] A story in *La Prensa*, Jan. 1, 1956, referred to 1955 as the year of *La casa barata que crece*.

[18] See *La Prensa*, May 11, 1961.

[19] *Report on Housing in Peru*, chap. 7.

[20] See Luis Dongo Denegri, *Vivienda y Urbanismo*, pp. 26–56.

that legislation was drafted which eventually became Peru's most important piece of squatter settlement legislation, Law 13517, passed in 1961.[21] The provisions of this law are discussed in greater detail below. In the present context, the important point is that though this law placed considerable reliance on the self-help potential of the settlements, it did not rely on the private sector in promoting housing development, but rather on the state. The passage of this law represented a major setback for Beltrán's approach. An important factor in the defeat of Beltrán's approach was the support of Apra for Law 13517. With the 1962 elections not far away, Apra was anxious to pass a piece of legislation which committed the governments to a complete solution to the problem of settlements.

The program of government aid for settlements authorized by Law 13517 got off to a vigorous start at the end of Prado's term of office and under the military government of 1962–63. However, after 1963, drastic budget cuts which resulted from congressional opposition and lack of support from President Belaúnde made it necessary to curtail the program.[22] Belaúnde's reluctance to aid the settlements reflected still another basic approach to the problems of settlements. The overriding concern of the Belaúnde administration was developing the rural areas of Peru.[23] It was felt that the expenditure of resources to improve low-cost housing in urban areas would only attract more migrants to the cities, thus increasing further the pressures of urban growth. The issue was not what form of aid was most appropriate for the settlements. Rather, it was whether it was appropriate to aid them at all.

Another reason for the lack of interest in settlements may have been Belaúnde's background as an architect and city planner. Though he brought progressive ideas to many areas of policy, he had been identified with the traditional approach to housing

[21] *Ley de Barriadas* (Lima: Distribuidora Bendezu, 1965). For an excellent discussion of this law, see Kenneth A. Manaster, "The Problem of Urban Squatters in Developing Countries: Peru," *Wisconsin Law Review* 1 (1968), pp. 23–61.

[22] The budget of the agency administering the law had been cut by 1967 to 11 percent of its 1963 level. See Junta Nacional de la Vivienda, *Obra de la Junta Nacional de la Vivienda de julio de 1963 a octubre de 1967* (Lima, n.d.).

[23] See Susan C. Bourque and David Scott Palmer, "Government Policy and Peasant Response in Rural Peru," Chapter 5 of this volume.

shortages that emphasized conventional public housing projects, having himself planned the Unidad Vecinal Número Tres, a middle- to low-income project that was constructed in the late 1940s. During Belaúnde's term as president, the most important government investments in housing had little relation to the housing needs of the poor. Instead, the emphasis was on handsomely designed projects for middle- and upper-middle class families, of which the San Felipe project is an outstanding example.

It should be emphasized that there were some innovations in settlement policy during the Belaúnde period. One of these involved the establishment of a settlement—Chacra Cerro—organized by the national housing office but financed by a private bank, which took direct responsibility for arranging the periodic payments by the residents for their lots. This was reminiscent of the emphasis of the role of the private sector in Beltrán's program and anticipated the active encouragement of the role of banks in settlements under the present government. Generally, however, the Belaúnde period was characterized by a deliberate choice not to take advantage of important opportunities for contributing to the development of settlements.

Legal Status

Another important aspect of government policy is that relating to the legal status of settlements. A basic feature of settlement development is, of course, their illegality. Not only do they violate the provisions of building codes and zoning regulations; they have, until recently, occupied land to which the residents did not have title.

Because governments have been involved in supporting the formation of settlements and because, for many years, no major effort was made to legalize the settlements, this illegality may be seen as a direct result of public policy. The relationship of the government to this illegality during the Odría period is particularly interesting. In spite of the extensive and public involvement of the Odría government in promoting settlement formation, and in spite of promises to grant land titles to the residents in certain cases, the Odría government in fact rarely granted titles in the settlements. When viewed in terms of Odría's concern with reestablishing a paternalistic relationship between the government and the lower classes, this failure is quite understandable. If squatters are simply located on public land, their security of tenure appears to depend on the willingness of the state, and particularly the president, to let them stay there. If they receive title, their security of tenure has a formal, legal basis that is independent of the good will of the president. The failure to give land titles thus reinforced the idea that the squatters were dependent on having a special connection with the president of Peru. It would appear that insecurity bred dependency.

Since the end of the Odría government in the mid-1950s, however, there has been a growing concern with the need to bring the existing settlements more nearly into conformity with zoning standards, to provide land titles to residents, and to provide a channel for the legal formation of new settlements. Although I have no definitive explanation of this shift in emphasis, it is certainly understandable in light of the changing political context. The relationship of the second Prado government with settlements was very different from that under Odría. Though Prado did occasionally use the settlements as a source of political support, this was far less important than it had been under Odría. Hence, Prado was not as concerned with perpetuating the dependency relationship which Odría had encouraged. There was also an attempt to discredit Odría's realtionship with the settlements, and it was therefore useful to adopt a fresh approach to settlement policy.[24] Finally, Apra was once again legal during this period—in an informal coalition with Prado—and was a major force in pushing for new settlement legislation. Apra did not rely on dependency relationships with the lower classes, but rather on strong organization of the lower classes, and likewise had no desire to perpetuate the legally ambiguous situation of the settlements.

The major piece of legislation through which the legalization of the settlements has been attempted is Law 13517 of 1961, which, along with its *Reglamento*, established a procedure for legalizing existing settlements as well as a legal basis for the formation of new settlements.[25] As a prerequisite for the granting of land titles, the law required extensive remodeling of the settlements, which was to include the rearrangement of lots in a

[24] Shortly after Prado came to office, *La Prensa* carried a number of stories about scandals involving the dwellers association in the settlement Twenty-Seventh of October which were obviously intended to discredit Odría.

[25] *Ley de Barriadas.*

more orderly pattern and the installation of city services. Full title would not be granted until this remodeling had been completed.

We have already referred to some of the problems that arose in applying this law. The work of the agency concerned with carrying it out was also hindered by the extensive remodeling that was required by the law before titles could be granted. Because of its limited resources, the agency concentrated its efforts on a few settlements which could be remodeled at relatively low cost, thereby narrowing greatly the scope of its legalization efforts.

Toward the end of the Belaúnde period, however, new pressures appeared which brought a change in policy regarding legalization. In anticipation of the 1969 elections, contending political parties vied to see which could offer the most attractive program to the settlements, and legalization was clearly a matter of high priority. León Velarde, the mayor of the settlement district which had been known as the Twenty-Seventh of October under Odría, successfully pushed for the passage of a law which eliminated remodeling as a requirement for granting titles in his district.[26] In mid-1968, in the face of a threatened march on the central plaza by settlement residents to be led by León Velarde, further decrees were passed which extended this change to all settlements.[27] Hence there was a brief upsurge in the granting of titles at the end of the Belaúnde period, since it could proceed without the expensive remodeling which had previously been required.

THE EVOLUTION OF POLICY FROM OCTOBER, 1968, TO THE PAMPLONA INVASION

The military coup of October 3, 1968, brought to power a new government, which quickly turned its attention to squatter settlements. The most important early expression of the government's approach to settlements came two months after the coup. In early December of 1968, the Organismo Nacional de Desar-

26 This law—number 16584—is included in Héctor E. Uchuya Reyes, Normas Legales de Pueblos Jóvenes (Lima: Ediciones Heur, 1971), pp. 71–77.

27 See Supreme Decree 066-69-FO of July 19, 1968 (La Crónica, July 20, 1968, p. 3) and Supreme Decree 014-68-JC of Aug. 2, 1968 (El Peruano, Aug. 5, 1968, p. 7).

rollo de Pueblos Jóvenes, the National Organization for the Development of Young Towns, later known as ONDEPJOV, was formed.[28] The importance given to ONDEPJOV was reflected in the fact that it was directly responsible to the president and the prime minister. The most visible innovation that accompanied the founding of ONDEPJOV was the introduction of a new name for settlements—young towns. This innovation followed a precedent already established in Peru of introducing a new name for settlements as a way of signaling a shift in policy. The most widely used term for settlements up through 1968 had been the somewhat derogatory expression *barriada*, though many different names for settlements had been employed.[29] An ONDEPJOV publication later suggested that the new term was intended to reflect the recent formation of the settlements, the youth of the settlement population, and the residents' desire for community improvement.[30] Judging from the wide acceptance of this new name in Lima, it would appear that the government's approach to settlements, as symbolized by the name, has been well received. Earlier name changes did not become part of the Peruvian vocabulary to the same degree.

The Role of Self-Help

The supreme decree which established ONDEPJOV discussed in detail the positive features of settlements, emphasizing the way in which settlement residents confront their problems of substandard living conditions through self-help. It suggested that the settlement residents had accomplished a great deal with little support from the state, and that if this local initiative were en-

[28] Supreme Decree No. 105-68-FO. This is included in *Documento Número 3, ONDEPJOV* (Lima, 1969). The name was changed a few months after the decree from Organismo to Oficina.

[29] Settlements have had many names in Lima over the last twenty years. The most frequently used has been *barriada*, originally meaning roughly "little neighborhood." Other terms have included *barriada popular, urbanización clandestina* (clandestine housing development), *barriada clandestina, barrio flotante* (floating neighborhood), *barrio marginado* (marginalized neighborhood), *pueblo en formación* (town in formation), and now young town. A change in name has been used at least twice in the past to reflect a change in policy—with the introduction of the term *town in formation* by Apra in the mid-1950s, and the term *barrio marginal* (marginal neighborhood) with the passing of the Law 13517 in 1960–61. However, the term *barriada* continued to be the most widely used, in spite of these earlier innovations.

[30] *Boletín Número 1*, ONDEPJOV (Lima, 1969), p. 5.

couraged and directed, even better results could be achieved.[31] The most important aspect of this encouragement has been ONDEPJOV's vigorous effort to build and strengthen community organization in the settlements through training local leaders and building local organizations based on a series of hierarchical layers that go down to the block level.[32]

The announcement of the members of the executive committee of ONDEPJOV a week after its formation provided further evidence regarding its orientation.[33] One of the most prominent members was the auxiliary bishop of Lima, Monseñor Luis Bambarén, who had the title "Bishop of the Squatter Settlements." Bambarén was strongly identified with the self-help approach. Another member was Diego Robles, an architect with long experience in settlements and author of an article about opportunities for self-help in settlements.[34] The executive committee also included three representatives from the settlements, all of whom were leaders in community organizations involved in self-help projects.

Another important figure in early settlement policy, Carlos Delgado, was not a member of the executive committee. Previously a prominent member of Apra, Delgado quickly emerged as an important adviser to the president at the beginning of the period of military rule. Delgado, like Robles, was the author of an article dealing with self-help development in settlements[35] and had worked in the period before the coup in a government planning office, PLANDEMET, with several people who were later involved in ONDEPJOV, including Robles. There is a striking

[31] Decreto Supremo no. 105-68-FO, in ONDEPJOV *Documento Número 3*, p. 4.

[32] This organizational arrangement is discussed in detail in Henry A. Dietz, "The Office and the Poblador: Perceptions and Manipulations of Housing Authorities by the Lima Urban Poor" (paper presented at the annual meeting of the American Society for Public Administration, 1973), p. 15.

[33] See *La Crónica*, Dec. 20, 1968.

[34] Diego Robles, "El Proceso de Urbanización y los Sectores Populares," in *Cuadernos DESCO* (Feb. 1969), pp. 49–63. This article was written before the military government came to power.

[35] See Carlos Delgado, *Tres Planteamientos en Torno a Problemas de Urbanización Acelerada en Areas Metropolitanas: El Caso de Lima* (Lima: Cuadernos Plandemet, Serie Anaranjada, Asuntos, Sociales, no. 1, 1968). This has also been published in English as "Three Proposals Regarding Accelerated Urbanization Problems in Metropolitan Areas: The Lima Case," pp. 272–299 in John Miller and Ralph A. Gakenheimer (eds.), *Latin American Urban Policies and the Social Sciences* (Beverly Hills, Calif.: Sage Publications, 1971).

similarity between the policy recommendations at the end of Delgado's article and the policies which the government has adopted.

Two private community-development organizations also had an important influence. Shortly before the coup, Monseñor Bambarén had established a private Oficina de Pueblos Jóvenes to promote self-help projects in settlements. The new name for settlements was originally proposed by a member of this organization, and the emphasis developed by members of this group on active community organization and self-help played an important part in later policy. Acción Communitaria del Perú has also played an important role. Acción was founded by Acción International of New York, a community-development organization which has initiated private community-development programs in several Latin American countries. One of the purposes of these programs is to introduce innovative approaches to community development in the hope that they will be imitated by government policy makers.[36] The Peruvian program is now autonomous, supported by the Peruvian private sector. During the first year of the new government, Acción initiated several pilot projects involving community self-help in settlements which became models for the projects later undertaken by the government. The most important of these involved a savings program established in coordination with a private bank through which settlement communities could accumulate capital for the installation of services, particularly electricity. Members of the ONDEPJOV executive committee followed Acción's efforts with considerable interest, making several visits to its main project in the settlement Pamplona Alta. It should also be noted that these two community-development organizations supplied between them all three of the settlement representatives on the ONDEPJOV executive committee.

Though civilians held important positions in ONDEPJOV, military officers played a very dominant role. As of 1970, all of the directors of the four zones of ONDEPJOV within Lima were military officers, as well as twenty of the twenty-one directors of the local ONDEPJOV offices in the provinces.[37]

[36] See *Encyclopedia of Associations*, 7th ed. (Detroit: Gale Research Company, 1972), p. 817.

[37] See ONDEPJOV, *Informe Preliminar del Censo*, 1970 (Lima, 1971) pp. 5–6 and 37.

The Role of the Private Sector

The association with Acción was just one aspect of the attempt by ONDEPJOV to increase the role of the private sector in the settlements. There was particular interest in coordinating the activities of the private sector with the self-help efforts of the settlement residents.[38] One of the most important aspects of this effort has involved encouraging the arrangement initially tried out by Acción in which savings plans are developed with private banks through which money is accumulated for community projects. An early publication of ONDEPJOV included a large table which suggested the ways in which seventeen different types of projects in settlements could be carried out by coordinating the efforts of different combinations of twenty private and public groups.[39] A massive 392-page catalogue of public and private institutions which provide services to settlements in Lima, Trujillo, Chimbote, and Arequipa was later prepared for ONDEPJOV by the U.S. Agency for International Development.[40] This catalogue, like many publications of ONDEPJOV, had on its cover a symbolic triangle representing ONDEPJOV's attempt to coordinate these efforts:

Settlement Residents

In some of the publications that have used the symbol the following statement appears below the triangle: "Only the combination of the public sector, the private sector, and the settlement residents can achieve the objectives of . . . the promotion of the economic development and the social and cultural development of

[38] ONDEPJOV, *Documento Número 3*, p. 1.

[39] ONDEPJOV, *Boletín Número 1*, pp. 18–19.

[40] ONDEPJOV, *Catálogo de Instituciones de Servico a la Comunidad: Trujillo, Chimbote, Lima y Arequipa* (Lima, 1971).

the settlements."[41] If this were a quote from the 1950s, one might assume that it was a statement by Pedro Beltrán. The fact that this government has expropriated many of the agricultural holdings of the sector of the rural economy which Beltrán represented and yet has adopted urban housing policies proposed by him illustrates how difficult it is to place the government on a Left-Right continuum.

The Legal Status of the Settlements

The government is also concerned about the legal status of the settlements. The question of legality has, of course, been an issue for some time. However, it takes on particular interest under the present government because it is an aspect of its overriding concern with law in general, and property law in particular.

The concern with law appears to stem from a belief that ambiguous law, and especially ambiguous property law, may be a source of political instability. This belief is in part a product of the military's experience with the rural land invasions and unrest in the Peruvian highlands in the 1960s, which were in considerable measure produced by serious ambiguities in land titles. Many of the land seizures in this period were carried out by peasants frustrated by years of expensive litigation over lands of poorly defined legal status of which they felt they were the rightful owners.[42]

It has been argued that the experience of repressing these peasant movements had a strong impact on the armed forces and convinced them that fundamental changes were required.[43] Other events in the 1960s doubtless contributed to the concern with law and authority as well. These included the scandal surrounding the Act of Talara of August 1968, also involving a question of property rights, and the smuggling scandals of the late Belaúnde period.

41 SINAMOS, Décima Región, *Organización Vecinal* (Lima, 1972), back cover. This particular example is actually from the period after ONDEPJOV was absorbed in SINAMOS.

42 See John Strasma, "The United States and Agrarian Reform in Peru," pp. 156–205 in Daniel A. Sharp (ed.), *U.S. Foreign Policy and Peru* (Austin: University of Texas Press, 1972), p. 172.

43 Luigi Einaudi, "U.S. Relations with the Peruvian Military," pp. 15–56 in Sharp, *U.S. Foreign Policy and Peru*, pp. 22–23.

The government's concern with law was emphasized immediately after the coup. Decree Law No. 1, issued the day after the government came to power, declared that one of the government's objectives was to "restore the principle of authority" and "respect for law" in Peru.[44] Since then, this concern has been reflected in a number of policy areas, including the reform of the court system carried out by the Consejo Nacional de Justicia, the more vigorous enforcement of tax law, the campaign for the "moralization" of public administration, and the attack on corruption in the Policía de Investigación Peruana (PIP).[45]

The concern with law is also reflected in policy toward settlements. It was clearly expressed in the decree which founded ONDEPJOV, which stated that it was necessary to deal with the problem of property rights in the settlements in the interest of their security and development.[46] Though the program of granting land titles in established settlements would become even more important after the Pamplona invasion in 1971, it was pursued actively from the beginning of the government, first by Junta Nacional de la Vivienda, the housing agency which had been responsible for the application of Law 13517 during the Belaúnde period, and then by ONDEPJOV. The legalization has been carried out under the terms of Law 13517, as amended by the laws of 1967 and 1968. Remodeling is therefore not a prerequisite for granting title, and the program can proceed with relative ease.

The government's concern with law is also reflected in the policy toward new squatter invasions. The first two and a half years of military rule saw a lull in invasions in the Lima area. A number of people involved with settlements and squatter invasions were given to understand that the government did not intend to tolerate new invasions. Though there were instances of occupation of new land at the edge of established settlements and one case of a land seizure which resulted from a dispute among members of a housing cooperative, there were no substantial new invasions.

[44] *El Peruano*, Oct. 4, 1968.

[45] See Marvin Alinsky, *Peruvian Political Perspective* (Tempe, Ariz.: Center for Latin American Studies, Arizona State University, 1972), p. 4; and *Latin America* (weekly newsletter), Sept. 10, 1971, pp. 293–294.

[46] ONDEPJOV, *Documento Número 3*, p. 4.

The government's determination to prevent invasions was also reflected outside of Lima in October 1969 when a squatter invasion in Talara which received national publicity was met with a firm reaction. This invasion occurred on the first anniversary of the nationalization of the oil complex there, during a visit by President Velasco. The new settlement was named the Ninth of October in honor of the date of the nationalization, and the invaders claimed to have a patriotic desire to commemorate the occasion, but the government moved firmly against them and cleared the site.[47]

Political Support

Another important aspect of the government's concern with settlements is the desire to use them as a base of political support. Early evidence of this interest may be found in a demonstration of support by settlement residents for the government's policy toward the United States which occurred in the main plaza in front of the presidential palace, just a week after the founding of ONDEPJOV in 1968. This demonstration was organized by Mayor León Velarde, who was involved in the effort to ease the requirements for granting land titles referred to earlier and who was also a close associate of President Velasco. However, León Velarde's demonstration was smaller and less successful than expected, apparently because his political rivals, particularly Apristas, made a major effort to discourage settlement residents from participating. It therefore did not have the desired impact, and it was some time before the government again attempted to arrange a demonstration of this type.

Following this demonstration, the most visible attempt to rally support involved periodic visits to settlements by General Armando Artola, the minister of interior and the member of the cabinet who had the greatest ability to mingle with settlement residents. In light of Odría's role in the settlements, it is noteworthy that Artola's father was a minister in Odría's government. In 1969 Artola made many visits to settlements, often arriving spectacularly in a helicopter and giving away used clothing and panetones (a sweetened bread that is a traditional Peruvian specialty), dancing traditional Peruvian dances, and occasionally

[47] *La Prensa*, Oct. 10, 1969, p. 4.

driving the army road graders which were being used to level the streets in settlements.[48]

Two interesting features of these early attempts to develop support in the settlements were the lack of involvement of President Velasco and the lack of coordination between these attempts and the activities of ONDEPJOV. The lack of a presidential role may have been related to the fact—heavily emphasized in the early period of military rule—that this was a government of the military as an institution, and not of the president as an individual.[49] The higher-level officers in the government were surely aware of the massive personal support which Odría generated in settlements, as well as of the attempt by Pérez-Godoy to undermine the institutional character of the 1962–63 military government and establish an independent base of power. There is even evidence that this attempt by Pérez-Godoy included a preliminary effort to establish a base of power in the settlements.[50] In light of these past events, it is understandable that the support-getting activity was carried out almost entirely by Artola. He was the odd man out in the cabinet, the subject of much of the criticism of the government which circulated in Lima, and the butt of most of the early jokes about the military regime. Permitting him to play a military populist role in settlements allowed the government to seek popular support in settlements without posing the danger that any member of the government would be able to use this as a major base of personal power. At the same time, however, the fact that Artola's father had been minister in Odría's government might have suggested that giving him free reign in the settlements would be risky. As it worked out, Artola later made a brief attempt to establish an independent base of support in the settlements.

The separation of the support-getting activities from the program of ONDEPJOV is also striking. ONDEPJOV did not seek wide publicity for its activities. An early ONDEPJOV bulletin emphasized the need to avoid excessive publicity and instead to

[48] See *La Prensa*, Feb. 28, 1969; May 2 and 19, 1969; and *Expreso*, May 26, 1969.

[49] Einaudi, "U.S. Relations with the Peruvian Military," p. 27.

[50] According to information collected in the interviews referred to above which were used in reconstructing the history of settlement formation, a close associate of Pérez-Godoy's was at one point recruiting people who would carry out invasions.

focus attention on the task of making ONDEPJOV projects effective as a means of gaining the confidence of the settlement population.[51] The difference between this approach and that of Artola was dramatized in May of 1969 when Monseñor Bambarén, an important member of the ONDEPJOV executive committee, held a press conference in which he criticized Artola, stating that the problems of settlements could not be solved "by gifts and used clothing" but rather by aiding the residents in building their own houses and helping to provide city services. The headline of an article in *Expreso* which reported the press conference—*Soluciones, no Panetones* (Solutions, Not Panetones)—clearly summarized the divergence in approaches.[52]

This separation between the government's development program and its support-getting activities continued until the founding of SINAMOS in 1971. León Velarde's demonstration might be cited as an example of the coordination of the two aspects of policy, since it occurred just a week after the founding of ONDEPJOV, giving the impression that the demonstration had been planned in part as an expression of gratitude for the new program. However, since one of the settlement representatives on the ONDEPJOV executive committee was a major political rival of León Velarde's, it would appear that the link between these two events was not close.[53]

The Pamplona Invasion

The government's policy of firmness toward invasions was subjected to a difficult test by the huge squatter invasion which occurred in early May 1971 in Lima, the Pamplona invasion.[54] This invasion began on an area of public land on April 29, spreading to neighboring areas, both public and private, in a series of invasions that continued until May 12. Tens of thousands of people participated. The government waited several days to initiate at-

[51] ONDEPJOV, *Documento Número 3*, p. 27.

[52] *Expreso*, May 23, 1969.

[53] The rival, from León Velarde's district of San Martin de Porras, was Alberto Díaz Jiménez. See *La Crónica*, Dec. 20, 1968.

[54] Much of the information regarding the invasion is taken from Manuel Montoya, "El Pamlonazo" (dissertation, Department of Sociology, San Marcos University, Lima, 1972). The newspaper clipping file of Henry A. Dietz was also a valuable aid in reconstructing the history of the invasion.

tempts to evict the invaders. A series of clashes then occurred which resulted in injury to many invaders and policemen, and one death. In one incident, police fired into a crowd of invaders; in another, the invaders captured a police commander and threatened to kill him. They agreed to spare his life when he promised to persuade the government to desist in its efforts at eviction. In the compromise which was finally reached, the invaders agreed to move to a government-prepared site to form a large settlement called Villa el Salvador. Only a small nucleus of the original invasion group remained in an area of public land which they had occupied in the invasion.

The invasion occurred during a meeting in Lima of the board of governors of the Inter-American Development Bank, an agency which in the past had given extensive loans to Peru to support low-income housing projects. The incident would have been a serious embarrassment to the government in any case, but the spectacle of a confrontation between poor families and police, and the implication that Peru was not satisfying the housing needs of its low-income population, was particularly embarrassing at that time. Invasions in Lima have commonly been timed to produce a maximum effect, and the timing of this invasion was surely no accident.[55]

Various rumors circulated as to who had planned the invasion. The most plausible version suggests that radical student groups were involved, though some sources hint that support may have come from a faction within the government that wished to dramatize Lima's housing needs and force the government to accelerate its programs in the settlements. It was even suggested that Monseñor Bambarén or Artola had taken part in planning it. Far more important than the question of who organized the invasion, however, was the massive, spontaneous growth of the invasion once it had begun. It demonstrated dramatically the seriousness of the housing deficit in Lima and the vulnerability of the government in the area of housing policy that results from the fact that poor families can meet their housing needs by simply seizing land. It was clear that the slow pace of expansion of

[55] A series of invasions occurred around Oct. 3, 1972, the fourth anniversary of the military coup. Under earlier governments, settlements had been formed on occasions such as Odría's birthday, Belaúnde's birthday, Christmas Eve, and Independence Day.

settlements during the first two and a half years of the Velasco government had left many families unable to get lots in a settlement and eager to join an invasion.

The Pamplona invasion is also of interest because it precipitated a second and final clash between Monseñor Bambarén and General Artola. Artola was identified with the hard line vis-à-vis the invaders, whereas Bambarén, after one of the invaders was killed, went to the invasion site and held a mass. Artola then had Bambarén arrested for disturbing the peace. The church vigorously protested the arrest.[56] Artola countered by arranging a demonstration by settlement residents which expressed support for his activities in the settlements.[57] Bambarén was released after thirteen hours, and Artola was forced to resign on May 17.[58]

Interpretations of Artola's intentions in this situation differ. Some argue that he deliberately delayed the first attempt to evict the invaders, thereby making it more difficult to evict them. It might be speculated that he hoped to increase his importance in the government when he finally succeeded in evicting them, or that he would dramatically choose not to, thereby becoming a hero to the settlement residents. It is difficult to find out which, if either, of these alternatives is true. In either case, Artola was removed from the picture, bringing to an end his spectacular visits to the settlements.

The Pamplona invasion posed a serious challenge to the government's policy of preventing people from obtaining land by simply seizing it, and the government attempted to emphasize that seizure was not a legitimate means of acquiring land. It was announced that "the government will not expropriate these lands in order to legalize the acts of agitators,"[59] perhaps referring to a 1969 law which had expanded the government's ability to expropriate land for low-income housing projects. It was further declared that "the government is revolutionary, but not disorderly, and does not believe that the people are ignorant of the proper means to obtain land."[60] Further, it was declared that whereas those who had invaded public land could receive lots in Villa el Salvador, those who had occupied private land could not.[61]

---

[56] *La Prensa*, May 12, 1971. [57] Ibid.
[58] *Correo*, May 11 and 18, 1971. [59] *Correo*, May 15, 1971, p. 14.
[60] Ibid. [61] Ibid.

THE FOUNDING OF SINAMOS

Though the Pamplona invasion by itself represented an important crisis for the government, the first half of 1971 was a period of other crises as well, particularly a series of strikes that brought considerable economic and political disruption. These included violent outbreaks in the sugar cooperatives on the north coast and numerous work stoppages in the mines of the central highlands. The miners' strikes had substantially reduced mineral exports, thereby damaging Peru's balance of payments, and were finally ended in late March with the arrest of large numbers of union leaders.[62]

All of these events made it clear that the government needed to increase its ability to deal with the sectors of society capable of mass political action. To help meet this need, the government founded SINAMOS, the Sistema Nacional de Apoyo a la Movilización Social, or National System for the Support of Social Mobilization. Because SINAMOS has taken over most government programs in settlements, this organization merits particularly close attention in the present analysis. It should be emphasized at the outset that in a number of areas the SINAMOS programs have been notably unsuccessful, though the program in settlements would appear to be among the more successful. Apart from the particular degree of success of SINAMOS programs, however, SINAMOS is of particular importance for the present analysis because there are striking parallels and contrasts between the tactics which Odría used to undermine Apra and the approach taken by SINAMOS to weaken political opposition.

Decree Law 18896 of June 22, 1971, which established SINAMOS, declared that this organization was to act as a link between the government and the people, helping to make government bureaucracies more responsive to the public and helping the population to express its desires to the government.[63] This latter objective would be achieved by actively organizing the Peruvian population as a means of creating links between the population and the government, and through "orienting" the participation of the population. Some of the language of the law resembled that which had been used earlier by the government

[62] *Latin America*, Apr. 23, 1971, pp. 129–130, and June 11, 1971, p. 186.
[63] *El Peruano*, June 24, 1971, p. 5.

with reference to settlements, particularly article 5a, which said that SINAMOS should help increase the capacity of the population to promote its own development, with the help of the government.

Squatter settlements represent only one sphere of SINAMOS activity. In addition to absorbing ONDEPJOV, SINAMOS is concerned with cooperatives, agrarian reform, and many other areas. However, as the organization of SINAMOS developed, it became clear that settlements occupied a position of special importance. SINAMOS is organized in terms of geographic regions which correspond to groups of departments. For instance, the Fourth Region corresponds to the departments of Lima and Ica, plus the constitutional province of Callao. There is one exception to this territorial pattern, however. The Tenth "Region" of SINAMOS is concerned exclusively with the geographically dispersed settlements of metropolitan Lima, despite the fact that everything else in metropolitan Lima falls within the Fourth Region.[64] Thus the settlements of Lima were singled out for special attention within the organizational structure of SINAMOS.

The special position of settlements in relation to SINAMOS became even more clear with the promulgation of the Organic Law—a fundamental, enabling law—of SINAMOS, the Decree Law 19352 of April 4, 1972.[65] The introduction to this law described as its goal the establishment of a basically self-directed (*autogestora*) economy in which the means of production are largely controlled by the workers themselves.[66] Squatter settlements obviously fit this model of control perfectly. Whereas in many areas, such as the recently expropriated sugar haciendas, SINAMOS must oversee the transfer of control from government supervisors to local cooperatives, the settlements have a well-established practice of *autogestión*. Both in the tradition of local initiative in building houses and community facilities and in the practice of electing community leaders, settlements have long had the organizational characteristics that the government seeks to develop elsewhere.[67] The self-help orientation of the settle-

[64] The regions of SINAMOS are described in the back of the official edition of the Organic Law of SINAMOS (Lima, 1972).

[65] Ibid. [66] Ibid., p. 3.

[67] For a description of local democracy in settlements, see William Mangin, "Squatter Settlements," p. 25.

ments is a model for what the government wishes to develop in other sectors of society.

There are various reasons why the government is interested in promoting this kind of organization in Peru, but one of them clearly lies in the types of problems that the government had with strikes in the period before the formation of SINAMOS. These strikes, and perhaps also the Pamplona invasion, had support from opposition parties, including the Left as well as Apra. The government is naturally interested in limiting the power of these parties and in competing with them for support at the local level. Though in some situations SINAMOS has permitted people from these parties to take over local associations—in part because it would be too costly to prevent it—the overall purpose is to create alternative organizations in all sectors of Peruvian society that will fill political space that has been or might be occupied by these parties.

The concern with the role of political opposition in squatter settlements has been particularly intense. Peruvians who were well informed about the thinking of the government in the early stages of the planning of settlement policy report that there was a great concern with the radical potential of the settlements. The attempts of university students to organize the settlements politically and the specter of urban guerrillas in other Latin American countries clearly provided a strong basis for these fears. The concern with radicalization in settlements was apparently expressed frequently by the members of the armed forces who were members of ONDEPJOV in discussions of policy within that organization, and the role of army intelligence in ONDEPJOV and in the settlements themselves has been large. There is considerable surveillance of outsiders who enter the settlements, and individuals known to be affiliated with the Left have on occasion been prevented from visiting them. SINAMOS is actively maintaining and strengthening the elaborate organization of settlements down to the block level which was earlier encouraged by ONDEPJOV, and this organizational structure clearly facilitates political control.

The SINAMOS program in the settlements is closely coordinated with the armed forces in a way that enhances political control. The armed forces have had a direct role in the settlements since the Velasco government came to power. In November 1968, a month before the founding of ONDEPJOV, President Velasco announced a substantial program of public works in settlements that would be carried out by the army.[68] This program has focused particularly on leveling and paving streets, and was responsible for major improvements in an important highway leading to the settlements located to the north of Lima. The Organic Law of SINAMOS specifically reaffirms the role of the armed forces in settlement projects.[69]

The links between the armed forces and SINAMOS go much further than this, however. SINAMOS uses the army radio communications system to conduct much of its business in settlements, which permits instantaneous communication among all of the settlement areas surrounding Lima. Three of the five generals who are commanders of the military regions of Peru, the basic units of territorial division of the command structure of the armed forces, are also the heads of the corresponding regions of SINAMOS.[70] In particular, the commander of the Lima military region is also head of the Tenth Region of SINAMOS, the one that is concerned exclusively with Lima settlements. It is striking that this commander is in charge of the region that includes only the settlements, and not the region that includes the department as a whole. Though I was not able to collect complete data on the administration of local offices for the period of SINAMOS administration of the settlements, it appears that there is a continuation of the dominant role of military officers in the directorships of local offices which was noted earlier for the ONDEPJOV period.

Without overstating the importance of the links between the formal structure of the army and the organization of SINAMOS, it is clear that they are related to the government's preoccupation with the potential for radical political activity in the settlements. If an urban guerrilla movement were to develop there, SINAMOS and the army would be in a good position to move quickly against it.

The relationship of SINAMOS with the local leaders in settlements is also a channel of potential control. SINAMOS does not prevent members of political parties from being elected as lead-

68 *La Prensa*, Nov. 7, 1968.

69 See title five, *Disposiciones Complementarias*, no. 6.

70 See *Actualidad Militar*, 11, no. 171 (Jan. 1972), p. 30, and the 1972 official edition of the organic law, pp. 33–34.

ers, but will remove them if they act for their party in their leadership role. The only formal requirements for leadership are living in the settlement, being at least eighteen years old and literate, having a known occupation, and having a "good background," that is to say, not having a police record.[71] Having a known occupation does not mean that a leader is excluded if he is temporarily unemployed. Rather, he must have had a regular job at some point. This provision, along with the requirement of residence in the settlement, is intended to exclude professional political organizers. SINAMOS maintains a central archive of records on all leaders.[72] Because SINAMOS has made student political organizing in settlements more difficult, has channeled private programs through the leadership structure which it created in settlements, and is keeping close track of these leaders, it has established a substantial degree of control over the political life of the settlements.

SETTLEMENT POLICY SINCE THE PAMPLONA INVASION

Since the Pamplona invasion, the government's development programs in settlements have become more extensive and visible, if for no other reason than the massive scale of the program in Villa el Salvador, the government-sponsored settlement formed to accommodate the families who participated in the Pamplona invasion. The government is attempting to develop the settlement through the prompt installation of city services and provision of land titles. The residents may build their own houses or select one of several models of prefabricated houses which are manufactured by the private sector and which are on display in the settlement.

The government's long-run goal is to turn Villa el Salvador into a vast "cooperative city" (ciudad cooperativa).[73] In 1972 this settlement, which had a population of over one hundred thousand, had more than a thousand local committees which formed the organizational base for the cooperative, and 130 people trained to teach methods for forming cooperatives were working there. The goal is to use the cooperative as a means of dealing not only

[71] SINAMOS, Dirigente Vecinal (Lima: 1972), p. 3.

[72] Reported by Alfred Stepan, personal communication.

[73] See the discussion of plans for this settlement in SINAMOS Informa, 1, no. 2 (Lima: SINAMOS, Oficina Nacional de Difusión), pp. 29–32.

with the need for housing and city services, but also with more basic problems of employment. A settlement of this size includes workers from a wide variety of occupations, and the goal is to bring them together in a cooperative which would sell goods and services to the community. To facilitate this, a large area of land close to the community was left unoccupied to provide space for the development of various types of light manufacturing. During the Belaúnde period, land was similarly put aside near a government-sponsored settlement, but this land was later occupied by invasion groups. One important indicator of the commitment of the present government to prevent uncontrolled invasions and to promote the economic self-sufficiency of Villa el Salvador will be whether it succeeds in keeping this reserved land available for its intended use.

President Velasco has developed a close relationship with Villa el Salvador, and he and his wife have made a number of personal visits to the settlement.[74] This departs from Velasco's earlier practice of not being personally identified with the settlement programs and corresponds to a decreasing emphasis on the institutional character of the military government. Thus Velasco, like Odría and Beltrán before him, finally has his own settlement and his own base of popular support.

Though the level and scale of activity is lower in other settlements, SINAMOS is actively involved in many other areas as well, promoting the formation of cooperatives for housing and the installation of services. The much stronger framework of community organization which ONDEPJOV and SINAMOS have built in the settlements is an important factor in projects such as the installation of water pipes which are based in part on labor contributed by the residents themselves. Each household is expected to contribute labor to these projects. If a household does not contribute labor and likewise fails to make a financial contribution equivalent to the estimated value of its labor, it will not receive the service. In order to accumulate capital for the acquisition of services, savings schemes have been established with the cooperation of private banks through which funds are accumulated. SINAMOS emphasizes that its role is not one of providing for all of the needs of settlements, but rather of coordinating the efforts of the residents and the private sector in promoting settlement development.

[74] Reported by Alfred Stepan, personal communication.

New Invasions

The basic pattern followed in dealing with the Pamplona invasion has been applied to other invasions as well. For instance, in the case of a small invasion of an archaeological site outside of Lima in 1972, negotiations between SINAMOS and the invaders resulted in an agreement that the invaders would move to land at the edge of an already established settlement.[75] On the other hand, the government has been unable to enforce this pattern in the case of four invasions which occurred along the Rímac River to the west of the center of Lima in October of 1972, timed to coincide with the fourth anniversary of the military coup.[76] Though SINAMOS was able to move two of the groups to other sites within the same immediate area, it has been unable to persuade the invaders to move to Villa el Salvador. Even police efforts to contain the invasions produced some violence,[77] and the government has been unwilling to apply the degree of violence that would be necessary to remove the invaders from the sites. In part in response to the failure to deal successfully with these invasions, the government promulgated Decree Law 20066 of June 26, 1973, which made involvement in invasions punishable by imprisonment of up to two years. This punishment applied not only to those who actually participated in invasions, but also anyone involved in organizing an invasion.[78]

Interviews in SINAMOS offices revealed that there exists a legal means through which families can obtain a lot in a settlement. This *vía legal* involves a program in which lots in government-sponsored settlements are sold to any family which applies for one. However, out of fear of stimulating a massive demand for new lots, this program has received little publicity and hence has operated only on a small scale. As of late 1972, a common way of getting a lot was to participate in an invasion and then get moved to a government-sponsored settlement. Invasions thus continue to be a major means through which families acquire land in settlements. Given the concern with adherence to

[75] *La Prensa*, June 3, 1972.

[76] There were articles on these invasions in *La Prensa* and *El Comercio* almost daily during the first week of October 1972.

[77] *El Comercio*, Nov. 13, 1973.

[78] *Peruvian Times*, July 6, 1973. I would like to thank Peter Cleaves for calling this law to my attention.

law, it is surprising that the government tolerates, and, because it moves the invaders to new sites, to some extent even provides an incentive for, the occurrence of invasions. The invasions that are occurring are clearly related to a continuing shortage of low-cost housing in Lima. Though opposition parties and land speculators might still be interested in invasions if this shortage did not exist, the elimination of the shortage would unquestionably eliminate one of the causes of these invasions. The program of offering lots to any family which applies for one could alleviate the shortage, but the government is reluctant to develop the program sufficiently to allow this to happen.

The reason for this reluctance presumably lies in the overall development strategy of the government. Through efforts to develop other parts of the Coast, extensive agrarian reform, and programs to develop the Jungle, this government hopes to stem the heavy flow of migration to Lima.[79] A massive program of offering land in settlements to any family that applied for it would make life in Lima easier for new migrants and would be a stimulus for new migration. It appears that the government is willing to tolerate the continuing occurrence of invasions in Lima as a price it must pay for holding down the rate of migration to the capital. This concern with the consequences of settlement development for urban growth has, of course, already been noted as an important aspect of settlement policy during the Belaúnde period.

Another ambiguity with regard to enforcement of law can be found in policy toward invasions in the provinces. There have been evictions in provincial cities.[80] However, on the basis of visits to provincial cities, Alfred Stepan reports that the reaction to invasions has been far less harsh outside of Lima.[80a] Interviews carried out by Stepan with SINAMOS officials suggest that there is a deliberate strategy of restraining invasions in Lima and letting them occur more freely in provincial cities. This is intended to discourage migration to Lima, and to encourage instead the concentration of migrants in secondary population centers. Concern

[79] For a discussion of the government's plans for regional development, see John P. Robin and Frederick C. Terzo, *Urbanization in Peru* (New York: Ford Foundation, 1973), pp. 25ff.

[80] See *La Prensa*, Nov. 2, 1969 (Chimbote), June 1, 1971 (Talara and Arequipa), and Aug. 25, 1972 (Chiclayo).

[80a] Personal communication.

with legality thus once again takes second place to the concern with restraining migration to Lima.

Legalization

SINAMOS is actively granting land titles in the illegally established older settlements and in 1972 was processing tens of thousands of applications for titles. Records examined by Alfred Stepan indicate that far more titles were granted from 1970 to 1972 than throughout the 1960s. An interesting aspect of this program of legalization is the requirements imposed for applying for a land title in a settlement. Among the documents that SINAMOS requires is a certificate of civil marriage.[81] This is a particularly significant requirement since a great many couples in settlements are joined only by common-law marriage. Though it is possible to make the application without the certificate, the belief that it will be required has produced a rash of mass marriages in settlements.[82] For conservatives who view the tradition of common-law marriages among cityward migrants and rural Indians as sign of national backwardness, these marriages are doubtless a source of great satisfaction. This is another way in which the government is extending the rule of law in the settlements.

SINAMOS is also attempting to force settlement residents to occupy the lots of which they claim to be the *de facto* owners or to give them up. The need to do this arises from the fact that many families have treated squatter invasions as an opportunity for land speculation, initially occupying a lot in a new settlement and building a minimal house on it but not living there. This is done with the intention of moving in later on, or renting or selling the house and lot at some future date. Law 13517 prohibits this, and housing agencies have tried, usually unsuccessfully, to prevent it. In September of 1972 SINAMOS began a major effort to end this practice.[83] Though obviously confronted by many of the same difficulties that earlier agencies faced in enforcing this aspect of the law, SINAMOS had a greater ability to recover the

[81] This was included in a mimeographed list of requirements which was available at local SINAMOS offices. Other personal documents and birth certificates for children were also required. In addition, the applicant had to be living on the lot and had to have a document showing that he did not own other real estate.

[82] For a report on one of these mass marriages, see *La Prensa*, Dec. 19, 1972.

[83] See *La Prensa*, Sept. 14, 1972.

unused lots because of its extensive efforts to organize the settlements. The local settlement organizations collect contributions from the residents for community projects, and to the extent that lots are not occupied, the ability to collect money is correspondingly reduced. SINAMOS therefore expected full cooperation from the settlement leaders in their campaign, and as of October 1972 they had already recovered a number of lots.

Popular Support

One of the important consequences of the formation of SINAMOS has been to bring together in one agency the government's programs in settlements and its attempts to mobilize popular support. These had previously been divided between ONDEPJOV and Artola. SINAMOS has arranged major demonstrations by settlement residents, such as the demonstration in Chimbote on July 29, 1972, the day after the national independence day, which a SINAMOS bulletin claimed was attended by 120,000 people.[84] SINAMOS literature on Villa el Salvador likewise focuses on popular support. An article on this settlement in *SINAMOS Informa*, a news bulletin put out by SINAMOS, included eight pictures of residents of Villa el Salvador engaged in large, enthusiastic demonstrations, waving Peruvian flags and banners which carried slogans supporting the government.[85]

There is a significant divergence between the reality of the political demonstrations arranged by SINAMOS and the officially stated objectives of SINAMOS of supporting "mobilization." The law which founded SINAMOS declares that one of its purposes is to create a dialogue between the people and the government and to stimulate the participation of the people in basic decisions.[86] The publicity regarding these demonstrations claims that they fulfill these purposes. On various occasions, settlement residents or members of other groups attending the demonstrations have been brought up to the platform to make a statement about their needs. This is referred to in the publicity as "dialogue."[87]

[84] *SINAMOS Informa*, 1, no. 1 (Lima: SINAMOS, Oficina Nacional de Difusión), p. 20.

[85] *SINAMOS Informa*, 1, no. 2, pp. 29–32.

[86] *Decreto Ley* 18896, article 5c.

[87] See, for instance, *SINAMOS Informa*, 1, no. 2, p. 32 and *Expreso*, Oct. 1, 1972 (the latter with reference to Velasco's visit to the Jungle).

Similarly, SINAMOS publicity regarding the July 1972 settlement demonstration in Chimbote states that demonstrations of this type are a "consequence of a coherent policy which is intended to encourage the participation of the citizenry in the tasks of development and progress.[88] The claims of SINAMOS regarding the significance of these demonstrations are also reflected in the main banner that hung below the speaker's platform at the Chimbote demonstration, which said *"Tu Presencia es Revolución"* ("Your Presence is Revolution").[89]

These demonstrations may reflect considerable support for the government. However, mass involvement in this kind of dialogue, participation, and "revolution" does not really involve the exercise of political power. The emphasis on this type of symbolic participation reflects a basic dilemma of military governments, even reformist or radical military governments, regarding the appropriate role of mass participation. The typical solution to this dilemma is nicely summarized by Stepan, who suggests that

in regard to participation, the desire of military radicals for control would tend to conflict with free democratic electoral campaigns, but would be congruent with a military populist plebiscitary style of politics. As regards mobilization, military radicals' preference for order and unity would make them . . . favorably disposed to mass parades.[90]

At the same time, however, the participation which is being encouraged in settlements by SINAMOS does affect decision making at the local level. Local associations are democratic, and within the limitations imposed on local political activity, settlement residents do exercise choice in decisions about local development programs.

To sum up the impact of the Pamplona invasion on settlement policy: It is clear that two basic elements of the policy already existed before the invasions—the self-help oriented development program of ONDEPJOV and the support-getting activities of Artola. The impact of the invasion and the other crises of mass

[88] *SINAMOS Informa*, 1, no. 1, p. 14.

[89] Ibid., front cover.

[90] Alfred C. Stepan, *The Military in Politics: Changing Patterns in Brazil* (Princeton, N.J.: Princeton University Press, 1971), p. 270.

participation which occurred at about the same time was to bring these two elements together in SINAMOS in such a way as to strengthen a third element—the capacity for political control. Though the concern with political control was present from the beginning, it was heightened by the crises of early 1971. It therefore appears that these crises of mass participation had an important influence on the way in which settlement policy is being carried out, and perhaps the scale on which it is being carried out. They did not alter the basic methods which are being used to develop the settlements.

Just as the crises of 1971 brought a sharp shift in the organization of the settlement program, so there have also been some changes within the SINAMOS period. Following a series of crises in a number of SINAMOS programs which did not involve settlements and a change in top SINAMOS leadership, there were, by 1974, some signs of a shift to a less populist, more low-profile approach which more nearly resembled the approach of ONDEPJOV. By early 1975, the weakened position of SINAMOS and the uncertainties about the future of the Velasco regime seemed likely to further encourage this tendency.

Analyzing the Policy

To place current policy in Peru in perspective, I will now point to certain contrasts with policies adopted in other countries, attempt to assess who benefits from the policy, and develop further the comparison with policy under earlier governments in Peru.

Contrasts with Other Countries

Contrasting present policy with settlement and housing policies in other countries is a useful means of identifying alternative policies which have not been adopted in Peru. For instance, the eradication of existing settlements has occurred under the present military government in Brazil, under Pérez-Jimenez in Venezuela, and in Korea and Africa.[91] This antisquatter policy

[91] Elizabeth and Anthony Leeds, "Brazil in the 1960's: Favelas and Polity, The Continuity of the Structure of Social Control" (unpublished manuscript); Talton F. Ray, *The Politics of the Barrios of Venezuela* (Berkeley and Los Angeles: University of California Press, 1969), p. 32; and Joan M. Nelson,

has been carried even further in the Central African Republic, where cityward migrants have literally been taken back to the countryside in trucks.[92] Such alternatives do not appear to have received serious consideration under the present government in Peru. Three reasons may be cited for this. First, Lima's unusual advantages as a setting for settlement formation have caused Lima's settlements to have a far greater potential for progressive development than settlements in many other countries. Hence, there is less reason to eradicate them. Second, it is obvious that the military are aware of the potential in the settlements for self-improvement and believe that they have played an important and positive role in the growth of Lima. Finally, though opposition parties have been reduced to a relatively weak position in Peru, they would probably be strong enough to encourage and organize forceful resistance if a systematic policy of eradication were adopted. The threatened eradication of established communities has frequently produced violent resistance in Peru. In Brazil, by contrast, the party structure is far weaker and the coercive potential of the government far greater.

Another important contrast with other countries concerns the extent to which traditional planners' standards have been relaxed in recognition of the contribution of settlements to urban development. Peru appears to be far ahead of most countries in this regard. The writings of Mangin and Turner on Peru were among the first anywhere to call attention to the need to relax traditional standards in order to take advantage of development opportunities in settlements,[93] and many of Turner's insights came directly out of his work in the housing institute associated with Beltrán in the late 1950s.[94] This relaxation of standards has obviously not been initiated by the present government. However, the decision to continue the earlier emphasis is significant.

"New Policies toward Squatter Settlements: Legalization Versus Planners' Standards" (unpublished manuscript). For an example of the apparently common phenomenon of eradication in Africa, see Michael A. Cohen, *Urban Policy and Political Conflict in Africa: A Study of the Ivory Coast* (Chicago: University of Chicago Press, 1974).

[92] Reported by Richard E. Stryker, personal communication.

[93] See Mangin, "Latin American Squatter Settlements" and "Squatter Settlements," and Turner, "Barriers and Channels" and "Uncontrolled Urban Settlement." Nelson's "New Policies" and personal communication with her helped to bring the issue of planners' standards into focus.

[94] Personal communication from John C. Turner.

Though Peru is innovative in terms of the relaxation of traditional planners standards, policy has been more cautious in two important areas—the extent of development of the *via legal* for applying for lots in settlements, and the initiation of urban reform. With regard to legal alternatives for the formation of low-income communities, the policy in Chile under Frei was far more ambitious.[95] However, the fate of the Chilean project suggests that the hesitancy of the Peruvian government in developing the *via legal* may be justified. Applications for the program ran far ahead of the government's ability to accommodate new families, and as the elections of 1970 approached, the opposition parties sought to call attention to the failures of the program by supporting the illegal occupation of proposed housing sites by the frustrated applicants.[96] Hence, the failure of a program intended to offer a legal channel for low-income housing development had the effect of encouraging further illegality. In light of this Chilean experience, the fear of the Peruvian government of raising expectations through a major program of offering lots in settlements seems justified. Such a program would also conflict with the goal of discouraging further migration to Lima.

Urban Reform

Another policy which has not been adopted is urban reform. Ever since the Cuban urban reform of 1960, reform governments in Latin America have had a model for the fundamental rearrangement of the ownership of urban property. The Cuban law eliminated renting, put all home construction in the hands of the state, imposed new norms for the inheritance of real estate, and placed future urban expansion under tight government control.[97]

The Cuban law was printed in Lima and circulated widely in the first years of military rule.[98] Support for urban reform came

95 See Robert North Merrill, "Toward a Structural Housing Policy: An Analysis of Chile's Low Income Housing Program" (Doctoral dissertation, Cornell University, 1971), pp. 11ff., and Peter S. Cleaves, *Bureaucratic Politics and Administration in Chile* (Berkeley and Los Angeles: University of California Press, 1974), chap. 8.

96 Cleaves, *Bureaucratic Politics*, chap. 8.

97 See Maruja Acosta and Jorge E. Hardoy, *Reforma Urbana en Cuba Revolucionaria* (Caracas: Sintesis Dosmil, 1971), chaps. 5 and 6.

98 Information on this and several of the following points was kindly supplied by Sinesio López.

from the Left—from the magazine *Oiga* during the first year of military rule when it was to the left of the government; from the most reform-minded members of the government—both civilian and military; and more recently, in 1973, from the Christian Democratic party, the party with the closest ties to the government.[99] The proposals of *Oiga* and the Christian Democrats included the expropriation of rented housing. In one version, back rent would have counted as partial payment toward purchase, and the government would have paid the balance.[100] This would not necessarily have involved all rented housing, and *Oiga* suggested that small-scale owners who were renting only two or three properties should be exempted.[101] The reform would also curb land speculation in areas of future urban expansion at the periphery of the city—an important factor in housing costs— through expropriation of areas of future urban growth and more careful planning of city growth.[102]

President Velasco's Independence Day speech on July 28, 1969, emphatically ruled out the possibility of a general redistribution of urban real estate but made it clear that some control over land speculation was imminent.[103] He declared that there would not be urban reform, as some had "self-interestedly" maintained (in part a slap at *Oiga*), and that the government would not eliminate the right to private property in the form of real estate, but rather would defend it. Instead, the concern of the government was with resolving the problems of squatter settlements and inner-city slums, and with eliminating land speculation. He was particularly forceful on this last point, declaring that

[w]e all know that in Peru, immense fortunes have been made through artificially driving up the price of . . . land. . . .
This is a situation of appalling injustice which cannot continue in the future.[104]

99 See, for instance, *Oiga*, Nov. 8, 1968, p. 13; Nov. 30, 1968, p. 11; Mar. 21, 1969; Apr. 11, 1969; Sept. 12, 1969, p. 14; and Nov. 16, 1969. See also the Declaración Política, published by the Christian Democrats in *Expreso*, Apr. 15, 1973.

100 *Oiga*, Nov. 9, 1968, p. 13.

101 Ibid.

102 This is mentioned in most of the statements on urban reform cited above.

103 Oficina Nacional de Información, "Mensaje a la Nación," July 28, 1969, pp. 13–14.

104 Ibid.

This speech naturally raised wide expectations of new measures dealing with settlements and slums and with land speculation. Endless rumors circulated about a new squatter settlement law. According to one version, the law would attack the problems of inner-city slums by offering new land to the slum residents and then eradicating the slums.[105] Another version suggested the law involved cooperative ownership of settlements by the residents which would preclude individual ownership of houses. A law based on this latter idea was apparently drafted and circulated in the government, but was not adopted. Rumors of imminent urban reform persisted through 1974—they were particularly widespread in July of that year—but as of mid-1974, settlement policy was still being carried out under the terms of Law 13517, as revised in the late Belaúnde period.

On the other hand, Law 17803, dealing with land speculation, came out a little over a month after Velasco's speech.[106] This law provided the basis for expropriating land for use in low-income housing developments and included fairly strict criteria for determining the price of expropriation and the terms of payment to the owners. The measure was generally well received, with some complaints from private developers about the terms of expropriation.[107] Since that time, the government has become involved in major low-income housing projects which involved expropriated land.

Why was there such hesitation in adopting urban reform? The parallel with agrarian reform was inviting. In rural areas, land invasions had threatened the stability of the system, and land was being redistributed to preempt future invasions. In urban areas, land seizures continued to occur, and it would seem reasonable to preempt them through the redistribution of urban property. However, there were major differences. Redistribution in the capital might conflict with the government's goal of diverting migration from Lima, whereas redistribution in rural areas was obviously consistent with it. Likewise, agrarian reform in the highlands took land from a class of traditional hacienda owners whose political power had long been declining. In urban areas, the private sector played an important role in the government's

105 *El Comercio*, Sept. 3, 1969.
106 *El Comercio*, Sept. 5, 1969.
107 *La Prensa*, Sept. 19, 1969.

housing plans, and the government perhaps did not wish to demoralize this sector by carrying out extensive expropriations. Other factors may have been influential as well, such as the fact that the government did not want to inhibit private investment in housing with a threatening law, and that some high-ranking military officers own significant amounts of urban real estate.

With regard to the possibility of new, comprehensive legislation for settlements and slums, the proposal for cooperative ownership of settlements was viewed in the cabinet and elsewhere as undermining the principle of private property, and hence was dropped. Because settlements make property owners out of the urban poor, a feature of settlements which has often been viewed as contributing to political stability, the government was apparently reluctant to eliminate this aspect of settlement life. The reasons why the massive relocation of slum residents was not carried out are less clear. If the old slum areas were eradicated, there was no reason why this measure should have stimulated further migration to Lima. It might also have helped to reduce the number and size of the squatter invasions which were occurring in Lima. On the other hand, it would have represented a major assault on private control of urban real estate. It would also have committed the government to a massive task of demolishing old slums and aiding new communities on the periphery of the city. It hence went considerably further than the government was ready to go at that time in aiding the urban poor. However, as the ongoing reforms of 1973 and 1974 touched more and more areas of private property, many observers in Lima felt that new reforms in the area of housing and real estate were likely.

Who Benefits from the Policy?

Another means of placing settlement policy in perspective is to ask who has benefited from it. We will not attempt to speculate about who benefits from all of the policy changes discussed in this chapter, but rather will identify the beneficiaries in the traditional pattern of settlement formation around Lima, note changes in the perception of who the beneficiaries were, and try to identify the principal beneficiaries under present policy.

To answer the question of who has benefited and who has lost in the traditional pattern of settlement formation around Lima, we must consider the broader context of patterns of landholding in Lima. One of the most important aspects of the landholding pattern has been the widespread illegal or legally ambiguous appropriation of land, not only by poor squatters, but by the wealthy as well. Many instances may be found of appropriation of land by the wealthy. Haciendas in the Lima area have been expanded by extending the cultivated land to neighboring publicly owned areas. Homesteading laws, which provide for the acquisition of land for agriculture and mining, have been violated by owners who instead build housing developments. Wealthy individuals who wish to claim a particular piece of public land have been known to sell it to a housing cooperative for low-income families, thereby gaining as allies for their claim an easy-to-mobilize group of poor families who will vigorously resist any attempt to evict them from the site.[108]

The occupation of land by low-income families—with or without encouragement from the government—is thus one aspect of a broad pattern in which many people, both rich and poor, have appropriated land in greater Lima. Policy arenas of this type have been labelled "distributive."[109] They involve a nonzero-sum game in which a highly divisible good is acquired in such a way that there are many immediate beneficiaries and no immediate losers—except, in this instance, for a few cases of conflict among contending illegal claimants.

The evolution away from this distributive pattern may be interpreted as resulting from a change in the political context which caused some groups to conclude that settlement formation was more costly than had previously been realized—that there were, indeed, losers. I suggested above that one aspect of the change in context was the rural instability in the Peruvian highlands in the 1960s and the link between this instability and ambiguous property law. The military apparently concluded that the ambiguous system of property law had already imposed a high cost by threatening the stability of the system in rural areas, and that it might do so in urban areas as well. The military gov-

108 For a further discussion of the illegal use of land around Lima, see my *Squatters and Oligarchs: Public Policy and Modernization in Peru* (Baltimore: Johns Hopkins Press, forthcoming, 1976), chap. 2.

109 Theodore J. Lowi, "American Business, Public Policy, Case-Studies, and Political Theory," *World Politics* 16, no. 4 (July 1964), pp. 677–715, at pp. 692–695.

ernment is therefore attempting to bring order to the system of property law, in urban as well as rural areas.

Though the military fears the radical potential of the settlements, it is important to note that this presumed radical potential has, in fact, not yet produced significant political disruption in Lima. The disruption occurred, instead, in the countryside. Following Hirschman, it may be argued that this is an instance in which a "neglected" problem—landholding arrangements in Lima—received attention in part because its solution is viewed as an aspect of the solution of a "privileged" problem—the landholding arrangements in rural areas.[110]

Other changes in the political context were important as well. The idea that settlement formation imposes a high cost by encouraging migration to Lima had already influenced policy in the Belaúnde period. The specter of urban guerrillas in other countries was another factor which affected the military's perceptions of the costs of uncontrolled settlement formation in Lima.

These changing patterns of the costs and benefits of settlement formation have caused a shift from a distributive, give-away policy to a policy of attempting to regulate land use. This regulation includes not only the attempted control of settlement formation, but also Law 17803, which laid the basis for regulating land speculation. The shift has resulted from the identification of new interests—the requirements of a particular national development strategy and the presumed requirements of national security—which are now perceived as having been jeopardized by the earlier policy.

There is a striking similarity between this evolution of settlement policy in Peru and Lowi's discussion of the way in which tariff policy in the United States has evolved from a distributive policy to a regulative policy. In the earlier part of this century, most strikingly with the Smoot-Hawley tariff of 1930, United States tariff policy was based on "giving limited protection [indulgence] to all interests strong enough to furnish resistance."[111] It involved a situation in which "a billion dollar issue [could] be disaggregated into many millions of nickel-dime items and each [could] be dealt with without regard to the others. . . ."[112] Beginning in the 1930s, however,

110 Albert O. Hirschman, *Journeys Toward Progress* (Garden City, N.Y.: Doubleday, 1965), pp. 301ff.

111 Ibid., p. 692.   112 Ibid.

the tariff began to lose its capacity for infinite disaggregation because it slowly underwent redefinition, moving away from its purely domestic significance towards that of an instrument of international politics. In brief, the tariff, especially following World War II and our assumption of peacetime international leadership, became a means of regulating the domestic economy for international purposes. The significant feature here is not the international but the regulatory part of the redefinition. As the process of redefinition took place, a number of significant shifts in power relations took place as well, because it was no longer possible to deal with each dutiable item in isolation. . . . Certain elements of distributive politics remain . . . [because] there are always efforts to disaggregate policies as the best way to spread the patronage and to avoid conflict. . . . But despite the persistence of certain distributive features, the true nature of tariff in the 1960's emerges as a regulatory policy.[113]

Thus with tariff policy in the United States, as with settlement policy in Peru, new, broader interests emerged which could not be served by the earlier distributive pattern.

Turning to the question of who benefits from present settlement policy in Peru, a number of different beneficiaries and losers must be identified. To the extent that it is harder to get a lot in a settlement in Lima, the present arrangement works to the disadvantage of low-income families who would like to move to a settlement. The fact that it is harder to get a lot in Lima may also reduce the overall supply of low-income housing and work to the disadvantage of families who would like to move to the capital but do not because it is more difficult to find housing. These families are the short-term losers in the government's efforts to divert migration from Lima.

On the other hand, the residents of Lima settlements have benefited, particularly through the granting of land titles. The importance of land titles to settlement residents was clearly reflected in a 1967 survey of settlement residents which measured the intensity of dissatisfaction over the absence of twenty-six different services and amenities in settlements.[114] The lack of land titles was tied for first in terms of intensity of dissatisfaction. It

[113] Ibid., pp. 699–701.
[114] Andrews and Phillips, "The Squatters of Lima," p. 218.

is clear that the settlement residents are getting something from the government which they very much want. Receiving title increases security of tenure on the lot, stimulates investment in housing, increases the value of the lot, and makes it easier to sell the lot. The active government support for community development projects likewise brings considerable benefits to the settlement residents. The government is unquestionably carrying out an enlightened program in the settlements.

With regard to the broader consequences of the policy, the sector which most obviously loses under present policy is the traditional party system. A major purpose of the policy is to insulate the settlements from the appeals of political parties. The government doubtless believes that the hoped-for slowing of the rate of migration to Lima and the attempt to raise the level of satisfaction of settlement residents will increase the stability of the political system. Determining who benefits from the stability of the present political situation obviously requires an elaborate assessment of the benefits and costs of many other government policies, which is well beyond the scope of this chapter.

Comparisons with Other Governments

The policies toward settlements adopted by the present military government appear to be guided by a number of concerns: a desire to stimulate the physical development of the settlements; concern with respect for law; the desire to avoid programs that further encourage the growth of Lima; the desire to reconstruct Peruvian society around partially autonomous units which operate on the basis of *autogestión* or self-direction; and the attempt to promote a particular type of popular support and controlled mass participation which is unrelated to political demand making, except for demands focused at the local level, and which precludes the traditional political parties. Though the government must occasionally choose from among these goals—as in the choice between respect for law and controlling urban growth—they form, overall, the basis for a fairly coherent and consistent policy.

At the same time, however, if one examines the precedents for current policy, one finds that it is a curious blend of policies pursued by an earlier progressive government and by the Right. Odría's use of settlements as a base of popular support and as part of his campaign against Apra anticipated current activities of SINAMOS. Beltrán's emphasis on self-help and the role of the private sector in solving the housing crisis have been revived. Belaúnde's concern with the impact of massive settlement programs on urban growth is also reflected in the present period.

It would, however, be a mistake to argue that the government is merely applying old policies. Even if many aspects of the policy have been tried out under earlier governments, it is an innovation to bring the different aspects of the policy together. Belaúnde attempted to shift development priorities to rural areas, but in the process totally neglected the settlements and failed to curb their extremely rapid growth in the 1960s. The present government, by contrast, is attempting to divert migration *at the same time* that it aids settlements. Likewise, Odría appears to have maintained political control in part by neglecting legalization, presumably at great cost to the settlement residents. The present government is controlling the political life of the settlements *at the same time* that it is granting land titles.

This difference between the Odría and Velasco periods merits close attention. The informality and paternalism of the policy under Odría involved a political relationship which Powell has called clientelistic. In discussing this type of relationship, Powell has written that the

contract between patron and client . . . is a private, unwritten, informal agreement, and highly personalistic in content. There is no public scrutiny of the terms of such agreements. . . . This stands in sharp contrast to the relationship . . . in modern systems of political transactions. In essence, the patron-client pattern occurs in the realm of private accountability, the modern pattern in the realm of public accountability.[115]

In the clientelist relationship, the lack of public accountability obviously works to the disadvantage of the client, because of

the degree of power asymmetry between superior and subordinate. Superiors in a clientele system are relatively free to behave in an arbitrary and highly personalistic manner

[115] John Duncan Powell, "Peasant Society and Clientelist Politics," *American Political Science Review* 64, no. 2 (June 1970) pp. 423–424.

in dealing with their subordinates. Subordinates in a
clientele system have relatively little recourse in such a
situation.[116]

The present government, by contrast, is relying on a system
of control which is quite properly called corporative.[117] It is
based on the comprehensive organization of the settlements
which has been carried out by ONDEPJOV and SINAMOS. By
channeling all aid programs, public and private, through this
organizational structure, SINAMOS has attempted to fill the political space in the settlements, drastically reducing the number
of alternative courses of political action open to settlement residents. The high degree of power asymmetry described by Powell
is still present, but a tendency for superiors to behave in an arbitrary and highly personalistic manner is not. Indeed, one of the
most important features of the organizational system set up by
SINAMOS is that it is consistent and predictable.

Though these methods for ordering political relationships in
the settlements would appear to be remarkably comprehensive
and complete, there is no guarantee that they will accomplish the
goals which the government seeks to accomplish. Questions about
the prospects for SINAMOS's role in the settlements also arise,
because the political position of SINAMOS is by no means secure.
SINAMOS has important enemies within the government, and
some of its programs have stirred strong opposition both in and
outside the government. The settlement residents themselves
may become dissatisfied with the SINAMOS program in settlements.

However, Dietz reports that as of 1973 the existing arrangement was quite satisfactory from the point of view of the settlement residents.[118] He suggests that in the absence of the earlier
party competition in settlements, the residents can now concentrate their demands for assistance with local improvements on
the appropriate SINAMOS officials, allowing the residents to be
more effective in their demand making with regard to local issues
and in their efforts to improve their own communities. It is precisely this kind of demand making and self-help that the govern-

[116] Ibid., p. 424.
[117] See Julio Cotler, "The New Mode of Political Domination in Peru,"
Chapter 2 in this volume.
[118] Dietz, "The Office and the Poblador."

ment wishes to encourage. Hence, although the political upheavals and the looming presidential succession crisis of 1975 appear to have weakened government performance in most areas of policy, it would appear that the government's program in settlements has made some important strides toward achieving its goals.

5

Transforming the Rural Sector: Government Policy and Peasant Response

Susan C. Bourque and David Scott Palmer

Today, the Day of the Indian, the Day of the Peasant, the
Revolutionary Government is making the best of all tributes to
him by giving the whole nation a law which will end forever
an unjust social order. . . . Today Peru has a government
determined to achieve the development of the country by the
final destruction of ancient economic and social structures that
have no validity in our epoch.[1]

On June 24, 1969, Juan Velasco Alvarado announced to the Peruvian nation the long-awaited Agrarian Reform Law. As indicated
in the passage above, the new law was to destroy those "unjust
social and economic structures" which had oppressed the peasantry. Further, the government would direct the destruction of
those institutions. We argue in this paper that the present military government has pursued a course of active interest in the
integration of the rural population and has taken the lead in developing a policy for restructuring rural institutions: production,
ownership, and organization. However, Peru's agrarian structure
and rural population are vast and diverse. This diversity, particularly its manifestation in differing levels of social mobilization,
represents a major constraint on the government's plans for rural
transformation.

This paper was originally prepared for delivery at the Seminar on Continu-
ity and Change in Contemporary Peru, Center for Inter-American Relations,
New York City, June 1, 1973. The authors are especially grateful for the ob-
servations made on an earlier draft by seminar participants David Apter,
Luigi Einaudi, Robert Kaufman, Abraham Lowenthal, Liisa North, John
Gitlitz, Luis Soberón, and Alfred Stepan. We are also indebted to Penny G.
Martin, Mount Holyoke College, Christian Potholm, Bowdoin College, and
Stanley Rothman, Smith College, for their comments on this paper.

[1] Juan Velasco Alvarado, June 24, 1969, from his speech to the Peruvian
nation announcing the Agrarian Reform Law, as reported in *Oiga* June 27,
1969; translated and reprinted in Paul Sigmund, ed., *The Ideologies of the
Developing Nations*, 2d rev. ed., Praeger, New York, 1972, p. 400.

In this paper we present a comparative assessment of the national integration policies[2] of the Belaúnde (1963–1968) and military (since 1968) governments. Their policies toward the rural sector, as well as the implementation process, are considered. Our discussion of the implementation process is an attempt to illuminate the change and modification necessitated by citizen—primarily peasant-citizen—response to government policy. Several case studies will illustrate the variety of results possible when a government consciously sets out to reorder a rural reality which is itself most diverse.

We frame our discussion around two hypotheses:

[1.] That the level of social mobilization affects the options available to government to achieve the integration of the rural population.[3]

Huntington argues that the earlier in the social mobilization process the government intervenes with a clear modernizing ideology, the more likely it is that it will be able to transform this ideology into organizations and then institutions capable of channeling the articulation of social forces as that articulation occurs.[4] The case of the present military government of Peru demonstrates some problems with this proposition. The military take-

[2] Integration is a most complicated process, whether seen in individual or aggregate terms. Karl Deutsch, drawing on Edward Shils, sees mobilization as a two-stage process, "moving from" and "moving into." Karl Deutsch, "Social Mobilization and Political Development," *American Political Science Review*, 55:3, Sept. 1961, p. 494. Old ties and loyalties must be broken down before a "traditional" citizen is capable of assuming the behavior patterns of "modern" society, including organizational membership and political activity. The distinction between the two stages of integration is analytical. In practice all integration processes involve the mixture of modern and traditional, whether for individual or institutional survival. In some societies, according to Geertz and Bendix, traditional structures adjust and adapt to modernizing forces, and on occasion they survive and become as dominant in the modern society as they were in the traditional one. Clifford Geertz, "The Integrative Revolution," in Clifford Geertz, ed., *Old Societies and New States*, Free Press, New York, 1963, pp. 105–157. Reinhard Bendix, "Tradition and Modernity Reconsidered," *Comparative Studies in Society and History*, 9, Oct. 1966–July 1967, pp. 292–346. One's past always plays a role in one's perception of the alternatives available and in the actual implementation of those perceptions.

[3] Samuel P. Huntington, "Political Development and Political Decay," *World Politics*, 17, 1965, pp. 386–430.

[4] Samuel P. Huntington, *Political Order in Changing Society*, Yale University Press, New Haven, 1968, chap. 4.

over did occur in Peru while overall social mobilization was relatively low.[5] Nevertheless, the Peruvian military government has been forced to rethink many of its policies in response to a relatively low aggregate level of previous social mobilization. This suggests to us the utility of examining the impact of differences in the levels of social mobilization. It appears that even the very partial social mobilization which precipitated the 1968 military take-over narrowed the limits within which the military must now operate.

Our second hypothesis is:

[2.] That political systems may be differentiated on the basis of whether social mobilization—in its critical dimension of integration—occurs fundamentally as a result of governmental or societal factors.[6]

In the case of Peru, it can be argued that the state's role in the Belaúnde and pre-Belaúnde years was basically one of responding to the demands placed on it by society. Rather than adopting an aggressive policy from the center, previous regimes responded largely by ignoring the rural sector, or else they responded on an *ad hoc* basis. As a result, the framework for integration was set by demands flowing from social forces, such as political parties, interest groups, unions, and peasant leagues, rather than the state apparatus.

Since the establishment of the Revolutionary Government of the Armed Forces of Peru, a conscious attempt has been made

[5] Peru was sixteenth of twenty Latin American nations in aggregate levels of social mobilization, according to ten indicators of various aspects of this phenomenon. D. S. Palmer, " 'Revolution from Above': Military Government and Popular Participation in Peru, 1968–1972," mimeographed, Latin American Studies Program, Cornell University, Dissertation Series, no. 47, 1973, table 1, pp. 8–10.

[6] The causal process of integration and the forms of representation induced by that process are obviously complex. They involve a calculus of both the role of government and that of society or social forces in stimulating the social mobilization which contributes to the breaking away from traditional patterns of behavior and in providing the alternatives in which new patterns may be adopted. As Apter has argued, either government or society may serve as the principal shapers, that is, independent variables, of the social mobilization, integration, and political development processes. David Apter, "Notes for a Theory of Nondemocratic Representation," in J. Rolland Pennock and John W. Chapman, eds., *Representation*, Nomos, vol. 10, Atherton Press, New York, 1968, pp. 278–317.

by the military to formulate and implement policies which designate the government as the dominant force in the creation of the structures for integrating the rural population.

In sum, we are suggesting that under the military government the state has taken the lead in creating institutions for the integration of the rural population.[7]

SOCIAL MOBILIZATION, THE DEMOCRATIC INTERLUDE, AND MILITARY CORPORATISM

Before addressing these hypotheses directly, let us sketch the historical relation between the rural and urban sectors in Peru. Independence from Spain did not include a profound revolutionary break with the colonial tradition.[8] A landed nobility independent of the crown had not emerged in the almost three hundred years of colonial rule.[9] The classical liberal ideology, which emerged with independence and permeated the region in the 1820–1860 period, legitimated the reestablishment and/or extension of the hacienda system throughout the rural areas, with its concomitant extension of dominance by the *gamonal* (the rural elite) over peasant *colono*.[10]

The bourgeoisie in Peru developed very slowly and was se-

[7] The analytical distinction between societal and governmental locus of initiative blurs in the face of reality. Government must take into account social realities when formulating policies. Nongovernmental groups likewise cannot implement strategies without consideration of governmental responses. The distinction that we make here is in the degree to which government assumes leadership in policy making. For a discussion of pre-1968 Peru in these terms, see M. S. Larson and A. E. Bergman, *Social Stratification in Peru*, Politics of Modernization Series no. 5, Institute of International Studies, University of California, Berkeley, 1969. Luigi Einaudi seems to be suggesting the same process in his article, "Revolution from Within? Military Rule in Peru since 1968," *Studies in Comparative International Development*, 8:1, 1973, pp. 71–87.

[8] Heraclio Bonilla and Karen Spalding, "La Independencia en el Perú: las palabras y los hechos," in Bonilla et al., *La Independencia en el Perú*, Perú Problema no. 7, Instituto de Estudios Peruanos (IEP), Lima, 1972, pp. 15–64.

[9] C. H. Haring, *The Spanish Empire in America*, Harcourt Brace and World, New York, 1963, p. 93.

[10] George Kubler, *The Indian Caste of Peru, 1795–1940: A Population Study Based upon Tax Records and Census Reports*, Smithsonian Institution, Institute of Social Anthropology, vol. 14, Wash., D.C., 1972, passim.

verely weakened by the loss of the War of the Pacific (1879–1883) and the subsequent remission of the country's resources to foreign interests for exploitation.[11]

The rise of a commercial or entrepreneurial class in Peru reflected more the *embourgeoisement* of the aristocracy than the establishment of an independent middle class. At the governmental level, this period was marked by a trade-off between civilian and military regimes. Both types of regimes resolved the problem of the peasantry by a *de facto* alliance between the upper classes and the *gamonal*. The problems of the rural sector were left in the hands of the rural elite; the urban coastal elite responded to highland unrest only when requested to do so by their rural allies.

During this period there were only the most limited efforts to integrate the rural sector. The peasantry was largely isolated from the national system, either in their Indian communities, or subject to the complete domination of the *hacendado* through the *colono* system.[12] The peasantry and their integration in the political system were not important factors in the political calculations of any national group.

Conditions in the Sierra changed dramatically in the 1940s and 1950s, which led to major political responses from the center by the 1960s. The expansion of rural education, extension of highways, increased commercialization and dramatic increases in the rate of migration to provincial and national capitals continually eroded the basis of *gamonal* dominance in the Sierra.[13] Many of those peasants who remained behind responded to change in the Sierra by organizing against the *gamonal* and by invading lands which had been taken from them in previous epochs. Such peas-

[11] This was in part to repay the massive debt incurred in the war. Ernesto Yepes del Castillo, *Peru 1820–1920: Un siglo de desarrollo capitalista*, IEP, Campodonico, 1972, pp. 127–180.

[12] Fernando Fuenzalida, "La estructura en la Comunidad de Indígenas tradicionales," in Robert G. Keith et al., *El Campesino en el Perú*, Perú Problema no. 3, IEP, Lima, 1970, pp. 61–104. Julio Cotler, "Actuales pautas de cambio en la sociedad rural del Perú," in José Matos Mar et al., *Dominación y cambios en el Perú rural*, IEP, Lima, 1969, pp. 60–79.

[13] Larson and Bergman, *Social Stratification in Peru*. See especially chap. 2. Paul L. Doughty, "Behind the Back of the City: 'Provincial' Life in Peru," in William Mangin, ed., *Peasants in Cities*, Houghton Mifflin, Boston, 1970, passim.

ant mobilization was especially widespread in Pasco, Junín, and Cuzco between 1959 and 1964.[14] This rural unrest in the Peruvian Sierra, with the rather limited goal in most cases of recuperating or retaining lands, served to precipitate new forms of governmental and nongovernmental response. The peasantry now found new channels of access to the national political system through fledgling attempts by political parties to organize rural areas.[15]

Up until the 1960s a "coalition of the whole" had prevailed among the political actors. The coalition was based on the neutralization of all new participants and the exclusion of the *campesino*.[16] Except for the efforts of APRA among the workers of the profitable coastal plantations, no political actor had attempted to mobilize support among the peasantry until the 1950s.

This coalition of the whole had broken apart by the 1960s. Once the traditional ruling groups in the Sierra lost local control, they simultaneously lost their legitimacy with the urban coastal elite. Thus the way opened for new efforts by national politicians in the Sierra. Belaúnde was the first national politician to perceive that socioeconomic change was creating new literate

[14] Starting with the invasion of the hacienda San Juan de Paria in Pasco by the adjacent Indian community Yanacancha in 1959, Lima newspapers reported 103 invasions of haciendas in Peru by the end of 1966, a figure which almost certainly underrepresents reality. All of the invasions were carried out by *comuneros* (members of Indian communities). Julio Cotler and Felipe Portocarrero, "Peru: Peasant Organizations," in Henry Landsberger, ed., *Latin American Peasant Movements*, Cornell University Press, Ithaca, 1969, p. 311. Howard Handelman reports 150 invasions in Pasco, Junín, and Cuzco alone between July and December 1963. "Struggle in the Andes: Peasant Political Mobilization in Peru," Ph.D. dissertation, University of Wisconsin, August 1971, pp. 90, 130–136. During much of this same period a very different kind of movement, involving *colonos* (tenants on haciendas who are given a plot of land to till in exchange for working the *hacendado*'s lands a fixed number of days per year) rather than *comuneros*, was able to achieve de facto ownership of La Convención and Lares valleys in Cuzco. Wesley W. Craig, "From Hacienda to Community: An Analysis of Solidarity and Social Change in Peru," mimeographed, Latin American Studies Program, Cornell University, Dissertation Series, no. 6, 1967, pp. 24–53.

[15] For further discussion of these attempts see Susan C. Bourque, "Cholification and the Campesino: A Study of Three Peruvian Peasant Organizations in the Process of Societal Change," mimeographed, Latin American Studies Program, Cornell University, Dissertation Series, no. 21, 1971.

[16] Jane Jaquette, "The Politics of Development in Peru," mimeographed, Latin American Studies Program, Cornell University, Dissertation Series, no. 33, 1971. Julio Cotler, "The New Mode of Political Domination in Peru," Chapter 2 of this volume.

groups in the countryside whose votes could provide the margin of victory in the evenly balanced national political arena.

Belaúnde's extensive trips through the Sierra following the 1956 election led to similar attempts by other political actors to tap the peasantry as a political resource. There followed during the early 1960s a proliferation of organizing activities among the peasantry by political parties. At the same time, the government created special programs designed to facilitate the inclusion of this sector into the national network on terms acceptable to the actors of the urban Coast; that is, without changing the rules of the national political game.

The Peruvian military was neither immune to, nor unaware of, the changes occurring in the rural sectors. During the 1962–1963 military government, they were forced to respond with *de facto* recognition of change by the agrarian reform decree promulgated exclusively for the La Convención and Lares valleys of Cuzco. The guerrilla movements in Junín, Cuzco, and Ayacucho in 1965 forced the military to bring its repressive potential to bear on the rural population and brought in their wake a number of lessons.

The operation against the guerrillas gave the military a new perception of the rural sector as a potential threat to internal security. It demonstrated the utter incapacity of the *gamonal* system for social control. It underscored the inability of the civilian democratic government to control rural unrest, suggesting the limited capacity of political parties to redirect rural ferment into suitable institutional channels. It demonstrated to the military their ability to handle peasant uprisings and thus increased their confidence in the military as an institution. But it also illustrated the extreme measures which might be necessary to maintain rural stability, and it thus enhanced the position of those elements within the military which had been urging nonrepressive alternatives.[17]

It can be argued, therefore, that the precipitating event for the rise of a modernizing military regime was the army's response to the entrance of the masses onto the political stage, as Samuel Huntington hypothesizes.[18] If General Manuel Odría (1948–1956)

[17] Luigi Einaudi and Alfred C. Stepan, *Latin American Institutional Development: Changing Military Perspectives in Peru and Brazil*, Rand Corporation, Santa Monica, Calif., publication no. R-586-DOS, Apr. 1971, p. 26.

[18] Huntington, *Political Order in Changing Society*, pp. 194–195.

was the first military president to see the need to cultivate the urban shantytowns, and Belaúnde was the first to perceive the political potential of the rural sectors, the Revolutionary Government of the Armed Forces was the first Peruvian regime to view the increasing mobilization of the rural population as a threat which required forceful intervention by government to create participatory structures to channel these emerging social forces.

This ushered in a serious attempt to establish a new relationship between government and society after 1968. The military underscored its new perception of the role of the state by attempting the rapid expansion of that role. Modernization, rather than emerging as the result of a series of *ad hoc*, reactive responses by government and national political actors to the demands of various groups in the society, would now flow in a structured and ordered fashion from government down to society.

Policy under the Military Government

The Revolutionary Government of the Armed Forces has adopted an aggressive policy toward rural Peru which attempts to extend state control and planning into the periphery. Paradoxically, one consequence of the government's initiatives has been to reduce the peasantry's alternatives for national political influence.

The military's policy has two dimensions. The first is the stimulation of local units of participation of a fully cooperative nature. Within these units, the military reasons, citizens can resolve those day-to-day issues of living and working which are of greatest concern to them. These local units of participation for the rural sector include Agricultural Production Cooperatives, Communal Cooperatives, Agrarian Social Interest Societies (SAIS), Integral Rural Settlement Projects (PIAR), and Integral Development Projects (PID).

The second policy dimension is the creation of a link between these various local units and a unitary national agricultural organization. The national organization would permit the involvement of various parts of the agricultural sector in the formulation and implementation of national policies. This national organization is called the National Agrarian Confederation (CNA).

The ideology of the Revolutionary Government of the Armed

Forces recognizes the crucial definition of participation: citizen control of decision making which affects society as a whole. Social mobilization is defined as

the process by which the emerging groups come to exercise a basic or structural participation by gaining access to the control of the society's key resources, basically the ownership of the means of production and the making of the central decisions which affect the most important aspects of society as a whole.[19]

However, ultimate authority remains outside the control of the local units. Basic policies continue to be determined by the governing apparatus at the center, and all actions at the local or regional levels must be taken in light of these determinations. The central government's control of the entire process is stressed on the grounds of internal security. Even at the local level, government agency rather than political party or union is designated the proper mechanism for the expression and resolution of citizen concerns. The dual commitments of the military government to the primary role of the state as the initiator and controller of policy and to full citizen participation create the major tension in the government's ideology and policies.

Beyond this ideological tension there are structural obstacles in the Peruvian rural sector: it is vast, severely underdeveloped, and encompasses several levels of social mobilization, integration, and economic development. Central government policies should take account of the variety of rural production and social patterns. However, the military's rural policies generally assume a commonality of interest which does not exist.

This emerges clearly in the government's policy toward cooperative organization. The Agrarian Reform Law of 1969 affirmed the government's concern with the expansion of the cooperative sector in rural areas.[20] It strengthened the cooperative provisions by designating the cooperative as the preferred form

[19] Peru, Presidencia de la República, Instituto Nacional de Planificación, *Plan nacional de desarrollo para 1971–1975, Plan Global*, Lima, 1971, p. 31.

[20] The law envisions affecting 24,822 farms encompassing 11,387,000 hectares and benefiting 242,088 families. From Peru, Ministry of Agriculture, Oficina Sectorial de Planificación Agraria, *Resumen del Plan Agropecuario a Mediano Plazo, 1971–1975*, vol. 1, Oct. 1970, Lima, pp. 89–99.

of landownership. The law provides for a number of different kinds of rural cooperative arrangements, including the Agricultural Production Cooperative and the Agrarian Social Interest Societies (SAISs).

The SAISs combine the land from expropriated haciendas and the adjacent peasant communities. This insures that large extensions of land will be maintained as a single unit. The SAISs also combine the former hacienda workers, and technicians with the *comuneros* of the indigenous communities.

This SAIS arrangement affects its various members differently. At one level, it is hoped, the inclusion of the poorer communities with the former hacienda will improve the economic basis of the communities through some redistribution of income in their favor. In addition, the more marginal *comuneros*, the representatives of the communities, have a majority in the governing body of the SAIS. They could, in principle at least, control its operation. However, this advantage does not balance the superior expertise of the former technicians. Further, the boundaries between the former hacienda and the communities are set in favor of the former hacienda workers. In addition, *comuneros* must help pay for the expropriation of the hacienda from its former owners even though they will not get direct use of the land.[21] Finally the SAISs require highly capitalized and profitable haciendas in order to insure profits which can be redistributed. Most haciendas of the Sierra are not of this nature, especially in zones where poorer communities are concentrated. As a solution to rural problems, therefore, the SAIS concept appears to be partial at best.

The Integral Rural Settlement Projects (PIAR) are another new rural structure created by the military government. These are intermediate forms of rural organization which permit, like the SAIS, the combination of different types of agricultural enterprises and the sharing of profits among the members.[22] They are likely to encounter the same problems as the SAIS. They cover all enterprises within a given homogeneous geographical area in order to permit the more efficient concentration of government

---

[21] This obligation appears to have been suspended by April 1973 legislation permitting some beneficiaries of the agrarian reform to forgo annual payments to the former owners through the government.

[22] Peru, Ministerio de Agricultura, Dirección General de Reforma Agraria y Asentamiento Rural, *Manual de normas y procedimientos para adjudicaciones de reforma agraria*, vol. 1, Lima, Sept. 1971, pp. 43–94.

resources. They assume, like the SAIS, the willingness of all entities and individuals located within the area—from individual holdings to peasant communities—to combine their efforts in a collaborative enterprise and to share in a more equitable distribution of future surpluses.

The Agricultural Production Cooperatives are the purest examples of the concept of social property, which the regime has stated is to predominate in all sectors of Peruvian society.[23] Ownership is to be the collective right and responsibility of all members of the enterprise. In the Agricultural Production Cooperative all land, except for small parcels, which can be held within the family, is to be cooperatively held and worked, and the profits equitably distributed to all. The SAIS, PIAR, and less-rigorous Agricultural Service Cooperatives (in which factors of production are not collectively owned) are viewed as transitional mechanisms toward the goal of full Agricultural Production Cooperatives.

The military government has created another administrative unit which will affect the rural areas, the Integral Development Projects (PID). The PID is intended to encompass all enterprises, agricultural and industrial, within a given geographic region. A certain portion of all the surplus generated by the enterprises within the PID would be held by the PID's central clearing house for distribution to the members on the basis of productivity and social welfare criteria. Thus the PID is seen as a mechanism for slowly redistributing the profits within each region of Peru on a more equitable basis to all residents of the region.

Under the Peasant Communities Statute of February 1970, the cooperative concept was extended to the 2,337 recognized Indian communities and their 390,000 families.[24] The statute establishes new membership criteria: only those *comuneros* who are full-time farmers and residents of the community may enjoy full membership. Secondly, the communities are to be reorganized along cooperative lines, with a new governing framework of administration and vigilance councils to supplant the old *junta com-*

[23] See Peter Knight, "New Forms of Economic Organization in Peru," Chapter 9 of this volume.

[24] Peru, Centro Nacional de Capacitación e Investigación para la Reforma Agraria (CENCIRA), "Reestructuración de las comunidades campesinas: Las comunidades campesinas contemporáneas," Elaborado por la Dirección de Comunidades Campesinas, Lima, 1970, p. 13.

munal and *personero*. In addition, the private holdings which prevail in the majority of communities are to be "restructured" into cooperatively owned land.[25]

The community statute disregards such traditional community structures as the *ayllu* and *varayoh*; it restricts elected positions in the new cooperative to those who can read and write Spanish. In addition, it prevents *comuneros* from seeking employment and maintaining plots outside the community. Previously this additional employment had added substantially to community and individual resources.

The National System of Support for Social Mobilization (SINAMOS) is the institutional expression of the concern of the military that the stimulation and channeling of participation be controlled by the state, rather than by such alternative structures as unions and parties. The initial law for SINAMOS was decreed in June 1971, although implementing legislation was delayed until April 1972 because of the strong differences among military factions and civilians within the government over the precise nature of the role which this agency should play.[26] SINAMOS has been given the responsibility for coordinating, stimulating, and channeling all initiatives relating to citizen participation. It incorporates a number of preexisting government agencies whose responsibilities related in one way or another to local organization and infrastructural development, including some previously associated with partisan political influence. SINAMOS is to promote participation of all kinds and to serve as an intragovernmental "transmission belt" for citizen concerns, as an alternative to the ministerial bureaucracies.

SINAMOS is directly tied to the Council of Ministers at the national level through a director who sits on the council with voice but not vote. It has zonal (departmental level) and regional (provincial level) units called OZAMs and ORAMs, which enjoy some degree of autonomy within national guidelines to adapt policies regarding participation to local conditions. This principle of decentralization provides, in addition, opportunities for the inclusion of citizen representatives from communities, co-

[25] The 1961 agricultural census of Peru suggests that communal holdings prevail in less than 33 percent of recognized communities. Peru, *Primer Censo Nacional Agropecuario*, Lima, 1966, pp. 14–24, chart 7.

[26] Noted by several high officials of SINAMOS in interviews with D. S. Palmer, Apr. and May 1972.

operatives, and the like in the ORAMs on a consultative basis. Nevertheless, the military retains overall direction of SINAMOS.

In May 1972, the National Agrarian Society (SNA), an old-line agricultural interest group dominated in the past by large hacienda owners, was abolished on the grounds that it did not represent the full spectrum of agricultural interests. In its place the National Agrarian Confederation (CNA) was established as the one legitimate organ of expression of farm interests.[27] This meant that all other peasant federations and associations lost government recognition as legitimate representatives of peasant interests before government agencies. Although agricultural unions registered with the Ministry of Labor are not eliminated by the legislation creating the CNA, they are left without a role in the new scheme of things.

All individuals who earn their livelihood principally from agriculture are eligible for membership in the CNA base organizations, which include members of SAIS, Agricultural Production Cooperatives, Peasant Communities, the Association of Small Landowners, and the Association of Peasants without Land. Day laborers are included within the respective base organization at which they work. Agrarian Leagues made up of elected representatives from each association are to be established in every province; these leagues will elect representatives to an agrarian federation for each department; these federations, in turn, will elect representatives to the CNA.

The inclusion of day laborers and landless peasants into organizations offsets to a degree their exclusion from the benefits of the 1969 Agrarian Reform Law. Another important provision is the extension of voting privileges to illiterates. The benefits that such provisions will bring to these most marginal farm groups will become clear only as implementation proceeds. The fine print of the law suggests that they may not be represented in accordance with their numbers. The day laborers will invariably be a minority in the community, SAIS, or cooperative in which they work, and thus will not be likely to elect their own representatives to the Agrarian Leagues. Peasants without land may form only one association per district, no matter how numerous they may be; hence, they too are likely to be underrepresented at the provincial level.

The CNA, like SINAMOS, is basically a mechanism to enhance

[27] Decree Law no. 19400, May 9, 1972, *El Peruano*, May 12, 1972.

the labors of the government: the interests of *campesinos* of diverse station are to be "defended" by the CNA, but only insofar as they are compatible with the national interest as determined by the Military Government.

Given the apparent effect of the CNA—to decrease the number of avenues open to the *campesino* to influence government agricultural policy—the role of the judicial system as an impartial arbiter of disputes assumes critical importance. The Agrarian Tribunal, established with the 1969 Agrarian Reform Law, appears to fill this role. It is designed to resolve all disputes arising between individuals or entities relating to land.

The land court system assumes that the peasant and the landlord are not able to defend themselves equally before the law, and sets up special provisions which benefit the subordinate. The peasant receives free legal assistance from a public defender who speaks his or her language, usually Quechua or Aymara. The length of processes and appeals is considerably shortened by law. In many cases, the judge is required to set up court *in situ*. Salaries are high, and judges are appointed for relatively long terms.[28]

As the above initiatives suggest, the Revolutionary Government of the Armed Forces has assumed during its first five years in office impressive responsibilities for the integration of the rural sectors into national life. The ideology of a fully participatory social democracy has been articulated. The principal policy initiatives have focused on the need to increase material welfare and provide a local and national structure for citizen participation. Although initiatives of prior governments and national political actors have been utilized on occasion (as with the cooperatives), they have more often been ignored or derided. Military policy is based on the assumption that solidarity of interest exists within the agricultural sector. This assumption takes its concrete form in the notion of social property in local cooperative structures. An embryonic notion of democratic centralism is emerging, preserving hierarchical distinctions. Throughout all this, the predominance of central government in all initiatives is justified on the basis of preparing the citizens to handle their own affairs.

[28] Peru, Tribunal Agrario, *Memoria del Presidente del Tribunal Agrario*, 1969–1970 and 1970–1971.

POLICY TOWARD THE RURAL SECTOR
UNDER BELAÚNDE, 1963–1968

In making and implementing policies, Belaúnde's regime had to take into account multiple political actors within a formally democratic framework, each responding to a climate of social ferment. Not surprisingly, the policies which emerged reflected the need for compromise and accommodation demanded by the exigencies of party politics. The result was the unplanned creation of a variety of channels of access to the national political system during this period. The political context of the Belaúnde years gave rise to an embryonic network of linkages between the center and periphery.

The Belaúnde government attempted to meet the needs of the marginal rural sectors with structural adjustments, increased government resources, and sensitivity to local perceptions of reality.

Belaúnde . . . did not insist, in his zeal for change, either on forcing the coastal way of life on the Sierra or on imposing the Sierra cultural patterns on the coast. He envisioned a genuinely pluralistic country in which the coast could advance with its westernized, capitalist traditions while the Sierra progressed through its at least semi-socialistic Inca customs. . . . Belaúnde called upon the native communities to advance themselves through the energetic use of the same methods employed by their distant ancestors. . . .[29]

One instrument chosen to advance these goals was Cooperación Popular, a program initially established in August 1963 by executive decree, which would combine governmental material assistance from several ministries with peasant self-help for local infrastructural development. Government centers were to be provided with equipment ranging from shovels to bulldozers and staffed with anthropologists and agricultural technicians, among others. These centers were to be complemented by Cooperación Popular Universitaria, a program through which university students would spend their summer vacations in the iso-

[29] Fredrick Pike, *The Modern History of Peru*, Praeger, New York, 1967, p. 307.

lated rural communities assisting the *comuneros* on community development projects.

An important symbolic gesture of Belaúnde's commitment to local control and autonomy was the implementation in 1963 of the municipal and local elections provisions of the Constitution of 1933. Such elections, originally instituted in the 1890s, had been abandoned in the 1920s by the central government in order to reassert its control and to maintain a patronage system. Whereas Belaúnde was willing to abandon these apparent advantages by reinstituting direct citizen participation, the restrictions in the 1963 Municipal Elections Law insured the maintenance of elite control. Council members must be over 21, reside in an urban area, be registered voters (i.e., literate), and not be related to each other or paid for their services. These criteria make clear that *campesinos* were not the intended beneficiaries. Nevertheless, the law did reflect an attempt to give local residents more control over decisions on local problems.

The persistent need for funding was confronted in the third prong of Belaúnde's rural policies: The January 1964 law was to provide monetary subsidies (about $4 million to the municipalities) from the central government to local government bodies.[30] This represents the potential to provide the newly elected leaders the means to insure their leadership: the financial resources to exploit the possibilities of Cooperación Popular and to shore up the new elective system.

Each presidential candidate in 1963 promised agrarian reform. An agrarian reform law was finally passed by Congress in May 1964 after key changes in the initial Belaúnde proposal were made. The most notable of these was the exclusion of properties which were highly productive enterprises and/or generators of foreign exchange. This guaranteed immunity for the large sugar haciendas on the coast and the few highly productive sheep and cattle haciendas of the Sierra, thus excluding the areas of APRA's greatest organizational and electoral strength.

The law established agrarian reform zones throughout the country and provided for the creation of agencies to supervise the reform and train the new owners. The law was judged by a

[30] Allan Austin, *Research Report on Peruvian Local Government*, Institute of Public Administration, New York, 1964, p. 3.

group of OAS experts to be "excessively broad, difficult to interpret, and in some cases impossible to apply."[31]

Belaúnde was the first president to promote actively the cooperative concept. A General Law of Cooperatives was passed by Congress in 1964 with APRA support. The law encouraged the formation of cooperatives throughout Peru, with tax exemptions and fewer import restrictions for cooperatively organized groups. Creation of the cooperatives at the local level was to be completely voluntary and to be accomplished largely through local initiatives.

THE POLITICAL PROCESS UNDER BELAÚNDE AND ITS EFFECT ON POLICY

Peruvian politics in the 1960s demanded accommodation and compromise; governments were frequently forced to respond to conflicting social forces. As did the others, Belaúnde operated in an atmosphere of political competition. From the outset both his administration and policies reflect that context.

The inauguration of Belaúnde as President on July 28, 1963, marked the beginning of a new phase of land invasions by *comuneros*. Within two months, two hundred thousand hectares were invaded in one Sierra department and forty communities occupied hacienda lands in another.[32]

The official government response was conciliatory. One department prefect defended the invasions as legitimate recuperations of community lands, and worked incessantly to avoid confrontations and to reach agreements between *comuneros* and *hacendados*. The police were not used in these areas to expel invaders during this period.

By the end of [1963] the number of invasions in the central *sierra* dwindled simply because most mobilized villagers were

---

[31] Comité Interamericano de Desarrollo Agrícola (CIDA), *Peru: Tenencia de la tierra y desarrollo socio-economico del sector agricola*, Organization of American States, Washington, D.C., January 8, 1965. Cited in James Petras and Robert La Porte, *Perú: ¿Transformación revolucionaria o modernización?* Amorrortu, Buenos Aires, 1971, p. 20.

[32] The departments involved were Pasco and Junín, *La Prensa*, Oct. 2 and 4, 1963, reported in Handelman, "Struggle in the Andes," p. 130.

in *de facto* control of disputed lands, or expected to
receive them from the government in the near future.[33]

The opposition-controlled Congress responded to these initiatives by dragging its feet on executive branch proposals and by
censuring the minister of the interior for ineffective handling of
the "communist-inspired" land invasions. As a result, Belaúnde
was soon forced to compromise with the opposition. This led to
the alteration of many of his original objectives regarding the
rural sectors, and included the repression of subsequent land
invasions.

Even with these difficulties, Cooperación Popular during its
first year provided for the construction of 2,600 kilometers of
roads, 500 schools, and 2,000 community buildings by the *comuneros*, assisted by 650 university students.[34] The program was
financed by an initial appropriation of about $2 million but was
almost constantly in need of funds after that.[35]

The Cooperación Popular concept and program ran into resistance immediately from the opposition majority in Congress,
who saw in it and in its offshoot, Cooperación Popular Universitaria, the seeds of Acción Popular (AP) party recruitment. In
addition, APRA recognized the potential of Cooperación Popular
for increasing AP's strength among the peasantry.[36]

The practical effect of this congressional opposition, since Congress controlled Peruvian government funding of the executive
branch, was to force Cooperación Popular almost from the outset
to a heavy dependence on outside capital and assistance, which
was uncertain at best.[37] Most of Cooperación Popular's operating

[33] Handelman, "Struggle in the Andes," p. 123.

[34] Jaime Llosa Larrabure, "Cooperación Popular: A New Approach to Community Development in Peru," *International Labour Review*, 94, Sept. 1966,
pp. 232–234.

[35] Ibid.

[36] In all fairness, Cooperación Popular was not free from partisan politics.
Communities complained that the political coloration of the voters determined the degree of willingness of Cooperación Popular technicians to help
with their projects or the ease with which funding or equipment could be
secured. Earl Morris et al., *Coming down the Mountain: The Social Worlds of
Mayobamba*, Socio-Economic Development of Andean Communities, report 10,
Anthropology Department, Cornell University, 1968, pp. 196–201.

[37] As Richard Goodwin points out, the United States held up or cut off
foreign assistance and loans to Peru during more than half of Belaúnde's

funds were provided by the Agency for International Development (AID). In addition it received assistance on a regular basis from AID advisers and Peace Corps volunteers.[38]

Belaúnde's proposal to hold local elections fared much better. It was approved by the opposition majority (APRA-UNO) in the expectation that they would win decisively any such local electoral contest.[39] To their surprise the Belaúnde party alliance won a national plurality both times such elections were conducted (46.8 percent in 1963; 47.5 percent in 1966).[40]

One unintended effect of the local election law in approximately six hundred Indian communities which were also district capitals was to undermine the communities' long experience in participatory democracy, by which all members of the community elect their community officials. Formalities such as slates of officers, an opposition, and political party labels were required for the first time, and only the literate minority (the usual case) was permitted to vote.[41]

Of the one hundred thousand families which Belaúnde claimed had benefited by the 1964 agrarian reform, more than seventy thousand received their land by virtue of de facto occupation of lands, which the law in effect legitimized.[42] Adjudications made through 1971 from properties expropriated under the Belaúnde Agrarian Reform Law totaled over 574,000 hectares and benefited about twenty-eight thousand families largely in departments such as Pasco and Cuzco in which major land invasions had taken

---

tenure in office due to the lingering and festering International Petroleum Company dispute. "Letter from Peru," *New Yorker*, May 17, 1969, pp. 41–108.

[38] Cooperación Popular also accepted the assistance of the International Development Foundation, later revealed to be a CIA conduit and hence a liability as far as Cooperación Popular's image was concerned.

[39] Pike, *Modern History of Peru*, p. 317.

[40] Figures from Carlos A. Astiz, *Pressure Groups and Power Elites in Peruvian Politics*, Cornell University Press, Ithaca, N.Y., 1969, pp. 110–111.

[41] D. S. Palmer was a witness to the utter confusion and dissension which the implementation of the local election law produced in one district capital in December 1963; that of Huancarayalla, in the *mancha india* province of Victor Fajardo, department of Ayacucho.

[42] Jean Piel, "Le situation actuelle della reforme agraire au Pérou," unpublished paper, Lima, 1967, as reported in Handelman, "Struggle in the Andes," p. 347.

place during the early Belaúnde years.[43] This process suggests again the degree to which government responded directly to the demands of society.

The figures suggest not only the reactive nature of the 1964 agrarian reform implementation process but also, due to the law's exceptions, the concentration by the government on the more marginal rural areas. Although many saw the exceptions (particularly the sugar haciendas of the coast) as a sellout, the unforeseen consequence of these provisions was to provide the marginal *campesinos* with a large share of agrarian reform resources.

During the Belaúnde government about 700 cooperatives of all types were constituted, of which 168 were agrarian cooperatives.[44] The name of the Ministry of Labor and Indian Affairs was changed to the Ministry of Labor and Communities, and more than 600 Indian communities were formally recognized between 1963 and 1968, thereby gaining exemption from most taxes and priority in the receipt of government assistance.[45] The number of recognized agricultural unions increased as well, from 230 in 1963 to 412 at the end of 1968.

Various national organizations began assisting the rural peasants to establish and operate cooperatives. APRA, AP, and the Catholic church offered both training courses in the mechanics of cooperative organization and some supervision over their establishment. However, the training was often cursory, and supervision ended before the peasants had adequately mastered the fundamentals, which led to *campesino* disillusionment in some instances.[46]

Such rural organizing by national actors took other forms as well during this period. After the 1956 presidential elections, in which APRA had agreed to support Manuel Prado in exchange

[43] Peru, Dirección de Planificación y Estadística, Dirección General de Reforma Agraria y Asentamiento Rural, Ministerio de Agricultura, Lima, Jan. 1972, as cited in Palmer, " 'Revolution from Above,' " table 10, pp. 190–191.

[44] Peru, División de Planificación y Estadística, Oficina Nacional de Desarrollo Cooperativo (ONDECOOP), Lima, 1971.

[45] The total number of recognized Indian communities at the time of Belaúnde's ouster in October 1968 was just over 2,300. This was estimated to be about 38 percent of all communities in Peru (about 6,000, according to R. MacLean y Estenos, *Sociologia del Perú*, Instituto de Investigaciones Sociales, Mexico City, 1959, p. 262).

[46] Bourque, "Chalification and the Campesino."

for recognition as a legal party, more or less open politics returned to Peru. APRA officially created the National Federation of Peruvian Peasants (FENCAP) in 1961 as a response to the needs of the party. With APRA control over the Peruvian union movement, the Confederation of Peruvian Workers (CTP), the party could count on trained union leaders to work with the peasants. The CTP provided a union framework into which FENCAP easily fit. It was to APRA's advantage to establish a peasant organization quickly and get it recognized as the national spokesman for the *campesino* (as it eventually was in 1965) in order to reap the benefits of the national political system—patronage including representation on appropriate government bodies. This status, they felt, would attract more of the peasantry to FENCAP and hence to the party itself, thus providing the new electoral support APRA required to retain a dominant political position.

During the 1960s peasant organizations proliferated. In addition to FENCAP some of the better-known groups were the Federation of Peasants of Cuzco (FCC), the Provincial Federation of Peasants of La Convención and Lares (FPCCL), and the Independent Party of Peasants and Workers (PITC). The FCC and the FPCCL were best known for their involvement in the land invasions of 1959–1963 in the Cuzco region.[47] The other group, PITC, was sponsored by the Cáceres brothers of Juliaca in the department of Puno.[48]

One of the critical failures of the Cuzco federations was their inability to institutionalize their organizations. Their attempts to establish a national organization similar to FENCAP failed, in part because they never enjoyed enough support from a powerful political group at the center after their split with the Communist Cuzco Federation of Workers (FTC). When the national system turned to repression of the land invasions, the peasants found themselves encapsulated: "a republic of *campesinos* within a hostile country."[49]

The split between the Cuzco Federation of Workers and the

---

[47] Wesley W. Craig, *From Hacienda to Community*, and Hugo Neira, *Cuzco, tierra o muerte*, Editorial ZYX, Santiago, 1968.

[48] Edward Dew, *Politics in the Altiplano: The Dynamics of Change in Rural Peru*, University of Texas Press, Austin, 1969, pp. 135, 139–141.

[49] Hugo Neira, *Los Andes, tierra o muerte*, Editorial ZYX, Santiago, 1968, p. 230.

campesino federation occurred primarily because the peasants were not anxious to support a sustained radical movement. Whereas they were willing to coordinate their efforts and take considerable risks for clearly defined short-term goals, once these goals had been achieved they were not willing to expand their activities into a movement which challenged the basic framework of the society.[50]

The PITC of the Cáceres brothers attempted to organize peasants into a political party in order to act directly upon the national system. Unlike FENCAP, PITC does not filter peasant relations to the political system through an alliance with other actors, even though it is basically a personalistic party and limited to the relatively small region of Puno.

The exclusively peasant base of PITC was an outgrowth of their understanding of the political system. From 1960 to 1961 the Cáceres brothers tried to organize peasant unions under the party umbrella of the Christian Democrats (DC). However, they ultimately decided that the existing Peruvian parties were unwilling to support meaningful reform. As relations became more and more difficult, the Cáceres brothers split from the DC and decided to build a national party from an independent *altiplano* peasant party.

The proliferation of rural organizations with institutional relations to the national political scene suggests the degree to which the mobilization occurring in rural Peru was being channeled through alternative structures to the center. In effect, government policy was only one facet of core-periphery relations in Peru between 1963 and 1968. Political actors had been working to mobilize the peasantry as power resources under their own respective banners.

The competition to recruit the peasantry carried over into the actors' responses to Belaúnde's policy initiatives. This reflected their perception of potential rewards from using the peasantry as a political resource. For instance, the APRA-UNO-controlled Congress went along with the government on the municipal election law and revenue sharing. The opposition recognized the need to expand their activities in the rural areas and were ready to compete in an electoral contest. However, the opposition perceived Cooperación Popular as a political instrument of AP and did what they could to thwart it. In order to get and keep Co-

50 Neira, *Los Andes*, p. 208.

operación Popular, Belaúnde was forced to accept an alternate development organization, the Departmental Development Corporation, which was tacitly a patronage agency for APRA-UNO. In sum, when a policy did not appear to be competitive, in the sense that it strongly favored one group over another, the party context under Belaúnde prevented the effective implementation of the policy.

This context was favorable in some respects for increasing rural participation and development.[51] Several political actors were concerned with gaining the support of the peasantry, and several acceptable means of communicating demands were available. However, this was a system that was prey to inefficiency, duplication of effort, and wastage. In some instances it induced further factionalism in a sector already plagued by divisions. During the Belaúnde years there were several actors concerned with gaining the support of the peasantry. However, such competition led to obstructionist politics, which cut off opportunities for peasant recruitment. The pluralist politics of accommodation and compromise worked as easily against the peasantry as for it.

POLICY IMPLEMENTATION UNDER THE MILITARY GOVERNMENT

The experience of five years of rule has forced the Peruvian military regime to adjust its initial notion of the ideal balance of power between government and society. Modernization has not proved to be a uniform process controlled from the top and accepted quietly by the bottom. On the contrary, the government has been forced to adopt far more tentative stances in its legislation and on occasion to change policy in fundamental respects.

Improved responsiveness to society has occurred without major bloodshed and violence. Massive repression has not characterized this regime. When it has become apparent that implementing a particular policy would require the sustained use of force, the military's response has been to alter the policy.[52]

Paradoxically, the reduction of alternatives available to the peasantry to influence the center under the military increases the

[51] Further, even when peasant participation increased, this was within the narrow limits set by a system dominated by nonpeasant groups.

[52] The examples of Huanta (1969), the Pamplona invasion (1971), and the North Coast sugar cooperatives (1972) indicate that the military would rather readjust policy than employ large-scale, long-term repressive tactics.

likelihood that peasants will resort to the "politics of violence" to achieve their goals.[53] The elimination of political parties as national actors in the policy formulation process has made it more difficult for the *most* mobilized peasant groups to make their demands known. To date the link between local units and the center envisioned by the military has not been implemented. In the interim, demands must be resolved either through clientelistic relationships with government officials in the bureaucracy or by direct confrontation through taking demands "into the streets."

Under the military government the preexisting bureaucratic apparatus has not undergone major alterations. Thus, to the extent that the old bureaucratic ties remain, so too does the old system of alliances, at least on the "output" side of government.

To circumvent this difficult problem the military has tried some bureaucratic reorganization. However, it has not achieved a massive infusion of new personnel. Throughout the country there is a shortage of trained individuals, especially in the rural areas. Many Peruvians willing to work for the government in Lima will not do so in the provinces. As a result, what ought to be the government's highest priority—its first point of contact with the population—is often its last and most ineffective.

In the marginal areas the government's rapid assumption of new responsibilities for modernization and participation has not been accompanied, to date, by a concomitant distribution of resources and personnel. Even so, changes have occurred in rural Peru since the military take-over. Through 1971 the military government had established seventy-seven Agricultural Production Cooperatives (and sixty of the less-rigorous Agricultural Service Cooperatives) and nine SAISs with lands adjudicated under the agrarian reform and the beneficiaries thereof.[54] About half of the seventy-four thousand families to benefit from the agrarian reform since 1968 are incorporated into one of these cooperative arrangements.

Although more than ten thousand families became part of SAIS through the end of 1971, the potential which exists for an important increase in participation and control by the members

[53] James L. Payne, *Labor and Politics in Peru*, Yale University Press, New Haven, 1965, esp. chap. 1.

[54] Peru, Dirección de Planeamiento y Evaluación, Ministerio de Agricultura, and the División de Planificación y Estadística (ONDECOOP), Lima, Jan. 1972.

of peasant communities in this structure is thwarted. In large measure this is due to the power of the technicians and managers, who retain their position through their monopoly of expertise and the need to maintain a high level of production.

The difficulties experienced in moving directly to production cooperatives in a setting often more accustomed to individual initiative, where large numbers of peasants were excluded, and where resources were very limited, resulted in a major policy adjustment. Beginning in 1971 experiments with less rigorous forms of land adjustment, known as Integral Rural Settlement Projects (PIAR), were attempted. The rate of increase of Agricultural Production Cooperatives declined, and the new mode was formally adopted on a national scale in May 1973. The new approach is more tentative and increases local options. The PIAR covers an entire geographical area, which permits greater efficiency in the utilization of scarce government resources.

For all intents and purposes, the application of the 1969 Agrarian Reform Law has been the only action of the Revolutionary Government of the Armed Forces which has brought about significant changes in the lives of residents of rural Peru since 1968. Even here, however, the benefits to date have affected a small portion of the farm families (about 10 percent); furthermore, the law has assisted to a disproportionate degree the most prosperous agricultural population. More than 65 percent of the families benefiting from the agrarian reform between 1969 and 1971 were from the Coast departments of Lambayeque (25 percent) and La Libertad (8 percent) and the wealthier Sierra departments of Pasco (15 percent) and Junín (15 percent).[55] A comparison between the prosperous Coast department of Lambayeque and the marginal Sierra department of Ayacucho reveals that only 8 percent of the *campesinos* of Ayacucho are scheduled to receive lands from the agrarian reform, compared with 50 percent of the farm population of Lambayeque.[56]

It has been pointed out that the agrarian reform of 1969 will result in some income redistribution when it is fully implemented (on the order of $86 million), effectively doubling the income of the permanent labor force on the expropriated farms.[57] However,

[55] Ibid.

[56] Palmer, " 'Revolution from Above,' " pp. 192–193.

[57] Hylke Van de Wetering, "The Potential Impact of Peruvian Agrarian Reform Law No. 17716 on Agricultural and Non-agricultural Production in

fully two-thirds of the benefits of redistribution will be realized by peasants and farmers in the Coast, not in the Sierra.[58] The total income transfer is estimated at less than 2 percent of 1967 national income.[59] Furthermore, even if it is fully carried out, the agrarian reform will benefit less than 40 percent of all farm families needing assistance and less than 10 percent of the Indian communities.[60]

Through 1972, government efforts to implement the Peasant Communities Statute were limited to the updating of the communities' membership rolls and the calling of elections for officials under the new cooperative framework.[61] Only twenty communal cooperatives have been established, and many of these do not involve a full restructuring of landholdings into cooperative patterns.[62]

In response to widespread protest among *comuneros* and efforts by some members of the Office of Peasant Communities, local adjustments to the statute were approved which formally relaxed some restrictions. For example, the residency requirement for *comunero* membership was relaxed in the more marginal areas to permit supplementing farm income through urban nonfarm employment. The prohibition on holding land outside the community was likewise relaxed. It is anticipated that with

Rural Areas," Convenio Para Estudios Económicos Basicos, Ministerio de Agricultura, preliminary draft, Lima, 1971, pp. 95–96.

[58] Ibid., p. 46.   [59] Idem.

[60] Estimate of Dr. Iván Pardo F., interview with D. S. Palmer, Lima, May 3, 1972. See Richard Webb, "Government Policy and the Distribution of Income in Peru," Chapter 3 of this volume.

[61] The Office of Peasant Communities depended for its funds through 1972 on the Agrarian Reform Office and usually found that its own priorities were subordinate to those of the agrarian reform. See Kevin Middlebrook, "Land for the Tiller: Political Participation for the Peruvian Military's Agrarian Reform," honors thesis, Department of Government, Harvard University, 1972, pp. 112–114. In 1971 there were fewer than twenty officials in the entire country working in the field directly on the application of the Peasant Communities Statute, according to Iván Pardo F., Subdirector of the Office of Peasant Communities, in an interview with D. S. Palmer, May 3, 1972.

[62] Peru, División de Planificación y Estadística, ONDECOOP, Lima, January 1972. This includes, for example, three such cooperatives for the department of Ayacucho, which D. S. Palmer visited in 1971; he verified that they consist of the much less rigorous service cooperative, in these cases the pooling of community resources for securing products needed in the communities.

the 1973–1974 biennial budget and with the full operation of SINAMOS, there will be a substantial increase in the resources available to carry out the government's work in the Indian communities and the marginal rural sectors.[63]

However, the SINAMOS budget for 1972 was approximately $92 million. This represented no new funds but, rather, the consolidated total budgets of the eight agencies now incorporated into SINAMOS.[64] The addition of new personnel, the expenses of integrating facilities, the establishment of new offices, and the intensive training (or retraining) provided most SINAMOS employees means that the actual budget available in 1972 for the implementation of ongoing programs has declined. The level of activity by government agencies with specific responsibilities for the "marginal" sectors of the population in at least one major rural area has fallen rather than increased during the first four years of the present military government.[65]

The military regime has manifested a genuine concern for the marginal sectors of rural Peru and has initiated a number of policies which could greatly affect their future well-being. To date, however, most of the benefits of implemented legislation have gone to a small, more prosperous, and more mobilized segment of the rural population. Furthermore, the emphasis by the government on stimulating local units of participation in rural areas, such as peasant cooperatives, agrarian cooperatives, and SAISs, has not been matched by a commensurate allocation of funds. This disadvantages the low-resource-base, or marginal, areas. In addition, the local participation units are established under criteria set by the central government. Ironically this often inhibits full local participation. The principle of participation within a corporatist framework is well advanced. However, the actual policy implementation process is such that in practice there remains sizable space for maneuver at the local level, especially in marginal areas. The Sierra in particular continues, as so often in the past, to work out local solutions to local problems whatever the policy initiatives emanating from the center.

[63] Iván Pardo, May 3, 1972, interview, anticipates a tenfold increase in the number of full-time field workers (*promotores*) working for the Office of Peasant Communities from twenty to two hundred.

[64] *Siete Días*, Apr. 21, 1972, p. 2.

[65] Ascertained by D. S. Palmer in interviews with employees of several government agencies incorporated into SINAMOS in Ayacucho, Apr. 28–30, 1972.

POLICY IMPLEMENTATION UNDER THE MILITARY GOVERNMENT:
CASE STUDIES

The policy of the Revolutionary Government of the Armed
Forces toward the rural sector has two principal dimensions: the
stimulation of social-property units at the local level and the creation of an integrated association of the entire agricultural sector
with representation at the regional and national levels.

This second dimension, discussed after the case studies, remains largely inoperative in terms of actual policy process. The
National Agrarian Confederation, although officially decreed in
May 1972, will not come formally into existence until departmental agrarian federations have been established in at least twelve
departments. As of May 1973, just one such federation at the departmental level had been officially established, in Piura.[66] The
regional associations of PIAR and PID are likewise still in the
very early stages of actual policy implementation.

The policy process regarding local units of participation is further advanced. The following case studies illustrate four responses to the implementation process: (1) successful implementation on the terms originally posited by the government;
(2) successful implementation after adjustments in policy by the
government in response to social pressures; (3) maintenance of
the *status quo ante*; and (4) a decline in peasant well-being as
a result of government policy implementation.

Successful Implementation: Loyanta

Loyanta was, until affected by the agrarian reform in 1970, a
rather typical small Sierra hacienda about two hours by gravel
road from the department capital of Ayacucho.[67] Thirty-seven
families eked out a subsistence living as *colonos* on the 515
hectares (1 hectare = 2.5 acres) which stretch in a thin ribbon
from fertile stream bottom at 10,000 feet to windswept *puna* at
13,500 feet. These families provided labor on the 27 hectares, cultivated for the benefit of the absentee landowner, and performed
services at her home in Ayacucho. In exchange, they received

[66] *Caretas* no. 473, Feb. 23–Mar. 8, 1973, p. 12.

[67] Drawn from field research by D. S. Palmer in the department of Ayacucho
between July 1971 and January 1972, some of which appears in " 'Revolution
from Above.' "

permission to live on the property, to cultivate small nonirrigated plots, and to graze their *puna* pasture.

The property was affected in its entirety under the 1969 Agrarian Reform Law for violations of the labor laws, and the proprietor was paid about $7,500 in cash and agrarian reform bonds for her holdings. Once all the official procedures were completed, in about a year, the property was provisionally adjudicated to the thirty-seven families and designated as an Agricultural Production Cooperative.

The former *colonos* are uniformly relieved to be rid of a *hacendada* whom they thoroughly disliked. They have eagerly turned to the cooperative cultivation of those lands once tilled exclusively for the *hacendada*'s benefit. They have followed the advice of the agrarian reform's local extension agent. This includes accepting a government program to plant five hectares in wheat, for which they receive seed and short-term credit for fertilizer from the Agricultural Development Bank. With equal enthusiasm they sought out and received a bilingual school for the cooperative, which opened the 1971 school year in the former *casa hacienda*. A small cooperative store has also been opened since the adjudication of the property.

Several members of the Loyanta community speak Spanish. The elected president of the Loyanta Farmers Council, the precooperative's chief decision-making body, has only a second-grade education. However, he spent several years in various jobs in the Coast and in the Jungle and has experience in dealing with outsiders. He returned to the hacienda permanently after the agrarian reform was declared in 1969 in order to be included as a beneficiary. He attended a peasant leaders training conference in Huancayo in early 1971. Because he spoke and understood Spanish, he was able to benefit from the experience.

This auspicious beginning suggests that this precooperative will develop into the type of local participation unit envisioned by the agrarian reform planners. Loyanta is favored with competent and experienced leadership and, perhaps even more importantly, an exceedingly favorable man-land ratio (one family for each seven hectares of cultivated land) in a department in which the average is exceedingly unfavorable (one farm family for each 1.5 hectare of cultivated land). The *campesinos* have been able to achieve a substantial increase in their incomes in a very short time with almost no alteration in their prior patterns of tilling the soil. They continue to maintain their own plots around their homes, and they continue to cultivate in a cooperative pattern the lands formerly utilized by the ex-owner. The crucial difference is that the profit from the sale of this land's product is now shared among those who till the land.

Government Policy Adjustment through Social Pressure: Cayaltí

Before the 1969 Agrarian Reform Law was decreed, there were eleven major sugar plantations which filled a number of the fertile river valleys of the North Coast desert.[68] Their holdings invariably extended up to the Sierra, but their most productive hectarage extended along the river courses. The sugar from these plantations provided Peru with substantial foreign exchange; the unions, which operated vigorously on all but one of the plantations, gave APRA one of its most important sources of political support; and the owners of the estates, who were Peruvian (only two of the estates were under exclusive or predominantly foreign control at the time of expropriation), formed the backbone of the national aristocracy. For these reasons the 1964 Agrarian Reform Law passed during the Belaúnde administration excluded these plantations from expropriation. For the same reasons, the 1969 law included them. Cayaltí was one of these estates.

Situated in the Zana River valley of the department of Lambayeque, Cayaltí contains approximately 30,750 hectares, of which 3,000 were cultivated in sugarcane and 4,885 in various foodstuffs.[69] Of the 2,385 employees at Cayaltí in 1969, about 1 percent were engineers and technicians, 14 percent were white-collar employees, 38 percent were factory workers (in the sugar mill), and 48 percent were cutters and field hands.[70] The old-line Peruvian owners, the Aspíllaga family, were in the process of

[68] Drawn in part from D. S. Palmer and K. J. Middlebrook, "Corporatist Participation under Military Rule in Peru," in David Chaplin, ed., *Peruvian Nationalism: A Corporatist Revolution*, Transaction Books, New Brunswick, N.J., 1975.

[69] Pontificia Universidad Católica del Perú, *La reforma agraria en los complejos agro-industriales, Cayaltí y Tuman: Informe preliminar*, Departamento de Ciéncias Sociales, Universidad Católica del Perú, mimeo, Lima, March 1970, p. 12.

[70] José Manuel Mejía, "Cooperativismo y reforma agraria en los complejos agro-industriales ayucareros del norte," typewritten draft, Lima, 1972, p. 28.

selling the estate to Cuban exile interests at the time of state intervention in June 1969.[71] The Aspíllaga family was intensely disliked by the workers because of repressive tactics used to maintain order on the estate. These tactics included the use of the police to shoot down striking workers, as in 1950, and the machinations to delay the formal establishment of the union. Facilities for the workers were perhaps the poorest among all the sugar estates.[72]

The adverse working conditions and a history of repression provided the conditions for the rise of an APRA-affiliated union at Cayaltí which was both vigorous and respected. The workers and the union both greeted the 1969 agrarian reform with enthusiastic support. The National Office for Cooperative Development (ONDECOOP) provided cadres of officials and assistants to conduct a series of classes explaining the agrarian reform and the theory of cooperative ownership. The labor union provided important assistance in preparing the population for the organization of a workers' cooperative.

When engineers and technicians at Cayaltí and the other sugar estates protested the proposed worker control and threatened to paralyze production by resigning en masse, the government imposed a number of restrictions on these former estates which would severely limit popular participation within the new cooperative structure.

For example, government decrees established that election to the 120-member delegate assembly of each cooperative would be determined by type of employment. Half of the representatives to the delegate assembly were to be chosen from the agricultural engineers and the white-collar employees, even though these two groups made up only 15 percent of the total work force at Cayaltí.

The administration and vigilance committees of the cooperative, responsible for the day-to-day conduct of some aspects of the enterprise, were to be selected from the delegate assembly in such a way that the engineers, administrators, and white-collar workers always had a majority of votes in each committee. The workers' union and political leaders were not to be permitted in

[71] Orlando Plaza Jibaja, "Historia del sindicato de Cayaltí," Tesis de Bachiller, Programa Académico de Ciéncias Sociales, Pontificia Universidad Católica del Perú, Feb. 1971, pp. 8–11, 15–23.

[72] Pontificia Universidad Católica del Perú, "La reforma agraria," passim.

the delegate assembly, which deprived the blue-collar and field workers of their most experienced representatives.

Since the government was the guarantor of the new cooperatives by its payment in cash and bonds to the former owners, it argued that it should name that proportion of the total number of delegates to the assembly which corresponded to the proportion of the net worth of the enterprise which it had guaranteed. This meant that the government named the majority of the delegates in all of the sugar cooperatives except Cayaltí, where the owners had declared the estate in bankruptcy.

In addition, the government established a "System of Advice and Fiscalization" (SAF) for the Agricultural Production Cooperatives of the North Coast. Its purpose was to oversee and coordinate the activities of the members of these cooperatives. In each of the North Coast cooperatives there was a military officer in residence in charge of the local SAF committee, who supervised the policies of the cooperatives.

At Cayaltí popular resistance to these multiple restrictions was channeled through the existing union. The labor union initiated a series of work stoppages between June 1970 and July 1971. Its strength was revealed when a massive seventy-two-hour work halt in July 1971 forced the government to return top union leaders to the cooperative's payroll in apparent violation of existing legislation. The government restrictions helped to maintain the union's vitality; the strike reaffirmed the union's importance as the workers' means of expressing material and political demands.

The government's perception of the basic incompatibility between the labor union and the cooperative structure was evidenced in ONDECOOP's effort to undermine the union organization through the creation of study circles. In the early months of 1971, ONDECOOP attempted to establish new communication channels at Cayaltí between the popular base and the unresponsive cooperative administration in the form of small discussion groups. However, worker apathy and governing council manipulation rendered the study circles meaningless as communication mechanisms between workers and officials.

Another strike broke out at Cayaltí in January 1972, after a key union leader was arrested on a charge of "sabotaging the agrarian reform." Workers at other North Coast Agricultural Production Cooperatives organized sympathy strikes in protest, precipitating a massive confrontation between the government and the workers. The initial government response was to jail numerous union leaders. In the intensive discussions within the government which followed, those advocating a policy of restraint and adjustment prevailed. The most onerous restrictions on participation in these local units were repealed in March 1972. SINAMOS was entrusted with overseeing the resident military advisers and with responsibility for increasing participation within the sugar cooperatives. When open elections under SINAMOS auspices were held in April 1972, blue-collar and unskilled workers were elected overwhelmingly.[73] Moreover, APRA union officials were elected as a majority of workers' delegates. Although they opposed the government in its attempt to legislate strict top-down control over these cooperatives, they certainly shared the government's interest in improving the well-being of the cooperative and its members. They were, in addition, by and large the individuals with the most experience in organizing and leading people. They could be counted on to continue to use these talents for the benefit of the cooperative, whatever their party affiliation.

This case underscores the dramatic reversal of government policy and the ability of the military to change policy in Cayaltí in the face of long-standing prejudices against APRA and against their perception of the crucial need to maintain production and profits in this highly industrialized segment of the agricultural economy. It also suggests the need for experienced and skilled leadership to reemerge within the new participatory structure of the cooperatives in this highly mobilized sector. At last the North Coast Agricultural Production Cooperatives obtained a real measure of local control.[74]

Maintenance of the Status quo ante: *Socos*

Contrary to general belief, in more than two-thirds of the 2,337 recognized peasant communities of Peru private rather than

[73] *Caretas*, no. 455, Apr. 17–27, 1972, p. 6.

[74] Nevertheless, military coordinators remain in each sugar cooperative, although controlled now by SINAMOS. In addition, the Center of Agricultural Production Sugar Cooperatives (CECOAAP) continues to make many of the basic policy decisions regarding production without worker participation. For additional details, see Douglas E. Horton, "A Preliminary Study of Agrarian History and Agrarian Reform in Northern Peru," dittoed manuscript, Land Tenure Center, University of Wisconsin, Madison, May 1, 1973, esp. part 5, pp. 80–128.

communal holdings predominate, according to the census of 1961. It is the present government's intention, as suggested by the Peasant Communities Statute of 1970, to restore legitimately communal property within the structure of a community co-operative. The dimensions of the problem in carrying out this objective are suggested by the highly privatized nature of the community of Socos.[75]

The main settlement of the 5,100-hectare community is nestled in a small intermontane valley of mixed property holdings of both hacienda and community, about thirty minutes by vehicle over excellent gravel highway into the hills to the west of Ayacucho. The community supports a total population of about 2,500 and has added to its lands on two occasions during the past generation by purchasing neighboring haciendas.

Socos has felt more than most communities in the department of Ayacucho the effects of modernization. The old customs and communal traditions have eroded gradually because of its proximity to Ayacucho. Teachers, government officials, and *comuneros* alike commute regularly from the capital to Socos, often maintaining homes in both places. Property in the community is divided almost exclusively into private holdings. The only communal lands remaining are a few small plots allotted each year to the person who is responsible for the annual community *fiesta*. When the community expanded its lands through purchase from its neighbors, lots were awarded within the new properties to individuals on the basis of the size of their contribution towards the purchase price of the entire hacienda.

As a result, those with wealth in the community have been able to extend their power in both land and positions of authority. A very stratified community has emerged. The proximity of the community to Ayacucho, however, has served as an escape valve.

The internal authority structure is somewhat confused by the recent change in status to district capital. The community council does continue to function at infrequent intervals now as the municipal council—but with little participation by the population at large. The only communal acts which are still practiced are the annual cleaning of the irrigation canal, construction or repair of community roads, and maintenance of the recently in-

[75] Drawn from D. S. Palmer, "'Revolution from Above,'" pp. 250–253. Based on field research between July 1971 and January 1972.

stalled potable water system; even in these limited cases, the wealthy pay to have the work done for them.

The representatives of the Office of Peasant Communities of the subzone have come to Socos to give lectures on the Peasant Communities Statute. However, the statute itself has not yet been implemented here. The Ayacucho Office of Peasant Communities indicated that it realizes Socos will be very difficult to deal with; thus they have not attempted to thrust the statute upon Socos to date. Authorities in Socos—the wealthy members of the community who have benefited most by the *status quo*—note that if the statute were applied, they would dissolve the community.[76]

In Socos implementing the statute would be difficult: individualism is high, communal collaboration low, and the *status quo* favoring the privileged position of the few is maintained (in part because the government has not pushed the implementation of the statute and in part because those less favored by the *status quo* have the option of "escaping" to nearby Ayacucho even while maintaining their residences in Socos). It is precisely this *status quo* which the military government has pledged itself to change by its new communities policy.[77]

Decline in Peasant Well-Being: Millpo

Millpo is the largest single hacienda expropriated thus far under the agrarian reform in Ayacucho.[78] It was also one of the first to be affected, in October 1969. It is comprised of 7,635 hectares, of which 93 are dedicated to dry farming and 6,540 to pasture. Situated between 11,000 and 14,000 feet about 70 kilometers south of Ayacucho, it is accessible to vehicular traffic over the most precarious of mountain roads. The road itself, built by the former owners in 1967, was virtually impassable by late 1971.

[76] What they do not seem to realize is that when a community formally disassociates itself, the Peasant Communities Office is empowered to reorder man-land relationships in the ex-community. Articles 112–114, Supreme Decree no. 37-70A, Feb. 17, 1970.

[77] Other examples could be cited, in which the maintenance of the *status quo* in marginal areas is beneficial to the community, as in that minority of communities in which communal holdings already predominate. See D. S. Palmer, " 'Revolution from Above,' " pp. 260–267.

[78] Drawn from D. S. Palmer, " 'Revolution from Above,' " pp. 247–250. Based on field research between July 1971 and January 1972.

Eighty-eight families residing on the property have been declared beneficiaries under the agrarian reform. The plans of the subzone call for Millpo to be included in a large associative enterprise (PIAR) of twelve ex-haciendas in the area, totaling some 25,000 hectares, which will specialize in cattle raising.

The property was valued in 1966 at over 2 million soles (about $70,000) by the Agricultural Bank when a loan of 1 million soles was granted for the raising of potatoes and for cattle improvements. In 1970, however, the same property was valued at 102,000 soles (about $2,350) by the agrarian reform for the purpose of paying the owner for the expropriated hacienda. The owners have initiated a legal battle under the law to protest this valuation. This accounts in part for the failure of the property to be adjudicated to the beneficiaries to date, and for the failure to begin a large-scale program of credit, technical assistance, and cooperative management training for the beneficiaries.

Before its expropriation, the farm was considered by many in Ayacucho to be a model hacienda in the process of modernization through the strenuous efforts of the owner's son, an agricultural engineer educated in Peru and abroad. He set up a school for the children of the workers, bought improved cattle for breeding stock, and led the establishment of an agricultural producers' cooperative. In addition, the owner's son and his wife established their residence on the hacienda itself. The family was astounded when its property was affected.

The son claimed that animosities between his family and that of the area's agrarian reform director, also a member of a family of large Ayacucho landowners, were the main reason for the expropriation, which, he said, violated the 1969 Agrarian Reform Law. He carried his case directly to the president and was told, he recalls, that he was indeed correct, but that the expropriation could not be reversed because it would suggest that the government was weakening in its resolve to pursue the agrarian reform to its fullest extent. However, the agrarian reform official in Ayacucho was soon replaced, and the owner's son was offered a high position with the government in partial compensation for the loss of the hacienda.

The son sold the entire herd of improved cattle on the farm for slaughter, and the debt to the Agricultural Bank was defaulted. The beneficiaries were left to their own devices. Because the hacienda was still at an intermediate stage between affectation and adjudication, no program of orientation and technical assistance was organized by the subzone office of the agrarian reform. The only assistance received through 1971 was an occasional visit by an extension agent. One Quechua-speaking beneficiary was sent in 1971 to a two-week leaders training program in Huancayo, which was conducted in Spanish. Understandably enough, he learned very little there.

In December 1971, the scene at Millpo was a desolate one. Families were on the verge of starvation. The improved pasturelands had been ruined by indiscriminate grazing by the families' own animals. A drought compounded the peasants' difficulties.

A combination of the elements, man, and the government had turned the peasants from hope to despair in a few short years. The government had affected the entire property under the law at the very moment the government's representatives had approved the plan by the owner's son to turn over a large portion of the hacienda to the *colonos* and retain a portion for himself and his family, also under the law. The cattle were sold by the former owners, preventing the *colonos* from receiving an income from them. The owners had alternatives available to them; most of the peasants had no choice but to stay on the land, waiting for governmental assistance, which was not forthcoming. The legal battle continued, resources and assistance were not available, and the plight of the peasants grew daily more desperate.

Alternate Peasant Organizations under the Military Government: The Problem of the National Linkage

The establishment of the Confederación Nacional Agraria (CNA) in May 1972 was perhaps the best indication of overall Military Government policy toward extragovernmental peasant linkages to the national system. FENCAP and other groups like it were free to continue to exist, but they were formally deprived of their ability to represent peasants in any official capacity. The fate of these organizations is suggested by a follow-up visit by one of the authors to some FENCAP facilities and conversations with government and federation officials from June through August 1971.[79]

As one high government official put it, the objective of the Mil-

[79] S. C. Bourque's interviews with FENCAP leaders. For earlier data, see Bourque, "Cholification and the Campesino."

itary Government was to reduce FENCAP's effectiveness by breaking its internal solidarity and by snipping off its ties to the party. In pursuit of that end, the military government offered various FENCAP leaders attractive government positions ostensibly dealing with the peasantry. Several FENCAP leaders accepted the offers, only to find them withdrawn. The credentials of these leaders were severely compromised. From APRA's point of view the leaders were collaborating with the military, whereas the peasants perceived that these leaders had lost access to their sources of assistance.

How were the leaders sucked into the scheme? On the one hand they received little support from APRA after 1968. Unlike in the Belaúnde and Prado years, when the party had access to patronage through congressional funds, government funding became more difficult to come by. In addition, FENCAP leaders were apparently dealing with a revolutionary military which espoused and was beginning to implement many of the same programs which FENCAP had advocated for years.

By 1971 the military's strategy toward FENCAP was taking its toll. The organization itself had split over differences in the degree of support to offer the military regime. While the national offices of FENCAP maintained APRA ties and discreet opposition, a group centered in the south split from APRA and maintained a policy of support. The central office in Huancayo was dormant, as was the office in Cuzco. On the other hand, there was a new FENCAP office in Tarma with a *campesino* training center, financed by USAID grants, which provided area farmers with technical skills and advice on stimulating the application of the new agrarian reform law.[80]

FENCAP's Federation of Rice Workers (FETAP) was working on all twenty-two rice-growing haciendas in the Jequetepequete valley in 1969. By July 1971 the office was quiet, the local FETAP newspaper was no longer published, and some leading FETAP *campesinos* had taken jobs with the military government in other parts of Peru. However, FETAP's remaining leaders argued that work went on as before.[81] They noted that

[80] Agency for International Development (USAID) Memorandum, July 7, 1971, USAID/Peru, Lima.

[81] Interview by S. C. Bourque with Pedro Cáceres, secretary general, FETAP, July 1971.

military officers had visited the office and agreed to leave FETAP alone. The FETAP leaders saw little change in their relationship with the government between 1968 and 1971 because the military regime had not shuffled local functionaries of the Ministry of Labor. This permitted FETAP to maintain the same situation of privilege and patronage under the military government which they had enjoyed during the Belaúnde regime.

The FENCAP case suggests that it is difficult though not impossible for alternate channels of access to maintain themselves under the present circumstances. Although the military government feels no need to overtly repress such groups, it does appear to view them as a threat. The military has deprived these organizations of their representational roles at the national level, has cut off some of their traditional sources of funding, and has made efforts to undermine their leadership. Current government policy toward these groups appears more guided by the military's fear of their close relationship with organized farm labor than by any objective assessment of their potential to provide the linkage presently missing between the peasantry and the national system.

CONCLUSIONS

The emergence of the masses on the national stage precipitated in Peru a shift from ineffective and incompletely institutionalized democratic forms to a modernizing regime directed by the military. Concomitantly, there has been a shift from representational forms of integration set essentially by society to forms set essentially by government.

The military's attempt to implement its policies in rural areas, with wide variations in social mobilization and integration, has posed problems. In areas where social mobilization and integration are high, such as the North Coast, the government faces a dilemma and a challenge. On the one hand, these are citizens who were relatively more favored under the old order and who often had organizational ties to the center. Consequently, they are the group most likely to oppose the modernizing regime's policies and the group most capable of organizing to make demands upon the government. At the same time, however, these citizens are best equipped and most able to run the institutions which the government wishes to impose. It is the complexity of dealing with the various levels of integration in the social-mobilization process which scholars emphasize in predicting the failure of reform-oriented military regimes.

The Peruvian government may be distinguished from most military regimes by its ability to recognize and act upon the demands of the most mobilized rural sectors. The pragmatic stance of the government in facing up to crisis, well-illustrated in the case of Cayaltí and the North Coast sugar cooperatives, has permitted it to utilize the creative capacity of citizens in organizations which it has promoted. At the same time, such a position maintains the military regime's image as a reformist force.[82]

While less-mobilized areas may be theoretically more submissive to the imposition of policies from above, they require most resources and attention if government is to have its way. In a context of scarce resources, however, the most mobilized areas are virtually assured of receiving a disproportionate share of those resources. Hence the marginal areas may well be left, by and large, to their own devices for the nonce, whatever the present military government might want to do there.[83]

In regard to our second hypothesis we have seen that the shift, in 1968, from representational forms flowing from society to an authoritarian form flowing from government, has freed decision-making bodies from constraints previously imposed by the intervention of disparate interest groups and political parties in the policy-formulation process. This allows a government which wishes to do so to extend its role in the wider society and rapidly embark on new ventures. Since 1968 Peru has witnessed a remarkable expansion of government's formal role in society.

The caveat, of course, is that increased power involves increased responsibility. The combination of a dramatic increase in the legitimate limits of state intervention with an ideology which declares the state's obligation to respond to these demands inevitably creates the most difficult of situations. As government becomes the sole legitimate channel for the satisfaction of de-

[82] The explanation for this ability rests primarily, we believe, on the internal dynamics of the Peruvian military and takes us beyond the scope of this paper.

[83] Only the massive infusion of new resources could appreciably change this picture, given the present regime's unwillingness to effect significant redistribution of internal resources. This unwillingness is one reason for the importance currently attached by the military to the exploration for oil in the Peruvian jungle and the willingness of the government to provide favorable terms to foreign oil concerns for that exploration.

mands, the number and level of demands placed upon it dramatically increase. Such a dynamic could jeopardize the ability of the regime to carry out its objectives. Extreme alternatives to a decline in the legitimacy of the government include social revolution on the one hand and increased authoritarianism and repression on the other.

Many Peruvian scholars have predicted the likelihood of such occurrences.[84] Our own conclusion, based on an examination of the experience of the military government in rural areas of Peru over the last five years appears less dramatic but more significant. We anticipate continued successful tension management by the military regime in its policies towards rural areas. That is to say, the military will probably continue to be able to construct a network of local and regional units of participation in rural Peru. The actual process of implementing this policy, however, is through continued adjustment of legislation—not to mention the eventual adjustment of ideology—when the government is confronted by strong citizen opposition. This is likely, whatever the objectives of the military organizers, to result in a much wider variation in practice than the organizers have envisioned in principle.

Successful tension management and policy adjustment are no mean tasks, particularly in conjunction with the government's objective of directing the social-mobilization process. If our expectation is correct, Huntington's hypothesis regarding the relationship between low aggregate social mobilization and success by reformist military regimes appears supported in this case. However, the distinction we have made regarding the importance of the various levels of social mobilization and integration within the rural sectors of a country reveals this regime's ability to respond effectively to the most-mobilized rural sectors. Such a demonstrated capacity by the Peruvian government distinguishes it from most other military regimes and suggests the basis for continued success.

[84] For example, Julio Cotler, Heraclio Bonilla, and Aníbal Quijano Obregón, among others, in the new journal *Sociedad y Política* (published in 1972 and 1973 until it was closed by the regime).

6

Land Reform and Social Conflict in Peru

Colin Harding

The agrarian reform program which the military government of Peru has been carrying out since June 1969 is the first serious attempt to make fundamental changes in the country's agrarian structure and to find overall solutions to problems that have been growing increasingly pressing in the course of decades of debate and piecemeal legislation. By 1976 some 11 million hectares of land should have been transferred to 340,000 families; by the end of July 1974, just under 5 million hectares had been allocated to 196,523 families, mainly organized into production cooperatives (CAPs) and *sociedades agrícolas de interés social* (SAISs) of various sizes.[1] Adjudications of land tend to be on a very large scale and are proceeding at a fast pace: in May 1974, for example, the first substantial transfers of land in the department of Huánuco involved 21,493 hectares, 1,200 families, 3 CAPs, and 2 *comunidades campesinas*, as well as several groups of individual peasants.[2] All this constitutes a far more radical assault on the problems of the rural sector than anything previously contemplated. Even so, the direct effects of the program of land redistribution will be limited in important ways. About two-thirds of all cultivated land in Peru will be affected by the reform, but only 25 percent of the natural pasture; only about one-third of the rural population will benefit directly from the land redistribution, and very small peasant proprietors (*minifundistas*) are likely to be as badly off after the reform is completed as they were

An earlier and briefer version of this essay appears in Rory Miller, Clifford Smith, and John Fisher (eds.), *Social and Economic Change in Modern Peru* (Centre for Latin American Studies, University of Liverpool, Monograph No. 6, 1976).

[1] *La Crónica*, Lima, 22 Sept. 1974.

[2] *La Crónica*, Lima, 7 Aug. 1974.

before it. About 43 percent of farmland will remain in private hands in 1976.[3]

Even within these limitations, the reform process has been a cumulative one: each new step has created new situations that require further action, new demands and expectations to be met, leading to further experiments and improvisation. The aim of this article is to show that, once a political decision had been made to carry out a thoroughgoing agrarian reform, the conflicting interests and claims upon the land released by the process itself made either increasing radicalization or tougher repression inevitable. In fact, there have been elements of both strategies present in government policy towards the rural sector so far, within the overall context of a move to bring the entire area under some form of central control.

SOME HISTORICAL BACKGROUND

As in other Latin American countries the "land problem" in Peru has traditionally been analyzed in terms of the opposition between the great estate (*latifundio*) and small peasant holdings (*minifundios*) surrounding it. The former are believed to monopolize land, water, credit, and other resources at the expense of the vastly more numerous *minifundistas*. On the coast of Peru this situation has been depicted as one of large commercial estates, employing wage laborers, dominating and destroying impoverished communities of independent peasant farmers, while in the Sierra, "feudalism" still prevailed into the 1960s, the landlord monopoly being exerted through the maintenance of precapitalist relations of production. Both views derive to some extent from the works of José Carlos Mariátegui, who saw clearly the penetration of capitalism into the export-oriented plantations of the coast but considered that this process had not yet reached the backward and isolated highlands, where the *gamonal* still held sway.[4]

[3] Douglas E. Horton, *Land Reform and Reform Enterprises in Peru*. LTC-IBRD Report (Madison, Wisc., 1974), pp. 78–79. Horton's work is the only comprehensive analysis of the Peruvian land reform to appear so far.

[4] "In the Sierra, the *latifundio* has completely retained its feudal character, putting up a much stronger resistance than the *comunidades* to the development of a capitalist economy." José Carlos Mariátegui, in *Siete Ensayos de Interpretación de la Realidad Peruana*, quoted by Carlos Malpica, *El Problema de la Tierra* (Lima, 1970), p. 300.

Although there are strong elements of truth in this view, the administrators of the current reform program have discovered that this presentation of the agrarian problem in terms of concentration of resources is misleading. Outside the big sugar plantations, there are many areas of the coast where small-scale commercial agriculture is well developed,[5] but it is in the Sierra that figures showing concentration of landownership are particularly deceptive. Legal ownership does not necessarily imply effective control over resources, and fragmentation of economic units turns out to be a greater problem for reform administrators than concentration. With the exception of a few modern ranches employing wage labor, Sierra properties were really clusters of tenants cultivating parcels of land or grazing animals on the pastures;[6] in other words, *latifundios* were frequently little more than shells containing large numbers of *minifundios*. Many estates on the coast, even some of the sugar plantations, also had many so-called *feudatarios*, with central administration either nonexistent or strictly limited.[7]

Since at least the 1920s, the Peruvian countryside has been the scene of bitter struggles between landowners and their tenants of one sort or another[8] (the Colombian term *usuario campesino* is convenient here, as it can cover *comuneros* and all others who

[5] Ford quotes a 1950 study showing that only 5 percent of farms in the departments of Tacna, Moquegua, and Arequipa were of more than five hectares each. T. R. Ford, *Man and Land in Peru* (Gainesville, Fla., 1955; reissued, New York, 1971), p. 62.

[6] Even the most modern ones had large numbers of tenants right up to 1969. The estates of the Cerro de Pasco Corporation in 1955 covered around 300,000 hectares and contained 52,000 sheep belonging to the workers and shepherds employed by the corporation; these sheep represented 17.33 percent of the total number of animals on the estates. Figures quoted by Juan Martínez Alier, *Los Huacchilleros del Perú* (Paris, 1973), p. 6. Many of the ideas on Andean haciendas expressed in this article are derived from the work of Dr. Martínez. Similar views are also developed in Horton, *Land Reform*, especially pp. 28–29.

[7] McClintock cites the case of CAP Santa Elena, in the Virú valley, which even in 1974 had one hundred *feudatarios* and only about fifty wage laborers. Cynthia McClintock, "The Impact of Agrarian Reform Organizations on the Attitudes and Behavior of Organization Members in Peru," unpublished manuscript, MIT, Department of Political Science (May 1974), p. 11.

[8] The early struggles of the different kinds of tenants in the department of Piura may be found in Hildebrando Castro Pozo, *El Yanaconaje en las Haciendas Piuranas* (Lima, 1947), passim.

have some claim on hacienda resources) over attempts by the former to exert effective control of land, either by collecting rent (in kind or labor) or by direct cultivation of the land. Tenants have done better in this struggle than some writers on the subject are inclined to admit, and in many cases they had already freed themselves from any sort of effective landlord control before agrarian reform came onto the political agenda.[9] The growing strength of some of the tenant groups on the coast was translated, from the 1920s onwards, into a growing body of legislation designed to protect their security of tenure and relative freedom to conduct their own businesses. By the 1950s, landowners in even the remote areas of the Sierra had decided that "feudalism" was no longer a paying proposition for the idlest absentee;[10] they either gave up altogether, abandoning their land to its occupants, or tried to sell it to them in individual parcels if they had any residual influence left. Alternatively, the most enterprising saw the way ahead in the introduction of wage labor on their estates, and the eviction of most of the tenants and pasture renters.[11]

During this period, a dual process was under way, influenced by the growing commercial opportunities brought about by better communications and the growth of internal and external markets for wool, meat, and grain. Both "landlords" and "peasants" sought to capitalize on the opportunities now opening to them and therefore had equal though conflicting interests in changing the *status quo*, or (in the case of tenants) preserving those aspects of it which suited them.[12] To the extent that tenants resisted conversion into wage laborers, or eviction, they can be said to have won this secular battle, and the fact that agrarian capitalism has had such a stunted growth in large areas of Peru is mainly due to the ability of peasants both inside and outside the haciendas to defend their perceived interests. It is this ability that the

[9] The growing political strength of tenants was noted by Ford in the early 1950s. Ford, *Man and Land*, p. 88.

[10] Malpica notes that only 11 percent of all rural properties in Peru still maintained precapitalist relations of production by the 1960s and that even in the Sierra they were in a minority. Malpica, *El Problema*, pp. 359–361.

[11] This is the process decribed by Solomon Miller in the 1950s in the highlands of the department of La Libertad. S. Miller, "The Proletarianization of a Tenant Farmer Society," in Julian H. Steward, ed., *Contemporary Change in Traditional Societies* (Urbana, Ill., 1967), vol. 3, pp. 133–225.

[12] These conflictive developments are well described by Virgilio Roel in his *La Economía Agraria Peruana* (Lima, 1959), 2 vols.

present agrarian reform authorities, and the institutions they are creating, are finding so troublesome.[13] The weapons used in the struggle were land occupations and the formation of unions, of tenants to begin with, and later of wage laborers, too; these tactics are still very much in use in the Peruvian countryside today, despite the vastly changed circumstances.[14] The army and police were traditionally a landlord monopoly; but violence was not, nor was the legal machinery, which some peasant groups learned to exploit with considerable skill. Political patronage, however cynically exploitative, also served its purpose in giving *campesinos* access to resources at certain times, particularly in the 1945–1948 period. In time, social differentiation in the countryside naturally increased, and some were better able to defend themselves than others—*yanaconas*, as a group, were far better off than migrant laborers or subtenants, for example, to such an extent that they are on opposite sides of the fence in the struggles that are still going on today. The government now finds itself caught between the extremes of sharecroppers and contractors who became, or were in the process of becoming, small proprietors of commercial farms, and casual laborers and genuine *minifundistas* who have never gained anything from any rural program. An account of the emergence of these differing interests should help to illuminate present government policy and some of the difficulties it is encountering in trying to transform structures that are only imperfectly understood.

The agrarian question in the early decades of the twentieth century revolved around various aspects of what was called the "Indian question"—in other words, the need of the coastal plantations for unskilled wage labor on a temporary basis, and the

[13] McClintock notes that in 1974, 40 percent of CAPs still contained private parcel holders (the former *feudatarios*) and that about 15 percent included more *feudatarios* than workers, though the percentages were declining with new adjudications. She noted that the parcel holders normally take little interest in the operations of the cooperative enterprise, and in some CAPs the private holdings are growing rather than declining (McClintock, "The Impact of Agrarian Reform," p. 8).

[14] See the discussion of the coordinated policy of land occupations by unionized *campesinos*, agreed upon at the fourth national congress of the Confederación Campesina del Perú, in the mimeographed newsletter *Informativo Político*, no. 3 (Lima, May 1974), pp. 1–21.

problems of "progressive" landowners in the Sierra with the thousands of tenants and *comuneros* who were preventing them from developing modern ranching operations. The labor problem on the coast could not be solved by taking over the land of local small farmers, so recruiting agents were appointed in the villages and *comunidades* of the highlands, which were also being drawn into the growing web of commercial influences. There were, of course, other problems—water rights, credit, marketing and transport facilities, and so on. Capital and credit were problems for all but the largest sugar plantations and were solved by using sharecroppers to bring land into cultivation from the mid-nineteenth century onwards. This system was found particularly suitable for cotton cultivation, and a variant of it was later adapted for use on the agricultural frontier of the *ceja de selva*.[15] *Yanaconaje*, as the system was called on the coast, suited landowners so long as capital was short, risks high, mechanization incipient, and unions nonexistent. The first rural unions appeared almost simultaneously around the time of the First World War on the sugar plantations of the north coast, which had the only large concentrations of rural laborers, and among *yanaconas* on cotton farms in Ica, south of Lima.[16] The tenants demanded security of tenure, written contracts, payment for any work done for the landowner, and freedom to dispose of their crops once the rent had been paid. In the highlands, efforts towards the technical development and economic rationalization of stock-raising farms was making some headway in the early 1920s, and there were frequent articles in specialized journals discussing what to do with Indian shepherds and the sheep they were traditionally allowed to graze on hacienda pastures when the fields were fenced off and imported breeding stock put on them.[17] The solution to this problem was seen by dynamic landowners as the liberation of the Indian from his situation of poverty and degradation. By this, they meant his conversion from a cultivator and

[15] Ford, *Man and Land*, p. 84; Malpica, *El Problema*, p. 202.

[16] See the journal *Campesino*, no. 5 (Lima, 1973). Little has been written on this subject, but some general information can be found in the working paper by Julio Cotler and Felipe Portocarrero, "Las Organizaciones Campesinas en el Perú," 2nd ed. (Lima, 1968).

[17] See *La Vida Agricola* 3–4 (Lima, 1926) for a description of a ranch in Puno. This article is quoted extensively in Martínez, *Los Huacchilleros*, pp. 21–22.

property owner into a wage-earning shepherd, a process which proved far from easy to carry out.

President Augusto B. Leguía, whose roadbuilding (the *Ley de Conscripción Vial*) and railway projects helped to fuel the growing enthusiasm in the 1920s for "opening up" the highlands and turning them into a second Australia,[18] perceived the dangers inherent in such a process. He attempted to head them off by granting Indian communities the right to land (without specifying how much or where) under his new constitution of 1920. In this way he hoped that historic conflicts over rights to land between haciendas and *comunidades* would be resolved without the commercial expansion of the haciendas (that is, in most cases, attempts by landowners to exert effective control over land they regarded as legally theirs) impinging too much on Indian communities, which had a history of bloody rebellion in such circumstances.[19] Leguía also created a department of Indian affairs in 1921 and set up the Patronato de la Raza Indígena in the following year. He was equally aware of the threat to stability contained in widespread tenancy and growing numbers of wage laborers, and he proclaimed his belief in the encouragement of a landowning middle class while defending the big commercial plantations as absolutely essential to technical and economic progress. He may have been sincere in his belief in the desirability of small and medium-sized properties, which his irrigation schemes were supposed to create,[20] but landowners and banks had no such interest at all, being more than satisfied with the short-term advantages of tenancy arrangements and the pool of seasonal labor provided by the shortage of land. "Land for the tiller" (which is also the slogan of the current agrarian reform) may have been seen by Leguía as the best long-term solution to the problem of tenants and landless laborers, but his acts tended to be confined to sporadic demagogic gestures, such as expropri-

[18] See, for example, Manuel D. Almenara, *El Ferrocarril de Chimbote a Recuay y Cajabamba (en construcción)* (Lima, 1929).

[19] There were several in the 1920s, the most serious being at Tocroyoc and Huancané, in the southern highlands. Castro Pozo, *El Yanaconaje*, mentions an uprising by the *comuneros* of Frías and Chalaco, in Ayabaca, in the northern Andes, in 1888, in protest against the encroachments of neighboring haciendas.

[20] See *Anales del Primer Congreso de Irrigación y Colonización del Norte* (Lima, 1929), 4 vols.

ating a few abandoned haciendas and yielding to pressures from *yanaconas* for regulation of their contracts.[21]

The collapse of Leguía's regime in 1930 briefly opened the door to the growing mass parties which had become increasingly active among the laborers, tenants, and *comuneros* of the rural areas. The Partido Socialista, founded in Piura in 1930, was closely associated with the Federación General de Yanaconas y Campesinos del Perú, while the 1931 agrarian program of the APRA party was mainly aimed at *yanaconas* and other tenants on commercial farms, promising them the security of tenure and written contracts they had been demanding, and a series of government-sponsored protective and developmental measures designed to convert them into a progressive rural middle class producing food for the home market. A bill containing these provisions was debated by the Constituent Assembly in 1933, but was never promulgated, because of opposition from the Sociedad Nacional Agraria, the landowners' association, who opposed the spread of private property.[22] In Piura, the Partido Socialista, under the leadership of Hildebrando Castro Pozo, a Deputy who had been the first head of the Indian affairs department, was active in organizing *yanaconas* into unions in the rice and cotton areas of the coast, and *colonos* in the highland province of Ayabaca. The labor bureau in Lima intervened thirteen times in landlord-tenant conflicts in this area in 1934 alone, thanks to the influence of Castro Pozo, and the tenants secured negotiated contracts in many of these cases.[23] The spread and activities of these unions, which have hardly been studied at all, were among the main reasons why landowners began to abandon tenancy arrangements in the 1930s, particularly on the commercial farms of the coast. Castro Pozo saw the beginnings of this process in Piura in 1935: "The northern landowners mean to avoid all the problems arising from the demands being made upon them by suppressing *yanaconaje* on their estates and cultivating the land themselves."[24] In 1937, the landowners' magazine *La Vida Agrícola* reported a wide-

[21] Roberto Mac-Lean y Estenós, *La Reforma Agraria en el Perú* (Mexico City, 1966), p. 24.

[22] See Alfredo Saco, *El Programa Agrario del Aprismo* (Lima, 1946), p. 12.

[23] Castro Pozo, *El Yanaconaje*, passim.

[24] Castro Pozo, *El Yanaconaje*, p. 31. See also Humberto Rodríguez Pastor, *Caqui: Estudio de una Hacienda Costeña* (Lima, 1969), pp. 182–193.

spread rumor that *colonos* were to be expelled from the Talambo rice farm, on the northern coast, and there were many similar instances.[25] In the Sierra, Castro Pozo was accused of encouraging *campesinos* to invade a cattle ranch in Cajamarca, and APRA was active in forming unions of *colonos*, who were being used increasingly as laborers on the landowners' commercial operations, demanding adequate pay and more time to work on their own plots.[26] The intense political activity among tenants from the 1930s onwards can be seen from the following report, taken from the files of the Casa Grande sugar plantation; it refers to a small estate in the Virú valley, south of Trujillo, in 1946:

> On Hacienda Tomabal, the workers, who are at the same time
> *colonos* of the hacienda, went out on strike, presenting a
> list of demands which included nonpayment of ground or
> pasturing rent for the land they occupy, absolute preference in
> the use of irrigation water, and release from having to
> work for the hacienda. In other words, these people would
> become owners of the hacienda.[27]

It can be seen that tenants in both coastal valleys and some increasingly commercial estates in the Sierra—where cash rentals were becoming more common by the 1950s[28]—saw themselves more and more as farmers in competition with the estate management, and anxious to free themselves from any remaining obligations to it, while retaining use of the estate's land. APRA, in preelection propaganda during 1945, had promised tenants in both the highlands and the coast that they would not have to pay rent any more after the party came to power and that the estates would be divided up among them. This did not happen, of course, but the unrest was sufficient to accelerate the process of

[25] *La Vida Agrícola*, vol. 14, no. 169 (Dec. 1937), p. 1045.

[26] References to unions of *colonos* in the sierra of La Libertad in the 1945–1948 period can be found in the archive of Empresa Andina San Leonardo, in the Centro de Documentación Agraria, Lima. There is an account of strikes on haciendas Campodén and Salagual, in the highlands of Cajamarca, in 1946–1947, in the archives of Empresa Agrícola Chicama, Casa Grande. Martínez, *Los Huacchilleros* (pp. 16–21) describes unions and strikes in the central Sierra during this same period.

[27] Confidential report in the archive of Empresa Agrícola Chicama, Hacienda Casa Grande, 1946.

[28] Ford, *Man and Land*, p. 95.

evictions, which was not effectively halted by the *Ley de Yana-conaje* passed, with APRA sponsorship, in 1947.[29] President Bustamante, who had three Apristas in his cabinet for a while, was moved to denounce APRA for stirring up the Indians,[30] and the general climate of rebellion helped to hasten the military coup which toppled the Bustamante government in October 1948.

The whole process of rural unionization was brought to an abrupt halt by the regime of General Manuel Odría, but even he was obliged to pass a series of laws halting evictions of tenants on the coast and fixing rents.[31] The 1947 legislation in favor of *yanaconas* had provoked a mass of litigation, mainly because it was not at all clear which people it applied to, with several different forms of rural tenancy lumped together as *yanaconaje*. Consequently, *aparceros, partidarios, colonos,* and others claimed that the legislation applied to them, while landowners in the Sierra insisted that it did not.

EARLY REFORM MEASURES

By the time political parties were functioning again, leading up to the 1956 elections, they were all promising agrarian reform. The winner that year, Manuel Prado, a prominent member of the traditional coastal oligarchy and director of Empresa Agrícola Chicama, appointed a commission soon after taking office to look into ways of fostering small and medium-sized private property in the countryside. By this time, large landowners with diversified interests had already begun to parcel up and sell their properties in the Sierra, sometimes as a defensive measure against "invaders."[32] Unions had begun to reappear, particularly

---

29 Thomas M. Davies, "The Indigenismo of the Peruvian Aprista Party," in *Hispanic American Historical Review*, vol. 51, no. 4, Nov. 1971, pp. 626–645.

30 "In some places in the Sierra Indian uprisings are being encouraged for seditious purposes." José Luis Bustamante y Rivero, *Mensaje a la Nación* (Lima, 1948), p. 7.

31 Law 11042 (27 June 1949) halted eviction proceedings and fixed rent in kind.

32 Mac-Lean y Estenós notes that the church was one of the first landowners to begin selling off its properties in the Sierra. Mac-Lean, *La Reforma Agraria,* p. 96. A similar point about the declining fortunes of the landowners in the Sierra department of Cajamarca and their decision to begin selling up in the 1950s is made by John Gitlitz, "Opposition to the Peruvian Agrarian Reform," unpublished manuscript, University of North Carolina, Department of Political Science (May 1974), pp. 9–10. An example of the sale of parcels of land

in the La Convención valley, a subtropical region in the southern department of Cusco. In response, the prime minister, Pedro Beltrán, set up the Instituto de Reforma Agraria y Colonización (IRAC) in 1959 and the Servicio de Investigación y Promoción Agraria (SIPA) the following year, both to stem the demands for land reform and help modernize agriculture. When the report finally appeared, in 1960, land invasions in the Sierra were becoming widespread, and alarm was turning to panic in some sectors in Lima. The commission's report spoke of the need to stop the process of concentration of landownership, to promote small and medium-sized farms, to abolish inhuman forms of labor relations, and so on, but the draft law they had prepared made few concrete recommendations beyond the creation of more land through colonization and irrigation schemes. Commercial estates were to remain untouched. The members of the commission, all closely connected with landowning interests, could quite sincerely say that inhuman labor conditions should be stopped, because it was clear that "precapitalist" relations were not in their interest; the rural unrest spreading like wildfire in the Peruvian Andes was mainly a consequence of the efforts of "modernizing" landowners to change these relations.[33] The abolition of "feudalism" meant the consolidation of wage-labor and a rural proletariat, and such a land reform was quite clearly favorable to the commercial landowning interests who were in power in Lima. Those estates already using wage-labor as the predominant form were exempted. But the commission's report was shelved, and nothing had been done by the time another military junta took power in mid-1962.

The attack on "feudalism" became the main object of the liberal agrarian reform programs that were put forward in the early 1960s. In 1962, Acción Popular's presidential candidate, Fernando Belaúnde, said:

---

as a defensive measure is found in the files of Empresa Agrícola Chicama, referring to a property in the highlands of Cajamarca, Hacienda Huacraruco, where in the late 1950s tenants were sold land on the boundaries to discourage incursions by the neighboring *comunidad* of La Huaraclla.

[33] A brief description of the events of this period in the Sierra can be found in Mac-Lean, *La Reforma Agraria*, pp. 124 ff.; Malpica, *El Problema*, pp. 239 ff. Malpica notes that the struggles in the highlands of Cajamarca were against "feudal remnants," yet he shows convincingly that conflicts there were provoked by landowners' attempts to evict their "serfs" (p. 235).

We understand by agrarian reform the elimination of the feudal structure, which is the greatest obstacle to the overall development of the country. With this in mind, we will encourage the redistribution of rural property, which presupposes the abolition of the feudal *latifundio* and serfdom.[34]

This sort of analysis of the problem had some important implications for policy. All forms of indirect tenure came to be regarded as feudal, as the term *feudatario* used in the 1964 Agrarian Reform Law (and the present one) indicates. Security of tenure was replaced by ownership of the land they worked as the promise made to all *feudatarios*. An early result of this kind of thinking could be seen in the valley of La Convención, where *arrendires* were given ownership titles following the strikes and land occupations there in the late 1950s and early 1960s. Many of the *arrendires* were substantial commercial producers of coffee and employers of labor (*allegados, suballegados,* and *habilitados*) and it was the *arrendires* who became owners of the land. The problem was not solved; the *allegados*, who had provided the militant rank and file of the union movement, were left leaderless when Hugo Blanco was arrested, and they had to make do with the military junta's reform, which left them no better off than before. Similar problems have dragged on to the present day.

The other implication, derived from the 1960 report, was that nonfeudal estates were blameless and should be left alone if they were efficiently run. An attempt by the vice-president in the government elected, with military support, in 1963, to introduce some worker participation in the running of the big sugar plantations was defeated in Parliament, and the law which was eventually passed in July 1964 was a compromise document which exempted commercial estates controlled by limited companies from the effects of the reform.

The period leading up to, and immediately following, the publication of the 1964 Agrarian Reform Law was one of intense rural conflict, particularly in the highlands; by early 1964, 114 haciendas had been occupied by *comuneros* and others in Cusco

[34] Mac-Lean, *La Reforma Agraria*, p. 69.

alone,[35] and it proved almost impossible to remove the "invaders" and their sheep, however much force was used. The struggle for control of resources between haciendas and *campesinos* was coming to a head, propelled, it seems, by population pressures within the communities that were exacerbated by the eviction of tenants and sheep from neighboring haciendas. The failure of "progressive" landowners to impose wage labor, or even cash rents, on reluctant *campesinos* was evident, and the effects of the 1964 reform were largely limited to recognizing that the *campesinos* had the land and could not be removed from it. The view that this constitutes "feudalism" persists, however, and is found today on the extreme Left: Bandera Roja, a Maoist group, has declared that feudalism has not been eliminated by the current agrarian reform program, because members of SAIS continue to cultivate small plots of land and graze sheep on the pastures while being obliged to work for the central administration, just like before.[36] But, the problem faced by the administrative councils of SAIS, like the modernizing landlords before them, is not how to keep the peasants tied to the land, but how to separate them from it; in this case, how to induce *conductores de parcelas* and *huacchilleros* to work longer and harder on the cooperatively-held land and not so much on their private plots.[37] It might be argued that the agrarian reform should never have promised "land to the tiller," but things were not seen in that light by most people involved in 1969.

Another common belief about *latifundios*, enshrined in article 47 of the 1933 Constitution, in the 1960 commission report, in the 1962 *ley de bases*, and in Law 15037 of 1964, is that they make inefficient use of resources and have unused land which should be expropriated, to be redistributed among neighboring *comunidades*. Landowners tend to reply that, in the highlands, grazing land is poor and has to be used very extensively. This was not accepted by the *comuneros* and shepherds, who saw themselves and their sheep excluded from fenced pastures, which were then

35 Ibid., p. 135.

36 *Informativo Político*, 3 (Lima, 1974), p. 33.

37 McClintock notes that the program to eliminate *huaccha* sheep on SAIS Cahuide has had to be delayed because of opposition from the members. McClintock, "Impact of Agrarian Reform," p. 18. In cooperatives in the Virú valley, workers typically earn twice as much from their own animals as they do from working on the CAP (p. 24).

left idle for months on end; they naturally cut the wires and put their sheep back on the paddocks which were being rotated.[38] They are still doing this in some areas in the Sierra, only the wires now belong to SAIS, and they are still excluded from the improved pastures, the victims of the logic of commercial stock-raising.[39] The other point about supposedly surplus land is that there are generally conflicting claims upon it—tenants consider they should get first priority in any redistribution of land, and outsiders should wait. Conflicts between hacienda tenants, *comuneros*, casual laborers, and *minifundistas* over who should benefit from the forthcoming reform became common in the early 1960s; Mac-Lean quotes one case in Cerro de Pasco where a hacienda was being parcelled up by the owners among its tenants when the estate was invaded and occupied by a neighboring *comunidad*.[40] This is the sort of problem that the SAISs are supposed to solve, but putting different groups of *campesinos* with different perceived interests together in a single unit and pretending they were all previously victims of feudal exploitation solves very little. The problems which continue are more the result of an advanced degree of individualism among the *campesinos* than a consequence of a precapitalist mode of production.

The first agrarian reform legislation in Peru, in 1962, which declared La Convención and Lares to be an agrarian reform zone, was still a piecemeal measure, designed to solve a particular problem and deal with a situation far away which was beginning to worry the people in Lima. This it did quite well, as mentioned previously, by favoring relatively well-off tenants at the expense of smaller subtenants and laborers; the reform in La Convención sealed the fate of landowners' attempts to use traditional tenancy arrangements to carry out a transition to wage labor. Instead, 260 tenants received titles to their land in July

[38] There is a case of this nature described in the files of Empresa Agrícola Chicama, referring to Hacienda Huacraruco and the *comunidad* of San Juan de Cachilgón, in 1943.

[39] A conflict between the administration of SAIS José Carlos Mariátegui and the *comuneros* of Cospán and La Huaraclla, in Cajamarca, over use of pastures is described in Hernán Caycho et al., *Investigación sobre Comunidades Campesinas y Reforma Agraria en Cajamarca*, typescript, CENCIRA, Lima, 1973.

[40] Hacienda Huarautambo, in Mac-Lean, *La Reforma Agraria*, p. 124.

1963, while 16,000 who were theoretically entitled to some benefits got nothing.[41]

The invasions in the highlands and, to a lesser extent, on the coast in the early 1960s generally came at the end of a long legal battle, which began in some cases in the 1920s. These generally seem to have been led by the wealthier *comuneros,* who needed more land for their sheep.[42] The eviction of invaders by the police, at the cost of many deaths (211 between 1956 and 1964, according to Carlos Malpica)[43] attracted most attention, but the majority of "invaders" stayed where they were or returned time and time again. Most of the expropriations made under Law 15037 were merely ratifying situations which already existed. The *comuneros* of the central Sierra who received 78,417 hectares of neighboring haciendas in 1964 objected strongly to being obliged to pay for land they already controlled and had always "owned" anyway.[44] The landowners' organizations were still powerful enough to launch a vigorous campaign in 1963–1964 against expropriation of anything other than "unused" land, and then with compensation in cash or negotiable bonds. They dominated the Consejo Nacional de Reforma Agraria, set up by President Belaúnde, as they had the 1956 commission, and they were successful in limiting the reform to land which they no longer controlled and for which they would be paid. The principle of payment in bonds was established, but they were made negotiable, exemptions from expropriation were allowed on grounds of efficiency, and industrial estates controlled by limited companies were excluded altogether, thanks to pressure in Parliament from APRA.

The quantitative achievements of Law 15037 were inevitably very modest. The present government says that 14,631 families received a total of 375,000 hectares between 1964 and 1969,[45] many of them getting only tiny *minifundios* they had previously worked as *feudatarios.* Clearly, the reform was understaffed and

[41] James Petras and Robert Laporte, *Perú: ¿Transformación Revolucionaria o Modernización?* (Buenos Aires, 1971), p. 33.

[42] This was the case in the conflict between the *comunidad* of San Pedro de Cajas and Hacienda Chinchausiri, described by Mac-Lean, *La Reforma Agraria* p. 141. A similar case between the *comunidad* of San Juan de Yánac and Hacienda Huacraruco, in Cajamarca, has lasted for more than forty years.

[43] Malpica, *El Problema*, p. 229.

[44] Mac-Lean, *La Reforma Agraria*, p. 135.

[45] Petras and Laporte, *Perú*, p. 156.

underfinanced, and the political will to push through a massive transfer of land was lacking—President Belaúnde continued to believe that what the country really needed to solve all its economic and social problems was roads, dams, and ditches.

THE MILITARY REFORM PROGRAM

It needed a change of minister before the military government which deposed Belaúnde in October 1968 could embark on its own reform program. The first minister of agriculture in the military government, General José Benavides, was closely connected with coastal landowning interests and had no intention of condoning a law which would involve expropriation of efficient commercial estates, particularly as payment was not to be made in cash. Practically all that was done of any significance between October 1968 and July 1969 was the completion of expropriation procedures for the Cerro de Pasco Corporation cattle ranches in the central highlands, which had been heavily "invaded." The resignation of General Benavides cleared the way for a more determined minister, General Jorge Barandiarán, and the publication of a new agrarian reform law on 24 June, the *dia del campesino*.

The current agrarian reform program, like its predecessor, set out with the orthodox reformist aim of giving "land to the tiller" in family farm-sized units, and also consolidating small and medium-sized private property organized along modern commercial farming lines. In many ways, it merely tidied up provisions of the previous law, ensuring that *feudatarios* received a workable plot of land and reducing the "unaffectable minimum" that landowners would be allowed to keep. There was also some mention of regional planning of the reform and of encouragement for production cooperatives, but early commentators on the actual application of the reform, including an FAO mission, said they saw little evidence that this was being put into practice.[46] In fact, few writers in the early months of the reform seemed to think it would really achieve very much, and judging by past experience, this seemed a reasonable assumption to make.[47]

[46] Petras and Laporte, *Perú*, pp. 89–92.

[47] "If the agrarian reform develops along the lines that its sponsors seem to have laid down for it, it will serve basically to strengthen and consolidate capitalism, by the creation of hundreds of thousands of small and medium

However, the immediate expropriation of the big coastal sugar plantations was an important departure from precedent; efficiency was no longer a reason for exemption. Expropriations concentrated overwhelmingly on the coastal region at first, the Sierra departments being declared agrarian reform zones only gradually. It was stated, later, that the greatest concentrations of economic power were to be found on the coast, so this region should be given priority treatment.[48] But the relative neglect of the Sierra, outside a few large ranches, has produced a great deal of resentment there, as well as giving landowners a virtually free hand to carry out their own agrarian reform and thereby help create or reinforce the problems of fragmentation of individual holdings that the reform officials now have to face.[49]

The spirit of the 1969 Agrarian Reform Law, as previously indicated, was not very different from its 1964 predecessor: the overall strategy was to strengthen commercial farming, preferably through the cooperative organization of small peasants, in order to increase the marketable surplus and expand the market for industrial goods. An AID-sponsored report of October 1969 summed up the aims of the new reform as follows:

The elimination of the traditional systems of excessively large and small landholdings, and the concomitant promotion of small and medium-size commercially viable holdings, and group operation for larger units where economies of scale would suffer from subdivision.[50]

Absolute preference was to be given for tenants of all kinds, including cash tenants and sharecropping contractors, to become owners of their land, in line with the general aim of ensuring that

---

proprietors, who are traditionally reactionary, and will work their plots individually or tied to service cooperatives of the German type" (Malpica, *El Problema*, p. 273).

[48] Jaime Llosa, "Reforma Agraria y Revolución," in *Participación*, no. 3 (Lima, Aug. 1973), p. 48. Horton (*Land Reform*) notes that nonsugar estates were not affected until the following year, 1970, but makes no attempt to account for this delay.

[49] John Gitlitz notes that private subdivisions of this kind were far advanced in the highlands of Cajamarca by 1970, with at least thirty-seven estates subdivided between 1962 and 1970. J. Gitlitz, "Opposition," p. 12.

[50] USAID-Peru, *Preliminary Analysis: Agrarian Reform Law No. 17716* (Lima, 1969), p. x.

land is directly worked by its owner and is a source of production and not of rent. The legislation made it clear that medium-sized commercial farms employing wage labor would not be touched—about 200,000 of them, according to one estimate[51]—and, if certain conditions were met, such as profit-sharing arrangements with the permanent labor-force, the unaffectable limit could be increased from 150 hectares of irrigated land on the coast, or the equivalent, to 200 hectares. This is still a very substantial holding in Peruvian coastal conditions; Thomas Carroll, in the *AID Spring Review* for 1970, noted that the law "apparently reflects the desire of the government to preserve the private entrepreneurial character of coastal agriculture."[52]

In order to encourage and consolidate this class of commercial farmers, within the socially-defined limits, landowners were given the option of carrying out their own voluntary reform, outside the areas declared agrarian reform zones. Limited companies were forbidden to hold land—another new departure—but were given time to convert themselves into general partnerships if each shareholder became the direct administrator of a portion of the estate. Estates of more than the permitted maximum could be parceled up among properly-qualified purchasers, and, as the bond compensation system did not look very attractive (the bonds were made nonnegotiable for the first time), most landowners on the coast, and many in the Sierra, took this opportunity, urged on by the minister of agriculture himself.[53]

Theoretically, those entitled to land under the reform are all *campesinos sin tierra*, which can mean anyone working on a farm who does not actually own the land—tenants of various kinds, sharecroppers, and laborers. One estimate gives a figure of at least seven hundred thousand qualified families, five hundred thousand of them in the Sierra.[54] But, in the original legislation, and following earlier examples, only the interests of tenants were protected in cases of "parcellation by private initiative," each of them being guaranteed a notional "family farm unit" of at least

[51] USAID-Peru, *Preliminary Analysis*, p. 150.

[52] Thomas Carroll, *Land Reform in Peru*. AID Spring Review Country Paper (Washington, D.C., June 1970), p. 33.

[53] See the text of a speech by General Jorge Barandiarán Pagador to the landowners of Cañete, Chincha, Pisco, and Nasca in the official publication, *Reforma Agraria Peruana: Balance a los 100 dias* (Lima, 1969), p. 21.

[54] USAID-Peru, *Preliminary Analysis*, p. 140.

three hectares. In the scramble to parcel up estates which took place all along the coast in the months following the publication of the law (and, in fact, the process was already far advanced under similar provisions of the 1964 law),[55] the permanent and temporary laborers came off very badly, despite the avowed intention of the ministry of agriculture that "permanent laborers should be furnished with land in zones not yet affected by the agrarian reform and in which parcellation by private initiative is carried out."[56] One author estimates that in the Cañete valley, south of Lima, two thousand permanent laborers (40 percent of the total labor force) were deprived of their jobs because of the smaller labor requirements of the new parcels of land.[57] There were complaints from all over the coastal region that people were being thrown out of work, or turned into casual laborers, and that purchasers of parcels were frequently not *campesinos* at all, but rather friends and relatives of the owners, who did not even live on the farm. Many "false" parcellations were also denounced, in which the estate continued to operate as a single unit, though nominally belonging to several different owners.[58] This process also threatened the existence of the laborers' unions, which had grown up along the coast since the 1950s, largely under Aprista control, but which were radicalized as a result of these experiences.

The uproar created by the laborers in the coastal valleys obliged the government to modify the conditions governing private subdivision of land after only five months (Decree Law No. 18003, 25 November 1969). The minister of agriculture explained a few months later that

[55] As noted by Gitlitz, "Opposition." In May 1974, a group of *feudatarios* from Hacienda Pomabamba, San Marcos (Cajamarca) complained that the owner of the estate had begun to parcel it up under Law 15037, and when Decree Law 17716 was published, she dismantled everything she could and left. Mimeographed leaflet, Lima, 1974.

[56] Dirección de Difusión de la Reforma Agraria, *Un Año de Reforma Agraria* (Lima, 1970).

[57] Ramón Zaldívar, "Elementos para un enfoque general de la reforma agraria peruana," in *Cuadernos Agrarios* 1 (Lima, Aug. 1971), p. 33.

[58] See, for example, the protests by the workers of Hacienda Hoja Redonda (Supe) that the 1,500-hectare hacienda had been parceled up among "ingenieros y otros allegados, miembros de la Sociedad Nacional Agraria." *Expreso*, 10 Oct. 1970.

Unfortunately, the results we had foreseen did not come about, and on the contrary we had ample proof of attempts to defeat the spirit of the Agrarian Reform Law. There was a noticeable feeling of unrest, and the normal dialogue with the unions ceased to operate. There were cases of massive dismissals of field workers, creating a climate of social tension.[59]

In all future subdivisions of land, the permanent work force would first have to be sold a piece of land to work in common, and in March 1970 subdivision of land among relatives was forbidden. However, this legislation was not made retroactive, and most parcellations were already completed by this time.[60] Nothing was done for the workers who had already suffered the consequences of private subdivision of land, to say nothing of the temporary laborers, who were not even included in the provisions of the new legislation.

In the face of continuing agitation and growing union militancy in many valleys,[61] demanding the take-over of all land and the formation of cooperatives, higher wages, and guaranteed work,[62] the government tried a number of measures, ranging from the creation of a general inspectorate of agrarian reform, to "detect and evaluate social tensions and conflicts arising in the countryside," to compulsory profit- and management-sharing schemes for permanent workers on farms created by, or untouched by, the reform legislation,[63] job security for laborers on subdivided estates,[64] and the implementation of a clause in the

[59] *El Peruano*, 23 Apr. 1970.

[60] One estimate says 90 percent of all estates were parceled up in the Ica valley south of Lima. *Expreso*, 3 Mar. 1971. One estate which had been privately subdivided and continued to operate as a single unit into 1973 was that of the Poblete family, in Barranca. See *Expreso*, 24 May 1973.

[61] A meeting was held in Cañete in August 1970 by the Comité Provincial de Trabajadores, to denounce private parcellations. See *Informativo Político*, no. 3 (Lima, May 1974), p. 8.

[62] See, for example, the letters from the Campesino Federations of Lima Department, published in *El Peruano*, 18 Mar. 1970.

[63] Articles 20 and 22 of the *Texto Unico Concordado* of Decree Law 17716 (18 Aug. 1970).

[64] *El Peruano*, 6 Mar. 1970, carried the text of Decree Law 18168, which set the penalty for dismissing permanent workers as a result of private parcellations at expropriation of the entire estate and a fine amounting to 50 percent of the value of the property.

Agrarian Reform Law—article 45—which authorized the total expropriation of estates where it could be shown that existing labor legislation was not being complied with. This clause, which was extremely vague, was now used to expropriate some of the subdivided estates in the early months of 1970,[65] under pressure from the unions, and in the teeth of violent protests from the landowners. The Peruvian Stockbreeders' Association (AGP) complained in August 1970 of a "climate of uncertainty and mistrust which discourages investment."[66] These protests had already led to the virtual suspension of article 45 in July 1970 and the subsequent appointment of committees to study the situation in the coastal valleys: for example, a commission was set up under the then head of military intelligence, General Enrique Valdez Angulo, to look into subdivisions in the Cañete valley, after a general strike there in November 1970.[67]

A famous test case arose when the 583 permanent laborers on a 1,800-hectare orange estate just north of Lima went on strike in October 1970, demanding the cancellation of a parcellation into 67 lots which had been authorized by the ministry in October 1969. The workers on this estate enjoyed high wages and good conditions, relatively speaking, won for them by years of pressure from the union, which was now fragmented, with many of the workers dismissed. The strikers demanded the conversion of the estate into a workers' cooperative and made several marches on Lima to reinforce their claim. The government clearly did not know what to do, but after a long delay the parcellation was finally annulled by executive decree in February 1971, and President Velasco hinted that there would be more to come.[68]

There can be little doubt that the government's hand was forced over private parcellations by pressures from the countryside. It had apparently underestimated the strength and determination of organized rural labor, and the expectations aroused by

[65] For example, thirty-seven parcels of Hacienda Jesús del Valle, Chancay, were expropriated (*Expreso*, 23 May 1970); the whole of Hacienda Casa Blanca Oeste, Cañete, was taken over (*El Peruano*, 18 Feb. 1970).

[66] *Boletín de la Asociación de Ganaderos del Perú*, 69, Lima, Aug. 1970, p. 9.

[67] See *Expreso*, 7 Dec. 1970.

[68] See the defence of this action by Director General of Agrarian Reform, Ing. Benjamín Samanez Concha, in *Expreso*, 21 Feb. 1971.

reform propaganda which promised social justice for all *campesinos*. The orange estate Huando was finally handed over to a production cooperative (CAP) in June 1973, after all appeals had been exhausted and government spokesmen had made repeated attempts to reassure landowners that this did not mean the imminent end of private property in the countryside and the complete collectivization of land.[69]

Cooperative forms of rural organization were, of course, one of the main aims of the 1969 law, as they had been of the previous one. The sugar estates were turned over to these theoretically self-managing enterprises by the end of 1970. But the climate of uncertainty which grew up while these battles were going on left many reform office staff uncertain about what they were supposed to be doing. For example, the director of the Ica office, Otto Schultz, complained in April 1971 that he was subject to pressures from both above and below. The Stockbreeders' Association returned to the attack in June 1971, complaining of the "justified uncertainty in many farmers and breeders, which is causing a most harmful paralysis of their activities."[70] Local landowners' associations alleged that cancellation of private parcellation constituted a threat to private property.[71] At the same time, the landowners' mounting offensive against a supposed "collectivization" of rural property was matched by growing militancy among the temporary laborers, who were excluded from both the subdivided estates and the cooperatives which were replacing them. These cooperatives were organized along strictly commercial lines, with their capacity to absorb labor dependent on their profitability,[72] which meant that sometimes even all the

[69] See the official communiqué published in *Expreso*, 23 June 1971, assuring the landowners of Ica, Pisco, and Chincha that they would not all be expropriated, small and medium property would be respected, and no massive program of collectivization was contemplated. This was reiterated in a declaration by the then head of SINAMOS in June 1973 that "the government is not heading toward forced nationalization or collectivization of the land." General Leonidas Rodríguez Figueroa, in *Participación*, no. 3 (Lima, Aug. 1973), p. 1.

[70] *Boletín de la AGP* 77/79, Lima, Apr.–June 1971, p. 5.

[71] See the statement by the Agricultural Association of the Chancay valley, published in *La Prensa*, 20 Aug. 1971; also that of the Agricultural Association of Palpa and Nasca, in *El Comercio*, 22 June 1971.

[72] Juan Martínez Alier quotes the case of Hacienda Pasamayo, in the Chancay valley, which was taken over in May 1970, under Article 45. A cooperative was formed for the thirty-three permanent laborers, excluding some twenty

permanent laborers could not be fitted in. One study estimates that 38 percent of all labor in crop farms on the coast in 1969 was in the temporary category, and goes on to explain why:

Temporary labor does not enjoy paid vacations or separation pay upon termination of employment. Because of this, producers usually try to negotiate informal short-term labor arrangements, even though the agricultural labor force is virtually permanent in character.[73]

Some of the sugar cooperatives continued, and continue, to use nonmember labor for some tasks, such as the hand-cutting of cane in the department of Lambayeque, and most rice transplanting and cotton picking is also done by contracted labor: thirty-two thousand *eventuales* in the cotton and rice areas of Piura alone.[74] The government had been forced to give way to the demands of organized rural labor but saw less need to take largely unorganized migrants and casuals into account, especially as their inclusion would make for uneconomic units of production and was generally opposed by the cooperative members.[75]

Even so, one lesson learned from the turbulent sugar cooperatives was that "closed" allocations of land, limited to full-time workers on an estate, are liable to create both pressures to get in from those on the outside and an equal determination to keep them out and maximize their own incomes by the beneficiaries. This *egoísmo de grupo*[76] has proved a serious problem for the authorities.

---

casual laborers living in the nearby village of Aucallama ("Some Rural Conflicts in Peru," mimeographed, Oxford, 1971, p. 14). Another case in the Mala valley had sixty-two permanent laborers for a cooperative that, according to the official calculations, could support only thirty-five.

[73] H. Van de Wetering, "Increased Agricultural Production through Land Redistribution: A Minor Possibility?" manuscript, Iowa State University, Ames, 1972, p. 6.

[74] "Informe sobre la Producción Agrícola, las Clases Sociales y la Situación Campesina en el Chira," mimeographed, Lima, June 1972, p. 18.

[75] McClintock notes, for example, that two CAPs in the Virú valley successfully resisted the incorporation of casual laborers as members of the cooperatives ("Impact of Agrarian Reform," p. 18).

[76] A term used by Jaime Llosa to describe the situation generated by the prosperous sugar cooperatives surrounded by areas of general poverty. *Participación*, 3, Lima, Aug. 1973, p. 51.

In order to calm down rural unrest and discipline workers' cooperatives that were taking the rhetoric of *autogestión* seriously, the government began to experiment with large-scale regional projects in 1971, taking over entire geographical areas and placing them under special commissions of administration while suitable organizational models were worked out for the different groups of claimants on the land.

One of the first of these experiments was begun in Piura, where rural militancy was becoming serious by mid-1971. Early in the year, groups of unemployed laborers and small peasants took over the landowners' association, aided and abetted by the local agrarian reform authorities,[77] but in June 1971 the Departmental Campesino Federation held its first congress and denounced both the slowness and inadequacy of the reform in the department.[78] Altogether, sixty-six estates covering forty-four thousand hectares were grouped together in a proposed Integral Project of Rural Settlement, designed to absorb more labor as well as take advantage of supposed economies of scale in production, administration of credit, extension, marketing services, and so on.[79]

The implementation of such large-scale rural reorganization projects implied a stepping-up of the tempo and scale of land expropriations. The criticisms made in 1970–1971 by Aníbal Quijano, Héctor Béjar, and others that—in Béjar's words—the reform was designed to benefit a "prosperous consumer-oriented rural bourgeoisie" which would "make the surest ally of the dominant class"[80]—valid enough at the time—were becoming less and less true, because of the dynamic that the reform had set in motion. The threat of imminent expropriation or occupation of their land made many commercial farmers abandon their estates, often taking the machinery and installations with them, and this in turn became a source of discontent and reason for expropria-

[77] See the report by the secretary-general of the Departmental Campesino Federation, in *Ediciones Voz Campesina*, 2, Lima, Dec. 1973, p. 3. Also Demetrio Reyes, "Luchas Campesinas en Piura," *Cuadernos Agrarios* 1, Aug. 1971, p. 79.

[78] Reyes, "Luchas," p. 80. See also report in *La Prensa*, 23 June 1971.

[79] Zaldívar, "Elementos," p. 43.

[80] Héctor Béjar, "La Reforma Agraria y el Momento Actual," mimeographed, Lima, 1970, p. 2.

tion.[81] In June 1971, the Agricultural Association of the valleys of Supe, Barranca, and Pativilca published a communiqué dramatically headed "We are doomed to disappear," reflecting the mood of alarm of many coastal landowners by this time and their determination to call a halt.[82]

The official political response to increasingly militant action by both sides was to draft in cadres from SINAMOS, the state social mobilization agency, in the first instance to preach the cooperative doctrine of social solidarity where the unions were strong, and organize potentially dangerous groups into controllable committees—the *asociaciones agrícolas* of *minifundistas* and casual laborers. Even at this stage, one American economist who was working with the agricultural planning office, OSPA, thought that the reform would take the road of parceling up estates among the permanent wage laborers, but he also noted the possibility that "the objective of the land redistribution program to give each agricultural worker his own parcel of land could gradually give way to the objective of creating equal income opportunities among rural people."[83] In fact, quite apart from political factors, the arithmetic of the situation was against the former solution: the land available for individual allotments, if the unaffectable areas laid down in the law were respected, would still leave some 350,000 landless laborers with nothing, quite apart from 300,000 families with less than one hectare each. On this basis, there was enough land on the coast to create 79,916 family farms, and 171,000 families qualified to receive one; in the Sierra the picture was even more bleak: 69,622 family farms for 681,000 families.[84]

Faced with this intractable situation, the government, through SINAMOS, concentrated on preparing the ground for the creation of more and bigger cooperative-style enterprises in the hope of both creating employment and equalizing incomes between enterprises of different sizes and economic potential. These activities earned the SINAMOS *promotores* the label of "agitators" from the Sociedad Nacional Agraria and its regional affiliates.

[81] An article in *Expreso*, 3 Mar. 1971, cited the case of Hacienda Santiago, in the Ica valley, where the owner refrained from sowing new cotton and removed everything he could from the property.

[82] *La Prensa*, Lima, 24 June 1971.

[83] Van de Wetering, "Increased Agricultural Production," p. 12.

[84] Figures from an official study quoted in *Peruvian Times*, 11 Dec. 1970.

This confrontation was the culmination of the conflict between the government and the commercial farmers who were originally supposed to be protected and encouraged by the reform program. The government's response was to abolish the SNA and its member associations in May 1972 and also, incidentally, to withdraw legal recognition from existing rural unions. In their place, SINAMOS proposed a hierarchy of functional organizations, grouping together the representatives of the new cooperatives, small proprietors, casual laborers, and unaffected landowners (now to be known as *trabajadores del agro*). These organizations were not to act as unions or pressure groups and were accountable to SINAMOS.[85] Not surprisingly, this initiative has been bitterly resisted by both sides, and the first congress of the Confederación Nacional Agraria (CNA), the highest body in the new structure, due to be held in mid-1974, had to be postponed repeatedly as the requisite number of local organizations had not been formed. The inaugural meeting of the CNA was finally held in Lima in October 1974.

The first local federation was formed at departmental level in Piura in February 1973. The choice of this area was again not accidental. After more than a year of peaceful demonstrations and petitions to the authorities, the *campesino* federation, FEDECAP, began a wave of land occupations in September 1972. The estates taken over had sometimes been parceled by the owner or had been exempted from expropriation, and in these cases the permanent laborers usually led the movement, as they had in other areas of the coast. In other cases, temporary laborers, who are unemployed for much of the year, took over estates that had already been allotted to cooperatives of permanent workers, and there were some clashes between these two groups, though FEDECAP claims that conflicts have generally been avoided: in one case, five hundred *eventuales* who had originally been excluded were made members of the cooperative following a *toma*.[86] SINAMOS did its best to keep up with this snowballing

85 Decree Law 19400, May 1972.

86 See the account of these occupations in "Enseñanzas de la Actual Etapa de la Lucha de Clases en el Campo Piurano," *Crítica Marxista-Leninista*, 6, Lima, Feb. 1973, pp. 58–69. For an account of clashes between permanent and casual laborers, see *La Prensa*, 17 Apr. 1973, which reports on the invasion of the Hacienda Montenegro-Houghton in the Chira valley, of 212 hectares, and two other properties. The newspaper comments: "The odd thing about this case is that the 150 occupiers of these neighboring estates are *campesinos*

movement and managed to recruit some supporters among the permanent workers of coastal estates—Zózimo Torres, the union leader at Huando, is the most notable case.[87] In most cases of land occupations—over eighty in Piura by mid-1973[88]—the reform authorities have been forced to accept the *de facto* situation, as in the Sierra in the early 1960s, and has expropriated the land with the minimum of delay. It is usually then adjudicated to a production cooperative of the permanent workers, despite the fact that "invasions" are defined as an act of sabotage against the agrarian reform.

There have been land occupations in many areas, including a general strike in the Chancay valley in May 1973, and an "invasion" by *comuneros* of a hacienda in Puno, which resulted in three deaths.[89] Other areas of the Sierra that have been scenes of bitter conflicts are Andahuaylas (land occupations in July 1974), Ancash (several *campesino* leaders killed in 1973) and Cajamarca.[90] Fearing a spread of rural violence that threatened to get out of hand, the government speeded up its plans to create regional central cooperatives and integral development projects

---

who do not work on them. They are, in fact, casual laborers excluded from the Chalacalá cooperative, which is near the occupied area. In this way, when the 59 workers of Montenegro-Houghton arrived for work this morning, they found the invaders blocking their way. . . . Two union officials went to complain to the First Agrarian Zone, as the estate was due to be adjudicated to the permanent workers in August."

[87] SINAMOS was particularly active in the Supe-Barranca-Pativilca areas, inducing unions of permanent laborers to affiliate themselves to the official Ligas Agrarias, and channeling demands through them for the expropriation of the entire valley. Complaints about SINAMOS activities by Barranca landowners can be found in *La Prensa*, 29 June and 23 July 1973. See also reports on the situation in these valleys in *Expreso*, 23 Mar. and 24–25 May 1973. This activity was probably spurred by the presence of strong antigovernment unions in the nearby Huaura valley. Opposition sources have accused SINAMOS of organizing "false" *tomas* in some areas. See *Debate Socialista* 1, Jan. 1974, p. 58.

[88] *Informativo Agrario* 3, Aug. 1973, p. 11. The *tomas* in Piura continued into 1974: in April, two hundred *campesinos* occupied Hacienda La Tina, according to *Informativo Político* 3, May 1974.

[89] "Ultimas manifestaciones de la lucha de clases en el valle Chancay-Huaral," in *Informativo Agrario* 2, June 1973. On Puno, see *Informativo Político* 3, May 1974, p. 14.

[90] See, among other sources, *Crítica Marxista-Leninista* 8, June 1974; *Voz Campesina* 22, n.d., and numerous leaflets put out by the Confederación Campesina del Perú (CCP).

(PID), which would give temporary workers the same rights and income as permanent ones, and would serve to redistribute profits from successful cooperatives to less successful ones.[91]

These policies have not generally been welcomed by permanent laborers, who are reluctant to share out the profits with "outsiders." This applies to both the CAPs, where private landholding is theoretically prohibited, and the SAISs, where it is common. The SAISs are a form of compromise between parceling an estate among the various claimants, and a fully-fledged cooperative. This formula was devised in the Sierra to tackle the problem presented by disputes over land between stock-raising haciendas and neighboring *comunidades*, which have sometimes been going on for decades. Under the SAIS arrangement, the few permanent wage laborers form a service cooperative and are represented on the administrative councils along with members of the neighboring *comunidades*, which are made members of the SAIS collectively rather than individually. Any profits are shared between the laborers' cooperative and the *comunidades*, which receive their part in the form of infrastructural investments rather than individual share-outs. This is a source of resentment for the *comuneros*, and the wealthier ones, who own the most sheep, object to the exclusion of their animals from the pastures of the former haciendas, which are invariably allotted to the SAISs for the production of improved breeds by scientific stock management. In effect, the *comunidades* have lost their battles for land against the haciendas as a result of the agrarian reform, and the higher profits to be made from the scientific use of the

---

[91] Gerardo Cárdenas, "La nueva estructura agraria," *Participación* 3, Aug. 1973, pp. 26–32. See the discussion of the problem of *eventuales* and their incorporation into the new rural structure carried on by SINAMOS officials in the columns of *Expreso*, particularly in the series on the "Nueva Etapa de la Reforma Agraria," in June/July 1973. The problem of income differentials caused by the new cooperatives was raised by Luis Pásara in the 9 June 1973 issue. See also "Estables y Eventuales en las Cooperativas Agrarias de Producción," by "Antonio Vela," in *Expreso*, 22 Feb. 1973. In this article, "Vela" called for "immense productive units to redistribute surpluses as a function of the work done." Most revealing is an article by "Emiliano Tantajulca" on 19 June 1973: "The tendency must be avoided for the agrarian reform to benefit only the *feudatarios* and wage laborers; the members of the most forgotten *comunidades campesinas*, and even the members of the less-profitable units of production must also be beneficiaries of the new agrarian structure." He recommended "a revision of the first schemes and models of adjudication carried out by the reform process."

pastures by the SAIS are not usually accepted by *comuneros* as valid arguments for the exclusion of their sheep. Similarly, former *colonos* are reluctant to vacate their parcels although the collective cultivation of the land within the SAISs should produce much better economic results, at least in theory. Consequently, the SAISs have not been very successful so far in eliminating social conflicts, and lack of cooperation from members has made them economically unsuccessful in the case of many crop-producing SAISs. In at least one case, in Cajamarca, a *comunidad* has withdrawn from a SAIS, and in other cases they have refused to join at all.[92]

By April 1973, there were 52 PIARs in existence on paper, made up of 468 enterprises, and 53 more planned by the end of 1974, most of them in the Sierra, where the focus of agrarian reform action is now to be found.[93] The problems in creating large-scale units in the Sierra are enormous; apart from reconciling laborers and *comuneros* inside SAISs, there is also the question of former *feudatarios*, who are most reluctant to give up their plots of land and flocks in return for a poor wage. Having resisted the efforts of landowners to dislodge them over a number of years, the *conductores de parcelas*, who are still numerous in both CAPs and SAISs, are reluctant to succumb finally to the agrarian reform.[94] Horton notes that problems have been partic-

[92] See the CENCIRA report on Cajamarca, mentioned above, note 39, and Horton (*Land Reform*), p. 141.

[93] Discontent had been growing over the low priority given to the Sierra before 1973. See the declaration of leaders of *comunidades campesinas* in Cajamarca, in *Expreso*, 24 July 1973, expressing support for the government but asking for the agrarian reform to be applied more rapidly in their department, since "until now we have not received any benefits despite the fact that the law was passed more than four years ago." McClintock notes the acceleration of activity in 1973 in forming CAPs (222 out of 497), many of them in the Sierra ("Impact of Agrarian Reform, p. 6). *El Peruano*, 20 July 1974, carried a report on the formation of SAIS Alpamayo and Grupo Campesino Cuatro Estrellas, within the framework of PIAR Callejón de Huaylas (Ancash). According to the report, the whole structure was set up by "equipos integrados de capacitación de Caraz y Huaraz," belonging to the Comité Zonal de Capacitación de Huaraz, made up of CENCIRA, the Third Agrarian Zone, and the local office of SINAMOS.

[94] See McClintock, "Impact of Agrarian Reform." Some of the problems involved in the reorganization of Sierra landholdings are discussed in José F. Elías Minaya and Mario E. Padrón, *Problemática Funcional de la Empresa Campesina y Alternativas para Su Consolidación Económico-social*, Ministerio de Agricultura, Zona Agraria III, Trujillo, 1973.

ularly acute in highland crop farms, which were generally badly run-down prior to the reform and were left largely in the hands of *colonos*, who operated as individual peasant farmers and have been most determined to resist any attempts at forms of "collectivization," which have, in practice, generally been abandoned.

The government hopes that, by the end of 1975, about 75 percent of productive land will be in the hands of various kinds of cooperative organizations.[95] In order to carry out these sweeping programs, the government, apart from canceling private subdivisions of land and condoning land occupations, has had to take over many farms that were theoretically exempt from the reform.[96] FEDECAP noted that

The type of agrarian reform that is being rapidly applied under the pressure of the land occupations is certainly not the one laid down in the bourgeois Agrarian Reform Law.[97]

Another publication representing a similar viewpoint makes the same judgment:

It is because of the pressures exerted by the *campesinos*, because of the struggles and resistance of the rural poor that some—not all—of the parcellations by private initiative were canceled and now the bureaucrats of SINAMOS and the Agrarian Reform Office find themselves obliged, however unwillingly, to expropriate some estates of the rural bourgeoisie, partly contradicting the original plans that the government had worked out.[98]

Landowners' associations have reacted strongly to this "radicalization" of the agrarian reform. There were protest marches in the early months of 1973 in a number of centers, and the rapid proliferation of committees for the defense of small and medium property, often joined by tenants who have seen their hopes of becoming proprietors frustrated by the wider expropriations and

[95] Lander Pacora, director general of production at the Ministry of Agriculture, quoted in *Andean Times*, 14 Dec. 1973.

[96] See, for example, the memorandum to the president of the Republic from landowners in Piura, published in *El Tiempo* (Piura), 17 Aug. 1973. Also *Crítica Marxista-Leninista* 6, Feb. 1973, and *Informativo Agrario* 3, Aug. 1973.

[97] *Ediciones Voz Campesina* 2, Dec. 1973, p. 30.

[98] *Informativo Agrario* 3, Aug. 1973, p. 7.

who refused to join cooperatives.[99] In May 1973, landowners in Arequipa succeeded in breaking up SINAMOS's Liga Agraria and set up a rival Frente de Defensa del Agro Arequipeño,[100] and delegates from the landowners' organizations obliged the president of the Republic and the head of SINAMOS to promise that they would not be taken over.[101] They also insisted on, and received, in some cases, certificates guaranteeing that they would not be expropriated, and, more importantly, legislation reaffirming the government's belief in small and medium properties directly cultivated by their owners (Decree Law No. 20120 of August 1973 and Decree Law No. 20136 of September of the same year). Subsequently, by Decree Law No. 20554, of March 1974, landowners were given the right to appeal to the Agrarian Tribunal against expropriation and were assured that they would be paid compensation in cash if their land had already been occupied. While tacitly recognizing the strength of the *campesinos*, this law also gave landowners the chance to hit back, and some appeals have been upheld by the tribunal; one such case in the Chancay valley in May 1974 led to violent demonstrations by the unions, and many arrests.[102]

[99] See, for example, the case of Hacienda Espinal, in the Zaña valley, where *yanaconas* already promised ownership of their land under the previous law refused to join the new cooperative. D. Horton, "The Effects of Land Reform on Four Haciendas in Peru," in *Land Tenure Center Newsletter*, Madison, Wis., Oct.–Dec. 1972, p. 19. See also the declarations of small and medium farmers from the Nasca and Palpa valleys in *La Prensa* 24 June 1973: "*feudatarios* [are] converted into proprietors of their land by the express mandate of the law, with the right to acquire the duly registered property deeds, and nevertheless the agrarian reform agents are pressuring them to give up their rights and join production cooperatives." One of the demands of the First Conference of Farmers of the Department of Lima (a landowners' defense organization), held in Huaral (Chancay) in June 1973 was for the "speedy handover of individual contracts of purchase to *feudatarios* in accordance with Title XV of the law." Some cases of *feudatarios* protesting against their inclusion in production cooperatives can be found in *La Industria* (Chiclayo), 14 July 1973, and *La Prensa*, 23 July 1973. A protest from the *comunidad* of Mocupe against the inclusion of its land in CAP Ucupe can be seen in *Movimiento Campesino*, 4, Chiclayo, Apr. 1974, p. 13.

[100] *Informativo Agrario* 3, Aug. 1973, p. 6. An account of the development of the movement of *pequeños y medianos propietarios* up to the first national congress in Arequipa in September 1973, can be found in *Informativo Político* 3, May 1974.

[101] *La Prensa*, 22 July 1973.

[102] *Informativo Político* 3, May 1974, p. 28.

The experience of the sugar cooperatives and the SAISs has shown that the formation of such organizations does not necessarily eliminate conflicts, and the rural unions see the PIARs are mere extensions of the same structures. The managerial and administrative hierarchies are maintained in order to keep up production, with the corresponding vast differentials of income among the members. The opening up of the internal elections in the sugar cooperatives in 1972 was forced on the government by workers' pressure, and even then real control was maintained by the central planning office in Lima. Cooperatives do not absorb labor, and in the case of the sugar operations, the problem of what to do with the temporary hands and the sons of members has become serious.[103] The sugar cooperatives and the SAISs are supposed to promote jungle colonization schemes to syphon off their excess labor[104]—excesses which are increased by the policy of rationalization and mechanization which the cooperative administrations are carrying out.[105]

The sugar cooperatives present a particularly acute case of the need to "open up" the benefits of the agrarian reform to wider social groups in the countryside, which is the thinking behind the PIARs and PIDs. Whatever their internal problems, which have been considerable, the sugar cooperatives, with one exception (Cayaltí), have been great successes economically, and their members are relatively privileged members of the Peruvian working class. For example, Tumán and Pucalá workers received 100-percent wage increases in 1972, and the share-out of profits among members amounted to 11,700 soles each in Casa Grande

[103] A delegation of workers from the Pucalá sugar cooperative to the Third Departmental Campesino Convention of Cajamarca included in its resolutions demands for security of employment and solidarity between permanent and seasonal workers on the cooperative. See *III Convención Departamental Campesina de Cajamarca*, Cajamarca, Feb. 1973, p. 23. The president of the Agrarian Tribunal admitted in June 1973 that "We have still not established a system of regulations to govern internal relations in the cooperatives, to reduce significantly the income imbalances between members and to do away with the marginalization of the temporary workers." Dr. Guillermo Figallo Adrianzén, quoted in *El Comercio*, 23 June 1973.

[104] Jaime Llosa has stated that 487,000 hectares will be colonized in the Huallaga, Chiriaco-Nieva, Alto y Bajo Mayo and Jaén-San Ignacio areas of the *montaña*. Participación 3, August 1973, p. 59. See the story headed "Voluntary colonizers will march tomorrow to the Pichis, Palcazú and Perené valleys" in *La Prensa*, Lima, 18 June 1973.

[105] Horton, "Effects of Land Reform," p. 20.

in 1973.[106] Perhaps not surprisingly, the members of sugar co-operatives are as reluctant as anybody to participate in regional PIARs, which would involve some redistribution of their wealth among the less-favored surrounding areas. Moreover, several writers have pointed out that economies of scale in the crop-producing areas of the Sierra are illusory, and the economic performance of PIARs created in these regions is liable to be indifferent, thereby provoking further hostility among the social groups who are supposed to be benefited by these formulas. It is up to the PIARs and PIDs to find a solution to the overwhelming problem of the *minifundios*, which abound in the highlands and which are not really going to be touched by the land redistribution program as such.

CONCLUSIONS

To sum up, the Peruvian agrarian reform has been pushed to the "left" in its program of land expropriations by pressure from rural groups originally excluded from it. The strength of organized rural labor, and later of casual laborers, forced the government into a conflict with the tenants and medium-sized proprietors who were to be the beneficiaries of the final defeat of "feudalism" in the countryside. The struggle between contending forces is by no means resolved yet, and the government has been forced to make important concessions to landowners while trying to cope with continued pressures from the other side in the shape of land occupations and strikes. But the increasingly sweeping nature of the rural reorganization program means that the government has chosen to resolve the conflicts that have been released by creating extensive units designed to accommodate the antagonistic groups in a single structure over which some form of central control can be exerted. The aim of encouraging private commercial agriculture within socially acceptable limits has been completely overtaken by events, and the problems being faced now are those of central planning and administration complicated by a rhetoric of self-management.[107] Government planners have become convinced of the advantages of a centrally planned and controlled

---

[106] *El Peruano*, 29 Dec. 1973.

[107] This conflict has been increased with the publication of the national crop plan and the greatly expanded role allotted to the state food marketing agency, EPSA. See *Peruvian Times*, 25 May 1973.

agricultural sector, with directives, credits, inputs, and so on emanating from central authorities to regional offices *(centrales)*, which have the job of distributing them among the various components of the regional units, and channeling the output of goods and payments into state agencies. The transfer of income from the countryside to the towns is a major objective of this land reform, as it is of every other, though the government claims that it is helping to correct the traditional imbalance between the two sectors. The problems of the new enterprises, often unwieldy and beset by social conflicts, are compounded by the official pricing policy for agricultural produce, as implemented by the state purchasing and marketing agency, EPSA (Empresa Pública de Servicios Agropecuarios). In order to keep prices to the (predominantly urban) consumers low, the prices paid by EPSA to the producers in the reformed and private sectors are uniformly low. This discourages production, and reduces the profits available for reinvestment, not to mention distribution among cooperative members. One fairly predictable consequence of this has been large-scale smuggling, in which EPSA officials have apparently been implicated. In October 1974 the agency was declared in reorganization and large numbers of its employees were arrested pending investigation. Whatever the outcome of this case, the extension of bureaucratic controls over the theoretically self-managing enterprises is inevitable, with the ultimate aim of maintaining the consumption patterns of the urban population. All the rural enterprises, from the wealthiest sugar cooperative to the poorest highland SAIS, may be expected to continue resisting these policies.

7

Continuity and Change: Peruvian Education

Robert S. Drysdale and Robert G. Myers

The traditional education system, an integral part of the overall socioeconomic structure, was designed to contribute to the maintenance of that structure. . . . Our criticism of the traditional education system is part and consequence of the critique we have made of Peruvian society, which society the revolution has begun to change irreversibly. . . . The educational reform of our revolution aspires to create an educational system that satisfies the necessities of the whole nation, that reaches the great mass of peasants, up to now exploited and deliberately maintained in ignorance, that creates a new consciousness among all Peruvians of our basic problems, and that attempts to forge a new kind of man within a new morality that emphasizes solidarity, labor, authentic liberty, social justice, and the responsibilities and rights of every Peruvian man and woman.

Juan Velasco Alvarado[1]

Education is a double-edged, if somewhat blunt, sword. It can accelerate or retard economic growth, facilitate or inhibit income redistribution, open or restrict employment opportunity, maintain or undercut privilege, and foster a liberating form of social participation or strengthen social control. While serving to integrate a society, it can also be a source of some tensions. Each modern government and each national political force struggles to position the cutting edge to shape the world according to its view. Examining the substance and dynamics of educational reform, proposed and promulgated, should, therefore, help us un-

This paper was originally prepared for delivery at the Seminar on Continuity and Change in Contemporary Peru, Center for Inter-American Relations, New York. The authors are grateful for observations and suggestions received on earlier drafts.

[1] From a speech by President Juan Velasco Alvarado at the second meeting of the Permanent Executive Committee for Education, Science, and Culture, Feb. 8, 1971. All translations are by the authors.

derstand more general views held and processes at work in any society.[2]

Because education both is conditioned by and conditions other social institutions, we must be extremely careful in our inferences. Whatever the educational innovation and no matter how well-intentioned the reformers, legitimate criticism can arise from those in society who choose to emphasize the "other edge." We will return to this general theme from time to time as we reflect on the differing analyses of the educational reform by various individuals and groups in Peru.

Education (not necessarily schooling) figures prominently in most strategies of revolutionary transformation as a force helping to produce desired changes or as a means of consolidating revolutionary achievements. (Whether or not education merits the attention it receives from social reformers and revolutionaries is, of course, a separate issue.) Intangible and diffuse, serving a variety of vested interests (students, parents, teachers, ministry bureaucrats), education is also one of the most intractable areas of policy with which any government, revolutionary or not, must deal. The task of would-be reformers is complicated further by popular faith in the ability of the educational system to satisfy multiple demands, and by the discouraging degree of immunity which the educational establishment derives from its role as custodian of knowledge. It is little wonder then that major changes in educational form and content are difficult even to legislate, let alone to effect.

In this essay we will examine the process of educational reform in Peru under the Revolutionary Government of the Armed Forces. We expect to see something of the philosophy and style of the military rulers mirrored in their attempts to cope with problems of educational change as part of their larger effort to transform Peruvian society. First we will examine briefly quantitative changes during the preceding two decades. We will then describe the educational reform promulgated by the Revolutionary Government of the Armed Forces, looking at major events

[2] The literature dealing with education and development is vast. As an introduction to that literature, two volumes that have worn well are: James S. Coleman, ed., *Education and Political Development*, Princeton, N.J.: Princeton University Press, 1965; C. Arnold Anderson and Mary Jean Bowman, eds., *Education and Economic Development*, Chicago: Aldine Publishing Company, 1965.

during the period of its preparation, setting out ideological underpinnings as contained in reform documents, and sketching the ambitious plan for a new system of Peruvian education. Next, we will focus on two problems that educational reform is supposed to help solve (the creation of a national society and the elimination of social privilege) and emphasize two areas of educational policy (rural bilingual education and university reform) presumably directed at the solution of those persisting problems. Finally, we will examine, in a comparative framework, other policies adopted or rejected and several problems encountered in the process of preparing the educational reform.

EDUCATIONAL EXPANSION IN PERU, 1950–1972

Educational reform by the revolutionary government accelerates change in a sector which, particularly under former President Belaúnde, had already experienced broad quantitative development. Table 7.1 indicates the substantial reduction in illiteracy, the dramatic increases in enrollments, and the growing percentage of gross national product (GNP) and national budget devoted to public education that occurred prior to 1968. Immediately evident, as well, is the rapid growth of Peruvian education at all levels during the late fifties and early sixties and throughout the Belaúnde years.[3] At the university and secondary levels, growth between 1968 and 1972 is more modest, even when adjustment is made for the shorter period covered. At the primary school level, growth is maintained at about the same rate, if slightly reduced —a reasonable balance, given the excessive expansion of the universities early in the decade and the continued demographic pressure for primary school enrollment.

To carry out the expansion, a large investment in education was needed. The rapid, if somewhat uneven, economic growth of Peru in the decade prior to Belaúnde's election in 1963, continuing during his first three years in office, generated a growing demand for education. It also created a bullish economic climate

[3] By way of comparison, Peru, during the first eight years of the 1960s, was second among Latin American nations in the rate of growth of its primary school system (after Honduras), third in its rate of growth for secondary school enrollments (after Mexico and Nicaragua), and third in the expansion of higher education (after Nicaragua and Colombia). Interamerican Development Bank, Social Progress Trust Fund, *Annual Report, 1969* (Washington, D.C.: IADB, 1970), pp. 141, 143, 145.

within which (what turned out to be) unrealistically large commitments were made to the educational sector. The increasing magnitude of the educational investment is reflected in Table 7.1. Indeed the military government inherited a heavy financial commitment to education that did not exist at the beginning of Belaúnde's term. Contributing to that growing burden during the 1963–1968 period were: the introduction of free education at the secondary school level, rapidly rising aspirations for education, general growth in school-age population, relative and absolute increases in teachers' salaries, and a lack of access to external financing.[4] With expenditures near 5 percent of GNP and 25 percent of the federal budget in 1968, there was relatively little room for increase. Even before the devaluation in 1967, Belaúnde found it necessary to cut back educational spending from the four-year plan prepared in 1966.[5]

As the military government approached educational reform, then, it faced a different set of financial constraints and a different level of educational development and demand than Belaúnde had faced. But, equally important, it also began its task at a time of broad disillusionment with so-called development efforts aimed narrowly at economic growth and at a time when a doctrine of "dependence" was ascendant, a point to which we will return. It is not astonishing, therefore, that the military began to talk and write in terms of a structural transformation of Peruvian society.

THE REVOLUTION PREPARES AN EDUCATIONAL REFORM

Unintimidated by the obvious challenge of reforming education, the military regime, in one of its first major decrees, ordered a controversial reorganization of higher education (Decree Law 17437, February 1969)—a move which brought intense reaction

[4] While other countries of the region, notably Brazil and the principal partners of the Andean Group, received massive loans from the international development agencies—Agency for International Development (AID), the International Bank for Reconstruction and Development (IBRD, also known as the World Bank), and the Interamerican Development Bank (IADB)—Peru was forced because of the assistance boycott to finance the growth from current national budgetary resources.

[5] See República del Perú, Sistema Nacional de Planificación, *Plan de Desarrollo Económico y Social, 1969–1970, Plan Sectorial de Educación*, Lima: Instituto Nacional de Planificación, 1967.

TABLE 7.1

Educational Enrollment, Illiteracy, and Educational Expenditures in Peru, 1950–1970

	Enrollments (000)						Illiteracy	
	Primary (1)[a]	% Increase	Secondary (2)[b]	% Increase	University (3)[c]	% Increase	% of Population over 15 (4)[d]	
1950	1,010.2		79.5		14.9*		1940	57.6
		19		52		36		
1956	1,204.8		121.2		20.2		1950	53.0
		34		98		101		
1962	1,615.0		239.9		40.7		1961	38.9
		46		139		130		
1968	2,360.0		563.5		93.9		1970	29.0
		17		46		37		
1972	2,759.6		821.1		128.2			

	Expenditures	
	% GNP (5)[e]	% Budget (6)[f]
1950	1.6	14.0
1956	2.4	—
1960	2.6	18.3
1962	3.2	19.9
1965	5.0	28.8
1966	5.2	30.0
1967	5.0	28.5
1968	3.9	25.3
1969	3.9	22.8
1970	3.8	20.8
1971	3.8	20.0
1972	4.5	21.4
1973**	4.6	21.5
1974**	4.6	20.4
1975**	4.7	20.3

*1951 Figures
**Projected in national plan
Note:

Reader should observe that the periods for (1), (2), and (3) are not all of six years. The percentage increases are not strictly comparable although average annual percentage increases can be estimated from the information provided.

The expenditures do not reflect the marked expansion of the public sector since 1968 and, thus, the continuing real increase in public expenditure on education indicated by an approximately constant share of the national budget. See the Peruvian national accounts data for real increase in public expenditure.

Sources:

ᵃ For 1950 and 1956: Ministerio de Educación, Dirección de Planeamiento, *La Educación en el Perú*, Lima, 1967, p. 51. For 1962, 1968, and 1972: Provided by Ministerio de Educación, Oficina Sectorial de Planificación Educacional.

ᵇ For 1950 and 1956: *La Educación en el Perú*, p. 51. For 1962, 1968, and 1972: Provided by Ministerio de Educación, Oficina Sectorial de Planificación Educacional.

ᶜ For 1951, 1956, and 1962: *La Educación en el Perú*, p. 51. For 1968: Consejo Nacional de la Universidad Peruano (CONUP), Programa de Desarrollo Universitario Peruano, "La Admisión Universitaria como Proceso Discriminatorio," Lima, July 1972, p. 17. For 1972: Provided by CONUP.

ᵈ For 1940: The data should be taken as rough point of comparison, since they are not very reliable. M. S. Larson and A. E. Bergman, *Social Stratification in Peru*, Berkeley, Institute of International Studies, University of California, 1969, p. 363. For 1950, 1961, and 1970: Interamerican Development Bank, Social Progress Trust Fund, *Annual Report, 1969*, Washington, D.C.: IADB, March 6, 1970, p. 137.

ᵉ For 1950: Rolland Paulston, *Society, Schools and Progress in Peru*, New York: Pergamon Press, 1971, p. 74. For 1956, 1962, and 1965: Calculated from *La Educación en el Perú*, p. 35. For 1960 and 1970: Calculated from *Estadísticas Básicas, Series 1960-1970*, Ministerio de Educación, Lima, 1972. For 1973, 1974, and 1975: *Plan Nacional de Desarrollo*, 7, Lima, 1971, table 7.02. For other years: Data provided by Ministerio de Educación, Oficina Sectorial de Planificación Educacional.

ᶠ For 1950: Paulston, p. 74. For 1962 and 1970: Luis Cangalaya et al., *Consideraciones sobre una metodologia para el estudio de costó-beneficio a nivel de sistema educacional*, Lima, Aug. 1972, p. 3. Cangalaya drew his original statistics from: *Presupuesto General de la República, 1960-1972*, Lima, 1972. For 1973, 1974, and 1975: *Plan Nacional de Desarrollo*, table 7.02. For other years: Data provided by Ministerio de Educación, Oficina Sectorial de Planificación Educativa.

and failed to reduce the debilitating unrest and political conflict prevalent within the Peruvian university system at the time of the take-over. The decree was followed by a series of legal modifications throughout 1969 bringing about significant compromise from the original government intent. In a move that further underscored the perils accompanying educational reform, the government attempted in June 1969 to impose fees on primary and secondary school students (specifically those students required to make up courses that they had failed), thereby touching off riots in the highland department of Ayacucho. A score of casualties, the imprisonment of a handful of teachers,[6] and the mobilization of parental opposition resulted.

Confronted by such undesired and unanticipated consequences, the government reconsidered and, on the counsel of high civil servants, appointed an Educational Reform Commission (November 3, 1969). Charged with fashioning a comprehensive educational reform, the commission's approximately one hundred and twenty specialists labored for almost a year before arriving at recommendations which were gathered together and published (September 1970) in a two-hundred-page report.[7] A best seller on the streets and in the supermarkets of Lima, the report immediately provoked open and vigorous debate involving teachers, parents, the church, private schools, and the press. For several weeks members of the commission and Ministry of Education officials were ubiquitous, appearing in Lima and in the provinces before concerned groups to explain, interpret, and defend the recommendations.

Despite extensive propagandizing, opposition to the proposed changes mounted. University officials sharply criticized what they considered to be a violation of the university's right to determine its own structure. Private school spokesmen, including church officials, voiced opposition to increased state control of their schools. At the same time, schoolteachers, many of whom had entered the profession in the late sixties on graduation from the politicized environment of provincial universities or the dull-

---

[6] The imprisoned teachers eventually became a thorn in the side of the regime, for the teachers' unions demanded their release as part of their more general demands, which have threatened and led to strikes closing the schools on at least two occasions since 1969.

[7] República del Perú, Ministerio de Educación, *Reforma de la educación peruana, Informe General*, Lima, September 1970.

ing confines of the normal schools, militated for economic and other benefits. Still smarting from the failure of Belaúnde to follow through with promised raises, the teachers were not in a mood to cooperate. Accordingly, they threatened to boycott a retraining program (begun even while the reform was still being debated) and raised the specter of a national teachers' strike. The capacity of national syndicates and their local affiliates to mobilize teachers was only reinforced by early comments issuing from the commission assigning to teachers part of the blame for the failure of education in Peru.

Under great pressure, the minister of education, in December 1970, terminated the contracts of most commission staff members (many of whom were rehired in the following year as permanent staff of the ministry). With instructions to complete their task quickly, the reduced commission produced a draft law by March 1971. Meanwhile, without public debate, the government moved ahead with a series of individual decrees and resolutions of limited scope.[8] The major recommendations simmered for another nine months, however, until a draft of the general law was eventually published in December 1971. Public airing of the draft stimulated over three thousand written suggestions for additional modifications, some of which were incorporated into the General Law of Education (Decree Law 19326), finally decreed on March 21, 1972, three and one-half years after the military takeover.[9]

According to the prologue of the law, education is to build upon and reinforce three ideological pillars: humanism, nationalism, and democracy.[10] In contrast with policy statements under

[8] For instance, during 1970 and 1971 the government began a reorganization of the Ministry of Education (*Decreto Ley* 18799 of March 1971), established norms for technical and normal schools, introduced a standard form that would follow students through their school careers, required a standard school uniform, set up pilot schools in *pueblos jóvenes*, and set in motion programs for teacher trainers.

[9] See *Ley General de Educación: Decreto Ley* 19326, Lima, March 1972.

[10] The authors of the new law place broad emphasis upon these three concepts in their writings and public statements but insist that the terms be understood in a "Peruvian context." According to their definition, humanism is, to some extent at least, antitotalitarian by definition; the emphasis is on the individual and not the state. Democracy is contrasted with manipulation, corresponding with the government's general assertion of creating a social democracy with full participation and a minimum of intermediation between

Belaúnde, explicit reference to Christian education is left out of the reform law.[11] Significantly, the thinking of Catholic radicals (and not the traditional church) is reflected clearly in the new law, particularly in the concept of realizing man's historic potential through social action. Echoing Paulo Freire and tying together the humanistic, nationalistic, and democratic elements in the educational ideology of the government is a central concept, *concientización*, or "awareness leading to liberation and participation in the historic process of removal of the old structures of dependence and domination." Awareness is defined in the law as

an educational process by means of which people and social groups adopt a critical attitude to the world around them and assume the responsibilities and take the measures necessary to change it. This process of making people aware of the world around them is not a temporary act imposed on them from outside, but a free, voluntary act of reflection through which they become aware of the world around them through a process of interaction and communication with their fellowman which will thus bring about this awareness. This process, therefore, excludes all forms of dogmatism, sectarianism, or control of persons.[12]

---

the individual and the state. Nationalism is anti-imperialistic or defensive of national interests from what is viewed as essentially economic aggression. See *Ley General*, Exposición de Motivos, section 1.

[11] "The objectives of national education have been elaborated on the basis of a society founded on principles which are humanistic, Christian, democratic, and nationalistic." República del Perú, *Plan de Desarrollo Económico y Social*, p. 108.

[12] *Ley General*, glossary. For a moving account of the Catholic radicals' attempt to reform education in Brazil in the sixties and the eventual consequences, see Emanuel de Kadt, *Catholic Radicals in Brazil*, London: Oxford University Press, 1970.

Paulo Freire, a Brazilian exiled from Brazil and later from Chile for his apparent success in organizing educational activities designed to develop awareness, has visited Peru, and his works have been read widely in Peruvian educational circles. His ideas have appeared in *Educación*, published by the Ministry of Education, and it is possible to purchase his *Educación como Práctica de la Libertad* from street-corner newsstands in Lima. In contrast with Freire, the Peruvian law places emphasis on "reflexive *concientización*," the means by which an individual processes information to enhance his own awareness. According to this definition, one person cannot *concienticize* another. This rather academic distinction could, nevertheless, lead to widely

Furthermore, in the rhetoric of the reform, awareness must be part of a larger process of creating a "new Peruvian"—of shaping men and women to the new morality described above by President Velasco. Rejecting the "personalistic" and "individualisitic" styles seen as fundamental to capitalistic societies, the regime claims to seek instead that awareness and behavior regarded as essential for the establishment of a "social democracy of full participation."

Elevating awareness or "consciousness raising" to a central goal of education and espousing a new morality clearly set this regime apart from previous Peruvian governments. This change accords with policy makers' conversion to a view of the Peruvian social order that was widely accepted among Peruvian social scientists, a view stressing dependency *relationships* among the four principal social groups—*indios, cholos, mestizos,* and *blancos*—relationships characterized by a concentration of power in the dominant *mestizo* and *blanco* sectors. Essentially urban, Spanish-speaking *mestizos* were seen to have employed their superordinate position to the disadvantage of the fundamentally rural, Quechua-speaking Indians of the Sierra and, to a lesser degree, to the disadvantage of the growing, intermediate, *cholo* population, partially differentiated from the Indian by participation in and identification with national culture.[13] In a fully dominant

---

differing practices. Emanuel de Kadt analyzes the interesting and parallel controversy in the Brazilian context of directed versus nondirected *concientización* and their separate results. The Hegelian and Marxist overtones of *concientización* as used by Freire are rejected in the Peruvian law. In the latter view, although two social groups may have interests which conflict, the resolution of this condition involves the merging of their interests, as opposed to the victory of one group. This will be achieved, the authors of the Peruvian law state, by gradual modification in the ownership of property and of the factors of production. Evidence of the influence of radical Christian thought within the Peruvian military leadership is given in an article recently published by a leading general of the Peruvian army, Jorge Fernández Maldonado, minister of mines and energy. See his article "Fuerza Armada, Cristianismo y Revolución," *Participación*, 2:3 (1973), p. 10. The goal of awareness fits well with the rhetoric of the Sistema Nacional de Apoyo a la Movilización Social (SINAMOS), the primary government agency for social mobilization.

[13] This section draws heavily on Julio Cotler, "La Mecánica de la dominación intensa y del cambio social en el Perú," Lima, Instituto de Estudios Peruanos, 1967, mimeo; and M. S. Larson and A. E. Bergman, *Social Stratification in Peru*, Berkeley: Institute of International Studies, University of California, 1969.

position relative to all others was the small cosmopolitan *blanco* group.[14]

Within this social hierarchy and as one component in its evolution and diversification, a national system of education has matured.[15] The government's public critique of that educational system (as reflected, for instance, in the quote from President Velasco used to open this essay) derives from the view that it has been a force for maintaining the unjust social order that has shaped it.

The concept of "dependence" has its economic dimension as well. In the opening paragraphs of the General Law of Education, for instance, an argument is presented that the structural causes of Peru's problems are underdevelopment and dependency.[16] Underdevelopment is defined as the existence of profound imbalances manifested by the unequal distribution of wealth and power favoring the dominant sectors. The privileged status of this minority is inextricably bound up with maintenance in a dependent position of vast sectors of Peruvian society. The law argues that the apparatus of the state, including educational services, has consolidated the privileges of the dominant group and the marginal position of the masses.

Within the existing social structure, economic growth, it is asserted, increases the already unjust disequilibria of Peruvian society. To pursue economic growth, which continues to be a basic goal of the military government's program, can only be justified, then, if a commitment to social transformation can be simultaneously and vigorously pursued. In the law and elsewhere it is argued further that the problem of underdevelopment is inseparable from that of external dependence. The economic phe-

[14] See François Bourricaud, *Power and Society in Contemporary Peru*, New York: Praeger, 1970.

Bases of social differentiation in Peru vary among regions, of course. Within each region, position in the social hierarchy is determined by a complex mixture of attributes including dress, family characteristics, occupation, property, language, and education. Larson and Bergman, *Social Stratification*, p. 40.

[15] One writer has argued convincingly that the social hierarchy is reflected in the school system. He also asserts, with some qualification, that social-class-linked education tends to perpetuate the hierarchical social system. See Rolland G. Paulston, *Society, Schools and Progress in Peru*, New York: Pergamon Press, 1971.

[16] See *Ley General*, Exposición de Motivos.

nomenon of external dependence, with its political manifestations in the social and cultural order, is a kind of mental colonialism which emasculates the work of creating national culture. Hence, the schools serve only to transmit "colonial values" and do not create new ones. This recognition of the essentially political nature of education in Peru is significant. In its analysis of education's contextual relationships with social and political processes, this regime contrasts markedly with previous governments.

To shift education from its position supporting the traditional social order, the military assigns several new roles to education. In the opening quotation from President Velasco, three goals are mentioned: eliminating ignorance among the previously exploited masses (primarily Indians), creating a new consciousness among all Peruvians, and forging a new morality. But the stated goals of education may not be the only, or even the most important, goals. Critics suggest several other functions of education that they think may reflect government thinking: the consolidation of disparate national groups within preferred political structures; a certification for and hence a barrier to social mobility, when access to quality education is influenced by social and economic factors; and a release valve for social pressures from lower-middle social strata.[17] This last purpose may be subtly fulfilled, they argue, by opening, ever so slightly, access to advanced secondary and higher education and hence to jobs, maintaining the flow at a level required to perpetuate the myth that social mobility is possible for all. At least as important, according to this argument, social harmony may be furthered by using educational expansion to appease the masses, satisfying their demand for education even though the rewards society provides those educated members of the popular classes will not be significant.

To meet its goals, the government has proposed, in the General Law of Education, a comprehensive and ambitious plan to create a new education in Peru. Under the new law the formal system includes three levels: (1) initial education for children up through age 5—a group virtually ignored by education policy makers in the past; (2) basic education for ages 6–15, extending the former primary cycle for three additional years; and (3) higher education, including the new vocationally oriented higher

17 See Felipe Portocarrero, "Universidad y Política: Situación Actual," *Sociedad y Política*, 1:2 (1972), pp. 34–49.

schools for professional education (ESEP), the university, and graduate school. Promotion will depend only upon successful completion of a given series of lessons, allowing students to progress through the basic cycle in less than nine years if they are able to do so. In monolingual rural areas the law demands that basic education be taught in the vernacular.

In an attempt to decentralize decision making, aid local participation, and rationalize resources, the law requires that school districts or *núcleos* be established throughout Peru. Each district will contain one central school and several satellite schools and is to be managed by a director who will be advised by a community educational council. Directors are appointed by the ministry from a list of three candidates recommended by the council, a body comprised of 40 percent teacher representatives elected by the teachers and 60 percent representatives of other local institutions of a social, cultural, or professional character, but explicitly not political parties (article 74). Educational facilities (including private school facilities) of each district are considered by the law as educational resources potentially available to children and adults of the district—although the full implications of this sweeping provision have yet to be worked out in practice. That this new organizational model is one component of a broader scheme for participation in the revolution is evident from a February 1973 article by Leopoldo Chiappo, former member of the Reform Commission and then a member of the Council of Advisers to the Ministry of Education. Chiappo writes:

In the context of the Peruvian revolution many things are changing. Even the instruments for formulation of educational policy have been adjusted to correspond with the other structural reforms, with the transfer of power from the oligarchy to the people. The institutionalization of participation in the educational field is manifest in one of the most original and daring concepts of the educational reform—*nuclearización* [roughly, the formation of school districts incorporating broad community participation]. The *nuclearización* of the educational community mobilizes the participation of the citizens of the district in the dual process of criticism and creation which will permit the definition of authentic educational models, rooted in the culture and needs of an organized community.[18]

All students in the reformed system who wish to attend the university must pass through an ESEP (the first cycle of higher education roughly parallels secondary school completion in most other Latin American countries), with the requirement of concentrated study in a subprofessional field. The work-oriented ESEP represents an attempt to modify traditional academic preferences and is supposed to encourage training of technicians and skilled workers of both sexes in fields for which there is a demand. By shifting to a single track, the reformers also hope to moderate the social discrimination accompanying traditional two-track systems separating academic from technical secondary schooling.[19]

Set in motion by the new law are two nonstandard out-of-school programs: basic education for school dropouts and young adults, and in-service training and upgrading of workers. Both programs will offer courses of general education and literacy,

[18] Leopoldo Chiappo, "Liberación de la Educación," *Participación*, 2:2 (1973), p. 33.

[19] The humanistic orientation of education as elaborated in the educational reform also centers attention on "self-fulfillment through work." The introduction to the General Law asserts that "education by work and for work is the cornerstone of any truly humanistic philosophy of education, and it, therefore, constitutes the basis of the present reform of education in Peru." This may be contrasted with a statement from Belaúnde's annual message in 1967, in which the humanistic ideal was set out thus: "Man is an end in himself, and, as such, he should seek his own goals while respecting others' freedom to do likewise." One finds no attempt in the planning documents of the Belaúnde period to tie a humanistic philosophy to a work-oriented education. Rather, work-oriented or vocational education is closely linked to a technocratic philosophy, stressing work as needed for production rather than as a source of individual fulfillment. From the technocratic approach follows a separation of academic and vocational streams in education, whereas the humanism of the revolutionary government leads toward integration of the two. In this difference we find an ideological underpinning for the new Escuelas Superiores de Educación Profesional (ESEP), an attempt to provide work-oriented education for all.

For an elaboration of the new academic technical synthesis, see Augusto Salazar Bondy, "Educación técnica, educación humanista: falso dilema," *Educación* 1:1 (1970), pp. 10–16. For the contrasting earlier approach, see Fernando Belaúnde Terry, *Mensaje Presidencial*, Lima, 1967, p. 543.

job training, and guidance. The law also sets the stage for an educational extension service via state-controlled radio and television. These extension programs and other social services will be assisted by university volunteers as authorized by the new law.

The horizon for full implementation of the law extends beyond the decade, and a cautiously planned and carefully budgeted year-by-year application is under way. Bylaws have been issued for private schools, bilingual education, and regional teachers' cooperatives. Reform-related projects for training teachers and developing new materials commenced in 1973. By the end of 1973, over two hundred and fifty *núcleos* were in operation. The 1973/74 educational budget registered an increase over that of 1971/72, and the allocation for new educational investments is up disproportionately. Education loan requests to the World Bank for $34.7 million have been approved. The Hungarian government has extended credits for the purchase of educational equipment at the level of $19 million. Negotiations continue with the governments of Canada, France, and West Germany, and with several international agencies.

This summary reveals the protracted nature of the government's attempts to institute an educational reform and the regime's willingness to include the public and the educational community in the elaboration of the ideas. With few exceptions, the legal structure incorporating innovative reform features is now successfully erected. The plans drawn up and actions already taken illustrate a long-term commitment to implement the reform program.

UNREMITTING PROBLEMS OF DEVELOPMENT IN PERU

Although the vocabulary of reform, the level of educational demand and development, the financial constraints, the social diagnosis, and the proposed remedies are different today from those of the Belaúnde years and before, many of the problems faced by the present government are the same. From among the myriad persisting challenges toward which educational rhetoric and policy have been and will be directed, we will emphasize two: national integration and social privilege. As we relate governmental style and policy to these two problems, in general and in the case studies which follow, we should keep in mind that each theme is complex, lending itself to various interpretations.

What to one commentator seems to be a flexible, participatory governmental style producing a change-oriented education law may be interpreted by another, with only a mildly sardonic twist, as a maneuver to prolong the status quo.[20] A policy judged by some to help solve a problem (e.g., dramatically expanding enrollment) may be looked upon by others as exacerbating the problem (e.g., expanding enrollment offers a greater opportunity for social "tracking" in schools).

Despite a century and a half of national home rule, Peru is not an integrated nation. Its legal and institutional character, reflecting urban, coastal, Spanish culture, remains remote from the Peruvian Indian, who, by birthright, is no less a Peruvian. Inability to integrate such a large portion of the Peruvian population into the national order is both cause and effect of an inability to articulate collective goals and to create a national consciousness. The analysis of this problem has long attracted the attention of Peruvian political theorists, many of whom saw education as at least a partial solution. Writing in the late nineteenth century, González Prada stated that the marginal status of the Indian masses lay in the economic and social order and was reinforced by widespread illiteracy.[21] Mariátegui elaborated the theme forcefully after the First World War. The revolutionary government echoes clearly these earlier concerns.

Extension of primary schools to rural areas was supposed to facilitate integration. However, many students do not remain in school long enough even to achieve literacy in Spanish. To compound the problem, recent evidence confirms in Peru the well-known tendency of the literate to concentrate in urban areas. The 1961 census revealed less than 40 percent literacy for the rural population as contrasted with 85 percent for the urban population. A census of *pueblos jóvenes* conducted in 1970 describes the

[20] It is argued that by providing the masses with more education, a little at a time, the government will be able to buy off some potential discontent. Peasants and workers, unaware that the schooling their children will receive will not help them get a better job, will be appeased at least in the short run. Furthermore, this line of reasoning asserts, graduates will presumably be willing to accept their lot more easily if, having had the opportunity afforded by education, they are not able to succeed. They will put the blame for failure on themselves rather than on the political or economic system.

[21] See, for example, Manuel González Prada, *Horas de Lucha*, Lima: Editorial Latinoamericana, 1961; José Carlos Mariátegui, *Siete Ensayos de Interpretación de la Realidad Peruana*, Lima: Biblioteca Amauta, 1968.

level of adult literacy among this relatively poor population as 89 percent[22] (the total urban literacy rate may be higher), but the national literacy rate for both urban and rural areas is no higher than 75 percent.[23] Most illiterates in the Peruvian national population, then, are Indian, are still located in rural Peru, and remain on the margin of the national order.

A second and related problem, perhaps less tangible but certainly no less real, is how to moderate, if not eliminate, the socially linked system of privilege and reward which has characterized the Peruvian social system. In contrast with the issue of integration, involving a mainly rural and Indian population, this problem unfolds principally in the cities with the gradual emergence of *cholo*, but principally *mestizo*, groups already integrated into national life. Although the dominant social system expands—incorporating into the national system individuals and groups emerging from excluded or subordinate social strata—economic resources, prestige, power, and most other rewards continue to be scarce. Under these circumstances advancement for underprivileged elements is not a necessary consequence of emergence onto the national scene.[24]

With demographic growth and economic expansion, the evolving middle and lower groups increase their demands for the benefits of development, including education and, particularly, higher education. Although it is generally resistant to the demands, the public sector and the groups which control it can respond by expanding the educational system. Larson and Bergman suggest that educational expansion in response to popular demand (particularly at the university level, where enrollments grew fastest between 1962 and 1970) was the principal nonpolitical, albeit temporary, reward available to compensate the new middle sectors for all that was unsatisfactory and precarious in their position.[25] For most people, however, education is not an end prod-

[22] See República del Perú, Oficina Nacional de Estadística y Censos, *Boletín de Análisis Demográfico*, vol. 13, *Los Pueblos Jóvenes en el Perú*, Lima, 1973.

[23] *Algunas Características Socio-económicas de la Educación en el Perú*, vol. 2, Lima: Centro de Estudios de Población y Desarrollo, 1972, p. 6.

[24] See Carlos Delgado, "Ejercicio Sociológico sobre el Arribismo en el Perú," in *Problemas Sociales en el Perú Contemporáneo*, Lima: Instituto de Estudios Peruanos, Campodónico, 1971, pp. 103–118. Delgado applies the concept of the "limited good" to analyze the conditions of individual social mobility in Peru.

[25] Larson and Bergman, *Social Stratification*, p. 125.

uct, and while the social base of the university broadens dramatically, the emergence of inferior education cheapens its value for aspiring new groups. The slow growth of jobs relative to enrollment gives a continuing inside track to those in the privileged universities and, at the same time, exposes unrealistic views held by the mass of students expecting better employment, increased prestige, and security to result from their educational experience. Consequently, the university, an institution with a long tradition in Peru and not noted for change, must handle intense and conflicting political pressures to eliminate educational elitism on one hand and to control it politically on the other. Educational policy makers anxious to create an "adequate" university system thus face an increasingly difficult task.

The two contrasting case studies that follow relate directly to the two problems highlighted above. The first case, reform of bilingual education for rural areas, is closely tied to the issue of national integration. Failure to master the dominant language makes integration difficult, if not impossible. The second case focuses on the key educational institutions—universites—affecting the distribution of social privilege among individuals competing fiercely for the limited rewards the system offers.

INTEGRATION, LANGUAGE, AND REFORM OF EDUCATION IN RURAL AREAS

According to the 1961 national census, approximately 40 percent of the Peruvian population claim an indigenous tongue, and about half of these are monolingual Quechua speakers. Quechua, in its various dialects, is the first language of approximately 6 million Peruvians today, most of whom are concentrated in rural areas of the Sierra, where they are a majority.[26]

[26] Multilingualism in Peru, as elsewhere in Latin America, is primarily the result of contact between native American (Indian) languages and a colonial (European) language, and, to a lesser extent, between different indigenous languages.

We will deal here primarily with Quechua. Of the other indigenous languages, only Aymara is spoken by a relatively large number (290,000) of individuals. About 210,000 people, concentrated on the eastern slopes of the Andes and in the Peruvian jungle, speak one of a multitude of languages. With the data from the 1972 census still in tabulation, this represents the most recent information on the national level. The error may be large, however, given an estimated 5 percent noncoverage of native groups and a tendency to under-

Alberto Escobar, one of Peru's foremost linguists, suggested several years ago to an official from the Ministry of Education that educational policy in rural areas should be reformulated on the basis of linguistic and anthropological analysis. The official replied, "What we really ought to do is brainwash the Indians so that they forget Quechua."[27] Perhaps the remark was sincere, illustrating a widespread attitude; perhaps it was a pathetic attempt at humor concealing frustration. Either way, it points to the prejudice and ignorance—or at best the level of indifference —that has prevailed in Peru with respect to the linguistic diversity of the population. In contrast, the new education law and the national policy for bilingual education published by the Ministry of Education in 1972 are not indifferent to the variegated cultural and linguistic reality that is Peru:

In consequence, bilingual education will seek to avoid the imposition of any single culture, but rather promote the uniform appreciation of the cultural pluralism of the country. . . . In the case of speakers of either a linguistic variant of standard Spanish or of an indigenous language, educational policy will include teaching the dialect of regional or national significance without the elimination of less prestigious dialects.[28]

What accounts for this apparently new awareness? Is there really a change from previous policy, as indicated by actions as well as words? What would prompt a change?

The few attempts at educational outreach to rural areas made under previous regimes betray their *mestizo* origins. For instance, the ambitious and innovative introduction of peasant

---

report native language as the first language. See Ines Pozzi-Escot, in Escobar, *El Reto de Multilinguismo*, p. 128.

In the coastal department of Lima, 15 percent of the population claim Quechua as their mother tongue, as compared with 95 percent in the department of Apurímac in the Southern Highland. Even greater differences appear if the population statistics are further disaggregated by urban/rural location and sex. S. K. Myers, "The Distribution of Languages in Peru: A Critical Analysis of the Census of 1961." Unpublished M.A. thesis, University of Chicago, 1967.

27 See Alberto Escobar, ed., *El Reto de Multilinguismo en el Perú*, Lima: Instituto de Estudios Peruanos, Campodónico, 1972, p. 6.

28 *Ley General*, Exposición de Motivos.

nuclear schools into the rural highlands beginning in 1944 and stretching over two decades did little to build programs constructively around the Quechua language and culture. Although an effort was made to adapt the curriculum to rural areas by emphasizing agricultural education and by including health instruction, and although a language barrier was explicitly recognized, classes were still given in Spanish.[29] Bilingual instructors were reportedly given preference in hiring for nuclear schools, but such individuals were typically anxious to reaffirm their ties with the "superior" coastal culture and to downgrade their origins in the Quechua culture from which they too recently had "escaped." The National Education Plan of 1950, prepared for General Odría by a commission of seven university officials, symbolized this disregard of language questions. The plan made no mention of bilingual education or of language as a factor of social differentiation.

Educational policies of the 1940s, 1950s, and early 1960s do not illustrate the influence of the *indigenistas* or the radical social thinkers and writers who, from the 1920s forward, had been religiously promoting the cause of the Indian. Policies were not linked to broader reform efforts, as Mariátegui and others argued they should be. Governments were not ready to accept the idea that any attempt to improve the position of Indians by reforming methods of instruction, public administration, police control, or public works would be superficial if it avoided the elimination of rural serfdom based on the concentration of property.[30] Indeed most policy makers still felt no need to worry about domination of the Indian. But analyses of reform-minded individuals are not easily converted into policy, even when heard. Moreover, the coastal *mestizos* responsible for policy were applauded by rural elites, themselves Spanish speakers and *blancos* or *mestizos*.

As a result, the language of instruction (and of the textbooks and tests issued by the central Ministry of Education) continued to be Spanish, even in rural departments such as Apurímac, where 95 percent of the population claim Quechua as their

---

[29] "The first problem and the most important one in *Transición* is language. Schools utilize Spanish exclusively." See John Baum, *Estudios sobre la educación rural en el Perú*, Mexico City: Centro Regional de Ayuda Técnica, 1963, p. 59.

[30] Mariátegui, *La Realidad Peruana*, p. 30.

mother tongue. Arriving at school with little, if any, knowledge of Spanish, rural students typically had trouble coping with the curriculum, creating a strange situation in which it seemed necessary already to know some Spanish in order to learn Spanish. Failure to acquire competence in Spanish in the schools, at least to the level of literacy, not only eliminated rural Indians from competing effectively for economic rewards in the ever-more-prominent "modernized" sectors, but also influence their view of their cultural identity and hampered political participation, making national integration virtually impossible.

An exception to the general inattention to indigenous languages by former regimes is found in the Summer Institute of Linguistics (SIL), a Protestant missionary group essentially dedicated to Bible translation, which, since 1945, has developed bilingual education programs in jungle areas of Peru.[31] The institute, although not a Peruvian organization, operated from the Ministry of Education and was given primary responsibility for literacy and community development education in the eastern jungle areas. The SIL approach involved making students literate in their tribal language first, then gradually working into Spanish, taught as a second language. Often, young Indian men who had served as informants to SIL language specialists also served as schoolteachers in the villages serviced by SIL. For twenty years, however, this program was restricted to the jungle areas, and only in the period of Belaúnde did similar projects emerge for highland dwellers.

Apart from the SIL literacy work, occasional "literacy" forays were made into the Peruvian provinces by ministry or international organization cadres. These efforts, including the 1962–1963 campaign mounted by the military during their brief rule (and during which bilingual instructors were employed), produced disappointing results.

By 1963, however, the Peruvian Indian community was radically different from that of the 1920s. The rapid increase in the highland population (a consequence of public-health measures taken in the forties and fifties) and the resulting pressure for land were making life increasingly precarious in some regions.[32]

[31] This paragraph draws upon Paulston, *Society, Schools and Progress,* pp. 234–37.

[32] *Algunas Características Socio-Económicas,* vol. 2, p. 2. See figures on population growth from 1940 to 1970 and the rural to urban shift: 35.4 percent urban in 1940 to 52.7 percent urban in 1970.

Sporadic violence resulted. Indian society was on the verge of revolutionary explosion. Incipient guerrilla groups commanded attention. Meanwhile in and around Lima the growth of sprawling slums and squatter settlements accelerated, making coastal city dwellers, including Lima politicians, even more aware of developing pressures in rural regions. As Bourque and Palmer point out in Chapter 5 of this volume, Belaúnde vigorously sought support in the rural highlands during the 1963 campaign. Once in office, he established Cooperación Popular, a grass roots rural development program building on local initiative. He also guided a land reform through the Peruvian legislature, presumably indicating thereby his regard for rural areas and their particular social problems. However, the reform fell far short of the structural changes Mariátegui and others had recommended.

The first five-year education plan, prepared in 1964 by an educational planning commission formed by Belaúnde, revealed a sensitivity to problems involved in extending primary education in the rural areas.[33] The plan repeated earlier ideas that schooling in rural areas should offer basic community education, that peasant children should learn techniques of raising productivity in agriculture, crafts, or small industry, and that only by instruction in a native language would an effective process of acculturation take place. While encouraging local adaptation of materials and curriculum, the document stressed, nevertheless, that peasant children must cover sufficient material to compete, in case of migration, with children in urban areas. Despite apparently good intentions, no large-scale education projects were organized for the national rural population during the 1965–1969 plan period, and an essentially urban curriculum taught in Spanish continued to prevail.

During the Belaúnde years, however, several significant developments were taking place: some bilingual teachers were trained; experiments in bilingual education were organized which eventually offered guidelines for the policy of the present regime; and the research on Quechua dialects by Peruvian and foreign linguists accelerated. Stimulated by the creation in 1964 of a special category of teacher called a bilingual teacher, the SIL conducted from 1964 to 1971, regular training courses of increasing sophistication in a project extending to teachers in

[33] See República del Perú, Ministerio de Educación, *Plan de Desarrollo Educativo, 1965–1969*, Lima, 1964, p. 39.

twenty-five rural primary schools.[34] In part, the project was an experiment to explore in the Sierra the effectiveness of the second language methodology applied in the jungle by SIL.[35] Another language experiment, carried out by San Marcos University, involving a peasant *núcleo* near Ayacucho, was designed to compare results of several approaches to teaching Spanish.[36] Each project created locally adapted texts. Each project used linguists and anthropologists, many of whom later became advisers to the military government. In them and in the projects one sees some roots of the current policy, as contained in the education law and related bylaws, and some seeds of the controversy which continues to characterize language reform efforts.[37]

By the time of the military take-over, then, conditions had be-

[34] According to the Ministry of Education, in addition to the 25 bilingual schools in the highlands under the direction of forty teachers, in 1971, 181 schools were operating in isolated jungle areas. Most of the 181 had begun to operate prior to the military take-over in 1968.

[35] For a description of the project, see Donald Burns, "Niños de la sierra peruana estudian en quechua para saber español," *Anuario Indigenista*, 27 (Dec. 1968), pp. 105–110. The experiments also seem to have roots in a round table discussion held November 20–24, 1963. See, for instance, the comments of Augusto Salazar Bondy in: *Mesa redonda sobre el monolinguismo quechua y aymara y la educación en el Perú*, Lima: Casa de la Cultura, 1966, p. 33. Participating in the round table discussion were Augusto Salazar Bondy and Emilio Barrantes, two key members of the reform commission appointed by the military government, and Alberto Escobar, presently serving as a consultant to the Ministry of Education. Donald Burns of SIL claims that students in the bilingual experimental program perform better on tests than students in a regular monolingual program and have a lower propensity to drop out. Donald Burns, "Five Years of Bilingual Education in the Andes of Peru," presented at the Inter-Branch Quechua Workers Conference of the Summer Institute of Linguistics, Lima, May 3–10, 1971. Throughout the various stages of each experimental project, the orderly execution of plans was impeded by the chaos which characterized the administration of rural primary schools. The ministry transferred teachers after the completion of special training and before the application of their new skills. Lack of supervisory personnel, scarcity of services, absence of materials and supplies contributed to delays and prevented in each case the orderly accumulation of experience. The ministry showed no inclination or capacity to control these problems. Actively involved in a massive program of primary school expansion, Belaúnde's government had no resources or personnel to spread for the execution of training or pilot programs in highland bilingual education.

[36] The nuclear school system included one central grade school, usually located in a small town, and approximately ten satellite schools.

[37] See Salazar Bondy, *Mesa redonda*, p. 7.

gun to favor rural bilingual educational reform. A respectable knowledge base was growing—an accumulation of efforts over many years by students of language, education, and indigenous organization in Peru. The rural areas were beginning to gain political attention, and this was at least in part because, despite outmigration, the absolute number of rural inhabitants continued to increase. The number of Quechua speakers was increasing as well.

It is argued that the military was more keenly aware of rural disparities and unrest than other mainly urban-confined elites.[38] During the sixties, organized popular protest in the countryside and occasional guerrilla movements required lengthy service in rural areas by young officers. Civic action, including some vocational education, was seen, increasingly, as a responsibility and duty of the military. These pressures and experiences may well have predisposed the revolutionary government toward approval of a so-called bilingual educational policy.

A desire for language reform also flows easily from the dependency analysis of Peruvian society and education mentioned earlier.[39] Committed, as it is to structural transformation, the revolutionary government cannot ignore the fact that for four centuries Spanish has been the language of those who exercise political and economic power in Peru while indigenous languages have served the subordinate sectors.[40] Interestingly, however, neither the rural experiences nor dependency theory nor the knowledge flowing from bilingual educational experiments provided the military with clear guidelines for a bilingual policy.

The Educational Reform Commission struggled with language policy. It argued explicitly that the exclusive use of Spanish in schools adversely affected the performances of highland peasants, thus reinforcing their marginal position.[41] The commission

[38] Víctor Villanueva, *La Nueva Mentalidad Militar en el Perú?* Lima: Juan Mejía Baca, 1969, pp. 51–69.

[39] See, for instance, SINAMOS, *La Voz de la Revolución: Discursos del Presidente Velasco*, Lima, 1972.

[40] See Alberto Escobar, *Lenguaje y Discriminación Social en América Latina*, Lima: Editorial Carlos Milla Batres, 1972.

As Bourricaud has written, the paradox of a regime such as that of Peru is that the majority is relegated to the state of a permanent minority. See Bourricaud, *Power and Society*, p. 89.

[41] *Informe General*, p. 23. See also Chiappo, "Liberación de la Educación," pp. 26–37. For example: "Nonparticipatory education represented an enclave

warned further that other reforms designed to change the structure of dependency and thus provide new opportunities for the Indian masses would be ineffective if a language barrier continued. The masses would not be able to take advantage of openings, either because they would be uninformed or because they would be unable to meet job requirements, one of which might be knowledge of Spanish.

The authors of the law stated clearly that the reformed educational system must face up to the linguistic reality of Peru in at least two ways. First, the goal of universal utilization of Spanish should be achieved, but, in the process, respect should be maintained for the cultural and linguistic heritage of the diverse groups composing the national population. Native languages should be used to facilitate the achievement of literacy in Spanish (article 12) and to preserve and transmit the values of local culture (article 246). Teacher-training programs in the normal schools and universities must include the teaching of one Peruvian indigenous language (article 312). Second, the law also states that learning of indigenous languages will be encouraged in its own right. Educational centers will provide facilities for the study of vernacular languages and for analysis of their influence on national culture (article 98).

These general principles of the law were made more precise in the bylaws for bilingual education, published on February 8, 1973, which required that the indigenous language be the language of instruction at the basic education level in areas of the country where little Spanish is spoken. Under these conditions, Spanish is to be taught as a second language, and teachers should be people whose mother tongue is the local vernacular. Teachers' records must indicate their capacity to work in a vernacular tongue. Those teachers with no working knowledge of a language other than Spanish will be obliged to study an indigenous language, most likely Quechua or Aymara. Although the teaching materials must be approved by the Ministry of Education, they should be appropriate to the particular area, taking into account the wide regional differences in culture and language.

---

which impeded any kind of participation. The systematic, psychological damage done to peasant children as a consequence (the results of which we see in the high school desertion rates) have, in our opinion, made nonparticipatory education a kind of spiritual genocide and an incredible crippling of the community" [p. 33].

Quechua has been recognized for several years as an unofficial second language. Official use of Quechua has been limited, however, since the language does not have a written tradition. In 1973, as a first step toward curriculum construction, a standardized Quechua alphabet was approved. It remains for the government to put the Quechua alphabet to use in its own work in the printing of laws, documents and manuals, or in subsidized reading material. Movement in that direction would indicate that the government is as serious about encouraging the learning of Quechua for its cultural value as it is about using it as a more rapid means of attaining literacy in Spanish.

The policy on bilingual education prepared by the ministry in 1972 asserts that "bilingual education will be ... a basis of *national solidarity*" (p. 9). National solidarity involves full participation. Language barriers, reinforced by bureaucratic and geographic distance, have prevented Indian parents in rural, predominately Quechua-speaking areas from participating effectively in policy decisions governing the education of their children. Accordingly, the education law, as indicated earlier, recommended formation of school districts and the organization of local school boards of parents responsible for the election of school principals. That system is just beginning to function. But solidarity and full participation may in the long run depend more on economic participation than on political participation as defined by this regime. And language reform by itself will not necessarily accelerate economic participation for Peruvian Indians.

The bilingual policy may flounder at an early stage for several reasons. First, the passage of a law and the mere existence of by-laws have not created a consensus among members of the linguistic and bureaucratic communities concerning the teaching of indigenous languages. Consequently, curriculum guidelines are not clear. Second, the talent and funds necessary to produce significant curricular reform are scarce. Moreover, Indian parents may block language reform efforts, not in an organized way at a national level, but in a series of local resistance efforts. They may use the very participatory devices the government is setting up or they may hold children out of schools. Opposition by parents to teaching in the native tongue might be expected on much the same grounds that many United States parents of black children object to the teaching of "Black English"—that the language does not help one get the preferred jobs. Indeed, Indians interviewed in the Ayacucho region believed not only that their lack of Spanish and of education reinforced their low social position, but also that an education equal to that of *mestizos* (a Spanish-language education) would allow them to compete for the same occupations.[42] If participation is defined to include economic as well as grass roots political participation, the parents may have a point. Finally, even assuming a new curriculum and parental support, we cannot be certain that other culture symbols, the teacher's style and method, the materials he or she employs, and the organization of the school can be sufficiently adjusted to promote the new cultural and linguistic goals.

In general, the education law, the national policy, the bylaws, and even early preparatory actions more closely approach a statement of idealized goals than a carefully analyzed policy taking into consideration costs, availability of personnel, and attitudes of the target population. The chances for achieving even a portion of the task must be regarded as slim. The policies have not yet been tested. If, in 1975, the new curriculum takes shape and is extended into rural areas, the government's bilingual educational policy will be open to proper evaluation. The concrete steps already taken in the ministry to make this aspect of the educational reform effective suggest a continuing commitment. How sustained that effort will be remains to be seen—although even modest progress in this difficult field would put Peru ahead of other Andean nations confronting the isolation of a rural Indian majority.

REFORM OF UNIVERSITY EDUCATION

In our second case we are concerned with attempts to expand and democratize Peruvian higher education in response to growing popular demand (while maintaining order and quality and while fending off counterpressures from entrenched academic and political elites). In general, pressure for mobility in the lower and middle strata is manifested by the search for improvement, principally for the young, via access to higher levels of the educational system. Only 20 percent of the national adult population express satisfaction with their educational attainment. On the average, they focus their own educational aspirations at the first

[42] Escobar, ed., *El Reto de Multilinguismo*, p. 24.

level beyond their own. In comparison, all literate sectors of the adult population show a strong preference for advanced secondary or university education for their children.[43] Access to higher education represents by itself a rise in status, as symbolized in Peru by the use of such formal titles as doctor, engineer, architect, professor. But education also provides access to economic security, even though the promise is less certain as educational opportunity expands downward.

When Belaúnde assumed the presidency in 1963, he inherited a university law approved in 1960 by a Congress in which the Apra party shared power with the traditional elements of the upper class loyal to then President Prado.[44] An unanticipated cost for Apra in their decision to work with Prado, and in the general centrist trend manifest in the party since the early fifties, was a serious thinning of the ranks of student leaders loyal to Apra.[45] The loss in militancy and control by Apra in the universities helped win Apra's support for and eventual approval of a university law in 1960—a law containing many elements of traditional student claims. Apra surmised that its loss of power among university students and professors could be reversed by a university law that offered student cogovernment, expanded student services, open competition for faculty posts, and career security

[43] See *Algunas Características Socio-económicas de la Educación en el Perú*, vol. 1, pp. 37–41.

[44] Prado negotiated the agreement in order to receive critical Aprista support. Apra accepted the arrangement on the promise of a lifting of the proscription of the party, in effect since 1948, and an offer to share the spoils that accompany a governing position in Peru. Apra may have also calculated that participation in government, even in a secondary role, would permit the construction of a base sufficient to win the elections of 1962. See Carlos A. Astiz, *Pressure Groups and Power Elites in Peruvian Politics*, Ithaca, N.Y.: Cornell University Press, 1969, p. 102.

[45] Since the founding of the Federation of Peruvian Students (FEP) in 1919, the student movement held a leftist position in Peruvian politics, and until 1956 the federation was solidly Aprista in leadership and policy. As Apra shifted to the right, as symbolized by association with Prado, student allegiance to Apra disintegrated. At the Trujillo student congress of 1959, the Apra party lost the presidency of the federation, an important source of influence in the universities. Haya de la Torre, the founder and long-time leader of Apra, brought the Reform Movement to San Marcos University in 1919 and led a strike at the university in struggle for increased autonomy and student participation. When the objectives of that strike were realized, at the end of four months, the students had mounted the federation as the basis of a political organization.

282—Robert S. Drysdale – Robert G. Myers

for professors. The 1960 law permitted the establishment of private universities and facilitated the creation of national universities, adding a potential element of payoff to provincial politicians loyal to Apra, and to Belaúnde after 1963. Those elements supporting Prado and Apra represented diverse currents, however, and no single philosophy was dominant in the law that emerged. The law failed to satisfy any single group, adding, thereby, a key factor for the general failure of university reform efforts throughout the decade. Indeed Dr. Luis Alberto Sánchez, a leader in the Apra party and then rector of San Marcos, commented in 1961 that the law was inoperable in at least 40 percent of its articles.[46]

During Prado's regime Apra presented little by way of a new program for Peruvian university reform, attempting instead to use the educational establishment to gain access to the power so long denied.[47] On the other hand, the sectors that united behind the Acción Popular of Belaúnde were formulating educational policies which later emerged as party doctrine. President Belaúnde argued that technicians armed with modern planning skills and backed by a strong economy could move the apparatus of government to supply the infrastructure needed for development. For Belaúnde, the university would produce the skilled human capital to keep the economy strong and growing and to increase the skill level of the public sector.[48] He recognized (as did the military junta preceding him) that the university would need

[46] According to Sánchez, contradictions in that law led to the rupture in the Faculty of Medicine in 1961 that resulted in the establishment of the private University Cayetano Heredia and the loss by San Marcos of over 60 percent of its professors of medicine. This particular conflict revolved around the refusal of the majority of the professors of medicine at San Marcos to accept student cogovernment. See Luis Alberto Sánchez, *La Universidad de San Marcos*, Lima: Universidad Nacional Mayor de San Marcos, 1962.

[47] Unlike earlier periods of Apra militancy, when Haya de la Torre, Luis Alberto Sánchez, and others wrote extensively on the university. Indeed Apra promoted, in the thirties, the founding of popular universities designed for adults, bypassing the limited secondary and higher education system of that period. See Luis Alberto Sánchez, *Testimonio Personal*, 3 vols., Lima, Ediciones Villason, 1969.

[48] For an early expression of the Belaúnde government on these points, see the speech by the president of the Council of Ministers, Aug. 1963, and *Plan Nacional de Desarrollo Económico y Social del Perú, 1962–1971*, Lima: Banco Central de Reserva del Perú, Oct. 1962.

rational planning, increased resources, including foreign grants and loans, and an improvement in quality accompanied by an emphasis on science and technology. With a strong Apra presence in the Congress and growing pressure for university admission from secondary school graduates among the expanding middle class and urban groups, the dramatic growth could not be planned or postponed.[49] From six universities in 1955, the system grew to ten by 1959, twenty by 1963, thirty by October 1968, and to its current number of thirty-five accredited universities with the creation of the University of Tacna in September 1971. Enrollment grew from a base of 31,000 in 1960 to 94,000 in 1968 and 120,000 in 1972.[50]

In 1964 the Apra party and several owners of private universities, under the leadership of Sánchez, convinced the Senate to approve a motion to form a commission for educational reform. Undoubtedly, Sánchez was motivated to promote the formation of a commission and to preside over its deliberations by a concern for Peruvian education and a desire to influence that sector. Another goal was to prevent centralization of control of the university, a policy which he and his party resisted. The resulting Sánchez Law, approved in the House of Representatives on December 1, 1967, concentrated on the universities in two-thirds of its articles.[51] The proposed law retained individual university

[49] The Apra-backed law of 1960 included tax incentives and autonomy to private entrepreneurs to create universities as businesses. The Congress willingly approved bills creating universities both because Apra hoped to gain and because many provincial capitals had long aspired to have a university.

[50] The number of secondary level graduates in 1965 was 187 percent of the corresponding figure for 1960; by 1968 the growth was 312 percent of the 1960 level. That university expansion, even at the accelerated rate, was unable to satisfy the growing demand is illustrated by the relation between applications for university admission and secondary level graduation. In 1960, 36 percent of the graduates were admitted although 74 percent applied; in 1968 the corresponding figure was 38 percent as virtually 100 percent applied (including a backlog from earlier years). See Consejo Nacional de la Universidad Peruana, Plan, *Sub-Sector Universitario, Versión Preliminar*, Lima, 1970.

[51] The picture is complicated by the fact that Sánchez was defeated in June 1964 in his bid to retain the rectorship of San Marcos. Not until June 1966 did he regain the rectorship, at which time his rival, Dr. Mauricio San Martin, was appointed by Belaúnde to head the National Inter-University Planning Office of the Inter-University Council, giving Sánchez additional incentive for resisting central control. See also "Ley Orgánica de Educación, Proyecto Ley Aprobado por la Cámara de Diputados," Lima, 1967; mimeo.

structural and operating autonomy but made little effort to modernize the archaic structure of university management. Most important, the proposal restricted the authority of the Inter-University Council created by the 1960 University Law of President Prado and given special authority by Belaúnde to recommend to Congress the opening or closing of universities. The law had not been passed by the Senate before the coup of October 3, 1968; the commission ceased to function on that date.

Although Belaúnde's efforts, and those of university officials sympathetic to his goals, to plan and to coordinate the university system were resisted by the 1960 law, by the traditions which it protected, and by a stubborn Congress, developments not directly related to the university further impeded his efforts. Belaúnde promised to resolve the dispute with the International Petroleum Company (IPC), but the case occasioned continuing U.S. government pressure on Peru. This conflict and the controversy associated with the purchase of Mirage jets from France resulted in a freezing of aid. The combined support available from the Agency for International Development, the Interamerican Development Bank, and the World Bank amounted to only a trickle, in comparison to the flow which had been promised. The proposed regional colleges Belaúnde had hoped to construct with international help did not materialize. Pressure to increase enrollment continued and was absorbed primarily in humanities and education faculties, which did not require large capital outlays to accommodate more students.

The growth in enrollments was accompanied by a widening of the social extraction of university students.[52] A former rector of San Marcos argued in 1966 that "compared with twenty years ago, when 95 percent of students came from middle- and upper-class homes, the majority of San Marcos students, over 65 percent, are of lower-middle and working classes."[53] The rapid ex-

---

[52] See Larson and Bergman, *Social Stratification*, p. 200.

[53] Ibid.

The occupational aspirations of these new students remain remarkably traditional. William Whyte established in an interesting study of secondary school students in 1963 that the goal of mobility via education for the middle class has its counterpart in the prevalence of an aversion to manual labor. Even among technical secondary students the prejudice against physical labor is powerful. In educational terms this is frequently translated into a need to continue to higher education. See William F. Whyte, "High Level Manpower for Peru," in F. Harbison and C. Myers, eds., *Manpower and Education:*

pansion of provincial universities is further illustration of the broadening social base of higher education. But a consequence was in some measure at least, the evolution of a system of universities reflecting the social composition of the society. A few elite universities, principally located in Lima, managed notable progress with selective support from Congress, foreign assistance agencies, and private foundations. Furthermore, with a tight rein on admission quotas, they chose only the best students, mainly graduates of the better private secondary schools. The other universities served the great mass of students emerging from the public schools, in search of the prestige and economic reward presumably attached to a university degree but unable to gain admission to the best universities.[54] Graduates of these universities increasingly discovered that the occupations that awaited them neither required university training nor offered an income proportionate to the investment they had made. Growing numbers of them accepted lower-level posts.

The expansion of a dual university system whose graduates faced a limited market for their skills undoubtedly heightened political consciousness among university students. At the same time there was a growing recognition of the failure of Belaúnde's policies on other fronts. The promised agrarian reform, finally given legal status, proved largely ineffective. Devaluation in 1967 and the related cutback in budgets brought student protest and opposition. Students who had supported the Belaúnde volunteer movement, Cooperación Popular, found themselves at the margin of the student political debate, as the integral Belaúnde program was brought into question. Despite the failure of the student movement to close ranks and present a solid front and even, perhaps, because of the resulting competition among the various

---

Country Studies, New York: McGraw-Hill, 1964, pp. 37–72; and Manuel Vicente Villarán, "El Factor Económico en la Educación Nacional," reprinted in Cuadernos, 12 (1973), pp. 11–22; Mariátegui, La Realidad Peruana, "El proceso de la Instrucción Pública," pp. 85–128.

[54] For further information, see Alphonse MacDonald and Catalina Romero de Iguíñez, "Investigación sobre estudiantes de la Pontificia Universidad Católica del Perú, 1968," Lima: Catholic University, CISEPA, 1969; and, Robert Myers and Baldomero Cáceres, "A Follow-up Study of Agrarian University Graduates, report no. 1," Lima, the Agrarian University, Apr. 1971; Rafael Roncagliolo, "La Universidad Peruana: modernización y democratización," in Modernización y Democratización en la Universidad Latinoamericana, Santiago: La Corporación de Promoción Universitaria, 1971.

leftist groups, considerable disruption and chaos reigned in the university system during the final two years of the Belaúnde period. Student action was catalyzed on September 18, 1968, in rejection of the Act of Talara of President Belaúnde, representing his government's solution to the long-standing dispute with the IPC. Students invaded San Marcos and took over the main facilities. When the police entered, thereby violating the immunity which students in Latin America claim as a right since the Reform Movement, the students counterattacked and captured several police investigators. The university system was paralyzed for several weeks.

In brief, Belaúnde sought to foment university development and democratization in order to promote the modernization of the country. He worked against important constraints, however, posed by a university law which tended to aggravate the problems in the system and by a Congress which refused to support his policies. His inability to realize his objectives on a scale adequate to resolve the problems he was confronting added to the developing crisis in the universities as his regime lost credibility among students and intellectuals.

The military government, which seized power on October 3, 1968, was presented with a sprawling, chaotic, highly politicized university situation. By dramatically expropriating IPC holdings, it bought, temporarily, student sympathy and gained time to attempt bringing the universities under control. It did not have to account to an opposition party as did Belaúnde, and, in theory, there was little to prevent it from acting decisively to structure a new university system.

The initial diagnosis the Peruvian military made of university education is not part of the public record. What ideas they shared about the university, however, are presumably contained in Decree Law 17434, prepared in secret and promulgated without advance warning in the fifth month of their rule, February 1969. The law was not prepared without civilian participation. A commission of military officers individually called together four veteran university professors and asked them to prepare a draft law to reform the university system. These professors, chiefly from elite private universities and engineering faculties, prepared a document which was circulated within the military, modified, and eventually signed into law on February 18, 1969.

By creating a National Council of the Peruvian University

(CONUP) of nine rectors and a professional staff, the law sought not only to plan and centralize the administration of government funds available to the universities but also to introduce a convenient buffer between the universities and the government. No longer were universities to negotiate budgets directly with the government, but rather with CONUP. The academic structure of the university was changed by eliminating the professional *facultades* and replacing them with departments and academic programs, a response again to advocates of efficiency and a functional structure. The law granted unusually wide powers to the rectors and eliminated student participation in governing councils. It also introduced a system of graduated tuition payments, reflecting both financial pressures on the education budget and a naïve notion of what might be done to make the system more egalitarian.

Reaction within the universities was, if not unanimous, essentially opposed to the vertical structure imposed and its violation of traditional principles of autonomy and participation. Throughout 1969 student protest closed various universities for several days or weeks. Opposition was also voiced by a small group of directors and owners of private universities who had benefited economically during the period of the previous law. On the other hand, support for the law was evidenced in sectors outside the university which approved of the order in the university that the law was supposed to establish. Support for many parts of the law also surfaced within the university among those groups (scientists and engineers in the main) most appreciative of planning, programming, coordination, and efficiency.[55] CONUP accepted the responsibility entrusted to it but officially expressed regret that the government had not sought consultation with the university prior to promulgating the law.

Continuing its unilateral approach to policy formulation, the government again acted confidently within several months to impose discipline and rationality in university operations in an area which would not have received effective attention by the council —professors' salaries and related compensations. A decree law was issued certifying that university officers and professors were members of the civil service and were therefore subject to regulations concerning salaries in the public sector. It is a reflection

[55] See Alberto Escobar, "El Problema Universitario o el Vacío Ideológico," in *Perú Hoy*, Mexico City: Siglo Veintiuno, 1971, pp. 260–304.

of concern for abuse and the conviction that the university was a shelter for unmerited privileges that professors' salaries were reduced and a new set of standard categories and statutes defined.[56] These have yet to be applied uniformly.

The regime's early approach sought modernization of the university, continuing, at this stage, policies of the Belaúnde regime. But in contrast with Belaúnde, the military enjoyed sufficient power to act decisively and create the legal framework and organizational mechanism they sought. The radical critique of Peruvian society which was to characterize later pronouncements of the military government in the education field had not yet appeared.

In its early effort to modernize and to relate the university system to the development needs of the country, the military government tried to control student political activity and moderate the effect of student cogovernment. It is not unlikely that the government hoped their action would mute political criticism as well as promote university modernization. Criticism of that policy was harsh, however, from social scientists and intellectuals in the university, some of whom had deeply influenced the military's analysis of Peru, and from students. Faced with the task of winning support from the university community for a cooperative reform effort, the military rejected the more extreme models of forceful intervention in the university to eliminate conflictive elements offered by recent military regimes in Argentina, Brazil, and Chile.[57] Instead the Peruvians sought to reduce conflict and tension by a combination of: (1) eliminating the unnecessarily authoritarian characteristic of the law, (2) broadening student participation in further definition of university policy, and (3) promoting progressive measures in other fields—for example, energetic foreign policy, agrarian reform, and the creation of the industrial community. By doing so they illustrated an unusual flexibility and a reluctance to use violence as an instrument for achieving their goals.

---

[56] *Decreto Supremo* 034–69, Ministry of Education, Sept. 1969.

[57] This gesture, which has characterized the regime's approach to conflict resolution in several sectors, is undoubtedly a product of their analysis that there is an essential harmony of interests among the various social sectors of Peru. Indeed the military have tended to seek throughout their rule reconciliation rather than repression to achieve goals. It is beyond the task of this paper to analyze in detail this important theme.

Opposition to the law continued in the universities throughout 1970. The government consulted broadly with the university community but learned, evidently to its consternation, how hard it was to arrive at a consensus.[58] With the capacity to define and initiate policy, the government was nevertheless frustrated by the inability of a consolidated (under CONUP) university to participate effectively and profitably in the definition of that policy. The difficulty of imposing one model upon the university system and of reducing the contest to one set of rules became apparent as the large student population and general poverty in the system inherited from the Belaúnde period maintained conflict at a high level of intensity. Retreat from the 1969 law was completed as the government agreed to allow the Educational Reform Commission to rewrite the University Law as part of a general law outlining education reform. With a new minister of education in 1971, a reduced commission, and the strong influence of the Higher Council of Education created in March 1971, a committee of five civilian advisers to the ministry, most of them former members of the commission, a new policy for the university system was designed. This policy included the participatory ethic applied to students, professors, and employers alike, in contrast to the University Law of February 1969, which represented the military government's first initiative in university affairs.

In his Independence Day address of July 28, 1971, President Velasco affirmed henceforth a significant role for students in university policy and proceedings. He further indicated that CONUP, the symbol of concentrated authority and the agency which had borne the brunt of opposition to adjustment demanded of universities by the 1969 law, would disappear and a new institution with broader participation from the university community would be created. By September of 1971 a final draft of the General Law of Education was submitted to the president by the minister of education and his advisers. A lengthy series of consultations followed in which each ministry was given an opportunity to review the document. The minister of education an-

58 During March, April, and May 1969, in accordance with the recommendations of CONUP, the government approved several minor modifications to the law favoring limited student participation and modifying CONUP's structure. The application of certain articles of the law, such as the policy regarding student failure and staff requirements for faculty positions, was postponed when that proved unrealistic.

nounced that the law would be issued by the end of December 1971 and that the universities would open in April under the new system—implying that the universities would adjust to the new system and elect new officers during the three months of summer vacation (January to March, 1972).

Despite the policy of including the law within the general educational reform, and the exhaustive consultations carried out by the reform commission, with the public, and within the government, the arguments did not cease. In December 1971, the President, reportedly after meeting with leaders of the church and the private universities, observed, with regret, that those affected directly by the law and the public at large had not been consulted sufficiently.[59] Probably in an effort to avoid further confrontation over the law, he called a halt to proceedings and asked the minister of education to publish and distribute the draft. The ensuing public debate, lasting throughout January 1972, resulted in significant changes. By February a further draft with approximately sixty modifications to the over four hundred articles of the earlier version was prepared in the Ministry of Education and again submitted to the president and the cabinet. On March 21, 1972, the final document was signed into law by the president and cabinet.

Well over one-half of the modifications made in the draft at this final stage concerned the university system, reducing considerably the detailed specifications characterizing the earlier versions. Reflecting the regime's growing reluctance to continue in the center of the debate over the structure of the university, the law presented general guidelines and elaborated a procedure by which universities would elect officials to determine for themselves the details of the system. By keeping its hands off the general statute and the bylaws, the regime may have hoped to decentralize conflict, eliminate the armed forces from the debate, and, perhaps, gain some new support for a direct intervention at some future point. The combined effect of consultation, of wresting authority from CONUP, and of turning the process over to the universities, however, was to open up and intensify the contest.

Even before passage of the General Law of Education, a dissident group of students, professors, and workers at the University of Cuzco protested, employing (by August 1971) a model soon

[59] Conversation with an official of the Peruvian Ministry of Education.

to spread to more than a dozen universities in the country.[60] In Trujillo in October 1971, in Cajamarca in April 1972, and in Arequipa in June 1972, attempts to take control of the universities led to temporary recess of the institutions concerned and considerable violence on the part of students and police. The National Agrarian University at La Molina was declared in recess in September 1972 after a lengthy dispute. A march of twenty-five thousand students was organized in Lima on June 7, 1972, by the Federation of Peruvian students, to protest the reaction which had been provoked at various universities by the duly authorized officers (student expulsions, withdrawal of funds) and to publicize student claims.

Despite the willingness by the government to reformulate the university policy laid down in 1969 and the continuing dialogue between the government and the universities, no consensus was reached on basic reform issues. For example, attempts to legislate greater student participation failed to resolve student opposition but brought a strong reaction from university administrations. A major concern of the government became removal from the controversy at minimum political cost. The full development of this final stage has been characterized by (1) a loss of confidence in the capacity of the university system to serve developmental goals and a search for alternatives, (2) a decision to hand the problem of university policy back to the universities and to accept a solution not involving political decisions by the regime, and (3) the co-opting of many university professors into the public sector by offering good salaries and by funding research institutes within the government. From a policy of decisive action to achieve the principal goal of the Belaúnde regime, the government has moved in the mid-seventies to a policy of near abandonment, in which inaction may be the preferred action.

Further evidence of the government's disillusionment with the universities is illustrated by the tight control on budget as symbolized by salary policies.[61] The government has been reluctant

[60] In demanding the immediate resignation of the rector, they also asked him to permit the formation of a freely elected body of students, professors, and workers to elect a new rector and new officers. Subsequently a new claimant was elected rector, and violence broke out, resulting in the detention of the pretender rector and sixteen students.

[61] Indeed the overall budgetary increase in recurrent expenditure awarded the university sector in 1973–1974 was approximately 500 million soles. The government published on January 10, 1973, figures showing a substantially

to increase salaries until norms decreed over four years ago to regulate the conditions of professors' appointments are adopted or modified. For example, there are professors who continue to teach at more than one national university, contrary to the terms of their contracts. It is also reported that certain professors with "exclusive dedication" appointments devote time to private employment, again in violation of the law. The official position remains that a reconsideration of the budget situation, and thus improved prospects for salary increase, depends on the elimination of these abuses. In April 1973, CONUP issued a resolution on salaries and norms for "rationalization" of expenditure. The reasonably generous increments (for example, from the 1969 rate of 14,400 Peruvian soles per month to a 1973 rate of 25,000 soles per month for the basic salary of a full professor) were tied, however, to firm regulations on teaching loads.[62] For example, full-time faculty would be required to put in forty hours of work at the university and assume a weekly teaching load of twelve hours minimum and fifteen hours maximum, a significant increase. But the increased teaching loads and threatened enforcement of conditions for exclusive dedication appointments received strong criticism in the universities. Opposition was dramatically emphasized by a one-day strike of professors at the National Engineering University on May 29. In September 1973, CONUP announced a slightly modified bylaw awarding the same salary schedule but modifying slightly the conditions regarding teaching load; CONUP warned that the increases would be made available only after suitable reform in each university and the approval of a new budget by the government. The controversy continues as opponents charge violation of university autonomy.

---

larger amount. The increase presented by the government, however, was the increment over the initial budget presented in December 1970 for the two-year cycle 1971–1972. There were increases on two occasions during 1971–1972 amounting to almost 25 percent, followed by reductions in 1972 and unspent balances at the end of the period. The new budget figure for recurring expenses is 9.3 percent higher than the amount actually expended in 1971–1972. Consequently, inflation (10 percent is as good as any other guess for average annual increase in an index of university operating costs) and an expansion in student enrollment would tend to reduce real current expenditure per student.

[62] See Resolución 1399-73, CONUP, Lima, Sept. 4, 1973, for the final version (now in effect, despite continuing protest).

EDUCATIONAL POLICY AND GOVERNMENTAL STYLE:
CONCLUDING OBESERVATIONS

The military bureaucracy may be one of the few elements of
Peruvian society for whom formal education has offered a socialization which is truly integrating, coherent, and functional. Education offered to recruits and career professionals by the military
system of schools, training colleges, and universities is closely
related to job qualification and to career advancement, thereby
helping blend Peruvians of diverse social and cultural backgrounds within the hierarchical structure. It is consistent, then,
that the Revolutionary Government of the Armed Forces moved
quickly to use the educational resources available to them for the
creation and consolidation of the new society which they are
seeking to construct.

That they have moved with a forceful but flexible and pragmatic style is evident in the two case studies presented here. In
part, their style reflects an organizational capacity to pursue a
broadly defined goal over time, adding precision to the objectives
according to the lessons of experience; in part, it reflects the need
to make compromises in order to maintain the stability and control felt to be essential for the military-guided transformation of
Peruvian society. A mix of military authority and broad civilian
participation also characterizes the formulation of educational
policy throughout these five years of military rule. Indeed, the
educational reform is not the intellectual property of the armed
forces. The best-trained and most talented civilian educational
specialists in Peru have, with few exceptions, provided counsel
and recommendations for the reform. Nor is the reform a copy
of an educational model developed elsewhere. That no foreign
missions participated in the planning illustrates increased independence and self-confidence among Peruvian intellectuals and
educational specialists, qualities unseen in previous major reforms or plans for education in Peru in this century.[63]

[63] Foreign missions of educational experts from France, Belgium, and the
United States have often influenced, if not directed, educational reforms in
Peru. As recently as the 1964 plan prepared for President Belaúnde, the mission from Teachers' College, Columbia University, received written thanks for
their assistance in the introduction to the plan. The *Informe General* of 1970
acknowledges, correctly, no foreign counsel. A parallel exists with the government's policy concerning the use of certain foreign curriculum and teaching
materials. The Ministry of Education prohibited the showing in Peru of a

In the area of rural and bilingual education, the military government seems able to move ahead steadily with reform—in marked contrast to the wavering efforts in higher education. Lines of opposition to bilingual education were not well drawn, and agreement on the problem, if not the details of the solution, appeared to be widespread. The church and the private educational sector, opposed to other aspects of the proposed law and able to induce significant changes in the draft, were, for the most part, unaffected by the bilingual reform proposals, given the concentration of their schools in urban areas. Nor did the majority of the teachers, or their spokesmen, choose to oppose bilingual reform; as high as 70 percent of the teaching force has rural origins and is already bilingual. As if to emphasize the validity of their social analysis, it did not seem necessary for the military to worry about objections from the dominated rural Indian population—the group to be affected most intimately by the reform (nor did they seek Indians' advice).

The bilingual educational policy borrows ideas from and builds upon work done in earlier years, including the Belaúnde period. The reform law and bylaws are not, however, mere *post hoc* legislative recognition of change that has already occurred; rather, they anticipate and require additional change consistent with the regime's desire to nationalize, democratize, and humanize education, and to extend participation. Nevertheless, the double-edged nature of language reform must be recognized. The central goal of language reform is incorporation of the indigenous population into national institutions and structures by teaching them Spanish and at the same time strengthening their attachment to and'pride in their mother tongue. The effect could be one of greater participation and influence of marginal groups, or it could be more effective management of these populations. From one point of view, the government seems to be responding to an evident need, but, from another, can be accused of creating conditions for tighter control of the Indian population.

We have no way of predicting how successful the bilingual educational reform will be (even if we could establish a clear definition and measure of success). Clearly an important and difficult challenge of this policy will be bridging the gulf between

Spanish version of Sesame Street, an educational television series now viewed regularly in its Spanish and Portuguese versions by thousands of children throughout Latin America.

the urban and rural worlds. To seek to build a revitalized Quechua world in Peru is not realistic. A return to a past that no longer exists, nor is desired, is not one of the options. But to find effective channels of communication and create the means, both educational and otherwise, to link these two worlds is an enormous task. Even more difficult is to link the two without totally destroying one.

The government's policy toward university reform provides a particularly good example of a shifting position over time in the face of strong opposition. From a nonparticipatory, authoritarian position the military moved to a participatory and conciliatory stance. But by mid-1973, the regime seemed to have abandoned its high hope that the university system could play a major role in the revolution.[64] To conclude, however, that the university community has been assigned a secondary position because the military hold an anti-intellectual ideological bias would be to oversimplify. One could argue, rather, that repeated attempts by the government to work out a viable university policy and obtain the support of a mobilized academic community have only weakened authority within the universities and catalyzed ever-present political contests in the universities. In the end, with the failure of the university and the government to work together effectively, the government has siphoned off much of the best talent, incorporating it into the public administration.

Although much of the legal debate and process analyzed here will not now result in realized educational change, a basis has been laid for further progress. Although there is as much evolution as revolution in these changes, promulgating the reform will surely be interpreted as a critical point in the development of Peruvian education.

Observers not accustomed to Peruvian practice and legalistic tradition could not help but notice the almost exclusive dedication in this process to the perfecting of a legal text. Has anyone asked if a law is necessary to reform education? Can the goals

---

[64] In virtually no modernizing country has the government received, for long, support from the intellectual community. Indeed, Huntington affirms, "If there is any cleavage which is virtually universal in modernizing countries, it is the cleavage between government and university. If the presidenial palace is the symbol of authority, the student union building is the symbol of revolt." See Samuel P. Huntington, *Political Order in Changing Societies*, New Haven: Yale University Press, 1968, p. 371.

asserted by President Velasco in the introductory quotation be achieved only subsequent to the enactment of an educational law? Richard Fagen's analysis of the campaign against illiteracy in Cuba in 1961 reveals the almost direct opposite of the Peruvian experience.[65] In Cuba, organization flowed from revolutionary activity, rather than the converse. The Cuban leadership believed that the act of trying, the struggle itself, opened up possibilities that could not have been imagined before the battle. The program was improved in operation. The Peruvian model, on the other hand, emphasizes analysis, planning, mobilization of consent, compromise (to the extent possible), and only then implementation—a model that in some aspects, but surely not all, parallels parliamentary procedure. While this process promotes the stability and—it is to be hoped—support for the eventual achievement of goals, a feature not without importance for Peruvian leaders as they have witnessed the weakening position and eventual overthrow of Chilean President Salvador Allende, it also provides ample room for reduction of revolutionary content.[66] Fidel Castro seized upon revolutionary educational goals, such as the campaign against illiteracy, to transform the attitudes, values, and behavior of Cuba's citizens. Peruvians have preferred a much safer approach. In so doing, they have foregone opportunities, to the disappointment of revolutionaries of a variety of casts.[67]

[65] See Richard R. Fagen, *The Transformation of Political Culture in Cuba*, Stanford, Calif.: Stanford University Press, 1969, pp. 62ff.

[66] The participatory ethic as applied since 1970 in the formulation of educational policy in Peru could be judged as an opportunity for conservative elements to cut back reform proposals. Education, unlike the agrarian sector or the industrial sector, does not counterpose two competing or, more commonly, conflicting groups—peasants versus landowners, workers versus capitalists. There is no one voice from those who would benefit from state control of preschool education, the formation of school districts, or a more equal sharing of the primary school resources. On the other hand, groups opposed to these policies, essentially elements of the church and private education sector, are ready and able to defend their position.

[67] By doing so, the regime has made itself vulnerable to the charge that revolutionary rhetoric does not correspond with subsequent action and that they are more concerned with symbol than with substance. Examples are the appeal in December 1972 to replace Santa Claus with "El Niño Manuelito"—the former representing an "alienating influence of foreign values," the latter "a more authentic figure from Peruvian folklore"—and the threatened cancel-

This reform is noteworthy, therefore, not only for actions which have been decided and initiated, but also for issues laid aside or rejected. Perhaps foremost among these is the treatment of private schools, including church schools, and the teaching of religion. In the enthusiasm and flush of historical opportunity, experienced after the formation of the reform commission in late 1969, the existence of privilege and status, as symbolized by the expensive private schools in Lima's suburban belt, drew early attention. The commission considered among other alternatives the direct management of the private schools by the community education council. According to this policy, elitist private education would disappear. Its resources would be opened up to children in the community. No longer could these schools select children on the basis of their capacity to handle a foreign language.[68] All texts and materials would be approved by the ministry and thus adhere to official dogma. Teachers' appointments and salary scales would be subject to ministry norms.

Reaction to these bold initiatives was swift and telling. Associations of private school parents, the Council of Bishops, and the major conservative newspapers in Lima conducted a lengthy campaign. In scarcely veiled attacks on members of the commission, the conservative daily, *La Prensa*, produced a series of articles on the political premises of the reforms. To illustrate, they observed that two Russian specialists in preschool education (visiting Peru in relation to relief work in the region affected by the 1970 earthquake) had offered a public seminar on preschool education. The paper prepared an editorial entitled "Soviet Model for Peruvian Education?"[69] The minister of education answered the charges by arguing that the reform was in harmony with the doctrine of Vatican II. He promised to respect the independence

---

lation of the bullfight season in late 1973 on the basis that these spectacles "drain scarce foreign exchange for events that are beyond family budgets of the popular classes."

[68] A second component of language policy involves the teaching of foreign languages. To many, Peru's dependency on the United States and European nations and the link between foreign and local aristocratic elites are symbolized by several elite private schools in Lima which use a foreign language for most, if not all, of their teaching. The draft of the General Law of Education proposed to eliminate teaching in a foreign language prior to age 11, but the opposition from private schools and their supporters led the government to strike that provision from the final law.

[69] *La Prensa*, Oct. 4, 1970.

of the private schools. The final version of the law omitted several major early proposals on private education, although the subsequent regulations prepared by technicians in the ministry, including former members of the commission, reintroduced somewhat more bite. In agreement with one of the objectives of the commission, the law did assure that parents had the right to determine religious education for their children. If they so desired, parents could exempt their children from religion courses in public schools. The ministry has since designed a new religion program, giving broader attention to concepts rather than to belief or practices.

An area which received remarkably little attention was the proposed policy of coeducation. Peru, like other Andean countries, displays a gap between the average level of education of the two sexes. In 1970, 40 percent of the female population five years of age or more was without formal instruction; the corresponding figure for males was 23 percent.[70] The quotation introducing this chapter promises a new education that emphasizes the responsibilities and rights of every Peruvian man and woman. But without a common educational experience, let alone equal educational opportunity, the two sexes cannot assert equal claims to responsibilities or rights. Spokesmen for private schools and the church opposed coeducation. Surprisingly, even the officials of the ministry and those in charge of teacher training were also against the policy. They claimed that neither the parents, particularly in the rural towns and villages, nor the teachers, who had themselves experienced separate education, were ready for this change. The law asserts that the ministry will implement coeducation gradually and only after careful study of the conditions in each area. The ministry plans no action at present.

A further "road not taken" involves the proposal for an early campaign for literacy and *concientización*, drawn up in 1970 by a subcommission on rural education. Financial pressure, recognition of the magnitude of the task, and perhaps the lack of persuasive ideology to provide the drive necessary to sustain an effort probably combined to produce a shelving of that plan. Another reason might have been the reluctance of the military to begin a program in rural areas that might stir up the population, particularly before the agrarian reform initiated in 1969 took full effect.

[70] *Algunas Características Socio-Económicas*, vol. 2, p. 5.

In this case, failure to move quickly does not necessarily indicate assignment of low priority to programs of rural education and adult literacy. On the contrary, early reports and plans emphasized the rural areas, in particular the southern highlands, an area of intense social conflict in the sixties. Peru is not alone in its measured pace on this front: Even Fidel Castro waited two and one-half years before mounting his war against illiteracy, which began from a much higher base and occurred in a more developed, more homogeneous, and less prohibitive national context. In 1973, with the burden of the law and the corresponding bylaws lifted, the ministry began an ambitious program for literacy, with priority attention to rural areas affected by the agrarian reform. This project began with the recruitment of students, teachers, and peasant leaders for training in literacy techniques, and emphasis on the Paulo Freire approach. Analyses of the experimental results in 1973 will be used for further efforts in 1974. In contrast with the political exuberance of the early proposal, the current initiative reveals a slower, lower-risk approach.

Perhaps the most intractable problem the educational reform has faced and has yet to solve concerns the opposition of teachers. In Peru, as the saying goes, one learns despite his teachers. While this may hold some truth for the secondary and university levels, it does not apply at the primary level. If the new education is to change the children of Peru, it will be by means of teachers committed to the reform. But Peruvian schoolteachers have every reason to resist initiatives issuing from the Ministry of Education. In many cases working under prohibitive physical conditions, frequently victims of unscrupulous administrators, often promised but seldom receiving, they have learned that opposition rather than cooperation holds more promise for the solution to their problems.[71] With the improved prospects for con-

[71] In a book first published in 1956, Luis Alberto Sánchez stated that "despite a low salary, teachers are a heroic bunch. . . . [The rural school teacher] resists the opposition and abuse of the large landholder, whose orders most public officials obey. The life of a provincial teacher is almost an odyssey. He's never secure. The Representative seeks him out as an instrument for political propaganda; the judge uses him as a scribe; the chief of police, as a counsellor; the priest, as a protector of morals. . . . [p. 192]" The charming little book has been reissued as one of a series of a hundred inexpensive works by outstanding Peruvian authors. The program is subsidized by the government in its general policy of cultural diffusion. See Luis Alberto Sánchez, *Retrato de un País Adolescente*, Lima: Biblioteca Peruana, 1973.

tinuing financial gain extended by Belaúnde in 1965, a larger proportion of males entered the teaching force. The wage freeze applied since 1967 to these new teachers, mainly graduates of the new universities and normal schools, reinforced growing political radicalization. Despite the substantial raises provided in 1972 and 1973, the more than eighty thousand schoolteachers of Peru continue to impede and block repeated efforts at reconciliation. Their opposition forced the government to form a commission in 1972 to examine the problems of the teachers. The recommendations of this commission resulted in salary increases awarded in 1973 and in the policy to form teacher cooperatives. These cooperatives are financed by a fraction of the increase and will offer social services and related consumers' benefits for teachers. Symbolic of the continuing conflict, the elections for directors of cooperatives led to broad victories, gaining over 80 percent of votes cast, for the representatives supported by the powerful teachers' union, and opposed by the ministry and SINAMOS. This experience, highlighting the political problem posed for the government by the teachers, surely contains the further lesson that producing educational change from within established structures will be more difficult than launching new educational programs not involving the schools.

In conclusion, the educational reform prompted by the military regime and their civilian advisers contains often innovative educational proposals which are, however, far from radical. That reformist tone should not come as a surprise to those who have followed Peruvian education for at least a decade. In retrospect, however, it is surprising that this educational reform so explicitly recognizes the hopelessness in Peru of merely expanding and improving education. Problems of the rural masses, the urban poor, and even the emergent, if precarious, urban middle groups, are seen in a structural and, therefore, political context. The resulting educational prescription is similarly structural and political. No amount of criticism or opposition between the publication of the commission report and the issuing of the General Law of Education eliminated the essential political justification of the reform. If anything, the clarification emerging from the debate of that era resulted in increased attention to mechanisms for reaching these groups. The further development of these means is largely the present task.

Looking ahead, one may predict many continuing problems resulting from the confrontation of educational demand and the rationing of limited resources. Indeed, one could even predict that without some measure of redistribution of resources and power on other levels, the allocation of educational resources will not correspond to the rhetoric of the reform. For some time, at least, those groups in Peru who have received the best education will continue to do so, and with some considerable margin.

If the regime is successful, however, in promoting and obtaining meaningful participation in education by a larger sector of the population (participation in formulating and managing educational policy as well as in attending school), then it will be faced with the need to deal with more intense criticism on a broader front than it has had to face in the past. As problems pyramid, disillusionment may set in, and the government will be under greater cross-pressures to become more radical or to draw back. The military rulers will no doubt struggle to maintain the civilian commitment but will find the task increasingly difficult in the growing contradiction between creating a dynamic economic order and obtaining the participation of a mobilized citizenry.

8

Direct Foreign Investment in Peru: New Rules for an Old Game

Shane Hunt

INTRODUCTION

The Peruvian Revolution has altered drastically the place of direct foreign investment in the nation's economic life. The dimensions of this change can be appreciated only if we begin before the beginning, tracing the evolution of policies and attitudes toward foreign investment in the twenty years preceding October 1968, when civilian government came to an end. The paper begins with a summary of that history. Then it describes how the present government has developed its foreign investment policy, first by reviewing the development of general laws and policy statements, then by surveying several case histories of expropriation and contract renegotiation. Next, it draws on further case studies to describe Peru's new approach to doing business with foreigners and assesses the foreigners' reaction to the new rules of the game. The paper then concludes with a summary of the extent to which foreign investment policy has changed under the Peruvian Revolution and the directions of further change that seem indicated for the future.

This study was supported by a grant from the Joint Committee on Latin American Studies of the Social Science Research Council and the American Council of Learned Societies. I am greatly indebted to Janet Ballantyne, Dan Cochran, Louis Goodman, Abraham Lowenthal, Stanley Rose, Guillermo van Oordt, Raymond Vernon, and Richard Webb, all of whom gave thoughtful criticism to earlier drafts, and to numerous businessmen and government officials who granted me confidential interviews. My debt is equally great to Doris Garvey and Jirina Rybacek, who assembled various facts in Princeton, and to Marcia Koth de Paredes, who dug up valuable materials in Peru. Finally, my special thanks to Jerri Kavanagh and Ann DeMarchi for their speedy and efficient secretarial efforts.

PERU UNDER THE OLD RULES OF THE GAME

The United States emerged from World War II at the zenith of its power and moral authority. The bastion of democracy, it had saved the world from fascism. The dominant economy in a shattered world economic system, its resources seemed essential to any effort at economic reconstruction and development.

Peru emerged from World War II a weak, underdeveloped economy, and immediately entered a period of divisive political conflict over fundamental issues of economic policy: inflation, deficit spending, exchange controls, and devaluation. Throughout the presidency of José Luis Bustamante (1945–1948), the economy remained paralyzed by political strife between an intractable APRA and an equally intractable conservative elite.

The issues that divided Peru held enormous significance for United States business interests. Their export operations became increasingly unprofitable as the authorities held grimly to the pegged official exchange rate despite a near doubling of wholesale prices in three years. The traditional elite, deriving much of its economic power from cotton and sugar exporting, also grew increasingly restive under exchange control. Despite intense Aprista opposition, the political and economic pressures for devaluation became irresistible. The first major devaluation came in September 1948, but it could not arrest the process of political deterioration. The following month General Manuel Odría launched his successful coup, returning conservative interests to full power and driving APRA undergound. When the official rate was abandoned in November 1949, exporters were able to exchange all their foreign exchange earnings at a new floating rate that represented a 141 percent devaluation.[1] Controls were dismantled and rates were unified. In a continent that was witnessing ever-increasing state intervention in economic life in country after country, Peru had turned around to begin a march in the other direction that continued for the next eighteen years.

Foreign investors could not have been more pleased. For minerals exporters, terms of trade increased from 117 (1945 = 100)

[1] The November 1949 certificate rate stood at 15.68 soles to the dollar, compared to the official rate of 6.50 soles. (15.68 − 6.50)/6.50 = 141 percent. This exchange rate experience is documented in Rolf Hayn, "Peruvian Exchange Controls: 1945–1948," *Inter-American Economic Affairs*, vol. 10, Spring 1957, pp. 47–70.

in 1948 to 169 in 1949.[2] Furthermore, the floating rate gave assurance of more rapid adjustment in future periods of domestic inflation or external recession. The new exchange rate system was followed by a new mining code, promulgated in May 1950, that replaced onerous export taxes with the more moderate income tax obligations then required of industrial and commercial firms. This change was further sweetened by a number of special ingredients: exemption from excess profits taxes, exoneration of import duties on mining equipment, provision of percentage depletion, and guarantees against new taxes for twenty-five years.[3] Through these changes the total tax burden of the mining sector declined from 35 percent of gross profits in 1948 to about 20 percent in the early 1950s.[4] For U.S. companies, the total decline was greater still, since the switch from export to income taxation permitted taxes paid in Peru to be credited against tax liabilities in the United States.

Besides these features of the Código de Minería, the famous Article 56 provided that, in deposits declared to be of marginal quality, especially low tax rates could be negotiated and would remain in effect until the investor had amortized his original capital outlay.[5] This clause provided legal basis for the Toquepala contract, signed with the newly created Southern Peru Copper Corporation in 1954. The Toquepala contract guaranteed a 30 percent tax rate until the investment had "earned net profits (after deduction of depreciation, mine preparation, amortization, depletion, and all taxes) sufficient to amortize therewith all capital investment."[6] This special provision gave virtually no extra margin of benefit, since other U.S. mining firms were paying

[2] Shane Hunt, "The Growth Performance of Peru," 1967, mimeo, p. 19.

[3] José Rocha Fernandini, "La legislación minera en el Perú durante el siglo XX," in José Pareja Paz Soldan, ed., *Visión del Perú en el siglo XX*, Lima, Ediciones Librería Studium, 1962, vol. 1, pp. 229–259. Also Romulo Ferrero, *Comentarios acerca de los impuestos en el Perú*, Lima, 1955, p. 8.

[4] Total taxes, including *arbitrios*, expressed as a percentage of gross profits plus tax payments, declined over 1948–1954 as follows: 35, 28, 27, 21, 12, 25, and 20 percent. Source: Banco Central de Reserva, *Renta nacional del Perú, 1942–1949*, Lima, 1950, pp. 94–95, and similar tables in other issues.

[5] Código de Minería, reprinted in *Peruvian Times*, Special Mining and Petroleum Number, Aug. 1951, p. 25.

[6] Toquepala contract, reprinted in *Peruvian Times*, Nov. 19, 1954, p. 7.

about 30.6 percent at the time.[7] However, it set the stage for acrimonious controversy twelve years later.

Thus Peru opened its doors wide to foreign investment, and for the first time in decades big investments poured in. Foreign business groups applauded Peru's new direction. "In its mining and oil codes," wrote *Fortune*, "Peru has viewed the modern wielder of power shovel and drilling rig not as an 'exploiter' but as the fulcrum for economic development. More important, it has maintained a scrupulous respect for private property and for the principle of free markets and convertibility."[8] The country's leading conservative proudly stated: "Peru has come to be looked upon as one of the most attractive countries for foreign investment in Latin America."[9]

The triumph of conservative economic policy was not brought about without controversy. Before Odría's coup, the political battle centering in the Congress found reflection in all parts of Peruvian intellectual life. After the coup the voice of APRA was silenced, and public discussion became distorted by the threat of censorship, but sufficient freedom remained to permit a raging debate on Odría's exchange rate policy between Lima's leading newspapers, *El Comercio* and *La Prensa*.

The curious feature is that so bruising a fight could have ignored foreign interests so completely. Critics of the new system tore into *La Prensa* and the export interests it represented as if such interests were exclusively Peruvian.[10] The deposed President Bustamante, sitting down in exile to write a defense of his administration, produced a political testament that never once mentioned foreign companies.[11] The major changes in mining

[7] This consisted of a 20 percent industrial profits tax; 12 percent on dividend remissions, and 1 percent on foreign branches. Cf. Ferrero, *Comentarios*, pp. 9–12. Also Charles W. Wright, "What Chance Has Foreign Capital in Peru," *Engineering and Mining Journal*, vol. 155, Dec. 1954, pp. 82–83.

[8] John Davenport, "Why Peru Pulls Dollars," *Fortune*, vol. 54, Nov. 1956, p. 131.

[9] Pedro Beltrán, "Foreign Loans and Politics in Latin America," *Foreign Affairs*, vol. 34, Jan. 1956, p. 302.

[10] The exchange rate debate is discussed in Wilson Brown, "Governmental Measures Affecting Exports in Peru, 1945–1962: A Study of Policy and Its Making," unpublished doctoral dissertation, Fletcher School of Law and Diplomacy, 1965, pp. 143–152.

[11] José Luis Bustamante i Rivero, *Tres años de lucha por la democracia en el Perú*, Buenos Aires, 1949.

legislation passed nearly unnoticed and totally uncriticized.[12] With the United States standing at its zenith, only *termacéfalos* (hotheads) would think of attacking North American investments in postwar Peru.

So remarkable a situation was destined to unravel with the passage of time. APRA, permitted to reemerge in 1956, soon began a steady drumbeat of criticism against the mining agreements signed during Odría's dictatorship. "The sellout of our natural resources during the eight years under the regime of official terror," wrote an Aprista columnist in 1958, "has no precedent in the history of our republic."[13] The tempo picked up after 1959, when a sharp increase in gasoline prices rekindled old animosities toward the International Petroleum Company (IPC). Then in 1963 Fernando Belaúnde captured the presidency and brought to power a new social group: middle-class, technocratic, and to a degree infused with Social Christian thought.[14] This new generation made Belaúnde's government more nationalistic than any of its predecessors. Yet despite occasional statements of impatience over economic relations with the United States and despite somewhat greater severity of terms for foreign investors in petroleum and mining, Peru's favorable view of foreign investment remained unaltered.

This favorable view is revealed by the absence of a general policy toward foreign investment. No policy existed because no problem was preceived. Thus when Belaúnde's economic strategy spoke of developing *"la industria nacional,"* this term merely referred to industry located physically within Peru, without reference to nationality of ownership.[15] In a similar vein, Belaúnde captured the rising nationalist sentiment of the time in the title of his political testament: *La conquista del Perú por los peruanos.*[16] Despite the title, however, the book had nothing to

---

[12] See, for example, *La Prensa*, May 13 and 24, 1950. *El Comercio*, Aug. 9, 1949, May 13, 1950.

[13] *La Tribuna*, Nov. 19, 1958.

[14] Arnold Payne, "Peru: Latin America's Silent Revolution," *Inter-American Economic Affairs*, vol. 20, Winter 1966, pp. 69–78.

[15] Fernando Belaúnde Terry, *El Perú construye: Mensaje presentado al Congreso Nacional por el Presidente Constitucional de la República Arquitecto Fernando Belaúnde Terry el 28 de Julio de 1965*, Lima, Minerva, 1965, pp. 264–266.

[16] Fernando Belaúnde Terry, *Peru's Own Conquest*, Lima, American Studies Press, 1965.

do with throwing out the foreigners; rather its concern lay in an engineering conquest of terrain, in mountains and jungle. Belaúnde's generation viewed development entirely as an engineering and technocratic problem.

The investment climate thus remained generally warm and sunny, but storm clouds began gathering over petroleum fields and copper mines. The case of IPC is so well known and so peculiar that it will not be discussed in this paper. Mining, however, cannot be set aside so quickly through claims of special distinctiveness. The changing treatment extended to the mining industry holds more general significance for what it says about changing attitudes toward foreign investment in general.

The first moves concerned tax rates. In 1950 mining companies had been required to pay the full industrial profits tax, but they were unaffected by the rate increase of 1958 that raised the top bracket from 20 to 35 percent. When Belaúnde raised the top bracket for mining companies to 30 percent in February 1964 and then to 35 percent in November of the same year, the companies protested that such increases violated the guarantee against new taxes contained in the Código de Minería.[17] The government's reply held that the new laws lay fully within the code, since they were not new taxes but rather new rates on old taxes. Indeed, the government was quite correct, such was the terminological looseness with which the Código de Minería had been drafted. The foreign companies grumbled, but they could do nothing as the total tax bite on profits rose from about 30 to 48.65 percent.[18]

With this change the Toquepala contract, guaranteeing a tax rate frozen at 30 percent, took on an entirely new significance. By the mid-1960s, the war in Vietnam had driven copper prices sky-high, and the owners of the "marginal" mine were making money hand over fist. Peru awaited the moment when Southern Peru would recover its capital, for the government's share of profits could then jump by 18.65 percentage points. One can therefore

[17] *Peruvian Times*, Mar. 6, 1964, p. 6; Nov. 6, 1964, p. 1; Nov. 20, 1964, p. 1. U.S. Embassy, "Some Factors Bearing on New Mining Ventures in Peru," Lima, Mar. 23, 1967 (mimeo), p. 6.

[18] On top of this, a partial exchange control was introduced in February 1964 with the ruling that depletion allowances could no longer be repatriated but had to be reinvested. See Hernando de Lavalle, *A Statement of the Laws of Peru in Matters Affecting Business.* Supplement no. 1, Washington, Pan American Union, 1965, p. 21. U.S. Embassy, "New Mining Ventures," p. 7.

image the consternation of those Peruvians who first looked into the fine print of the Toquepala contract to discover that the 30 percent rate remained in force until *net* profits, net of taxes, *depreciation*, and *depletion*, had accumulated to equal the original investment.

Very quickly, Southern Peru found itself under attack from several directions. In 1965 the director of tax collections (Superintendente de Contribuciones) ruled that Southern Peru had already recovered its capital and would thenceforth be liable to the normal tax rate. This declaration, apparently based on a definition of capital recuperation that blithely ignored the fine print of the contract, found only faint support within the government itself. Southern Peru appealed to the courts but violated Peruvian law by failing to pay up pending the judicial decision. The government permitted this illegality and thereby outraged vocal sectors of Peruvian opinion. The finance minister even attempted to quash the Superintendente's initiative.[19]

Also in 1965, the Congress formed a special commission to investigate the Toquepala contract. Its labors covered two years, and its articulate, detailed final report excoriated the Código de Minería, the contract, and the company itself.[20]

As congressional hearings and fiscal quarrels dragged on through months and years, various critics, led particularly by the newsweekly *Oiga*, widened the attack to every aspect of the government's copper policy. Criticism on other issues accumulated rapidly: underpricing of exports, manipulation of account books, falsification of metallic content, particularly of gold and silver traces, unreasonably low tax rates.[21] Again and again, critics hammered home the message that the assertion of Peruvian sovereignty required much tougher bargains to be driven with the foreign miners. Characterizing Toquepala as "a fabulously rich

[19] *Oiga*, May 19, 1967, p. 8. The case is reviewed in *Oiga*, Nov. 28, 1969.

[20] Peru, Congreso. *Dictamen de la Comisión Bicameral Multipartidaria encargada de revisar el convenio celebrado entre el Gobierno del Perú y la Southern Peru Copper Corporation, para la explotación de las minas de Toquepala y Quellaveco, y su amplicación para las de Cuajone*, 2 vols., Lima, Feb. 1967. The findings are summarized in Carlos Malpica, *Los dueños del Perú*, 3d ed., Lima, Ediciones Ensayos Sociales, 1968, pp. 176–181.

[21] *Oiga*, Nov. 19, 1965, pp. 15–16; May 27, 1966, pp. 10–11; May 12, 1967, p. 11; June 21, 1968, pp. 8–9; Nov. 28, 1969. *Dictamen . . .*, pp. 90–93. Malpica, *Los dueños*, pp. 173–187.

mine" (una mina riquísima), Oiga brushed aside any fears that foreign investors would be scared away from Peru's mineral wealth:

Throughout the world there exist capital funds interested in investing in copper mines. If the present holders of concessions decide that our conditions are not suitable, we can anticipate, with absolute certainty, that other investment sources from other countries will come forward.[22]

As we shall see below, later events have not substantiated this view, such has been the international investment community's skittishness about risk taking in a revolutionary setting. Nevertheless, my own preliminary estimates suggest that Toquepala had indeed become una mina riquísima and that foreign investors generally secured very healthy profit rates in Peru under the Ancien Régime. These estimates, which are discussed in a separate paper, show that Toquepala earned an after-tax return of about 19 percent for Southern Peru, whereas Marcona earned about 28 percent on its iron ore venture.[23] The corresponding figures for U.S. manufacturing investment in Peru stand at about 16 or 17 percent. Although these profit estimates are not nearly as high as the figures used by some critics, they indicate that Peru had indeed become an attractive country for foreign investors. The aspirations articulated by conservatives in the 1950s had come true, even at the same time that the critics of the 1960s were starting to make Peru look less attractive. Reflecting the alarm of U.S. investors who witnessed the attacks on Southern Peru and other companies, the U.S. Embassy's survey of the situation spoke of "political ideologies in Peru [that] counterbalance somewhat the benefits offered by the geological and mineralogical situation."[24]

The Toquepala question remained unresolved until Finance Minister Ulloa reached a new agreement with the company as part of his emergency fiscal measures in mid-1968. That agree-

[22] Oiga, May 12, 1967, p. 11; June 21, 1968, p. 8.

[23] Shane Hunt, "Direct Foreign Investment in Peru under the Ancien Régime," Conference on External Finance in Latin America, University of Cambridge, June 1974, mimeo.

[24] U.S. Embassy, "New Mining Ventures," p. 8.

ment required Southern Peru to give up its favored treatment and pay normal tax rates retroactively, but only from the beginning of 1968.[25] Although this perhaps represented a reasonable compromise between the maintenance of legal fine points and acquiescence to absurd contract provisions inherited from the past, three years of acrimonious debate could not be so quickly washed away. The special disadvantages of direct foreign investment remained more obvious than ever before to important sectors of public opinion. The fundamentally favorable view of the Belaúnde government toward foreign investment had not been altered, but this perhaps merely indicated the continuing failure of that government to recognize the power and importance of changing attitudes. The storm clouds were gathering over the Palacio de Gobierno as well.

THE PERUVIAN REVOLUTION AND THE NEW RULES OF THE GAME

From the moment that the armed forces took power in October 1968 and declared Peru to be entered into a revolutionary process, official pronouncements on questions of economic development changed significantly in both language and substance. In part, this change merely reflected regional intellectual currents, as Latin America moved (leftwards) from *cepalismo* to *dependencia*. But the change in Peru was particularly abrupt and drastic. Here one beheld a government whose access to power had been triggered by the historic abuses of a foreign company and whose first year of rule was marked by intense diplomatic and economic pressures exerted by the United States. It is hardly surprising that the Peruvian leadership was quick to incorporate concepts such as external dependence and imperialism into its official diagnoses of the Peruvian development problem. Thus in the words of President Velasco:

The structural root of the great problems that beset Peruvian society . . . arises in final analysis from its double, interrelated condition of being a society that is underdeveloped and subject to imperialist domination. . . . For this reason it is not possible to resolve any of our major problems without

25 *La Prensa*, June 19, 1968. *Oiga*, June 21, 1968, pp. 8–9.

confronting the crucial questions of dependence and underdevelopment.[26]

Clearly the development problem was no longer considered essentially technocratic.

Throughout Latin America, the U.S.-based multinational corporation has commonly been marked as the principal mechanism for the exercise of imperialism and the perpetuation of dependence. In the Peruvian case, this link to foreign direct investment remained conspicuously absent in revolutionary ideology, except in the case of the International Petroleum Company. Time and again, however, Velasco and others emphasized that the IPC affair was an exception and, "for that reason, a case which has no relation to the policy followed by the Revolutionary Government with other foreign companies that exploit the country's natural resources and whose legitimately acquired rights are respected and will always be guaranteed."[27]

The analytical link between foreign investment and imperialism was avoided by the Peruvian government because it decided not to throw the foreigners out. Rather, it has chosen to tame the multinational beast, to make it work better for national interests. This approach, being more pragmatic than ideologically elemental, has given foreign-investment policy low ranking among the points rattled off in any summary of the Revolution's accomplishments.[28]

The pragmatic approach to foreign investment emerged in President Velasco's first Independence Day speech of July 1969. The old way of doing business was rejected, since "private invest-

[26] Speech of Oct. 28, 1971, reprinted in Comité de Asesoramiento de la Presidencia de la República (COAP), *La revolución nacional peruana, 1968–1972*, Lima, 1972, p. 95.

[27] Juan Velasco Alvarado, speech of Jan. 31, 1969, reprinted in *Velasco, La voz de la revolución. Discursos del Presidente de la República General de División Juan Velasco Alvarado, 1968–1970*, Lima, Ediciones Peisa, n.d., p. 15.

[28] For example, a study of the Centro de Altos Estudios Militares (CAEM) lists five objectives and thirty-four accomplishments of the Revolutionary Government without ever mentioning foreign investment ("Today's Peru," Lima, mimeo, 1972). The 223 pages of the national economic plan for 1971–1975 contain precisely one paragraph on foreign direct investment, and that paragraph restricts itself to generalities (Presidencia de la República, *Plan nacional de desarrollo, 1971–1975. Plan Global*. Lima, 1971, p. 46).

ment, even if it creates points of economic modernization, serves under present conditions as a mechanism for removing wealth from Latin American countries." But Velasco immediately went on to state flatly: "Latin American development requires foreign capital."[29] Clearly the foreign investment game needed new rules.

When Velasco next returned to the subject of foreign investment in a public speech, in April 1970, he began by arguing that Peru indeed held the power to write new rules and obtain better bargains:

We are not a weak group of nations at the mercy of foreign capital. They need our raw materials and our markets. And if we need capital goods and advanced technology, the evident bilaterality of these needs must lead to new arrangements that protect the present and future interests of Latin America.[30]

This stated, Velasco proceeded to outline the two main rules of the new game. First, natural resources and basic industries would be reserved for state enterprise. Second, in other nonbasic sectors, foreign investment "would be channeled through joint ventures or through private companies, subject to a fixed period of reversion to the state once the total investment and an acceptable return have been covered by profits."[31]

With these words Peru adopted the fade-out joint venture as its principal new instrument of tightened control over foreign investment. This new so-called Velasco Doctrine, emphasizing bargaining and joint ventures, carried a message vaguely familiar to anyone whose memory stretched back forty years to similar proposals put forward by such dissimilar advocates as Haya de la Torre and Víctor Andrés Belaúnde.[32] The difference lay in the fact that in 1970, for the first time, the government was prepared to do something about it.

When implementing legislation followed a few months later, it went well beyond new rules for foreigners and encompassed

[29] Speech of July 28, 1969, reprinted in *Velasco, La voz de la revolución,* p. 62.

[30] Speech of Apr. 6, 1970, reprinted in *Velasco, La voz de la revolución,* p. 203.

[31] Ibid., p. 204.

[32] Víctor Raúl Haya de la Torre, *El antimperialismo y el APRA,* 2d ed., Santiago, Ediciones Ercilla, 1936, pp. 33–36. Víctor Andrés Belaúnde, *La realidad nacional,* 3d ed., Lima, 1963, p. 197.

the total restructuring of industrial enterprise. The major provisions of the Ley General de Industrias affected all private enterprise, both national and foreign.[33] Only a few firms would be affected by the reservation of basic sectors to state enterprise. But every firm was shaken to its roots by the prospect of compulsory profit sharing that would lead to eventual joint ownership and joint decision making with the firm's workers. Although the law contained special provisions for reducing foreign ownership in any firm to minority participation, this involved little extra burden in a situation where all firms were required to surrender 50 percent of equity to the workers. The only difference, which could be a very important difference, concerned the period required for divestment. For national enterprises following the dictates of the Ley de Industrias, the time required for raising worker participation to 50 percent depended on the firm's profit rate and reinvestment policy.[34] The special provisions for foreign firms could result in a more rapid divestment for foreigners. Provision for such an eventuality was established in the Reglamento of the Ley de Industrias, but the actual pace of divestment was left open for subsequent negotiation.[35]

The Ley de Industrias avoided all but the most basic outlines of a foreign investment policy because such a policy had first to be developed within the Andean Group. Decision 24, when it emerged from the Andean bargaining table in late 1970, contained many of the controls and restrictions implicit in the idea of tougher bargaining but missing in previous Peruvian legislation.[36] Thenceforth, it stated, foreign investors would be subject

[33] *Decreto Ley 18350*, July 27, 1970. This and other relevant legislation is reprinted in Confederación Nacional de Comerciantes (CONACO), *Régimen industrial del Perú*, Lima, 1972. Important provisions are summarized in Price Waterhouse Peat and Co., *Information Guide for Doing Business in Peru*, Feb. 1973.

[34] In fact, a high rate of reinvestment from profits could keep the workers' share below 50 percent permanently. See Pedro de las Casas, Angel de las Casas, and Augusto Llosa, *Análisis de la participación de la comunidad industrial en el capital social de la empresa*, Lima, Universidad de Pacífico, Centro de Investigación Interdepartamental, 1970, mimeo.

[35] See articles 16 and 17 of the law and articles 215, 216 and 229 of the reglamento, CONACO, *Régimen Industrial*, pp. 83, 216–220.

[36] Decision 24 was ratified by Peru as *Decreto Ley 18900*, dated June 30, 1971. The text is reprinted in CONACO, *Régimen Industrial*, pp. 282–303. The history of Decision 24 is reviewed in John Lindquist, "The Merits of Forced

to regulations regarding permission to invest, terms of overseas borrowing, and access to local credit. Contracts for licensing patents or trademarks, or for obtaining technical assistance, would be subject to review. Annual profit repatriation would be limited to 14 percent of invested capital. The most publicized feature of Decision 24, however, was its endorsement of the Velasco Doctrine; it required forced divestment to a minority position, under an explicit deadline of fifteen years. Last-minute compromise between Peru and Colombia partially dissipated the impact of this provision, however, by exempting already-established foreign firms that did not intend to take advantage of trade liberalization under the Andean Common Market.

In subsequent legislation of early 1972, the Peruvian government reasserted its application of forced divestment to all foreign manufacturing firms, not just those exporting to other parts of the Andean Group; but the time period remained open to case-by-case bargaining.[37]

The new rules of the game, thus set up in general form, called for a massive bureaucratic effort to fill in the details. Each control provision implied a new regulatory agency, a new series of procedures, and a new area of administrative jurisprudence. Once these details are established, the new system will be normalized.

This has not yet happened. The government, preoccupied throughout 1972 and 1973 with more immediate problems in the functioning of industrial communities and the industrial programming negotiations of the Andean Group, has left many of the most important details hanging unresolved.[38] While little progress has been made in the refinement of general rules, however, new developments in foreign investment policy have taken place on two other fronts. The first concerns expropriation and reorganization as the government has dealt with foreign com-

---

Divestment: The Experience of the Andean Group," Research Program in Economic Development, discussion paper no. 31, Princeton University, Oct. 1972, mimeo.

37 CONACO, *Régimen Industrial*, pp. 328–329; Price Waterhouse, *Information Guide*, p. 63.

38 Such as, for example, the definition of foreign investment upon which the 14-percent profits repatriation is based. Note the bewilderment of Price Waterhouse, *Information Guide*, p. 70.

panies in basic sectors earmarked for transfer to state control. The second concerns negotiations with particular foreign investments required to achieve governmental targets for industrial and export development.

EXPROPRIATION AND REORGANIZATION IN BASIC SECTORS—SOME CASE STUDIES

For some foreign investors, the process of clearing private companies from the basic sectors meant expropriation with highly satisfactory settlements regarding compensation. Consider two cases from telecommunications and banking.

In the early years of the Belaúnde administration, the Compañia Peruana de Telefónos, an affiliate of ITT, provided Lima with terrible telephone service. It did so because its regulating agency, the Junta Nacional de Telecomunicaciones, refused rate increases. Finding itself locked into such a low return on past investment, the company refused to expand that investment despite the acute need for expansion of facilities.[39] On the other hand, the Junta felt a rate increase to be an inappropriate reward for such poor service. This impasse was finally broken in 1967 by an agreement that called for the company to double the number of telephone lines within three years, in return for which rate increases would be granted sufficient to earn a 12 percent return. Both parties carried out their sides of the bargain. The company's expansion program improved service dramatically; the government authorized rate increases even at moments of political difficulty.[40]

This new harmonious relationship notwithstanding, in October 1969 the Revolutionary Government suddenly announced the expropriation of ITT's 69 percent share in the telephone company. Final agreement was reached quickly and called for ITT to receive $14.8 million for shares that had been carried on the books at a value of $18.5 million. Four million dollars would be paid in dollars, the rest in soles or value in kind. With these local accounts, ITT agreed to build and operate a major new hotel, valued at $12 million, and a telephone equipment factory that

[39] The company's annual return on investment averaged 6.8 percent over 1958–1966. *Peruvian Times*, Apr. 11, 1969, p. 6.

[40] *Peruvian Times*, Mar. 15 and May 10, 1968.

would be 40-percent government-owned. In addition, Bell Telephone of Belgium, an ITT subsidiary, would receive various contracts for telephone lines and equipment supply.[41]

ITT emerged quite satisfied from negotiations that had set total compensation at 80 percent of book value. Although this result could have been lamented as a 20-percent loss, one must remember that the values were based largely on equipment purchases made from other subsidiaries of the same corporation and thus could have been challenged and even rejected by government negotiators suspicious of inflated asset prices. The incentive for such inflation was clear, since the higher the value, the greater the allowable profit under controlled rate setting. Suspicions notwithstanding, the government accepted all of ITT's equipment valuations. ITT got out of a tight corner with most of its capital not only intact but also invested in more promising sectors.

If ITT was content, so was the Peruvian government and Peruvian public opinion. The same cannot be said with respect to the terms upon which Chase Manhattan's share of the Banco Continental was bought out. Even before the price was announced, it was evident that the government would treat Chase well. Anticipating the announcement of favorable terms, the *Peruvian Times* commented on the government's desire to avoid an acrimonious expropriation, "because this could well create an unfavorable reaction in banking circles outside the country, some of which, it appears, were stunned by the sudden way the [Banco] Popular was taken over."[42] But even with this forewarning, the sober *Peruvian Times* gasped at the "sky-high prices" announced the following week: Chase was to get $6.3 million, as compared to the $1.7 million it had invested six years earlier. At a moment when the market value per Banco Continental share stood at 102 soles and the book value at 188, the government had agreed to a share price of 586 soles.

While the *Peruvian Times* was merely incredulous, other reactions in Peru ran from glee to outrage. Among the gleeful were to be found various politicians from the Belaúnde era, happy to grasp an opportunity for embarrassing the government on an issue of *entreguismo*. Among the outraged were the Loyal Left, *Oiga* and *Expreso*, who kept asking for more clarification to an

---

[41] *Peruvian Times*, Mar. 27, 1970.
[42] *Peruvian Times*, Aug. 28, 1970.

event they found difficult to comprehend. The clarifications that were issued consisted largely of accounting exercises that were remarkable for three reasons.[43] First, all valuation estimates were based on future profitability; the possibility of a valuation instead based on past investment costs was not even considered. Since the Banco Continental had become a very profitable business, this meant that the government freely conceded Chase's right to capitalize its high profit rate into the expropriation price. Second, within the possible calculations based on future profitability, the numbers actually chosen were particularly generous; they included an initial profit total taken from a very prosperous year, and a low discount rate on future profits which undoubtedly lay below Chase's opportunity cost of capital. Third, the detailed calculations underlying the valuation estimates can only be described as travesties of proper accounting practice. Crucial numbers were plucked from thin air; valuations based on past cost and future profitability were added together.

In fact, the price was not arrived at by such tenuous calculations, which rather represented ex post facto rationalizations. The price had been set by Chase Manhattan. In the economical words of *Caretas*, "Chase decided to sell dear."[44] Chase having named its price, take it or leave it, the Peruvian government took it and spent the following two months explaining itself. Public critics remained dissatisfied, and within the government even President Velasco felt obliged to express his unhappiness with proffered explanations.[45] In the end, however, the government stuck to the announced terms. It emerged from the experience with revolutionary credentials somewhat tarnished but with the consolation that in the future Peru would have a friend at Chase Manhattan.

ITT and Chase Manhattan emerged unscathed from the expropriation process, but other companies fared much less well. At this other extreme, consider the cases of two companies driven to the wall, a railroad and a refinery.

In the 1960s, major railway systems remained in private hands in only three countries of the world: United States, Canada, and Peru, where the Peruvian Corporation, that ancient artifact of

[43] Official valuation reports were reprinted in a special supplement of *La Prensa*, Nov. 13, 1970.

[44] *Caretas*, Nov. 15–19, 1970, p. 10.

[45] *Oiga*, Nov. 6, 1970, p. 8.

the British bondholders, continued operating the engineering marvels built a century ago by Henry Meiggs. As in so many countries, however, railways in Peru were a sick industry, in need of substantial infusions of capital for new equipment if trucking competition was to be fought off and economic survival assured. In 1962 the Peruvian Corporation obtained a loan of $19.5 million from the World Bank and Export-Import Bank, the Peruvian government serving as guarantor, in order to rejuvenate itself through the introduction of diesel engines and other new equipment. The effort failed. In 1967 the corporation defaulted on these loans, which were assumed by the government's Banco Industrial. Acting as an unpaid creditor, the government took over administration of the corporation in 1971 and in 1972 auctioned off and bought the assets for $21 million.

The passing brought little mourning but some recrimination. The president of the corporation charged that bankruptcy had been forced upon the railroad by the government's refusal to permit required rate increases. *Peruvian Times* commentary suggested the same thing, at the same time pointing out that road competition for Cerro de Pasco mineral output always represented a competitive threat that effectively controlled railroad rates. Government officials went even further, charging that road competition had obliged the corporation to set rates lower than those permitted by government regulation.[46] The controversy carried over to auction price as well. A government-approved valuation of 1971 set the corporation's assets at $62 million, but at the moment of auction in 1972 a new valuation of $31 million was produced. Since auction rules stipulated that the price paid had to be at least two-thirds of the valuation, the final price therefore came to $21 million. As chance would have it, this turned out to be just enough to cover outstanding indebtedness to the World Bank, Export-Import Bank, and workers' compensation fund.[47]

It appears that saving the Peruvian Corporation would have required vigorous government support, involving not only rate increases but also some control over trucking competition, perhaps in the name of avoiding wear and tear on the Central Highway. This the government had been unwilling to do under both

[46] *Peruvian Times*, Apr. 28 and Oct. 13, 1972.
[47] *Peruvian Times*, Aug. 25 and Nov. 17, 1972.

Belaúnde and the armed forces. Perhaps the corporation would have been permitted to reorganize under a continuing civilian government. As it turned out, the military government took over with a surgical incisiveness. No complaints were raised about excessive payments to corporation shareholders, because the corporation shareholders didn't get anything.

Refinería Conchán Chevron S.A. was set up in the early 1960s as a joint venture between Standard Oil of California and Prado interests. Warmly welcomed to Peru as a means of giving competition to IPC in the domestic market, the company was exempted from payment of turnover taxes under special provisions of the Ley de Promoción Industrial, declared by the government of President Prado. The exemptions were later challenged by government tax authorities, and litigation begun under the Belaúnde administration came to an end in May 1972 with a disallowal of the exemption and a claim of back taxes amounting to 86 million soles ($2 million).[48]

In the meantime, things had not gone well for Conchán. Standard of California found itself saddled with a wholly owned subsidiary, since its Peruvian partners never put up their capital subscription; moreover, they were saddled with a chronic loser, thanks to the severity of gasoline price controls in recent years. Payment of the back taxes would have obliged Standard of California to put more money into an operation that had no future. This they refused politely to do, so in June 1972 the company was intervened by the government, and, the following March, put up for auction. Only one bidder appeared, Petroperú, which offered an amount exactly equal to the amount of unpaid taxes.[49]

Throughout the whole procedure, the government scrupulously avoided any charges of corruption or bad faith on the company's part. Thus no tax penalties were claimed. However, neither was the government prepared to consider a negotiated settlement, letting the company off the hook for having perhaps made an honest mistake. Nor did it show particular generosity regarding the sale price. The official valuation, which exactly equalled the amount of back taxes, represented only a third of the company's own valuation.[50] Quite evidently, the government

48 *Peruvian Times*, June 9, 1972.

49 *Peruvian Times*, Mar. 23, 1973.

50 *Peruvian Times*, Mar. 2, 1973.

really didn't want Conchán around any more. Under new legislation, Petroperú is granted a monopoly of petroleum refining in Peru, so Conchán's very presence was an anachronism. Furthermore, any enterprise associated with Prado interests had to be viewed with a certain distaste.

Automotive Reorganization

From the extremes of expropriation experience, we next turn to a case of reorganization in that most reorganized of all industries, automobiles. In recent decades the conventional wisdom of economic development has made industrialization synonymous with economic progress. At the same time, particular industries have acquired fame as the key elements of industrial progress. The steel industry held this distinction for several decades until the close of the 1950s, when the mantle was transferred, first by Khrushchev to petrochemicals and then by Servan-Schreiber to computers.[51] For Latin America in the 1960s, this distinctive role was surely assigned to the automotive industry.

Like so many of its neighbors, Peru pushed ahead rapidly and decisively in the early 1960s to create its own automobile industry. Within the general provisions of the Ley de Promoción Industrial, a decree of late 1963 announced a number of special tax incentives for automobile assembly.[52] The decree held the line on the already high tariff rates for imported assembled vehicles and provided special exonerations on the importation of unassembled CKD (completely knocked down) kits. The kits were relieved of all specific tariffs and sustained only an ad valorem charge of between 10 and 15 percent. In addition, companies were exempted from the 5-percent turnover tax on sales between manufacturer and dealer, as well as certain additional charges, provided that only 10 percent of the car's value consisted of Peruvian parts. The government announced that it was prepared to sign five-year contracts on these terms, at the end of which period it would expect the local content share to have reached 30 percent.

The terms proved attractive enough to automobile assemblers. The first contract was signed with General Motors only three

[51] Jean-Jacques Servan-Schreiber, *The American Challenge*, New York, Atheneum, 1968.
[52] *Decreto Supremo 80*, Nov. 22, 1963.

months after the decree, and by April 1964 two contracts had been signed and nine other applications received from various automobile and truck producers.[53] This is hardly surprising: the rate of effective protection being offered the assembly industry amounted to something around 200 percent.[54] The figures in Table 8.1 give an indication both of the industry's growth and of

TABLE 8.1

The Automobile Industry in Peru, 1965–1972

(Units and millions of soles)

	Units Produced	Gross Value of Production	Imported Inputs	National Inputs	Wages and Salaries	Value Added
1965	2,824	S/. 314	S/. 173	S/. 21	S/. 54	S/.120
1966	13,170	1,437	911	155	142	371
1967	17,414	1,936	1,330	161	169	445
1968	10,119	1,576	919	127	178	530
1969	16,860	2,739	1,662	313	207	765
1970	14,456	2,441	1,544	338	205	559
1971	16,639	2,616	1,360	401	213	856
1972	23,796	3,899	—	785	284	—

Sources:

Asociación Peruana de la Industria Automotriz, *Boletín*, no. 68, January 1973, and special tabulations. Banco Industrial del Perú, *Situación de la Industria Manufacturera*, 1966 and 1967. Ministerio de Industria y Comercio, Dirección de Estadística, *Evolución de la Industria Manufacturera Peruana, 1968–1970*, Lima 1973. The 1971 data are from a special tabulation by the Ministerio de Industrias.

its financial condition. Value added is obtained by subtracting the value of inputs from the gross value of production and is in turn divisible into wages and salaries and profits gross of taxes and depreciation. Gross profit therefore came to the following:

[53] *Peruvian Times*, Apr. 10, 1964.

[54] In the early 1960s new cars sold for about double their c.i.f. value. Assuming a 33-percent distributor's markup, this implies a 50-percent nominal tariff rate. The c.i.f. value of CKD kits was about 80 percent that of an assembled vehicle. The rate of effective protection on value added is given by $[.50 - .8(.15)]/.2 = 190$ percent. Local content requirements lower this effective rate, however. Assume that the 30-percent local content is also priced 50 percent above c.i.f. value. The CKD component would then decline to 50 percent, and the rate of effective protection to 137 percent.

Year	Millions of soles
1965	66
1966	229
1967	276
1968	352
1969	558
1970	354
1971	643

Total investment in the early years of the automobile industry has been estimated at approximately 675 million soles.[55] Therefore, gross profits during 1966–1968, the first full years of operation, averaged about 36 percent, i.e., the gross payback period was from two and one-half to three years. Assuming a length of life for assembly plants as short as ten years, this implies a net return on investment, after taxes and depreciation, of about 16 percent. Since total profitability is given by this 16-percent figure plus those profits generated elsewhere in the multinational system from sales of parts and kits, it becomes clear that the automotive stampede into Peru was the economically rational thing to do.[56]

This congenial arrangement was interrupted after only a few years, when in 1967 the Belaúnde government attempted to change the rules of the game. By a series of decrees, it shut major foreign firms out of local borrowing opportunities, raised the ad valorem duty on CKD kits from 12 to between 20 and 44 percent depending on the kit's c.i.f. (cost, insurance, and freight) value, and redefined CKD kits more stringently, charging that "some assemblers have done little more than loosen the bolts and pass the vehicles off as CKDs."[57] Moreover, the tariff increases were

[55] The dollar figure is $25 million. *Peruvian Times*, Aug. 21, 1970, p. 3.

[56] The reader must be cautioned, however, that this profit estimate is tenuous. It assumes that tariffs on CKD kits are included in the cost of imported inputs reported in the various sources of Table 8.1, but that social security contributions are not included in wage costs. Isidoro Korngold and Josef Maiman, "La industria de ensamblaje automotriz en el Perú," mimeo, 1969, p. 45, show that in 1968 the automobile industry paid 76 million soles for social security contributions and all taxes except customs duties. Expressed as a share of the gross value added in Table 8.1, this comes to 28 percent, a figure used for all years in the calculation of net returns. In separate interviews, two representatives of the industry claimed substantially longer payback periods for their respective companies.

[57] *Peruvian Times*, June 30, 1967.

declared to be retroactive and thus imposed essentially as fines amounting to as much as $706,000 in the case of General Motors. The automobile companies responded by refusing to pay retroactive tariffs and threatening to sue the government for breach of contract. They refused to claim CKD kits on the docks and started cutting production. The Belaúnde government backed down and reached a compromise under which CKD tariffs would rise to 20 percent without retroactive provisions.

Curiously enough, Peru passed through this 1967 controversy without anyone, in or out of government, suggesting that the companies were making too much money under the terms of the original contracts. The stated reason for the government's move was the fiscal crisis. The only expression of dissatisfaction with previous contractual arrangements was technical—the failure of some companies to do enough assembling—rather than financial. To be sure, Carlos Malpica blasted the automobile companies for excess profits, but Malpica's work did not command respect in the days of Belaúnde as it would later under the Revolutionary Government of the Armed Forces.[58] Furthermore, nobody stumbled onto the opportunities for additional profit taking through pricing of CKD kits.[59]

Two years later, in the last days of 1969, the military government unleashed the first policy thunderbolt to fall on the automotive sector. It called for new concession bids under drastically changed conditions:

1. Local content requirements were escalated dramatically. From between 15 and 20 percent in early 1970, they were to be raised by steps to 70 percent by February 1, 1973. Choice of composition for local content was

[58] Carlos Malpica, *El mito de la ayuda exterior*, Lima, Moncloa, 1967, pp. 120–124.

[59] Automobile companies customarily price the complete CKD kit at full average cost. As parts are removed from the kit during the process of import substitution, the kit price is reduced by only the marginal cost of the deleted components. Thus as local content rises, imported kits become increasingly overpriced. Companies allegedly follow this practice as a means of discouraging import substitution and thereby preserving economies of scale obtained in the centralized production of parts for a worldwide network of assembly plants. See Sebastiaan J. Kleu, "Import Substitution in the South African Automobile Industry," unpublished doctoral dissertation, Harvard Business School, 1967, pp. 67–73. Also Jack Baranson, *Automotive Industries in Developing Countries*, Baltimore, Johns Hopkins Press for IBRD, 1969, p. 37.

also to be restricted. Any Peruvian automotive parts certified by the government as equivalent to international standards of price and quality had to be used. Importation of motors was to be prohibited after January 1974.

2. Foreign companies were given just one year for fading into minority ownership.

3. CKD tariff rates were shifted to a scale, depending on engine size, ranging from 5 to 85 percent.

4. The number of models produced was strictly limited.

5. Importation of assembled cars was prohibited. Prices of assembled cars were to be set annually by the Ministry of Industries.

Ten producers hurriedly assembled formal proposals by the March deadline, and then waited. In August, the government announced the winning bidders. Four automotive producers remained, and five were shut down. One truck producer remained, and three were shut down.

The survivors of this shake-out found themselves in a new environment of tightened control and heightened uncertainty. The controls reduced price-cost margins (dealer markups included) from about 45 percent in Belaúnde's time to about 20 percent. The return on investment did not decrease so drastically, however, because each remaining company increased production volume. Two-shift operations, formerly unheard-of, became the industry norm, and in some cases profit rates even increased. The uncertainty of the new environment derived from the widespread realization that the new rules of 1970 were not the last changes that would be visited upon the industry. Some of the subsequent changes, however, involved easing the severity of the new rules. For example, the local content targets announced in 1970 were lowered or postponed time and again. Similarly, CKD tariffs were lowered in 1972, and 1974 dawned with the fade-out rules on foreign ownership yet to be implemented.

But while pragmatic accommodation thus set to rights some of the disarray created by old thunderbolts, new storm clouds appeared. Only one month after the August 1970 announcement of who would stay and who would leave, new bids were called, this time for monopoly rights to produce gasoline engines and power trains. This tender produced great confusion, since it failed to allow sufficient engine variety to accommodate the eight automobile models authorized the month before.[60] The government dropped the tender, apparently for lack of takers. The line of industrial expansion that it had begun could be continued only after further contraction in the number of companies and models.

By early 1972, the government appeared to have surrendered completely on the local content issue, having lowered the end-of-year goal from 70 to 35 percent. Yet in fact it had not surrendered its vision of an integrated automotive industry. Quietly casting about for new ways in which to reorganize the industry, in mid-year the government approached General Motors and one or two other companies regarding the possibility of a monopoly concession—cars, trucks, engines, everything to be handled by one producer. When nothing came of this approach, it returned to an earlier formula—new bids from the remaining producers. In January 1973, for the fourth time in the ten-year history of the industry, new terms of operation were announced. The most important rules of this new game were the following:

1. The number of automobile producers would be reduced from four to one or perhaps two.
2. The producer(s) would build an engine and transmission plant, and also contribute capital to a forge and foundry for casting basic automotive parts.
3. The producer(s) would export automotive parts equal in value to the kits imported. This so-called *intercambio compensado* provision was offered as a more flexible substitute for local content regulations.[61]

Once again, proposals were hurriedly prepared and submitted, this time by the end of May 1973, and then the companies waited. In December 1973 the government delivered what may be the last thunderbolt in the revolutionary reorganization of the automotive industry: Toyota was named the chosen company. If a second company is needed, it will be Volkswagen. Chrysler, the only one of America's Big Three to survive the first shake-out, finished dead last.[62]

---

[60] *Peruvian Times*, Oct. 2, 1970.
[61] *Peruvian Times*, June 1 and Sept. 7, 1973.
[62] *Andean Times*, Dec. 7, 1973.

Copper Negotiations

Automotive reorganization has been characterized by frenetic competition, as each company attempted to salvage what it could of past investments and future market potential. Although loss of a bid, with consequent explusion from the local market, has come as a crushing blow to local executives, their companies can view the loss of the Peruvian market as a matter of limited importance. By contrast, the major mining companies cannot afford to treat Peru with such detachment. The stakes are far bigger, as are the risks. For our final case for examination, we return to the storm clouds that have hovered around the Southern Peru Copper Corporation.

More than with any other single project, Peru's economic and political prospects in the first years of the Revolution have turned on Cuajone, a mammoth open-pit copper deposit recently estimated to require $550 million for full development. Cuajone has formed the key element in plans for an expanding mining sector, the sector that gives firmest prospects for future growth in export earnings.

Before its demise in October 1968, the Belaúnde government had begun negotiations over Cuajone with the same New York-based Southern Peru Copper Corporation that had provoked such nationalistic resentment over the Toquepala contract. Once the dust had settled from the IPC expropriation and the Hickenlooper menace, the military government returned to the issue of Cuajone and found itself confronted with a delicate choice between political solidarity and economic necessity. Clearly the ideal solution lay in awarding the Cuajone concession to a European or Japanese group. Yet despite a certain amount of brave talk about others who might come forward, in fact the worldwide supply of potential investors was highly limited.[63] Few companies possess familiarity with the technology of open-pit copper mining. Fewer still have access to the enormous amounts of capi-

---

[63] Persistent rumors of Russian financing came to nothing. Apparently the Russians weren't interested. See Aníbal Quijano Obregón, *Nationalism and Capitalism in Peru. A Study in Neo-Imperialism*, New York, Monthly Review Press, 1971, p. 46. Also, Janet Ballantyne, "The Political Economy of Peruvian Gran Minería," unpublished doctoral dissertation, Cornell Business School, Jan. 1974, chap. 3, p. 15.

tal required. Moreover, the potential difficulties of sharing transport, refinery, and export facilities with Southern Peru in its adjacent Toquepala deposit essentially ruled out the entry of a new company. The choice available became clear: It was Southern Peru or nothing.

Matters came to a head in late 1969, at a time of great uncertainty about Peru's economic prospects. The foreign debt needed refinancing and the domestic economy needed more spending to pull it out of recession. Neither foreign creditors nor domestic investors were prepared to commit funds without a solid indication that Peru intended to maintain regular business connections with the centers of world capitalism. The indication that they wanted was the Cuajone contract.

Politically, it was no easy matter for the government to sign. In the weeks following the first announcement that the contract was nearly ready, the Peruvian Left mounted an all-out campaign of opposition. The terms hardly mattered; any contract would bind Peru more closely into the capitalist orbit. In the words of one critic: "Any foreign investment whatsoever is enslaving. The task of the Revolution must be to enable Peru to exploit its own resources."[64]

Journalistic opposition from outside reflected the far more important opposition that lay within the government. The cabinet met in crisis sessions, and the government's position changed somewhat to accommodate the inner stresses. The signing was postponed, slightly tougher terms were demanded of Southern, and a new mining law was promised. The government denied all the time that it felt any pressure connecting Cuajone to the refinancing of Peru's foreign debt, yet President Velasco's perhaps unguarded response to a reporter's question tells a different story:

The government doesn't have any money. When we assumed power we found a disastrous situation. Huge debts, both external and internal. The Peruvian economy is in large part paralyzed. Lines of credit are closed. The country needs capital for its development.[65]

[64] *Caretas*, Nov. 11–21, 1969, p. 10. See also *Oiga*, issues of Nov. 7, 14, 21, and 28; also "Voz y Voto" column in *Expreso*, Dec. 30, 1969.

[65] *Oiga*, Dec. 5, 1969, p. 9.

Two weeks after these unrevolutionary remarks, the government signed on the dotted line. Perhaps never before or since has the meaning of external dependence seemed clearer in the context of the Peruvian Revolution.[66]

Southern Peru Copper Corporation began the new decade with a contract, but without the required investment funds. No longer could it step up to the window at the Export-Import Bank as it had done before for Toquepala. That particular funding source had been shut down as part of the U.S. financial boycott against Peru, a boycott imposed in retaliation for the expropriation of IPC.[67] As for private lenders, they viewed Peru somewhat more favorably after the signing of the Cuajone contract, but no surge of funds into Peruvian mining materialized. After all, expropriation was in the air in Latin America, in Chile, in Bolivia, even in Venezuela, and the Peruvian Revolution's ultimate political direction seemed to change with every month. Lenders persisted in waiting a bit longer before committing funds to Peruvian mining, and so months dragged into years as Southern Peru doggedly kept up its search for finance.

That search had received an early setback with the Mining Law of April 1970, which converted the minerals exporting business into a government monopoly and reserved all future metal refining for state enterprise. These moves appeared to break all possibility of guaranteeing copper deliveries to favored buyers in exchange for finance from those buyers.[68] The government came forward with sufficient assurances to allay those fears, only to create new fears later in the year through regulations that threatened loss of mine concessions if companies failed to develop them rapidly.[69] Financing negotiations with a consortium

[66] In leftist circles throughout Latin America, the Cuajone contract produced substantial disillusionment regarding the Peruvian Revolution. This is reflected in Ricardo Pumaruna-Letts, *Perú: Mito de la revolución militar*, Caracas, Ediciones Bárbara, 1971, pp. 70–75, and Quijano Obregón, *Nationalism and Capitalism*, pp. 22–26.

[67] U.S. government decision making that led to the policy of "nonovert economic sanctions" toward Peru is analyzed in Jessica Einhorn, "The Effect of Bureaucratic Politics on the Expropriation Policy of the Nixon Administration: Two Case Studies," unpublished doctoral dissertation, Department of Politics, Princeton University, Jan. 1974.

[68] *Peruvian Times*, Mar. 13, Apr. 24, 1970.

[69] *Latin America*, Sept. 25, 1970, p. 309; *Business Week*, Aug. 29, 1970, p. 26. *Peruvian Times*, Oct. 2, Oct. 9, Nov. 6, 1970.

of Japanese smelters were well under way at the time, and optimistic announcements in November suggested that the deal was nearly settled. In fact, the final settlement never came.[70] A sharp decline in world copper prices apparently turned Japanese investors away from Cuajone, but only because higher prices were required to make the political risk worth running. In the words of *Metals Week*, "with the new left-wing military government in power, financing is understandably a very tricky proposition."[71]

Through most of 1971 and 1972, Cuajone financing remained at a standstill. Southern Peru continued to invest depletion allowances and net profits from Toquepala into Cuajone, thereby maintaining the investment schedule called for in the contract. In the meantime, Peru's creditworthiness in the eyes of the world's major lenders slowly but steadily improved. The government consistently demonstrated its intention of honoring debts to foreign lenders, no matter how embittered the fights with certain foreign companies. Moreover, fairly tight fiscal and monetary policies produced that aura of fiscal responsibility so cherished by potential lenders. The premium over London interbank rate required of Peru diminished steadily.

By late 1972 the price of copper was high again. Peru was a better credit risk. The Eurodollar market was loaded with funds looking for projects. These factors encouraged formation of a consortium that arranged a $200 million loan to Southern Peru for Cuajone. The consortium was organized and led by the Chase Manhattan Bank of New York.

Yet even with this major breakthrough, Southern Peru was not entirely out of the woods. Nearly a year was to elapse between acceptance of the Chase consortium proposal by Southern in December 1972 and actual signing in late November 1973. Furthermore, an additional $200 million was still required to complete the financing package. While announcement of the Chase consortium loan included a confident prediction that the remainder would be collected without difficulty from suppliers' credits and long-term sales contracts, in fact a fundamental obstacle remained.[72]

[70] *La Prensa*, Nov. 4, 1970; *Correo*, Nov. 5, 1970; *Metals Week*, May 10, 1971; *La Prensa*, May 21, 1971; *Peruvian Times*, Dec. 3, 1971.

[71] *Metals Week*, May 10, 1971.

[72] *Peruvian Times*, Mar. 9 and June 1, 1973; *Andean Times*, Dec. 7, 1973, p. 7.

Both members of the Chase group and other potential lenders still required further guarantees. It was all very well that Peru's creditworthiness had improved, but the loans for Cuajone were being made not to the Peruvian government but to a U.S. company. Thus the lenders' perception of default risk by the company was inevitably influenced by Peru's treatment of expropriated companies. The risk surely appeared real and nonnegligible. To the early casualties of IPC and the Grace properties expropriated by the Agrarian Reform had been added not only Conchán but also all the U.S. fishmeal companies plus a couple of road construction firms. Then, during 1973, negotiations for the purchase of Cerro de Pasco became increasingly tense, threatening a new diplomatic crisis of IPC magnitude.[73] In this environment the potential lenders insisted on the additional protection of U.S. government participation in the financing package. Some loan, however small, had to be obtained from the Export-Import Bank. The U.S. government would not permit such a loan, however, without a general settlement of outstanding expropriation issues. The Cuajone project remained stuck on dead center.[74]

Although prospects for such a settlement appeared more remote than ever in mid-1973, in fact it suddenly materialized in the first days of 1974, capping many months of quiet diplomacy undertaken by James Greene, a New York banker designated as special emissary of the U.S. government.[75] The terms illustrate neatly the potential of imaginative diplomacy in finding compromise between apparently irreconcilable opposing positions.

Faced with positions which, on the one hand, demanded some compensation for IPC and, on the other hand, insisted that IPC was absolutely nonnegotiable, the settlement formula called for a lump-sum payment to the U.S. government, with subsequent distribution to the various companies undertaken by the U.S. government in accordance with U.S. law. In an appendix to the agreement, the Peruvian government listed the companies whose claims it considered included within the agreement. The IPC

[73] *Peruvian Times*, July 13, Sept. 28, 1973. *New York Times*, Sept. 25 and 30, 1973.

[74] Ballantyne, "Political Economy," chap. 4, pp. 16, 17. *Andean Times*, Feb. 22, 1974.

[75] *Andean Times*, Jan. 4, Jan. 18, Feb. 22, 1974. *New York Times*, Feb. 20, 1974. The full text of the agreement is reprinted in the *Andean Times*, Feb. 22.

was, of course, not included in the Peruvian list. However, the appendix was also stated to be a unilateral declaration by the Peruvian government that did not modify the provisions of the basic agreement. Thus the Peruvian government declared itself to be no party to any arrangement involving compensation to IPC. Nevertheless, IPC will undoubtedly claim compensation under U.S. law and get it.

As compensation agreements go, this one is not particularly generous to expropriated companies. The funds available for distribution amount to $76 million, as compared to the companies' claims in the order of $250 million. Peru's bargaining stance over previous years had been sufficiently tough to convince the companies that their alternative to half a loaf was none. Therefore they settled, and the U.S. government agreed to the following article in the final text:

The Government of the United States declares that the
payment of the sum referred to in Article II cancels any
liability or obligation of the Government of Peru to United
States nationals, their subsidiaries, branches and
affiliates.[76]

The financial war was ended. The U.S. companies had been swept out of the basic sectors to Peru's satisfaction.

As for Cuajone, within a matter of weeks the Export-Import Bank announced a $55 million loan for equipment purchases, and a few days later the President of American Smelting and Refining Company, which owns majority interest in Southern Peru, was able to announce that the financing package was at last complete.[77] At the same time, however, he also announced further difficulty with the Peruvian government over the guarantee of copper deliveries to certain participants in the financing package. Although the difficulty will most likely be settled expeditiously, it serves to remind foreign investors that in the newly normalized investment climate of revolutionary Peru, risk is reduced, but not to zero.

[76] *Andean Times*, Feb. 22, 1974, p. 5.

[77] The Export-Import Bank loan was announced on Apr. 11, 1974. The ASARCO president's remarks were made at the company's annual meeting of Apr. 23, 1974.

The Pattern of Outcomes

These various cases show that as state enterprises have taken over in the basic sectors, foreign investors have been bought out or swept aside in arrangements ranging from sky-high prices to confiscatory expropriation. Despite this range of results, the outcomes are by no means random. In large part they have depended upon the particular bargaining strength of each foreign company, where this strength has derived from the company's capacity to provide financial or technical services needed by Peru. Chase Manhattan was able to offer technical assistance and access to the New York financial market. It was well paid. The Peruvian Corporation had nothing to offer. It was driven to the wall. Other cases are intermediate to these extremes, but they all illustrate the remarkable pragmatism of Peru's approach to foreign investors, a pragmatism advocated by President Velasco and evidently adhered to by negotiators.

These considerations seem not to apply in the case of IPC itself, since Peru has undoubtedly lost far more in blocked loans and withdrawn aid than would have been involved in a moderate plan for compensation. The political capital accumulated by the IPC expropriation, however, must not be forgotten; after all, it provided political sanction for the armed forces to take power in the first place.

It is sometimes suggested that old, long-established companies may find particular difficulty in their dealings with government.[78] By this view, a foreign firm is greeted most warmly on arrival, but as years stretch into decades the welcome wears thin, as the host country becomes increasingly aware of the negative factors deriving from the company's presence. The company's position weakens both because old firms belong to traditional industries where oligopolistic bargaining power has been eroded by competitive forces, and because the frictions generated by past dealings are never entirely forgotten, but rather tend to accumulate over time.

This view suggests that the big old-time companies would be first to get the ax. In the case of Peru, four companies fall into this category—Cerro de Pasco, the Peruvian Corporation, IPC, and Grace—and sure enough, all four are gone. It is not obvious, however, that they left specifically because of resentments that

[78] Raymond Vernon, *Sovereignty at Bay*, New York, Basic Books, 1971.

had built up over the decades. Cerro asked to be bought out, and the final price seems likely to make Cerro content. The Peruvian Corporation was a basket case. IPC was a special case, so everyone says, although it does fit this view very well. The frictions generated from its past dealings were, to say the least, substantial. As for Grace, most of its operations were either in agriculture or in basic industrial sectors. Other holdings have been sold off as part of a long-standing company objective to get out of South America.[79]

THE SHAPE OF THE FUTURE IN MINING, PETROLEUM, AND INDUSTRY

While old foreign investments were being reorganized in some sectors and expropriated in others, elsewhere in the economy the government pushed ahead with plans for industrial and export development that included foreign participation under new terms. We must examine a few more case studies concerning these terms in order to gain a better sense of the role being reserved for foreign investors in a reorganized Peruvian economy.

In early 1972, the *Peruvian Times* forecast the future of Peruvian mining with these words: "The chief entrepreneur in the search for mining capital is clearly Mineroperú: The development of the Cuajone deposit by Southern Peru Cooper Corporation is the last big new mine that will be financed solely by private enterprise."[80] Mineroperú, the new state mining company, holds rights to innumerable promising ore bodies that reverted to the state when private companies were slow to develop them. It has chosen to cut its teeth as a big-time mining enterprise by developing an open-pit copper mine at Cerro Verde. This seemed an appropriate choice, since Cerro Verde's proximity to Arequipa reduced greatly the need for infrastructural investment, thus cutting down on both capital costs and planning problems.

The organizational changes at Cerro Verde mark stages in the entrepreneurial development of Mineroperú. First plans called for a joint venture with Anaconda, which had been holding on to the Cerro Verde concession for fifty years. In late 1970, however,

[79] *Peruvian Times*, Apr. 30, 1971, Nov. 17, 1972. *New York Times*, Feb. 16, 1974.

[80] *Peruvian Times*, Apr. 14, 1972, p. 17.

negotiations collapsed with Mineroperú's insistence on majority ownership. Stating that required loans could not be raised in world markets on such a basis, Anaconda dropped the concession, wrote off $4.3 million of development expenditures, and left Peru.[81]

Only two months after Anaconda's announcement, a Belgian delegation was in Lima offering a financing and technical assistance package. Similar offers soon came from a British-Canadian consortium, and the following October Mineroperú signed a memorandum of agreement with the British and Canadians. The agreement called for a turnkey job. British Smelter Constructions, Ltd. (BSCL), was charged with all aspects of opening the mine—finance, equipment purchase, construction. Engineering design work was to be subcontracted to Wright Engineers of Vancouver. Once put onstream, BSCL would stay on for an additional year and then hand the key over to Mineroperú.[82]

More tough bargaining was to follow this preliminary agreement, and when the final contract emerged nine months later, the terms had changed significantly. Now Mineroperú was to run the project instead of British Smelters, although BSCL still held responsibility for the three principal functions of finance, purchasing, and construction. Having passed through the stages of silent partner and turnkey project recipient in Cerro Verde negotiations, Mineroperú as manager forms the shape of the future in Peruvian mining.

Yet that future is not yet assured. Mineroperú's plans for mine development require enormous sums of foreign capital, which will probably become available only if its managerial record is a successful one. In Mineroperú's only venture thus far, finance has proven to be no problem. Most funds for Cerro Verde came from export credits of the British and Canadian governments. The remainder came from the first loan Peru ever floated on the Eurodollar market.[83] However, Cerro Verde has been delayed by technical problems that are not yet resolved.

The difficulty arose with the decision to begin operations on a veneer of oxide deposits using a refining process that has several

[81] *Peruvian Times*, Oct. 16, and Dec. 4, 1970, and Feb. 12, 1971.

[82] *Peruvian Times*, Feb. 5, June 11, and Oct. 8, 1971. Ballantyne, "Political Economy," chap. 4, pp. 17–26.

[83] *Peruvian Times*, July 7, 1972.

unique and untried features.[84] Despite the best efforts of the Canadian consulting firm, the process has not been made to work on Cerro Verde ores. While the experiments continue, the development schedule has been set back. In the words of one authority on Peruvian mining:

What most mining people in Peru and New York are now saying is that Minero Perú made its first big mistake in even attempting to process the oxide ores—that it should have stripped the oxide zone away as overburden . . . and gone straight to work on the lower levels. Its second mistake, they continue, is in not realizing it made the first mistake, and just abandoning the oxide-electrowinning process now.[85]

Financing sources in the United States and Europe read this experience as evidence of Mineroperú's inexperience. The shape of the future in Peruvian mining depends greatly on successfully overcoming that inexperience during the next few years.

Whereas Mineroperú had to start from scratch, Petroperú sprang full-grown from the ashes of IPC. Petroperú inherited a production and distribution system and also an efficient administrative organization. All it lacked was capital for exploration. Whereas Mineroperú chose to bypass foreign mining companies and obtain finance through suppliers' credits, Petroperú could not do this. The risks are such that suppliers cannot consider similar terms for petroleum exploration. Yet the old-time concession contracts appeared particularly unappealing in the petroleum sector. Accordingly Petroperú hit on the idea of a service contract that shared output instead of profits, an approach that had been tried previously only in Indonesia, and in somewhat different form. Petroperú sought out Occidental Petroleum, a company widely reputed to be venturesome, and signed them to the first service contract in June 1971.

Perhaps the two outstanding features of the Occidental contract are its emphasis on assertion of sovereignty and its simplicity.[86] In the words of General Fernández Baca, "The con-

[84] *Peruvian Times*, Special supplement on Cerro Verde, Mar. 23, 1973, pp. 18–27.

[85] Ballantyne, "Political Economy," chap. 4, p. 21.

[86] The contract is described in *Peruvian Times*, June 25, 1971, and Marco Fernández Baca, *El contrato de operaciones modelo Perú*, Departamento de Relaciones Públicas de Petroleos del Perú, Lima, 1973.

tract naturally puts special emphasis in affirming, at every instance, the sovereignty of the Peruvian nation. Experience has taught us much in this respect."[87] Thus the contract emphasizes that the concession is held by Petroperú and that the petroleum flowing from the wellhead belongs to Petroperú, which then pays half of it to Occidental as a service fee. In the calculation of tax liability, however, Occidental receives a tax credit for the 50 percent petroleum share kept by Petroperú. This more than covers tax liabilities and renders the tax calculation an exercise having only arcane legal significance. Its economic insignificance furnishes the basis for the contract's simplicity: Systems of tax audit control become unnecessary. Everything reduces to the fifty-fifty split at the wellhead.

The contract held two other features important to Peru. First, it pushed Occidental to rapid development of the assigned area. Geophysical exploration had to begin within six months and drilling within thirty months, with three wells drilled within four years, and ten within seven years. Petroperú had no difficulty with Occidental on these points. Within twenty-six months of signing, Occidental had drilled five wildcats and hit oil on every one. These combined with three successful Petroperú wildcats to set off a stampede for Petroperú service contracts. By late 1973, when the government called a halt to new contracts, eighteen had been signed with various companies, all similar in terms to Occidental's except that the output division was forty-five to fifty-five, in favor of Petroperú.[88]

The contract's second important feature lies in the absence of a capital commitment from Petroperú. All the risk is shifted to the foreign companies. This is of course an advantage, particularly if no petroleum is found, but it also means that the profits tax implicit in output sharing will be lower either if truly spectacular discoveries are made, or if ordinary discoveries are made at a time of spectacular increases in world petroleum prices. In no case could the implicit profits tax fall below 50 percent, which is a respectable tax bite in most industries.[89] But petroleum ex-

[87] Fernández Baca, *Contrato de operaciones*, p. 11.

[88] *Peruvian Times*, June 8, Aug. 10, and Sept. 7, 1973.

[89] The relation between output share and equivalent profits tax is as follows. For the foreign company, let Q be output, P the price of output, C the production cost per unit of output, s the output share paid to government, t

porting countries are accustomed to tax rates in the order of 75 percent these days. The recent dramatic escalation of world petroleum prices, an event very hard to have foreseen in 1971, may make the fifty-fifty output division too generous a contract, thus generating a political head of steam that will force renegotiation of the percentage division at the wellhead.

Petroleum service contracts became a political volcano in Argentina in the early 1960s. Careful management and attention to issues of sovereignty by Petroperú have thus far averted a similar development in Peru, even as the country passes through a nationalistic revolution. Output sharing contracts probably obtain foreign capital and technology in as antiseptic a manner as possible. Their only danger is that they shift the risk all too well.

The shape of things to come in industry is perhaps best judged not by the new terms offered the automobile industry, but by the course of negotiations with companies lacking preexisting investments in Peru. Only by examining such cases can we say something about Peru's prospects for driving automotive-type bargains without first having lured the foreigner into the country on substantially easier terms.

Other sections of Peru's motor vehicle industry provide instructive examples. In April and May 1971, six months after the first shake-out of the automobile producers, the government

---

the equivalent profits tax rate, pb profits before taxes and pa profits after taxes. Then:

and

$$QP - QC = pb \tag{1}$$
$$QP\,(1 - s) - QC = pa = pb\,(1 - t) \tag{2}$$

Substituting (1) in (2) and rearranging terms gives an expression for the equivalent profits tax rate:

$$t = \frac{Ps}{P - C} \tag{3}$$

Let k be the margin by which price exceeds cost, i.e., $C\,(1 + k) = P$. Then:

$$t = \frac{s\,(1 + k)}{k} \tag{4}$$

The greater is k, the more profitable is the operation and the lower t (the equivalent profits tax rate) becomes. If $k = 0$, cost and price are the same, and the company makes no profit but must pay its output share. The equivalent profits tax rate is infinite. Alternatively, let price be the double of cost, i.e., $k = 1.0$. Assuming a fifty-fifty output share, then the equivalent profits tax rate t is 100 percent. Finally, if costs are trivially small, then k is infinite and t is 50 percent, its lowest possible value.

called for bids on the production of tractors and diesel engines. The terms offered were similar in the two tenders. The foreign company would be minority partner in a joint venture with Induperú, the government's industrial development corporation. The number of models to be produced would be carefully stipulated, local content requirements would be high, around 75 to 80 percent within five years, the plants would be located in Trujillo and would have prospect of near-monopoly positions in the Andean Common Market. A capital contribution to the forge and foundry would be required, by direct subscription from the diesel company, from reinvested profits in the case of the tractor company. Local content regulations would be less onerous for tractors, since locally produced diesel engines would count, but in addition the tractor tender included *intercambio compensado* provision (that exports equal imports) two years before this feature cropped up in automobile negotiations.[90]

Both tenders received strong responses. Seven companies bid for the tractor contract—three from England, two from Italy, and one each from Romania and the Soviet Union. The closest thing to an American bidder was Ford of England. Apparently the major U.S. tractor producers weren't interested.

The same was not true in the diesel bidding, where three of the seven bidders were American—Cummins, Caterpillar, and Continental Motors, engine maker for Checker cabs. Continental made the most spectacular proposal of all, offering a production volume seven times what the government had asked for, the bulk to be directed to export markets outside the Andean Group.

Eighteen months later, the tractor contract was awarded to Massey-Ferguson, an English-Canadian company, and the diesel contract jointly to Volvo of Sweden and Perkins of Great Britain, the latter a Massey-Ferguson subsidiary. Contracts were not actually signed until July and September of 1973. This extraordinary delay testifies to the complexity of the contracts and to the difficult trade-offs that confronted the government. The fundamental trade-off lay between efficiency and backward linkages. Despite the apparent usual fixation with local content, government negotiators were in fact preoccupied with what they them-

---

[90] *Peruvian Times*, Mar. 12 and Oct. 8, 1971. Also Council of the Americas, *Andean Pact: Definition, Design, and Analysis*, New York, [1973], mimeo, Part IV, pp. 12–18.

selves referred to as the "inefficiency cost" of local supply.[91] Partly to avoid that cost, the tractor contract called for at least one-third of local content to be produced by the company itself, where presumably the inefficiency cost would be lower.

Another important trade-off lay between cost and bargaining position within the Andean Group. The final choice on the tractor contract lay between Massey-Ferguson and the Romanians, who offered a lower-cost financing package. The government, however, feared that a Romanian tractor contract would carry little weight in future Andean negotiations. And if Peru fails to get a tractor assignment in those negotiations, neither Romanian nor any other tractor producers would have much future in Peru.

Peru's position in the crucial Andean negotiations is therefore strengthened by having a contract with a name brand. It may also be strengthened by the compensatory export provision, which serves as a partial guarantee that the quality of the Peruvian product will not be allowed to slip below Massey-Ferguson's worldwide standard. In addition to improving Peru's bargaining position, this provision can encourage the technology flow that Peru wants from foreign investors.

In tractors, in diesels, and in every new major industrial enterprise, the technology possessed only by foreign companies is indispensable. Peru wants that technology and is prepared to offer in return protection from competition, a minority share of the equity, and a constrained form of managerial control. This represents an unceratin bargain, since countless details will surely remain to be worked out long after investment is begun. Also, government policy makers are still feeling their way, and may well change the terms in the future. Nevertheless, the lesson of the tractor and diesel tenders is that many foreign companies are prepared to accept these terms and take their chances in joint ventures with Peruvian state enterprises.

THE RESPONSE OF THE FOREIGNERS

It's been some years since I lived in Peru, but I visited there recently, and was really impressed. You hear all this pessimism about business in Peru these days, but I think

---

[91] *Peruvian Times*, Nov. 24, 1972, and July 13, 1973.

it's exaggerated. From what I saw, I think you can really do business, and make money. But I wouldn't want to invest there.

This comment by an American businessman neatly captures the prevailing outlook among the more progressive elements of the foreign business community in Peru today. Most feel in some sense captive, unable to get their money out, obliged to make the best of a situation not of their choosing. In the meantime, they make good profits. But they bring in no more investment funds.

Even before the beginning of the Peruvian Revolution, in the friendly days of Belaúnde, one knowledgeable observer described typical business strategy as follows: "Make a minimum investment, plow back profits, borrow locally, and grow to maintain your market share with a minimum commitment." New investment funds were brought in so sparingly because of fears of devaluation, exchange control, and political instability. Today, this same observer characterized business strategy as more concerned with quick payoffs rather than growth and reinvestment. Defensive investment has given way to Take the Money and Run.

Foreign businessmen see risk of expropriation and loss of managerial control as the major deterrents to investment. The expropriation risk arises partly because the government has not yet established definitively which sectors are to be reserved for state enterprise, as the fishmeal expropriations demonstrate. It also comes from a lingering concern that the revolution may well shift dramatically to the left, perhaps socializing all industry. Without any shift in the revolution's direction, foreign businessmen find themselves staring straight at the specter of lost management control. The government views the Comunidad Industrial, through which 50 percent of the firm's equity will ultimately pass to the workers, as a means for bringing harmony of interests between management and labor. Most foreign businessmen view it as an invitation to chaos. To put off the day of reckoning when the workers' share rises to 50 percent, businesses have strong incentive to reinvest and expand, thus increasing their own share. Thus firms already in the country do invest, but the incentive that moves them contains rather more of the stick than the carrot.

While risk of expropriation and loss of control constitute the major drawbacks to further investment, the drain on management time under the new rules of the game is often mentioned as an important secondary factor. One manager commented, "All our department heads are in the Ministry three or four days every week." The extra effort derives partly from the complexity of labor relations in the era of the Comunidad Industrial, partly from proliferating regulatory mechanisms, particularly those concerning profit repatriation. Some foreign subsidiaries have repatriated profits without difficulty but have hit snags on royalty payments to the parent corporation. Other companies have had repatriation requests delayed from one to three years.[92] The apparent arbitrariness of treatment increases risk for all foreign investors.

Profits available for repatriation are substantial. A profit squeeze is not often mentioned as an important deterrent to foreign investors in Peru today.

For these various reasons, nearly all new investors coming into the country do so through special contracts, as in the cases of petroleum, tractors, and diesels. Being partly owned by the government and judged important in government development plans, such firms can be more confident of entering a facilitating environment. The government wants them to succeed.

As we have seen in some of the case studies, not all foreign companies look with favor even on the opportunities of special contracts. Company reaction often depends on the idiosyncratic response of individual managers, but in general American companies seem particularly skeptical about investment prospects in Peru. The reasons advanced for this are many. The Europeans and Japanese are said to have greater experience in joint ventures with governments.[93] It is also suggested that big American firms, already well established in the larger markets of Brazil, Argentina, and Mexico, feel that they already have enough investment in Latin America and are therefore less interested in the Andean Group. Then again, the rhetoric of the new nationalism is aimed more directly at Americans, building a stronger sense of rejection on top of what had probably been a stronger ideological antipathy in the first place. Perhaps some such com-

---

[92] Ballantyne, "Political Economy," chap. 3, p. 32.

[93] It should be noted, however, that much of Japan's new flurry of investment activity in Peru consists of loans rather than equity. See special survey of Japanese investment in the *Peruvian Times*, Sept. 29, 1972. Japanese caution about major mining investment is described in Ballantyne, "Political Economy," chap. 3, p. 25.

bination is required to produce the viewpoint of one American businessman that "Decision 24 cannot be considered a satisfactory body of legislation. It is entirely negative," or of another, who characterized the new rules of the game as built on "a legal structure so precarious that any company putting its faith in it is just putting its head into a trap."

Business decisions that spring from such viewpoints sometimes acquire surprising form. One company, for example, was described as making enormous profits, yet the board of directors of the parent corporation remained persistently unhappy about the situation. Their unhappiness arose not merely from a perception of the proper risk discount to be applied in calculating expected future returns, but also because of an abhorrence of the prospect of being expropriated per se. The board's agitation finally convinced the Latin American manager that he should sell out at a bargain price, but he could find no takers.

The American business community does not speak with a single voice on the proper response to Peru's new rules. The opinions just described are likely to be challenged increasingly in boardrooms across the United States.[94] Out of such challenges, American corporations will no doubt make their grudging accommodations with the new way of doing things in Peru. The accommodation will be easier to make if the rules are loosened, as has been predicted recently.[95]

THE NEW FOREIGN INVESTMENT GAME— HOW DIFFERENT IS IT?

Looking over the Peruvian economic landscape in the first days of 1974, one sees dramatic changes in the foreigner's role compared to what it had been five years earlier at the end of Belaúnde's administration. In that Peru of the *Ancien Régime*, the largest and most visible firms in nearly every sector had been foreign. Almost without exception, Peruvian firms were small-scale operations. Peruvian state enterprise consisted of little more than a moribund steel company, a modest shipping line, a shipyard, a few fertilizer plants, and some sectoral development banks.

[94] For one such challenge, see Jon Basil Utley, "Doing Business with Latin Nationalists," *Harvard Business Review*, vol. 53, Jan.–Feb. 1973, pp. 77–86.
[95] *Andean Times*, Dec. 21–28, 1973, p. 4.

After five years of the Peruvian Revolution, most of those large and visible foreign firms are gone, replaced or absorbed by state enterprises. In transport and communications, Lima's power company, the national telephone system, the railroads, and Peru's international airline have all been transferred to the state. In manufacturing, the cement, chemical, and paper industries were defined by the Ley de Industrias as basic, to be reserved for the state, and have been taken over. The government steel plant has been expanded considerably. Among export sectors, the entire fishmeal industry was nationalized at a stroke; so was the sugar industry, through the 1969 Agrarian Reform Law. The petroleum industry, where it all started, consists of one firm: Petroperú. Only in mining were major foreign firms still to be found. But in mining too the state has become dominant. Cerro de Pasco was expropriated on the first day of 1974, to be re-created as the state-owned Empresa Minera del Centro.[96] Elsewhere, the most promising ore bodies are reserved for Minero-perú, to be developed in coming years along the lines of Cerro Verde.

Outside of commodity-producing sectors, state enterprises have acquired marketing monopolies of all major commodity exports and a major share of domestic food distribution. In finance, most of the insurance industry has been nationalized, along with three of the major commercial banks.

Thus it turns out that state enterprises have become the chosen institution for achieving the objectives of the Velasco Doctrine. Transferring the commanding heights of the economy from foreign to national ownership has not meant a substitution of local capitalists for foreign capitalists. The government has little interest in developing powerful local capitalists, even if it could. A private sector, reformed by its sharing of power through the Comunidad Industrial, is still counted on to play an important role, but only in sectors of secondary importance. These are also the sectors where scale economies are thought to be less important, firms are smaller, and no one firm need grow to politically threatening size.

In this new Peru declared to be *"ni capitalista ni comunista,"* what role remains for direct foreign investment? The question is surely answered by the recent Greene compensation agreement if it was not answered earlier by the Cuajone contract: The Peru-

[96] *Andean Times*, Jan. 4, 1974, *Latin America*, Jan. 4, 1974.

vian Revolution has no intention of severing economic relations with Western capitalism. On the contrary, it desires to normalize and thus strengthen those relations. Normal relations would imply renewed credits from international lending agencies, but Peru is after bigger game than that. Most important of all, Peru needs access to the Export-Import Bank and to New York and European capital markets for the enormous volume of funds required to expand the mining and petroleum sectors.

These relations involve more than finance. Peru also remains in the market for technology, both scientific and organizational, and so the government will want to continue dealing with direct investors. The organizational forms will surely vary from one deal to the next—joint ventures in some cases (such as the tractor and diesel contracts), petroleum-type production agreements in others, and in still others management contracts that will resemble Cerro Verde.

The government's plans for industrial investment concentrate on massive projects in a few basic sectors—the automotive complex, petrochemicals, paper. Peru is forging ahead quickly in these sectors, partly to improve its bargaining position in Andean Group negotiations, partly to fulfill the government's vision of the most promising path to development. Along this path foreign participation will be required at every step of the way, in order to obtain and incorporate foreign technology. Although the government will always prefer a joint venture or coproduction agreement, it is not inconceivable that an occasional wholly-owned foreign subsidiary will be let in, if the foreigners bargain from great strength (as IBM is able to do) and are able to extract such a price. In every case, the foreign firm will justify its presence to the government by forming a key link in the government's own chain of industrial projects.

Outside these major project areas, foreign investment is technically welcome under the conditions stated in the Ley General de Industrias and Decision 24 of the Andean Group. As mentioned above, however, these conditions are bureaucratically complicated, with many procedures and policies not yet fully worked out. Companies are liable to find themselves caught in a variety of possible crunches on issues such as price policy, profits repatriation, royalty payments, import permits, and permission to expand through reinvestment of profits. In most cases, these issues are processed smoothly by the bureaucracy. But when obstacles arise they cannot be gotten around by the smooth accommodations generally available under earlier governments. And they arise often enough to lend substance to the impression that Peru's general welcome to foreign investors is highly qualified.

From what nations are foreign investors sought? From all nations, even the United States. Peru has deliberately diversified its economic and diplomatic relations, and has given special effort to expanding trade with new markets in China, Cuba, Eastern Europe, and other parts of the Third World. This diversification extends to foreign investment as well. New investment proposals have been welcomed not only from Japan and Western Europe, but also from such unexpected sources as Romania, Bulgaria, and Albania. Yet at the same time, the government does not want to lose contact with American industry. It was a source of disappointment to many officials that all the automotive contracts wound up without a single American entrant. Some were angered at what they saw as an American corporate boycott of their industrialization plans. On the other side, some Americans have seen discrimination in the quick dismissal of the Continental diesel proposal and the fourth place finish of Chrysler in the final automotive crunch. Ministry officials explain both these results in technological terms. The automobile contract, which involved a small vehicle, saw Chrysler pitting its Hillman against Toyota and Volkswagen. It was not to be.

These continued associations with multinational corporations and major banking houses have caused some critics to conclude that Peru's new rules of the game involve cosmetic change without altering the fundamental realities of imperialist penetration and economic dependence.[97] The conclusion depends very much on one's definition of imperialism and dependence. One could, for example, see the essence of dependence in the formation of consumer preferences through the communications media of Western capitalism. Once the media have done their work, the public craves and the government must deliver the trappings of Western, middle-class existence. By this view the Peruvian Revolution is no revolution at all.

Another view of dependence is more concerned with lack

[97] E.g., Quijano Obregon, *Nationalism and Capitalism.* Also César Germaná, "Si es Bayer . . . ¿Es bueno?" *Sociedad y Política*, no. 2, Oct. 1972, pp. 31–33.

of bargaining strength and vulnerability to manipulation by imperialist pressure.[98] By these criteria the present military government differs substantially from its civilian predecessors. Foreign businessmen and diplomats view it as sometimes unreasonable and sometimes erratic, but always a formidable adversary over the bargaining table. It is a government highly impervious to political penetration by outsiders, whether they be foreigners or Peruvian civilians. Furthermore, it is likely to remain that way, as the growth of large state enterprises in basic sectors limits the concentration of independent economic power.

It might be argued that multinational corporations and major foreign banks acting in unison could exert overwhelming power against so small a country as Peru. In fact this seems unlikely. Peru has already won a fight against the world's largest corporation. Moreover, while Exxon blustered, and General Motors turned up its nose, Massey-Ferguson made a deal. Peru bargains from strength so long as it can find enough companies like Massey-Ferguson.

Assessing the Costs and Benefits

One finds greater difficulty in deciding if Peru is really better off as a result of the new rules for foreign investment. I suspect, however, that Peru is indeed better off, for three reasons.

Perhaps the most frequently mentioned reason concerns the gains that closer supervision can provide through enabling a host government to obtain foreign capital and technology at lower cost. Effective supervision would make supranormal monopoly profits less likely and would make it more difficult to hide any such profits in royalty payments, transfer prices, or other time-honored gimmicks.

Such gains are undoubtedly real, significant, and worth pursuing, yet I suggest that they represent the least important of the three forms of gain that the new rules can provide Peru. This is because the mythology of foreign-company profit rates has probably outrun reality by a wide margin. My impression is that foreign companies in Peru have generally earned profits that could be described as healthy but not extravagant. The few cases verg-

[98] This view is important in the well-known article of Osvaldo Sunkel, "National Development Policy and External Dependence," *Journal of Development Studies*, vol. 6, Oct. 1969, pp. 23–48.

ing on the extravagant have generally involved old mining and petroleum concessions. Virtually everywhere in the Third World, concessions as they were written twenty years ago were give-aways. In most countries the terms have been tightened greatly in recent years, however, without recourse to revolution.[99]

The second source of gain lies in the general satisfaction a society obtains by doing things for itself. Economists have incorporated this idea into their frameworks by considering nationalism as a collective consumption good.[100] Although this may seem a rather artificial construct, the phenomenon is real and important. The accomplishments of a nation reflect on every citizen of that nation. A nation obliged to employ foreign companies to accomplish its significant tasks of production can feel little pride in itself. Inevitably, its citizens will sense that the nation's lack of economic accomplishment reflects poorly upon them.

The creation of Peruvian enterprises and Peruvian leadership within the national economy undoubtedly provides satisfaction. It also provides the most severe challenge that Peru has faced in this century. Having constructed a network of state enterprises destined to control the commanding heights of the economy, Peruvians will become obliged to manage, to administer, and to perform entrepreneurial functions as never before. The benefits to be obtained from successfully meeting this challenge are the greatest of all. It involves nothing less than changing a nation's character in a way that can bring development out of under-development. I have suggested elsewhere that the greatest obstacle to economic progress in Peru's history lies in the fact that the traditional elite consisted of rent collectors rather than entre-preneurs.[101] The social cost of this economic fact is incalculable. The opportunity of escaping from that sorry heritage is the greatest potential benefit that can come from the present government's

[99] See Louis Wells, "The Evolution of Concession Agreements," Harvard University Center for International Studies, Economic Development Report no. 117, mimeo, 1968.

[100] Harry Johnson, "A Theoretical Model of Economic Nationalism in New and Developing States," in Harry Johnson, ed., *Economic Nationalism in Old and New States*, University of Chicago Press, 1967, pp. 1–16. Also Albert Breton, "The Economics of Nationalism," *Journal of Political Economy*, vol. 72, Aug. 1964, pp. 376–386.

[101] Shane Hunt, "Growth and Guano in Nineteenth Century Peru," Research Program in Economic Development, discussion paper no. 34, Princeton University, mimeo, Feb. 1973.

decision to assume a managerial role in its dealings with foreign enterprises.

To speak of this opportunity is also to speak of the danger that confronts Peru along the course it has chosen. In the next decade, the Peruvian economy will prosper or atrophy according to the effectiveness with which the new public enterprises are managed. This concern has already been emphasized above, particularly with respect to mining development at Cerro Verde, but the challenge lies in every sector with every state enterprise.

The new rules of the game present a challenge for the regular bureaucracy as much as for the state enterprises. The new rules are complex and involve all the various dimensions of control mentioned above as part of Decision 24. The bureaucratic challenge lies in achieving this control without inadvertently driving potential investors away from Peru. The danger of the system lies particularly in its bringing discouragement to small investors, both foreign and domestic, who lack special influence and who might never be rescued from bureaucratic snags through special intervention.

The investment plans of larger, more visible, more influential firms are not freed of similar problems. A review of the tractor and diesel contracts, for example, creates fears that from their very complexity industrial progress could founder in an ocean of red tape. The principal guarantee that this will not happen lies in the importance the government attaches to the development of these enterprises. Such contracts may therefore be workable only in key industries that hold the government's continuing attention.

At the moment, these are the industries that Peru wants out of Andean bargaining. The haste to get started and thus improve negotiating position tends to sweep all cost considerations aside. Unfortunately, a country can't develop efficiently according to an evolving comparative advantage if next century's industrial structure is to be decided tomorrow. One can only hope that the efficiency loss will not be too great the day after tomorrow. Many foreign companies hold this same sense of urgency. They aren't sure where the Andean Group is going, but they would rather not be left behind. Having lost the tractor contract in Peru, for example, Fiat secured a contract in Bolivia and has sought other footholds in Colombia.

In the next few years, therefore, the flow of new investment and new technology must be left to the Fiats and Massey-Fergusons of world capitalism, companies whose worldwide strategies call for aggressive expansion in new markets like the Andean Group. Such companies will probably be able to provide Peru with its basic technological needs in coming years. Nevertheless, it must be recognized that in moving to a new set of rules for direct foreign investment, Peru has inevitably traded quantity for quality. The quantity is reduced not because the terms available in a transformed Peru are undesirable terms, but rather because of risk. The future is still murky, and uncertainty confronts the investor on all sides. The loss of some foreign investment is a price that must be paid for the rapid institutional change of the Peruvian Revolution.

To sum up, then, the benefits to Peru lie in the impetus to development of the nation's human resources, national pride of accomplishment, and lower payments to required foreign factors of production. The costs lie in the efficiency losses caused by reliance on inexperienced public enterprises, complicated bureaucratic control procedures, hasty commitment to massive projects in the scramble for Andean Group bargaining positions, and loss of some foreign investors unwilling to incur risks in Peru's changing political environment. The present Peruvian government has developed these new rules, confident that the benefits outweigh the costs. I believe that most foreign observers, perhaps after a moment's hesitation, would agree.

New Forms of Economic Organization in Peru: Toward Workers' Self-Management

Peter T. Knight

INTRODUCTION

Since taking power in October 1968, President Velasco and other Peruvian government spokesmen have stressed the important role they assign to new forms of economic organization in moving Peru toward their professed goal, a fully participatory social democracy. Under the 1969 Agrarian Reform Law the government has transformed the vast majority of affected private land-holdings into collective enterprises—the Agrarian Production Cooperatives (CAPs) and the Agricultural Societies of Social Interest (SAISs)—rather than parcel them out to individual tenants and workers. Beginning in 1970, firms in manufacturing industry, mining, fishing, and telecommunications have been reformed by the introduction of "labor communities" designed to gradually increase worker participation in ownership, profits, and management. All these measures potentially augment the workers' control over the decisions which affect their lives most directly, while distributing income more equitably than was the case in the past and diminishing the political power of the groups previously dominating Peruvian society—the landed oligarchy, the industrial bourgeoisie, and their foreign partners.

I gratefully acknowledge useful comments on earlier drafts which were received from Roberto Abusada, Jorge Avendaño, Giorgio Alberti, Michael Anderson, Gerardo Cárdenas, Reynold Carlson, Peter Cleaves, Edward Dew, Robert Drysdale, Marie Jones, Lillian Knight, Abraham Lowenthal, Mechthild Minkner, Abner Montalvo, Luis Pásara, César Peñaranda, René Rodríguez, Jorge Santistevan, Martin Scurrah, Alfred Stepan, John Strasma, James Trowbridge, and Carlos Zuzunaga. The opinions expressed in this chapter, however, are my own and do not necessarily represent the views of any of the aforementioned. I also wish to thank Diana Davis for long hours spent typing several drafts.

But as early as 1970 it became apparent that the government was contemplating an additional form of economic organization. Articles 6 and 8 of the General Industries Law (July 1970) had foreseen the existence of "social-property" firms, and both the General Fishing Law (March 1971) and the General Mining Law (June 1971) contained similar references. At the end of August 1973 the government unveiled a draft law defining a social-property sector (SPS) as a sector composed of firms managed by their workers and owned collectively by all the workers of that sector rather than by the workers of each enterprise, as in the case of production cooperatives. The public was invited to submit written comments to the Council of Presidential Advisers (COAP),[1] and an extensive public debate ensued. The Social-Property Law was finally promulgated on May 2, 1974.

According to repeated official statements, the future Peruvian economy is to be divided into four sectors, each characterized by a different form of property—social, state, reformed private, and fully private. The social-property sector is to become "predominant," though neither the exact meaning of this term nor the period required has been spelled out. Social-property firms may undertake any activity not specifically reserved for the state. A group of *state owned and operated firms* in basic and strategic industries is to be "important," and there will also be two *private sectors*, one consisting of firms reformed by the introduction of labor communities, the other being a residual classification including all small-scale activities such as artisanal industries and small commercial and service establishments. The cooperatives and SAISs do not fit into this four-sector scheme, and this suggests that the government would like to convert them into social-property firms. Political realities, however, may force their recognition as part of a fifth sector.

Although President Velasco has declared this pluralism to characterize the Peruvian model of economic organization, he has emphatically asserted the transcendental importance of the social-property sector, which is to "express in the economy the Revolution's fundamental political option"—that is, its neither capitalist nor communist nature.[2] Indeed, he has claimed that the

[1] See Chapter 1 of this volume for an explanation of COAP's role in the legislative process during the Velasco government.

[2] Message to the nation, Oct. 3, 1973.

creation of the social-property sector is "perhaps the most important step of the Revolution."[3] All rhetoric aside, a decision to proceed with establishing the social-property sector appears to be a fundamental choice, one that goes considerably beyond the creation of agricultural cooperatives or the introduction of labor communities. Although these earlier steps represented important departures from conventional capitalist economic organization, the social-property sector would go much further, possibly at the expense of reforms introduced by the Revolutionary Government itself—whether or not this is desired by the regime. For example, the presence of a liberally financed and self-managed alternative could undermine attempts to induce worker collaboration with skittish capitalist partners in the reformed private sector. But paradoxically, given the nature of the Social-Property Law which emerged, vested interests of workers in existing cooperatives and reformed private-sector firms may grow over time, imperiling the regime's declared objective of achieving a predominant social-property sector despite or, in some cases, because of defects of the earlier reforms. Another major challenge to future social-property sector predominance is posed by the rapid growth of powerful state enterprises already commanding massive amounts of limited investment resources.

In attempting to introduce worker-managed firms on a national scale, within a pluralistic economy including important private and state sectors, and without relying upon a single dominant political party, Peru's military government has launched a unique experiment in economic and social change. Many intellectuals and politicians in the Third World perceive both Soviet-style socialism and private capitalism as unattractive models for development, and this view is shared by a growing number of analysts in "advanced" countries on both sides of the rapidly-disintegrating iron curtain. Both the origins and the outcome of the Peruvian experiment are thus of great interest not only in Peru but in other countries as well.

Just what is meant by workers' self-management, the concept which underlies the Peruvian definition of social property? What issues may arise in designing and implementing self-management systems? How and when did major political actors begin advocating the adoption of workers' self-management in Peru? What

[3] Message to the nation, July 28, 1974.

are the principal characteristics of the CAP, the SAIS, and the reformed private-sector industrial firm, and what role did these earlier creations of the Velasco regime play in the decision to proceed with the social-property sector? What can be learned about the nature of economic policy making under Velasco by examining the regime's treatment of the social-property issue? What are the salient features of the Social-Property Law which finally emerged? And finally, assuming the creation of a predominant social-property sector is indeed a high-priority goal, what problems are likely to arise in the implementation process?

In this chapter I seek to provide at least tentative answers to these questions, more or less in the order they have been raised here. I will argue that the process of defining social property is best viewed as the most recent phase of a long-standing debate among Peruvian intellectuals and politicians—primarily among civilians, but with increasing military participation. Though Velasco and his army supporters came to power committed to a series of structural reforms, the particular characteristics of the social-property sector appear to have emerged as a function of the revolutionary process itself. As analysis of accumulating experience revealed shortcomings of the regime's earlier economic reforms, the intelligentsia was able to play an important role in designing the new sector. The multiple issues associated with the maintenance of economic pluralism were at the forefront of the debate during the design phase of the social-property sector and are likely to remain predominant during implementation.

WORKERS' SELF-MANAGEMENT: DEFINITION, OBJECTIVES, AND POLICY ISSUES

Before analyzing the social-property issue in the Peruvian process, it will be helpful to define in general terms what is meant by workers' self-management and to pose more precisely the principal policy issues which arise in the design and implementation of self-management systems. A useful description of a market economy composed of worker-managed firms is provided by Jaroslav Vanek, a Czech-American economist who has developed the relevant economic theory most completely.[4] Though Vanek's

[4] The best technical reference is Jaroslav Vanek, *The General Theory of Labor-Managed Market Economies* (Ithaca and London: Cornell University

model offers a convenient point of departure for comparative analysis, it does not correspond precisely to any existing economy, and other definitions of self-management are possible.

Vanek distinguishes five characteristics of such an economy: democratic management of each firm by its workers (defined to include all individuals employed by the firm): sharing by all workers in net profits; decentralized decision making, with firms and individuals guided by a free market in goods, labor, and investment funds; rental of capital assets from an agency external to the firm, with members of the firm collectively enjoying usufruct, but not full ownership; and freedom of employment. In the strictly economic realm, the fundamental difference between a self-managed firm and a traditional capitalist firm is that the self-managed firm will seek to maximize net income per worker rather than net profits on capital employed. This distinction arises from the autonomous and democratic nature of decision making within the self-managed firm, where capital receives a fixed rental and acquires no rights to management.[5] Among the objectives posited by advocates of self-management are increased worker participation, education, and solidarity, as well as a more equal distribution of income and faster capital accumulation.

In practice, policy makers who contemplate the adoption of some or all elements of self-management must wrestle with three difficult trade-offs. The first may be called the problem of *economic pluralism*. For a number of reasons (including political constraints, a desire not to precipitate a flight of capital and technical personnel, or fear of introducing an untried form of economic organization without a long initial trial), policy makers may prefer to permit and even encourage the maintenance of one or more modes of economic organization other than self-management. This may either condemn the nascent self-management sector to economic strangulation or provoke costly conflict between competing modes. It also requires establishing criteria for

---

Press, 1970). A more philosophical and speculative work is Vanek's *The Participatory Economy: An Evolutionary Hypothesis and a Strategy for Development* (Ithaca and London: Cornell University Press, 1971).

[5] See Vanek, *General Theory*; Benjamin N. Ward, *The Socialist Economy: A Study of Organizational Alternatives* (New York: Random House, 1967); and J. E. Meade, "The Theory of Labor-Managed Firms and of Profit Sharing," *Economic Journal* 82:325s (Mar. 1972, supplement) 402–428.

deciding which firms and/or types of economic activity will have any given mode.

Secondly, there is the problem of *growth versus distribution*. A strong reliance on material incentives and the market mechanism may stimulate production and capital formation but accentuate income differences between individual workers within a given firm, between different firms within the self-managed sector, and/or between workers in the modern and traditional parts of the economy. Although in principle income redistribution within a pluralistic economy may be carried out most efficiently through a national system of taxes and expenditures, in practice political realities may not favor such a frontal attack on inequality. In such circumstances the design of compensatory mechanisms within a self-managed sector may help pave the way for more comprehensive measures. On the other hand, strong redistributive mechanisms confined to a self-managed sector may aggravate the problem of economic pluralism.

Finally, decisions must be made regarding the *degree of decentralization*. The very concept of self-management implies considerable decentralization of economic decision making. Nevertheless, variations on the theme are possible, particularly concerning investment. At one extreme consider a system of self-managed firms, each of which would be free to dispose of all after-tax income as it desired, and at the other a system in which capital and rental income of all self-managed firms would be channeled to a central financial agency, to which existing or prospective firms would then apply for investment funds. Policy makers must weigh the benefits of autonomy and decentralization, which favor more rapid implementation of initiatives originating at the base of the system, against those of central planning and control. Of course, between an atomistic and a centralized system, many federal systems with three or more tiers are possible.

WORKERS' SELF-MANAGEMENT IN PERUVIAN POLITICO-ECONOMIC THOUGHT PRIOR TO OCTOBER 1968

Three significant political movements in Peru's recent history have departed from an adherence to orthodox liberal capitalism or authoritarian socialism to advocate some form of workers' self-management—the Peruvian Aprista party, the Christian Democratic party, and the Social Progressive Movement. In the following paragraphs I examine the basic ideas regarding the organization of the firm developed by each of these movements prior to October 1968.

The Peruvian Aprista Party (APRA)

Even before the founding of the Peruvian Aprista party in 1931, Víctor Raúl Haya de la Torre had sketched the basic outlines of a pluralistic economy within what he called the anti-imperialist state, emphasized the need for gradualism in implementing reforms, and called for an alliance of peasants, workers, and the middle class against imperialism and the oligarchy.[6] The dominant economic sector within the Aprista scheme would be state capitalism, reducing the economic power of the domestic capitalists and their foreign allies, who would nevertheless retain control of a traditional private sector for some time. But the anti-imperialist state would also favor development of a third sector, cooperatives. We may consider production cooperatives to be self-managed firms as defined in section two of this chapter except where capital is held internally in unequal amounts by individual members who receive correspondingly unequal returns on this capital.

Although the declared goal of APRA was socialism, in practice the party did little which might move Peru in this direction. APRA supported a rather capitalistic cooperative law passed during the Belaúnde regime, but successfully opposed the inclusion of coastal sugar plantations (APRA strongholds) within Belaúnde's agrarian reform. Although once considered a revolutionary threat by the Peruvian establishment, by the 1950s, most observers agree, APRA could not claim to be either revolutionary or socialist.[7] Nevertheless, APRA's strategy and the instruments

[6] Víctor Raúl Haya de la Torre, *El Antimperialismo y el Apra*, 4th ed. (Lima: Editorial-Imprenta Amauta, 1972), p. 85.

[7] An account in English of the degenerative process may be found in François Bourricaud, *Power and Society in Contemporary Peru* (New York and Washington: Praeger Publishers, 1970), pp. 139–185. For a particularly vitriolic denunciation by a former Aprista, see Hernando Aguirre Gamio, *Liquidación Histórica del Apra y del Colonialismo Neoliberal* (Lima: Ediciones Debate, 1962).

proposed to carry it out bear some resemblance to the Velasco government's approach prior to the emergence of the social-property issue.

The Christian Democratic Party (PDC)

The PDC was the first Peruvian political movement to base itself solidly on Christian thought as exemplified in the social encyclicals. It is the civilian political organization which probably has contributed most to the Velasco government's thinking on economic organization. Born in January 1956 as a party of the center right strongly supporting private enterprise and the free market as a necessary condition for democracy,[8] it has always sought a more complete integration of labor and capital within the firm as a means of achieving class conciliation. The party's declaration of principles (*ideario*) approved by its first national convention in January 1956 urged that this be accomplished by "profit sharing, participation in management, and access to the property of the enterprise" achieved gradually in accord with the economic possibilities of each firm.[9] The bias toward private enterprise has eroded over time, more or less accompanying a progressive radicalization of international social Christian thought.

The seeds of this radicalization were present within the newly born PDC as well as in social Christian thought. Indeed, the final section of the PDC *ideario* of January 1956 contained a repudiation of individualism, unregulated capitalism, imperialism, and colonialism as well as of totalitarianism, dictatorship, and Marxism. The ideas of joint ownership (*copropiedad*) and joint management (*cogestión*) of the firm by capital and labor were also included in the *ideario*. By the end of the decade they had become key elements in the PDC's proposals for enterprise reform, by which the party sought to define a "third position" distinct from capitalism and communism.

In 1961 Héctor Cornejo Chávez, the principal PDC theoretician and party candidate for president, introduced a new term

[8] See "Plan de la Economía Nacional," a speech by Ernesto Alayza Grundy, in Ernesto Alayza Grundy et al., *Una Tercera Posición: Discursos Demócrata Cristianos en los Ultimos Cuatros Años* (Lima: Editorial Universitaria, Colección Pensamiento Político, 1960).

[9] "Ideario del Partido Demócrata Cristiano," *Democracia* (a weekly newspaper published by the PDC), Mar. 23, 1956.

into the Peruvian political lexicon, the *empresa comunitaria*.[10] By this he meant a firm in which all members contributed capital as well as labor and where the influence of external capital would be minimized. Cornejo Chávez and his colleagues have legitimized the concept of the *empresa comunitaria* by citing the Gospels, the early popes, the social encyclicals, and recent Christian social philosophers such as Mounier, Maritain, Berdyaev, and Lepp.[11] A French Dominican priest, Louis-Joseph Lebret, who founded a school of thought known as "economics and humanism," was an important influence on their evolving ideas.[12] Lebret, who first visited Peru in 1954, induced many Peruvians to question the relationship between private property, Christian social values, and the existing sociopolitical structures in Peru. In particular Lebret influenced a group within the PDC youth movement which worked closely with Cornejo Chávez[13] and also gave lectures in the universities and at the Center for Higher Military Studies (CAEM).

After the 1962 electoral defeat of Cornejo Chávez and the refusal by the military to accept the results of those elections, the PDC entered into an alliance with Popular Action (AP) for the 1963 elections. The program of the AP-PDC coalition called for "a progressive reform of the private firm destined to encourage

[10] "Que Propone Realizar en el Perú el Gobierno de la Democracia Cristiana," speech given May 13, 1961, and reproduced in Héctor Cornejo Chávez, *Que Propone la Democracia Cristiana* (Lima: Ediciones del Sol, 1962). The term *empresa comunitaria* was not new in Latin American Christian Democratic circles. One of the conclusions of the Fifth International Christian Democratic Congress held in October 1959 urged the gradual substitution of the capitalist firm by the *empresa comunitaria*. The idea of the firm as a community of persons may be found in Pope John XXIII's 1961 encyclical, *Mater et Magistra*, and the concept has deep roots in Christian social doctrine.

[11] See Héctor Cornejo Chávez, "Memorandum sobre la doctrina del partido" and "Conclusiones sobre la ideología del partido" (Oct. 31, 1969), included in *Sociedad Comunitaria* (Lima: 1969, mimeo) and Carlos Blancas Bustamante, "Pensamiento Cristiano y Propiedad Social," *Expreso*, Sept. 27, 1972.

[12] A systematized compendium of Lebret's thought available to Peruvians in the 1950s is Louis-Joseph Lebret, *Guia del Militante* (Montevideo: Editorial Mosca Hnos., 1950).

[13] Among these students were Helán Jaworski, now a high official of SINAMOS, and Fernando de Trazegnies G., now a professor of law at the Catholic University and for a period in 1973 an adviser to the commission which prepared the draft Social-Property law.

and protect *empresas comunitarias* and cooperatives."[14] Many of the key ideas included in the AP-PDC platform of 1962 were later incorporated in the labor communities introduced by the Velasco regime to reform the capitalist firm. Among these ideas were gradualism, class conciliation, pluralism of organizational modes, and worker participation in ownership, profits, and management of the firm.

In February 1968 PDC Deputy Rafael Cubas Vinatea introduced a draft law defining the *empresa comunitaria* and providing for several national institutions to foster this new form of organization.[15] Cubas Vinatea's draft law and the speech he made when introducing it in the Chamber of Deputies are the most complete elaboration of the PDC ideas concerning the reform of the firm developed prior to October 3, 1968.

In essence, the *empresa comunitaria*, as defined in this draft law, would be a self-managed firm (as described in the second section of this chapter), except that self-financing would be permitted, even forced. Capital could be obtained through issuing bonds, but the ultimate goal of an *empresa comunitaria* would be to operate only with collectively owned capital called the Common Fund, formed by reinvestment of all or part of the firm's profits. Voluntary conversion of firms with other modes of organization into *empresas comunitarias* as well as the creation of new firms would be encouraged, within a pluralistic economy. A federal system along geographic and functional lines was specified to link individual firms. Its higher organs would serve as interest groups and provide services to member firms.

Cubas Vinatea's draft law elicited virtually no reaction or comments from members of the Peruvian legislature or the Lima press, probably less because of the nature of the subject matter than the continual political crises which characterized the last months of the Belaúnde regime. This PDC proposal was the sole

[14] Published in *Alianza Acción Popular–Demócrata Cristiano, Bases para el Plan de Gobierno: Síntesis de las Principales Recomendaciones* (Lima: Librería e Imprenta Minerva, Apr. 1963), p. 9.

[15] The draft law, an introduction by Cornejo Chávez, and the speech made by Cubas Vinatea when he presented the law in the Chamber of Deputies on February 14, 1968, were published in a pamphlet entitled *La Empresa Comunitaria* (Lima, 1968). This draft law was prepared by a group of PDC members with experience in cooperatives and industrial management; the group began its work in November 1967 by studying the experiences of other countries.

systematic attempt to design a self-managed sector of the Peruvian economy prior to the advent of the Velasco regime.

The Social Progressive Movement (MSP)

The MSP arose as a Peruvian adaptation of socialist humanism. Though influenced by European thinkers and experience, it drew heavily on modern social science analysis of the Peruvian reality. The MSP was officially formed in December 1955, and its following—primarily intellectuals, technical personnel, and youth— never reached significant proportions.

The "economics and humanism" school of Louis-Joseph Lebret and François Perroux influenced MSP thinking on economic organization. During his visits to Peru in the 1950s, Lebret was in close contact with MSP members such as Jorge Bravo Bresani, Germán Tito Gutierrez, and Alberto Ruiz Eldredge. An important editorial published in the MSP newspaper *Libertad* in June 1961 used the concept of the *empresa comunitaria*, which was already current in PDC circles, but went much further in describing a concept of socialism which rejected "collectivist and totalitarian statism." The MSP sought to create a series of intermediary institutions between the individual and the state designed to permit direct participation in the decisions affecting the individuals concerned.[16]

In its platform adopted in preparation for the 1962 elections, the MSP proposed an enterprise reform to achieve self-management in an evolutionary fashion by passing through a range of forms of comanagement to arrive at a socialist form of the *empresa comunitaria*.[17] This "new socialist firm" would participate in the elaboration of economic plans, but would conserve autonomy of management, operating within a market subject to institutional controls. Not only the firm's workers, but also representatives of consumers, client firms, and in some cases the state would participate in management decisions, the exact scheme being determined by the scale of the firm and type of activity in which it was engaged.[18] The capitalist as such would disappear,

16 "El Estado Socialista," *Libertad*, June 28, 1961.

17 "Reforma de la Empresa: Una Base Institucional para la Justa Distribución de la Riqueza," *Libertad*, June 21, 1961.

18 "La Nueva Empresa Socializada," *Libertad*, May 16, 1962.

though private capital might be accepted in return for fixed-interest-bearing securities.

The MSP never proposed any legislation to implement these ideas. But although the MSP disappeared as a political party after 1962, a number of its members have occupied posts in the Velasco regime. The newspaper *Expreso* has been a stronghold of *social-progresistas* and has been an important forum for writers favoring social property.

INITIAL STEPS TOWARD WORKERS' SELF-MANAGEMENT UNDER VELASCO

Within two years of taking power the Velasco regime introduced three new forms of economic organization at the enterprise level: the Agrarian Production Cooperative, the Agricultural Society of Social Interest, and the labor community within the industrial sector. Each of these fell short of establishing full workers' self-management. Moreover, their inability to achieve all the multiple goals set for them has become increasingly manifest. That this in turn has influenced the design of the social-property sector shows the dynamic nature of the Peruvian revolution. It is thus important to review the principal features of these earlier creations.

The Agrarian Production Cooperative (CAP)

In principle, a CAP is an indivisible unit of land, associated livestock, buildings, and processing facilities under common administration by its members.[19] In many CAPs, however, members retain small private parcels for their own use. The CAP mode is preferred under the agrarian law for reforming agricultural production complexes whenever a rational exploitation of the unit would permit the provision of permanent work for all the members at acceptable levels of income. The best-known and economically most important CAPs are those that were established

[19] The document setting forth the characteristics of the CAP is ·Decreto Supremo no. 240-69-AP of November 1969. Technically it is a *reglamento* of Ley 15260 (the General Cooperatives Law), Decreto Ley 17713 (which created the National Office of Cooperative Development), and Decreto Ley 17716 (the Agrarian Reform Law). A useful reference is Alberto Bustamante B., "Legislación sobre Reforma Agraria y Cooperativas Agrarias" (Lima: DESCO, Aug. 1974, mimeo).

in the former sugar plantations of the northern coast beginning in 1970. Much of Peru's irrigated and most productive lands, principally in the coastal valleys, is included in CAPs; by the end of 1974, the agrarian reform had incorporated 86,597 families into 348 CAPs.[20] Even if it is assumed that each family included two members of the labor force, this mode embraced only about 3.9 percent of the economically active population of Peru, or only 8.8 percent of the rural labor force.

A CAP's membership consists of field, industrial processing, white-collar, technical, and administrative workers. Part-time workers (*eventuales*), including seasonal cane cutters, are excluded from membership: approximately one out of every four workers in the coastal sugar CAPs was a nonmember in 1972.[21] Monthly monetary income and income in kind of member fieldworkers has run about four times as much as for *eventuales*.[22]

That part of the CAP's capital received under the agrarian reform cannot be individualized. In return for this property, the members of the CAP as a group must contract a debt with the agrarian reform agency, paying a portion of each year's surpluses for amortization and interest on the outstanding balance until the debt is canceled.[23] In addition to basic wages and salaries, which vary according to the type of work performed, members earn a fraction of the CAP's yearly profit, which is distributed in proportion to the number of days worked during the previous year. Nonmembers do not receive this dividend, nor do they participate in many other benefits such as subsidized housing and food.

Self-management as defined in the second section of this chapter does not really exist in the CAP, because the Ministry of Agriculture selects the general manager from a slate proposed by the

[20] Ministerio de Agricultura, Dirección General de Reforma Agraria y Asentamiento Rural, Dirección de Asentamiento Rural, "Reforma Agraria en Cifras" (Lima, Dec. 1974, mimeo), table 1.

[21] Santiago Roca, "La Distribución del Ingreso en las Cooperativas Azucareras del Perú, 1968–1972" (Lima: ESAN, 1973, mimeo), table 12, p. 29.

[22] Calculated from ibid., table 25, p. 78 (see Roca's footnote 25 for his method of estimating full-time equivalents for the *eventuales*) and Jaime Llosa, "Reforma Agraria y Revolución," *Partcipación* 2:3 (Aug. 1973), table on p. 50.

[23] In addition to collectively owned fixed assets, a CAP's capital normally includes a social fund initially composed of the accumulated social benefits of individual workers against which the CAP issues nonnegotiable certificates bearing a maximum interest rate of 2 percent. These certificates are the property of individual workers.

CAP and the fixed capital of the CAP is the collective property of its members rather than capital rented from an external financing agency. The former provision tends to generate conflict between managers and technicians on the one hand and field workers on the other. The fact that the capital of the CAP is owned by the members collectively, rather than by an external agency, helps perpetuate pronounced inequalities in income distribution, since different firms in the agricultural sector are unequally endowed with high-quality land, infrastructure (especially access to irrigation and transportation systems), and other forms of capital. Consider the example of the eight largest sugar cooperatives studied by Santiago Roca. In 1972 blue-collar workers of all kinds (*obreros*) in the richest cooperative (Casa Grande) received incomes almost three times as high as those in the poorest (Cayaltí); the average earnings of *obreros* in the four richest sugar cooperatives was 63 percent higher than in the four poorest.[24] Such differences no doubt will become even more striking when payments on the agrarian debt, which are related to the value of the complexes, have been completed.

The provision that at least 15 percent of surpluses must be used to reinvest in the operations of the CAP may further aggravate the problem of unequal endowments of land and capital. This forced reinvestment is likely to exacerbate the already highly unequal income in rural areas if a tendency to raise the level of direct and indirect remunerations does not eventually wipe out the profits from which reinvestment funds are drawn.[25]

Well-documented research on CAPs other than those established in the former sugar complexes is scarce. Perhaps the most comprehensive study to date is one by Douglas Horton.[26] Horton presents data showing that the CAPs established in the coastal

[24] Calculated from Santiago Roca, "La Distribución de Ingreso," table 24, p. 74.

[25] Detailed financial projections for one of the coastal sugar CAPs suggest that if trends established in the first three years of operations continue, the CAP will not make needed reinvestments and is headed for total decapitalization by 1980. See Luis Blomberg et al., "Análisis y Programación Financiera Preliminar de la Cooperativa Agraria de Producción Pomalca Ltda. No. 38," master's degree project, ESAN, Jan. 1974.

[26] Douglas E. Horton, "Land Reform and Reform Enterprises in Peru: Report submitted to the Land Tenure Center and the International Bank for Reconstruction and Development" (Madison, Wis.: Land Tenure Center, June 1974, mimeo, 2 vols.).

region—where the wage labor system prevailed prior to agrarian reform and year-round irrigated crop production favors the establishment of large units—have been relatively successful at maintaining or increasing production and investment. But in crop-producing parts of the Sierra, the semifeudal *colonato* system is still prevalent, and ecological conditions tend to favor smaller production units. There is thus a strong economic basis for peasant resistance to collectivization of production, and CAPs have proven both difficult to establish and prone to serious production problems. On the other hand, in higher regions within the Sierra, where livestock production predominates, CAPs have had a better record. This seems to be because livestock production is less influenced by climate, and the nature of the production process itself favors large-scale enterprises.

In most economically successful CAPs it appears that while production has been maintained or increased, many decisions are still made from above in rather hierarchical internal organizational structures. At least in the coastal sugar CAPs the real income of all workers has risen substantially as part of the profits previously accruing to the owners has been distributed as wages, salaries, and benefits. But in the sugar CAPs studied by Roca, member *obreros* have enjoyed percentage increases over three times as great as those received by *eventuales* (many of whom in practice work for the CAPs year round), who are still in the position of providing cheap hired labor without acquiring any voting rights.[27] Perhaps a more serious problem is that rather than being "a dynamic agency for the achievement of a society characterized by solidarity" (as proposed in the implementing regulations creating the CAP mode), the CAPs appear more interested in expanding their own members' incomes. They have not contributed to solving the rural employment problem. In fact there is some evidence that employment in the CAPs has actually decreased.[28]

This complex of behavior has been widely referred to as "group egoism" and has moved many observers to consider integrating the CAPs into much larger agricultural units embracing entire valleys or regions.[29] Another frequently mentioned possi-

[27] Calculated from Santiago Roca, "La Distribución de Ingreso," table 25, p. 78.

[28] Calculated from ibid., table 25, p. 78, and table 19, p. 49. See also p. 109.

[29] Advanced thinking within government agencies on this topic is reflected

bility is the incorporation of the CAPs within the new social-property sector.

The Agricultural Society of Social Interest (SAIS)

A SAIS generally consists of one or more expropriated estates transformed into a cooperative and a group of surrounding peasant communities (comunidades indígenas) which participate in management of the cooperative and receive income generated by it but do not directly contribute capital, land, or labor.[30] The rationale is that peasant communities invariably have suffered encroachment upon their lands by neighboring estates, which have grown at their expense over the centuries. Thus a SAIS attempts to reconcile actual or potential conflict within the same institutional structure rather than break up the relatively productive estates.

The SAIS mode has been widely used in the Andean highlands (the Sierra) but not on the coast. It tends to be implemented when the beneficiaries are legal entities (e.g., peasant communities and cooperatives) and when the reorganized enterprises have low manpower requirements in relation to their profitability and the number of qualified beneficiaries. By the end of 1974, 54,561 families had been incorporated into 48 SAISs under the agrarian reform.[31] This means that the SAIS mode embraced about 2.6 percent of the economically active population of Peru, or 5.3 percent of the rural labor force.

As in the case of a CAP, all lands, livestock, processing facilities, and other assets of the former estates are turned over to a SAIS, become property of its members as a group, and cannot be divided. The cooperatives, which usually occupy more productive lands and have lower man-land ratios than the surrounding communities, generate all of the SAIS income. They retain a fraction of the surplus for internal reinvestment and for distribution to their own workers.

The innovative feature is that member peasant communities

in Gerardo Cárdenas, "La Nueva Estructura Agraria," and Jaime Llosa, "Reforma Agraria y Revolución," Participación 2:3 (Aug. 1973) 22–23 and 44–59 respectively.

[30] The legal documents regulating a SAIS are the same as for the CAP. See note 19.

[31] Ministerio de Agricultura, "Reforma Agraria en Cifras," cuadro 2.

are also entitled to receive a percentage of this surplus, determined by a complex formula which provides income in inverse relation to each community's wealth. There is no explicit use to which such income must be put by communities, except that it must be used on communal projects, never for direct distribution to individuals. The cooperative may also provide technical services to the communities to help upgrade their production technology.

The SAIS is explicitly designed as a transitional form which could lead toward the incorporation of the member communities into an enlarged cooperative, thus creating a CAP. The unilateral transfer of resources and technical assistance to member peasant communities by the cooperative of the SAIS is designed to break down a distrust of the agrarian reform on the part of many communities as well as to redistribute income. But, in practice, since community representatives normally have a strong majority in the administrative council, the result sometimes has been an alliance of community representatives with the cooperative's technical and managerial personnel to hold down incomes of the cooperative's workers.[32] If the cooperative's workers receive lower wages, the surplus channeled to the communities is correspondingly increased. A percentage of the surplus must also be reinvested in the cooperative.

The aims of the SAIS mode are to reduce social tension and redistribute income while increasing production and investment within the region it embraces, and it appears to have been reasonably successful in achieving at least the last two of the goals.[33] But there is no distribution to groups outside the SAIS other than through taxes and that small part of governmental expenditure going to rural areas. Even in a rich SAIS the profits distributed to communities may be small in comparison with needs. The internalization within the SAIS of long-existing tensions between estates and peasant communities may threaten the viability of this form of organization in the long run if eventual transition to the CAP mode does not prove feasible. Regional integration of

[32] See Horton, "Land Reform and Reform Enterprises in Peru," and Carlos Aramburú, "Sais Cahuide Ltda. No. 6, Huancayo, Peru" (Lima: Centro Nacional de Capacitación e Investigación para la Reforma Agraria, n.d., probably 1972, mimeo).

[33] Horton, "Land Reform and Reform Enterprises in Peru."

various SAISs and the establishment of industrial activities such as textile plants are possibilities that have been much discussed. Both the SAIS and associated industrial activities may eventually be brought into the social-property sector under special arrangements foreseen in the Social-Property Law.

The Reformed Private-Sector Industrial Firm

The labor community concept first appeared in the General Industries Law and was subsequently introduced in the fishing, mining, and telecommunications sectors.[34] If the government carries out its announced plans to reform all private firms other than small-scale businesses, labor communities will eventually exist in other types of economic activity such as services and commerce. More than three years' experience with the labor community in the largely private manufacturing sector were evaluated along with the experience of CAPs and SAISs by the drafters of the Social-Property Law. Since fishing, mining, and telecommunications are increasingly dominated by state-owned enterprises, this analysis will be limited largely to the reformed private-sector industrial firm.

All industrial firms with six or more workers or a gross annual income of more than 1 million soles (approximately $25,000) must have a *comunidad industrial* (CI) composed of all permanent employees of the firm. (As of September 1974 there were 3,446 CIs with approximately 200,000 members.) Each year the CI of a private firm receives 15 percent of the firm's pretax net income, which must be used to purchase shares in the firm until

[34] The key legislation determining the nature of the reformed private-sector industrial firm is Ley 16123 of May 6, 1966 (Law of Mercantile Societies); Decreto Ley 18350 of July 30, 1970 (General Industries Law); and Decreto Ley 18384 of September 1, 1970 (Industrial Community Law). A number of other laws and regulations are also applicable. A summary of those issued before 1974 may be found in Ministerio de Industria y Turismo, Oficina Sectorial de Planificación, "Descripción y Concordancia de los Dispositivos Legales sobre Comunidades Industriales," Doc. 002-AES-DESP-OSP-MIT-1/74 (Lima, Ministerio de Industria y Turismo, Jan. 1974, mimeo). A complete legal analysis may be found in DESCO, "La Comunidad Laboral" (Lima: DESCO, 1973, mimeo) and Marcial Rubio, "Evolución de la Legislación de comunidades Laborales" (Lima: DESCO, Sept. 1974). A popular guide, designed for use by members of industrial communities, is DESCO, *Manual del Comunero Industrial* (Lima: Campodónico, 1972).

50 percent of the shares has been acquired.[35] If sufficient re-investment is planned by the firm, new shares are issued by the firm and purchased by the CI. Otherwise, existing shares must be purchased from other shareholders.

When the CI obtains 50 percent of the outstanding shares, it issues its own securities (representing CI ownership in the shares of the firm itself) and distributes these to its individual members in proportion to the time they have worked in the firm. These securities of the CI are not transferable and must be redeemed at their full cash value by the CI when a member leaves the firm. Thus they are *not* shares in the firm itself. Before the CI securities are issued to workers, a worker who leaves the firm is entitled to receive only one-half of the value of his contribution to the CI's ownership in the firm. This value is based on that of the firm's shares acquired by the CI and the worker's time of service independent of his wage. After 50-percent ownership has been achieved, the 15 percent of net income continues to accrue to the CI to be used for a variety of purposes including investment in other firms or government securities, but not direct distribution to members of the CI.

In addition to the 15 percent of net income turned over to the CI, the reformed industrial firm must distribute an additional 10 percent to its workers, half in proportion to their basic remuneration and half in proportion to the number of months worked during the previous year. From the outset the CI has at least one member on the board of directors, and this number increases over time in proportion to the shares owned by the CI.

The CI is self-managed, having as its maximum authority a general assembly composed of all members which elects an executive body, the council, responsible to the general assembly. However, within the firm itself, worker participation in management is required by law only in the form of representation of the CI on the board of directors, where CI shares must be voted as a bloc. Thus management remains a function of property rights,

[35] State enterprises in "basic" industries and state, mixed, or private enterprises in industries designated by supreme decree as "strategic" are also required to have industrial communities; these do not purchase voting shares in their firms, but rather bonds or state securities. At the end of September 1974, there were thirteen state-owned industrial firms with 8,229 workers. (Source: Ministry of Industry and Tourism, Statistical Office.)

as in a traditional capitalist enterprise, even though the workers become part owners of the firm. Eventually the CI should be able to gain control and thus implement a more democratic internal structure within the firm. This could happen well before it owned 50 percent of the shares, assuming it could form alliances with some other shareholders.

Only 10 percent of net income is shared within the reformed private firm; but if the CI obtained control, it might raise this percentage, either by increasing the portion distributed to workers or by raising remunerations. Capital is internally owned by the CI, and although reinvestment is not forced, generous tax incentives and customs rebates for reinvestment under the General Industries Law effectively make the cost of fixed investment to the firm very low. This in turn implies that new investments by the firm are likely to use more capital and less labor than would otherwise be the case, thus aggravating the employment problem while providing additional capital income to existing workers.

Although the General Industries Law specifies that the reformed private-sector industrial firm is to operate within a pluralistic economy, the private firm as reformed by the CI could serve as a transitional stage leading toward self-management. The rather ambiguous control mechanism implied in the planned fifty-fifty split of ownership between traditional capitalist and the CI suggests that its legislators may have had this objective in mind. In any case, with the increasing emphasis placed on the sector of social property by government spokesmen, strong pressures have been generated to convert many if not all reformed private-sector firms into social-property firms.

A principal objective of the industrial reform was clearly to increase production and capital formation. Gradually increasing worker participation in property, profits, and management was intended to achieve class conciliation. Considerable emphasis was given to the educational process which would be initiated by the reform, a process that would lead, it was hoped, to a new type of relation between labor and capitalists.[36] In the course of this process the regime apparently expected that labor unions would wither away, or at least undergo substantial modification

---

[36] See President Velasco's speech at the closing of the Annual Conference for Executives (CADE), Nov. 15, 1970.

in functions, as the traditional adversary relations between capital and labor were transformed into teamwork.[37] Higher profits made possible by augmented productivity would stimulate investment, which would be further encouraged by generous tax incentives.

In practice, the goals of stimulating industrial investment and social peace have not proved easy to achieve. Whether due to the presence of the CI within the reformed industrial firm or to uncertainty regarding the stability of the "rules of the game" caused by the debate over social property, new private investment in industry has been very low since 1970 (the government has not published precise figures), although reinvestments of profits picked up notably beginning in 1972. Further, businessmen used a number of ploys to deflate net income, thus reducing profits distributed to workers and transformed into shares owned by the CI. Common practices included inflating the costs of inputs and holding down prices of outputs in favor of service or commercial firms controlled by the same private capitalists and not yet required to have labor communities, paying exorbitant fees to directors, and padding the payroll of the firm with highly paid shareholders, relatives, or even "phantom employees" who existed only on paper.[38]

In addition to deflating net income, it was possible for businessmen to frustrate the goals of the industrial reform in many other ways. Industrial firms which would otherwise have had to establish CIs could be broken up into a series of closely related firms smaller than the minimum standard set down for establishing CIs. If a firm had a CI, the objective of promoting worker participation in management could be bypassed by holding unannounced informal meetings of the board of directors to decide all really important matters without inviting the CI representatives or by bribing or otherwise influencing *comunero* members of the board to act against the interest of the CI as a whole.

[37] See Velasco's message to the nation of July 28, 1971.

[38] All of these ploys and many others were quite well known to students of the CI and were amply ventilated in the Lima press, especially *Expreso*, which ran a series of case studies in June 1973 and has given heavy coverage to the issue. Most of them were mentioned by the minister of industry in a speech closing a seminar for businessmen dealing with CIs on October 28, 1972. See *El Comercio*, Oct. 29, 1972.

Many of these and innumerable other ploys could be foiled by alert and well-trained members of the CI sufficiently loyal to their fellow workers. But this combination of qualities was not always easy to find among the members of many CIs. The workers' exposure to management via the board of directors has been more useful in the early stages of the reform for obtaining information of interest to the CI and the union in pressing union demands on the firm than for assuring any substantial participation in management. In May 1974, although the CI share exceeded 25 percent in some firms, the national average was around 8 or 9 percent, far from sufficient voting power to have a substantial influence on management.[39]

The objectives of economic growth and social peace are far from being achieved via the existing industrial reform, but it appears that distributive justice is virtually impossible to obtain—especially if the question of income distribution is viewed nationwide. The CIs embrace only some two hundred thousand workers in the most capital-intensive part of industry, roughly 4.3 percent of the economically active population. An additional one hundred thousand workers (another 2.1 percent) are members of labor communities in the increasingly state-dominated fishing, mining, and telecommunications sectors. Adolfo Figueroa argues that "the Industrial Law takes income from the highest quartile [of the income distribution] and transfers it within the same quartile."[40] Thus, even if some form of compensation mechanism were adopted within industry (as it has been in fishing, mining, and telecommunications) to help even out interfirm inequalities in worker income, at the national level the industrial reform would not transfer income to the lower three quartiles of the labor force. This observation does not ignore the sometimes substantial increases in income which the CI has obtained for individual workers; it merely places this achievement in a national context.

[39] Those figures were given by the minister of industry in a speech. See *Oiga*, May 24, 1974.

[40] Adolfo Figueroa, "El Impacto de las Reformas Actuales sobre la Distribución de Ingresos en el Perú," *Apuntes* 1:1 (1973), 67–82. See also César Peñaranda, "El Impacto de las Reformas Actuales sobre la Distribución de los Ingresos en el Perú: Aspectos Adicionales y Comentarios," and Richard Webb, Adolfo Figueroa, and Jurgen Schuldt, "Conversatorio sobre la Redistribución del Ingreso en el Perú," *Apuntes* 1:2 (1974), 73–80 and 81–92.

Peruvian experience with the CAP, the SAIS, and the reformed private-sector industrial firm has revealed some notable successes. The coastal CAPs, livestock-producing enterprises in the Sierra (both SAISs and CAPs), and existing industrial firms have generally maintained or increased production and investment while increasing the incomes of member workers, all during a period of structural change. The reforms have also provided workers with access to information regarding the functioning and administration of their enterprises. These accomplishments may have helped create a base of civilian political support for the military government.

But a number of less encouraging aspects have surfaced as experience with the new modes of economic organization has accumulated. Collectivization of Sierra crop production within CAPs or any other large-scale enterprise has been resisted by the peasantry, apparently at least in part for sound economic reasons. The medium-term impact of the CAP on investment is subject to question, since a tendency of members to raise remunerations may eat deeply into profits and hence investment. New private investment in manufacturing industry has fallen sharply. The extent of effective worker participation in management appears to be very low both in industry, where it is largely confined to the board of directors, and in the agricultural enterprises, where educational, social, and even ethnic differences between managers and technical personnel on the one hand and production workers on the other are even greater than in industry. These differences impede communication and weaken the production workers' ability to fully exploit the formal mechanisms of participation provided by the reforms. In any case, only about 13 percent of Peru's economically active population has benefited directly from these reforms, none of which has made a significant contribution to increasing employment.

There are reasons to believe that the economic problems may become more severe. In industry part of the problem is investor uncertainty regarding stability of the "rules of the game." A more basic issue is that the new types of firm are not enmeshed within any larger system, other than the state itself, which would facilitate what Richard Webb calls horizontal income redistribution via the extraction of surpluses which can be used to create new firms or to expand existing ones in ways likely to increase employment significantly.[41] Rather, assuming the reformed firms are economically successful, benefits tend to accrue to those already employed and therefore to accentuate existing inequalities in income distribution except at the very top of the income pyramid. The accumulation of vested interests as labor community ownership increases in industry and the agrarian debt is repaid by the CAPs may make it politically more difficult to change this situation in the future.

Yet the workers' experience with these new forms of economic organization has whetted the appetite of some for a higher degree of participation—if not control. Such aspirations can only have been heightened by repeated government declarations that the reformed private-sector firm, the CAP, and the SAIS are not the regime's preferred models, and that a predominant sector of self-managed social-property firms will be created, enjoying massive technical and financial aid from the state.[42]

POLICY MAKING ON ECONOMIC ORGANIZATION DURING THE VELASCO REGIME: SOCIAL PROPERTY

Military Predisposition toward Enterprise Reform

When a revolutionary group within the Peruvian army deposed the Belaúnde regime in October 1968, the military, through CAEM and the Higher War School, their intelligence operations, and other contacts with civilians, had been exposed to currents of thought regarding forms of economic organization departing from capitalist orthodoxy. During the 1960s at least some groups within the military came to the conclusion that rather than defend the established socioeconomic order they must take the lead in transforming it, if only to save their own institution from potential revolutionary upsurge of the masses.

---

[41] See Richard Webb, "Government Policy and the Distribution of Income in Peru, 1963–1973," Chapter 3 of this volume.

[42] See for example, Prime Minister Mercado Jarrín's speech to the closing session of the First National Congress of Industrial Communities published in *Expreso*, Mar. 3, 1972, and the speech by the then head of SINAMOS, General Leonidas Rodríguez Figueroa, published in *Anales de la XI Conferencia Anual de Ejecutivos CADE '72* (Lima: IPAE, n.d.), 79–106.

The sobering experience of putting down several guerrilla movements no doubt was an important factor in this conversion.

Influenced by these educational and military experiences and possibly by the philosophy of civil action instilled by North American military mentors, Peruvian military leaders, particularly in the army, came to believe that national security was not a purely military question but one intimately related to development. In their analysis of the national situation, they concluded that development would require a radical transformation of social, cultural, political, and economic relations, including the creation of mechanisms permitting all strata in Peruvian society to have "direct participation and growing power of decision in the process of structuring the new power of the State."[43]

Although the concept of participation may seem foreign to military thought, some officers may have been attracted by the argument that establishing a system of decentralized worker-controlled enterprises would not only give the working population a greater sense of identity with their firms, but also with the national government which took this step. That strategy had been used in Yugoslavia, in the Israeli *kibbutzim*, and in the Chinese commune system as one of the principal bases of national defense. The menace of a potentially hostile Brazil, possibly in alliance with one or more of Peru's other neighbors, may well have moved the defense-conscious military to consider these examples of socioeconomic organization used as a bulwark against large and powerful neighboring states.

According to an officially sanctioned account, prior to taking power Velasco and a small group of Peruvian army officers drafted a plan of government including specific actions to transform the country's economic, social, political, and cultural structures. Neither civilians nor officers of the other armed forces participated in these deliberations.[44] In his Independence Day speech almost six years later, Velasco finally made public what he claimed was the text of this plan. It called for creating labor communities in private and state firms, reserving basic industry for the state, and promoting social-property firms. No further

[43] Edgardo Mercado Jarrín, "La Seguridad Integral en el Proceso Revolucionario Peruano," *Participación* 1:1 (Dec. 1972), 10.

[44] See Augusto Zimmerman Zavala, *El Plan Inca—Objetivo: Revolución Peruana* (Lima: Empresa Editora del Diario Oficial "El Peruano," 1974), especially pp. 33-53, 75-77, and 105.

explanation of what was meant by social-property firms was contained in the plan.

The first public pronouncement by the new regime regarding economic organization was by Prime Minister General Ernesto Montagne in December 1968; in it he specified that a medium-term goal of the government was "to reform the firm, orienting it toward worker participation in profits and management, and to protect cooperative firms organized by their workers."[45] But within COAP a group of colonels was already working on enterprise reform, albeit sporadically given competing demands on their time. They began by studying initiatives like the draft law of *empresas comunitarias* prepared by the Christian Democrat Cubas Vinatea, the experience of other countries including Yugoslavia and Algeria, and an important group of industrial cooperatives centered on Mondragón in northern Spain. According to General Arturo Valdés Palacio, Sub-Head of COAP, social property was not mentioned in General Montagne's speech in order not to alarm the reaction, which was still very strong, and because COAP had not yet had time to develop a Peruvian definition of social property, a concept which has different meanings in different countries.[45a]

Civilian Influence and Initiatives

It appears that prior to taking power, and probably for several years thereafter, the military government did not have very precise ideas concerning either the nature of the social-property enterprises it planned to promote or the relationship of these firms to one another within a larger sectoral framework. Official spokesmen repeatedly declared the regime to be neither capitalist nor communist, but the only forms of economic organization introduced which departed significantly from private or state enterprise were the CAP and the SAIS. A number of creative civilians were, however, willing and able to help fill this organizational void.

Among them were the members of a loosely knit group known as the *libertarios* because of their belief in a form of socialism

[45] Ernesto Montagne, *Lineamientos de la Política Económico Social del Gobierno Revolucionario*, 2d ed. (Lima: Oficina Nacional de Información. 1969).

[45a] Authorized interview by the author, November 21, 1974.

emphasizing self-managed production units and placing a high value on individual freedom. Many of the *libertarios* had been activists in the cooperative movement, the left wing of Popular Action, and various offshoots of the Communist movement. Despite their inherent distrust of bureaucracy, a number worked in government agencies during the Velasco regime, and one of their leaders, Jaime Llosa, eventually became both a high official of SINAMOS and a member of the COAP commission charged with drafting the Social-Property Law. The other principal *libertario* theoretician was Gerardo Cárdenas.

Both Llosa and Cárdenas were associated with Lima's National Agrarian University, studied cooperativism in France in the early 1960s, and came to see in the cooperative movement a potential for developing a modern version of libertarian socialism inspired by the ideas of Proudhon, Bakunin, Kropotkin, and other thinkers in the anarchist tradition. Yet by 1968 they were convinced that cooperatives could not fulfill this function if they were isolated entities within a hostile, essentially capitalist, environment.

Another group which had an important influence on the social property legislation was composed of lay Catholic lawyers and sociologists, many of whom worked in an independent research institution known as the Center for Studies and Promotion of Development (DESCO) and/or in Lima's Catholic University. DESCO and the Catholic University have both published a number of influential works on the labor community and social property.[46] One DESCO associate, Luis Pásara, has written extensively on the labor community and social property in the Lima daily

[46] Mimeographed DESCO publications include "La Comunidad Laboral" (2d enlarged ed., Feb. 1973); Henry Pease et al., "Propiedad Social: Análisis del Anteproyecto de Ley" (Dec. 1973); Luís Jiménez, "Propiedad Social: El Debate" (Jan. 1974), and Rubio, "Evolución de la Legislación." Three important works on social property by socially inclined lawyers have been published in the Catholic University law school review: Luis Pásara, "Propiedad Social: La Utopía y el Proyecto"; Jorge Santistevan, "El Régimen Laboral en el Anteproyecto de Decreto Ley de la Propiedad Social"; and Fernando de Trazegnies G., "¿Existe la Propiedad Social?" all in *Derecho* no. 31 (1973), 211–267. For economic analyses see Roberto Abusada, "Propiedad Social: Algunas Consideraciones Económicas" and César Peñaranda, "Anteproyecto de Decreto Ley de Propiedad Social: Comentarios y Planteamientos Alternativos," Centro de Investigaciones Sociales, Económicas, Políticas y Antropológicas, Serie de Documentos de Trabajo nos. 12 (Oct. 1973) and 14 (Jan. 1974), mimeo.

Expreso as well as in academic publications. Another, Rafael Roncagliolo, was a leader of a left-wing group which split from the Christian Democratic party in 1971. All were familiar with the concept of the *empresa comunitaria* but unlike the Christian Democrats felt that property should not be directly owned by the group of workers in any given firm. The ideological position of most had much in common with that of the *libertarios*. Many of these lay Catholic intellectuals had regular contacts with government policy makers, including members of the commission which drafted the Social-Property Law.

Finally, mention should be made of two foreign experts in workers' self-management, both economists, who came to Peru as consultants invited by various government agencies working on the social-property issue. Jaroslav Vanek made three trips to Peru between August 1970 and December 1971, and Branko Horvat, a Yugoslavian, came once in January and February of 1972. Both men have written extensively on the theory and practice of self-management.[47]

Work on what must be considered the first draft of the Social-Property Law began in August 1969 when a small group of *libertarios*, on their own initiative, began preparing a law to establish a "National Cooperative Sector" (SNC) including institutions to support and promote the kinds of cooperatives they sought to create. Later joined by dissident leftist Christian Democrats (many of whom left this party in 1971) and other lay Catholic intellectuals, the *libertarios* had as their initial focus of activities the National Center for Cooperative Training, then directed by Gerardo Cárdenas. This Center was a dependency of the National Cooperative Development Office (ONDECOOP), absorbed by SINAMOS in 1971. The fact that article 6 of the General Industries Law specified that, in addition to a private and public sector, there would be a "cooperative sector" composed of "industrial social-property firms which are governed by special

[47] Vanek's principal books are cited in note 4. Among Horvat's many works are *Towards a Theory of Planned Economy* (Belgrade: Institute of Economic Research, 1964), *An Essay on Yugoslav Society* (White Plains, N.Y.: International Arts and Sciences Press, 1969), and "Yugoslav Economic Policy in the Post-War Period: Problems, Ideas, Institutional Developments," *American Economic Review* 61:3. part 2 supplement "Surveys of National Economic Policy Issues and Policy Research" (June 1971) 69–196.

legislation" suggests that the government was aware of the SNC proposal by July 1970 and viewed it favorably. Indeed, COAP was aware of the work being done by the *libertarios* and lay Catholic intellectuals, and followed it with interest without establishing direct contacts.

In August 1970, Vanek visited Peru for the first time, invited by General Luis Barandiarán, then head of the National Integration Office (ONIT). He conducted a seminar at the National Planning Institute (INP) met with those preparing the draft law of the SNC, and also spoke in COAP. His views were given a public airing in an interview published by the Lima fortnightly *Caretas* shortly following his departure.[48]

The draft law of the SNC was completed in September 1970.[49] The SNC was to constitute a sector differentiated from the private and public sectors by its forms of property, management, participation, and accumulation. The basic principles of the SNC specified in this draft law are essentially the same as those spelled out in articles 2–5 of the Social-Property Law finally promulgated in May 1974. Many other aspects, including the organization of SNC firms and sectoral institutions, bear a striking resemblance to features of the Social-Property Law.

After the completion of the draft SNC law, which was never published, the social-property issue seems to have been dormant for some time. This may be because the government's energies were fully occupied with the implementation of the labor communities, the CAPs, and the SAISs, as well as the creation of SINAMOS (in gestation at this time). However, in his July 28, 1971, speech, President Velasco brought social property prominently into the public view for the first time, indicating that the government would give priority support to the formation and development of self-managed social-property firms. On October 28, 1971, in his address to the second ministerial meeting of the Group of 77, he went further and indicated that the economic base of the regime's social democracy of full participation was to

---

[48] "Con Vanek, Teólogo de la Autogestión," *Caretas* no. 421 (Aug. 31–Sept. 11, 1970).

[49] Most of the details referred to below are contained in Gerardo Cárdenas, "Hacia el Sector de la Cooperación" (Lima, Comité de Educación, Cooperativa de Crédito Santa Elisa Ltda. no. 39, 1972, mimeo). This article was written in November 1970, two months after the draft law of the SNC was completed. It does not contain explicit references to the draft law, however.

be fundamentally self-managed, with the means of production being "predominantly social property."

These two speeches heralded much activity within the government. Vanek made two visits in the latter half of 1971, during which he worked closely with a committee including members of SINAMOS, the INP, and the Center for Training and Research on Agrarian Reform (CENCIRA). With the assistance of the Peruvian economist César Peñaranda, he prepared an extensive report providing detailed advice on the creation and development of a self-managed sector within the Peruvian economy.[50] In early 1972 Horvat was invited to the INP and met with the INP-SINAMOS-CENCIRA joint committee. He was asked to give his comments on the report and did so orally and in several memoranda.[51] Although Peruvian policy makers listened to Vanek and Horvat, many of their suggestions were not adopted.

By the middle of 1972 it was increasingly clear to the government that neither the CAPs nor the industrial reform were achieving all their objectives, particularly those of stimulating investment, creating new jobs, correcting the highly unequal distribution of income and, in the case of the reformed private-sector firm, eliminating the traditional antagonism between labor and capital. In July 1972 President Velasco called a series of meetings with a group including the Ministers of Industry and Finance and the heads of the INP, ONIT, SINAMOS, and COAP to discuss the social-property issue. A number of civilian and military advisors also took part in these meetings, accompanying their military superiors. In his message to the nation of July 28, 1972, President Velasco emphasized the intention of the government to accelerate the creation of a predominant social-property sector within a pluralistic economy.

The Legislative Process

The legislative process in the Velasco regime has been both simpler and harder to follow than in most parliamentary govern-

---

50 Jaroslav Vanek with César Peñaranda, "Creación de una Economía Autogestionaria en el Perú" (Lima: Departamento de Producción y Difusión, ONDECOOP-CENACOOP-SINAMOS, Dec. 1971).

51 Part of what is alleged to be one of Horvat's memoranda to the INP was published in La Prensa over two years later. See Pedro Bellrán Ballen, "Recomendaciones Yugoslavas para el Futura del Perú" La Prenza, Apr. 29, 1973.

ments: simpler because, in the last analysis, crucial decisions have been made at the apex of the pyramid by President Velasco himself with the counsel of his most-trusted advisers, harder to follow because the channels through which these decisions have been influenced are less visible than in a parliamentary democracy, and the power of contending participants in the bureaucracies and the military has been difficult to gauge for the participants themselves as well as for the outsiders.

Precisely because of the government's authoritarian nature and its need for original solutions to difficult problems requiring the application of skills not previously developed within the military, relatively small groups without any significant mass power base, such as the *libertarios* and the lay Catholic intellectuals, have been able to exert a major influence on such critical decisions as have been involved in the social-property legislation. It is obvious, however, that the final decisions and responsibility have rested with the military, especially Velasco and his closest associates in the army.

As mentioned above, in July 1972 a ministerial-level commission was formed and thereafter met on various occasions with President Velasco to discuss the basic concepts of social property. As a result of these meetings a working group was formed in COAP, and various civilian advisors representing ministries and other key government agencies participated in its deliberations. During the remainder of 1972 the working group met many times, and various draft laws were prepared and studied. Nevertheless, the result of the group's efforts did not satisfy President Velasco, who insisted that "the Revolution wants a social-property firm not copied from anywhere, but authentically Peruvian like the labor community."[51a]

In March 1973, when he had not yet officially reassumed his presidential functions following two operations in February that cost him a leg and almost his life, Velasco chose General Arturo Valdés of COAP, a lawyer who at one point had been attracted by the Christian Democratic concept of the *empresa comunitaria*, and who had participated in the COAP working group, to head another commission charged with drafting the Social-Property

[51a] *El Comercio*, Jan. 23, 1973. It is important to emphasize that President Velasco personally directed the initial stages of the social-property law's gestation and closely followed the entire legislation process.

Law. Valdés in turn chose three civilians—Jaime Llosa of SINAMOS, Luis Giulfo of the INP, and Angel de las Casas of the Ministry of Industry—to assist him. All three had participated in both the ministerial commission and the earlier COAP working group.

In the period between August 1972 and the end of August 1973 many other persons were involved in the technical work on the social-property legislation—as many as twenty-five at one point, some of them not regularly employed in government agencies. In addition to COAP, SINAMOS, the INP, and the Ministry of Industry, the principal government institutions represented in this work were the Ministry of Finance, the Development Finance Corporation (COFIDE), and the National Supervisory Commission for Securities and Enterprises. Among the civilian groups represented (on a personal basis, not as delegates of these groups) were the Christian Democrats and the former Social Progressive Movement as well as the *libertarios*.

In the new Peruvian political system, bureaucratic politics also clearly plays a role, especially at the stage during which key draft legislation leaves COAP and circulates to government agencies for comment, and even more so during implementation. In the case of social property, for example, the draft law of the SNC proposed the creation of what amounted to a state within a state, with its own financial and planning systems. This certainly must have been considered a threat by almost all bureaucratic participants in the drafting process with the possible exception of SINAMOS. The Social-Property Law, on the other hand, strengthened COFIDE, created no new financial institutions, clearly established the responsibility of the INP for developing national plans (within the limits of which the institutions of the social-property sector would carry out their own planning with the help of representatives of the INP), and maintained firm state control at the top of the system. It did provide, however, for the new sector's integration into traditional capital markets. It was made extremely difficult to convert private firms or cooperatives into social-property firms. The stiff provisions governing conversions may well have been designed to satisfy the Ministry of Industry's private-sector clients and allay the fears of the Ministry of Finance regarding possible disruption of the economy (and tax revenues) by massive attempts at conversion.

Rather than create wholly new support institutions for the social-property sector, the government seems to have felt that it would be wiser to reorient the existing state apparatus toward social property and its needs. Though the risk that traditional clients of existing bureaucracies might successfully resist this reorientation may have been recognized, it was apparently judged that the risk of creating wholly new institutions, which would also be subject to attack, would be even greater.

Public Debate

All these phenomena suggest a process of compromise and trade-off among a limited group of bureaucratic participants in a legislative process initiated by decisions taken in the highest spheres of the military government and fueled by the creativity of an elite of civilian experts. But it is important to realize that the drafting process was accompanied by much open debate, particularly in the Lima press, academia, the church, and the labor movement. This helped to clarify the issues and probably to legitimize the concept of social property, though the degree to which it influenced the basic outlines of the resulting legislation is questionable.

Civilians knowledgeable about the subject took the lead in this debate. All of the issues described in the second section of this chapter were publicly vented more than a year before the regime revealed one of the many drafts of the Social-Property Law at the end of August 1973. Most of the writers seemed to be privy to at least the principal questions being debated by the drafting commission, and indeed it is likely that there were deliberate leaks of information as one of the strategies employed by contenders within the government. For example, at one point portions of a draft law and its *reglamento* (later substantially modified) were published in *Caretas*.[52] Perception of the new law's paramount importance by groups outside the government resulted in repeated requests for publication of a draft and were probably an important factor in the decision to request comments from the public.[53]

On several occasions, notably in September 1972 and again in

[52] "Un Borrador," *Caretas* no. 479 (June 21–July 5, 1973).

[53] For example, see Partido Demócrata Cristiano, "Declaración Política," *Expreso*, July 22, 1973.

the months following Velasco's illness in mid-1973, the intensity of the press debate was particularly great, because many interested parties expected the government to promulgate the Social-Property Law first on October 3 (the fourth anniversary of the regime's seizure of power) and then on July 28 (national independence day). That the law was not then decreed no doubt showed there was not a sufficient degree of consensus within the government over this controversial and extremely complicated piece of legislation.

The final phase of the social-property debate began with the publication of the draft law at the end of August 1973. In the following months the newspapers and magazines of Lima were filled with the expositions made by members of the drafting commission, editorials, and the official comments of political and interest groups.[54] Numerous meetings were held to elaborate comments or educate various constituencies.

The most fundamental disagreements with the draft law during the official public debate centered on the issue of economic pluralism. Groups representing the center left—such as the PDC, the radical priests' movement (ONIS), and the Communist party —as well as those on the right—including the Society of Industries, the Lima bar association (*Colegio de Abogados*), the Arequipa Chamber of Commerce and Industry, and APRA—claimed that the new social-property sector could not long coexist with the private sectors. The right argued that it would be necessary to place strict limits on social property in order to protect private enterprise. On the contrary, the center left urged the conversion of many private and, in the case of the PDC, state enterprises into social-property firms in order to avoid confining the new sector to a marginal role in the economy. The extreme left did not participate significantly in the public debate.

In order to limit the degree of income inequality within the sector, the lay Catholic intellectuals of DESCO proposed setting a single salary scale for the new sector and fixing interest charges on capital conceded to social-property firms so as to absorb differences in profitability due to location or capital intensity. On the other hand, the PDC and even more so APRA, by insisting

[54] See Jiménez, "Propiedad Social: El Debate," for a summary and analysis of these pronouncements, including dates and places of original publication. Unless specifically noted all the comments referred to in the text are summarized in this publication.

that property rights should lie within the firm rather than the sector as a whole, implicitly favored a greater reliance on market forces and a correspondingly greater inequality in income distribution.

DESCO and ONIS both called for measures to insure that production in the new sector would be in accord with basic social necessities rather than a function of a market distorted by a highly unequal distribution of income and consumption aspirations "irrationally" induced by advertising often originating in wealthy capitalist nations.[55] The Episcopal Social Action Commission, headed by Bishop Luis Bambarén, issued two statements,[56] both of which were generally supportive of the government's initiative. They probably helped legitimize the concept of social property in the eyes of those Peruvians, including many in the military and their wives, who take the teachings of the church seriously.

Almost all commentators argued in favor of increasing direct worker participation in management, including questions of labor discipline, at the expense of sacrificing some of the prerogatives attributed to (worker-elected) management or to government agencies in the draft law. Particularly strongly attacked were provisions calling for selection by lot rather than election to some internal positions in the firm.

The PDC, ONIS, and APRA, among others, complained that the state's supervisory role as proposed in the draft law could result in excessive bureaucratization and centralization of decision making in the new sector. The Communist party and its labor unions, however, suggested even stronger planning and programming functions for the state, maintaining that the highest form of social property is state property. Nevertheless, the Communist party, while criticizing some aspects of the draft law, has given strong public support to the new sector.[57]

[55] DESCO's comments are contained in Henry Pease et al., "Propiedad Social: Análisis del Anteproyecto de Ley."

[56] This first statement is dated September 18, 1973, and was published in *El Comercio* on September 22, 1973. The second was published in *La Nueva Crónica*, October 10, 1973.

[57] The Communist party's attitude toward the industrial community is clearly delineated in Jorge del Prado, "Is There a Revolution in Peru?" *World Marxist Review*, Jan. 1971, p. 23. The party's comments on the draft Social-Property Law may be found in *Unidad*, Oct. 25, 1973. A summary is contained

The Social-Property Law of May 1974

The law finally promulgated as a result of the debate and drafting process did not drastically alter the general outlines of the system proposed in the draft of August 1973, but there were a number of important changes.[58] Most of these appeared to respond to the more constructive criticisms published in the Lima press. Thus in a limited sense the public may be said to have participated in policy making. The significance of the changes is heightened because almost without exception they either increased the degree of internal democracy and worker control in the institutions of the new sector, increased the chances that distribution of income will be more equal within the sector and nationally, and/or potentially facilitated more rapid growth of the social-property sector. But the law also contained provisions, not explicitly included in the draft law of August 1973, for the finance of housing, health, education, and recreational services for workers of the social-property sector. These provisions were reportedly included at the personal insistence of President Velasco, who has strongly supported the social-property concept.[59]

According to the law, a social-property firm (EPS) is to be composed exclusively of workers (which eliminates capitalists or their representatives within the firm), and characterized by "full participation, social ownership of the firm, social accumulation, and permanent training." Full participation consists of the right of all the workers to participate in the direction, management, and economic benefits of the firm. Ownership of the firm is social in that it resides in all the workers of the social-property sector rather than in individual firms or workers. Accumulation is social because part of the income generated by firms of the social-property sector is to be used to expand the sector, thus creating new jobs and benefiting society as a whole. Social ownership and ac-

in Jiménez, "Propiedad Social: El Debate," 21–22. Following the promulgation of the law, it was praised in an official party declaration published in *Expreso*, May 7, 1974.

[58] The establishing legislation is Decreto Ley 20598 of April 30, 1974. Quotations in the remainder of this section are from the text of the law unless otherwise indicated. The description provided is by no means exhaustive and is in some places simplified.

[59] See the declarations of General Valdez in an article entitled "Pueblo Dio Ley de Propiedad Social: Presentó más de 2 mil Sugerencias," *La Nueva Crónica*, May 4, 1974.

cumulation represent major advances as compared with the CAP, the SAIS, and the reformed private-sector firm. Permanent training is to help achieve worker participation at all levels of decision making within the social-property sector as well as to increase technical skills. It will be promoted by allowing deduction of training expenditures as a cost of production.

A social-property firm may engage in any form of economic activity not reserved exclusively for the state (strategic and basic industries as defined by the General Industries Law and other legislation) and may be formed in one of three ways: creation of an entirely new firm, conversion of an existing firm, or merger of two or more social-property firms.

In the case of a wholly new firm, the law specifies a process which may be initiated by private individuals, groups, special firms formed to develop projects, or institutions of the public sector. All projects must fall within the framework of national development plans and be submitted to the National Social-Property Commission (CNPS), composed of twelve representatives of different state agencies and three workers of the sector elected by the Assembly of the Social-Property Sector (ASPS). If preliminary approval of the CNPS is obtained, the project must then be sent to the state development bank (COFIDE) and/or the National Social-Property Fund, which are responsible for feasibility studies and initial financing.

The CNPS must approve the statutes of each enterprise so constituted, including its scale of wages and salaries. This provision, which is an important limitation on self-management, was probably inspired by the experience with the CAPs, where surpluses have tended to be absorbed by higher direct remunerations voted by the workers, thereby diminishing tax revenues and reinvestment. Fixing of remunerations by the CNPS will, however, be subject to certain constraints imposed by the labor market, given the continued existence of the two private sectors.

The conditions for conversion of non-social-property firms are strict, apparently in order to maintain economic pluralism by impeding the massive transfer of reformed private-sector firms. The basic requirements are the approval of the CNPS; the agreement of two-thirds of the owners, shares, or members; and verification that the firm is in good economic and financial condition. Provision is made for the constitution of special variants of the social-property firm under certain conditions, apparently opening the way for the eventual conversion of various types of co-operatives and SAISs.

All workers of a social-property firm, both permanent and temporary, will be members of the firm. Temporary workers have the same rights and obligations as permanent workers except that they cannot be elected to leadership positions. These membership provisions represent an important advance for temporary workers compared with the provisions of the CAP and the reformed private-sector firm.

Within a social-property firm the basic source of authority is a general assembly composed of all the firm's workers. The general assembly elects a directing committee to oversee day-to-day operations. This committee in turn selects the general manager, who must be approved, and may be fired, by the general assembly. A number of other committees elected within the firm have specialized functions, including planning, elaborating and conducting training programs, and handling disciplinary matters. In the draft law many of these committees were to be selected by lot, but this provision was retained only in the committee that supervises elections. At the express consent of more than 50 percent of the workers of a social-property firm a union may be formed, but its leaders are required to be the same as those of the social-property firm, presumably the directing committee. This provision appears to confuse the functions of a union with those of a firm and may constitute additional evidence of the regime's hostility to unions, which it seems to consider unnecessary. In any case, an EPS provides many internal channels for the resolution of issues normally handled via unions in capitalist firms (whether state or private), and the principal function of the union in an EPS may be to represent the firm in its dealings with the CNPS and other institutions of the SPS, the state, or the private sector.

The social-property sector will also have a number of institutions at the regional and national levels. The relationship of these institutions to one another and to government agencies so far as membership is concerned is indicated in Figure 9.1. The regional units will carry out a number of planning and coordinating functions, make sure that their member firms do business on a preferential basis with other firms of the sector, and otherwise promote the growth and interests of the social-property sector within their respective regions. The ASPS performs similar functions

FIGURE 9.1

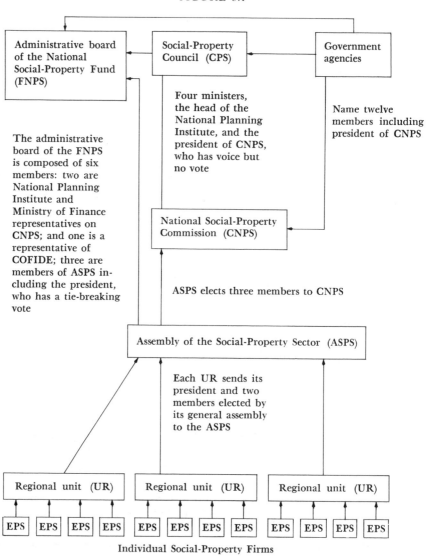

Individual Social-Property Firms

The general assembly of each EPS elects three delegates to the
corresponding regional unit

at the national level. Unlike private-sector firms, the social-property firms are required by law to share economic, financial, and technological information.

The law makes no specific provisions for regional financing of social-property firms, concentrating these powers in the National Social-Property Fund (FNPS) and COFIDE. The workers of the sector have an effective majority on the administrative board of the FNPS, which may share certain wage- and salary-fixing functions with the CNPS if a member firm is not able to meet its financial commitments.

Above the CNPS, the FNPS, and the ASPS, all of which include workers of the sector, is the Council of Social Property, composed of the head of the INP and ministers of finance, labor, commerce, and industry. This council is clearly designed as a high-level control over the social-property sector to assure that the new sector evolves in line with overall government economic policy, but it may also represent the interests of the social-property sector within the Council of Ministers.

The Social-Property Law clearly establishes the principle of net income sharing. A worker's income will be divided into three parts: direct remuneration, a share of the distributable surplus (*renta de trabajo*), and access to common services (including housing, education, health, and recreation). Although direct remunerations are effectively subject to control by the CNPS and the FNPS, the size of distributable surplus is influenced by the economic performance of the firm, providing a collective incentive to greater work effort. The *renta de trabajo* is distributed in equal parts to all workers of the firm according to the number of days worked during the previous year.

The financial provisions of the law are complex and innovative. There are essentially three ways in which a social-property firm may obtain fixed capital: loans from COFIDE and/or the FNPS (*aportes transitorios*), reinvestment of funds generated by the social-property firm itself, and the issue of redeemable variable income securities (*accio-bonos*) which confer no rights to participate in management or control of the firm and must be held by financial intermediaries, not individual investors.

The *aporte transitorio* mechanism permits any individual or group capable of developing a viable project approved by the FNPS and/or COFIDE and by the appropriate public agency (the Ministry of Industry, in the case of industrial projects) to obtain the capital necessary to start a new enterprise, including the costs of feasibility studies. Among the objectives of this provision is giving all those capable of creative entrepreneurial activity, not just those with access to private capital, an opportunity to express their talents, thereby harnessing this potentially important national resource.

The agreement establishing the *aporte transitorio* will specify an amortization schedule for the loan and may also require the payment of an annual additional sum which can be considered a rental charge on the capital. These charges will be set "taking into account the economic and financial conditions and the environment in which the firm will develop, favoring decentralization." The payment of the capital charge would continue indefinitely even after the *aporte transitorio* had been amortized by the social-property firm. This feature is extremely important since, in principle, it will permit the socialization of income derived from favorable locations and monopoly power, which are unrelated to labor effort. This would favor more equitable income distribution than in the CAP, the SAIS, or the reformed private-sector firm both directly and through providing an additional source of finance for new firms or expansion of existing ones.

The requirement that a new firm amortize its original capital may place excessive strain on the firm, but the law does specify that the timetable of amortization payments will be established taking into account a projection of funds which will be available to the firm. The amortization payments will be deducted from the firm's income for income tax purposes.[60]

Once the amortization has been completed, the social-property firm must continue deducting annually from its income a sum equal to the average of the five years of highest amortization payments. This deduction may be reinvested in fixed assets of the social-property firm. A social-property firm may also assign a fraction of its economic surplus for reinvestment, even before the

[60] A complex series of accounting practices is established whereby each amortization payment by a social-property firm creates a collective debt of the firm's workers to their firm, part of which is canceled from a reserve fund constituted by 5 percent of annual economic surpluses when a worker leaves the firm. The net effect of this scheme is to increase the distributable income of the firm in its first years, as the amount of the amortization of the *aporte transitorio* is added back to the taxable surplus when calculating the distributable surplus.

aporte transitorio has been amortized. An additional *aporte transitorio* may also be obtained to finance expansion. Finally, each year a social-property firm must transfer to the FNPS 10 percent of the sum of its economic surplus (essentially gross profits) and that portion of wage and salary payments exceeding an average of twice the minimum wage times the number of workers in the firm. All of these financial provisions are designed to facilitate a rapid rate of capital accumulation within the social-property sector yet guard against potential overcapitalization within individual firms, thus favoring a more equitable distribution of income at the national level.

The issue of *accio-bonos* is designed to tap private capital markets to obtain additional investment funds for the social-property sector, and it is subject to a number of controls. First, both an absolute majority of the workers of the firm and the appropriate regional unit must approve the issue. The CNPS will then (1) establish a maximum percentage of *accio-bonos* which can be issued as a fraction of the capital of each social-property firm and (2) fix the maximum percentage of *accio-bonos* of any given social-property firm or type of economic activity which can be held in an investment portfolio of a financial intermediary. These provisions are clearly designed to prevent excessive issue of *accio-bonos*, which might dangerously reduce material incentives to greater worker effort by draining away an excessive proportion of distributable surpluses, and to prevent concentration of control over surpluses generated by any given firm or branch of economic activity. Financial intermediaries may purchase portfolios of *accio-bonos* and government securities against which "certificates of participation" will be sold to the public. What an individual saver will purchase, then, is something like the security issued by a mutual fund.

In summary, the social-property sector comes very close to being a self-managed market economy as characterized in the second section of this chapter but operating within a framework of national development planning in a pluralistic economy. The principal differences are (1) the degree to which superior organs of the sector can intervene in investment decisions and in the fixing of basic remunerations and (2) certain aspects of the financial mechanisms which depart from a system of pure capital rental. These modifications seem designed to increase the rate of growth of the social-property sector, reduce the degree of inequality in incomes, and insure that investments in the new sector correspond to national goals. But they require very sensitive and well-informed intervention by the CNPS, the administrative board of the FNPS, and COFIDE—essentially Lima-based bureaucracies. Very little effective power is conceded to the regional units, especially financial power.

The Political Economy of Implementing the Social-Property Sector (SPS)

What are the principal requirements for success in implementing the social-property sector, and what problems are likely to arise? I address these questions by referring again to the three policy problems mentioned in the second section of this chapter: economic pluralism, growth versus distribution, and degree of decentralization. Underlying the discussion is the theme of developing political support for creating a predominant social-property sector.

Economic Pluralism

Given the regime's commitment to maintaining economic pluralism, the social-property sector seems destined to be composed almost entirely of new firms. If conversion of existing firms is to be minimal, and the new sector is to become predominant within, say, fifteen years, a very high percentage of all new investment must be channeled toward the social-property sector. For from five to ten years the bulk of this investment will have to be diverted from other sectors, since accumulation within the social-property sector cannot become an important source of investment until the sector has achieved a significant weight in the economy. Thus the state will have to engage in heavy pump-priming in the initial years before investment in the social-property sector becomes self-generating.

The required funds could come from greatly increased tax rates, foreign grants and loans, or increased revenues derived from natural-resource-based exports controlled by the state. Another source of finance might be the sale of *accio-bonos* and certificates of participation. But given the problem of making the certificates attractive to the investing public, it is likely that the most acceptable form of generating investment resources would be directly through the tax system.

A social-property sector composed entirely of new firms will also require massive numbers of skilled technicians and managers capable of operating in a highly participatory environment. At present, such crucial human resources are scarce—and already employed in private, state, or cooperative enterprises. The problem, of course, is that the private, state, and cooperative sectors cannot afford to lose the investment funds and human talent they currently enjoy. This explains why the issue of economic pluralism generated the most heat during the social-property debate. The cries of protest from the private sectors and cooperatives will probably intensify as the government moves to implement the social-property sector. Opposition from within the public sector is likely to be largely passive.

The government has not yet published figures on output, value added, investment, or employment broken down by type of enterprise. Preliminary indications show that the state sector has expanded most rapidly during the Velasco regime and may already control as much as half the value of output in the Peruvian economy. Since the government appears committed to strengthening and further expanding the state enterprises—at least those in the capital-intensive basic industries such as petroleum, steel, cement, fertilizers, mining, metal refining, paper, telecommunications, electric power, and air transport—it is obvious that the private sectors and cooperatives are most likely to feel the pinch if the government moves toward rapid implementation of the social-property sector.

The implication is clear: if the private and cooperative sectors expand at even modest rates, and if there is no significant conversion of existing firms into social-property firms, the social-property sector will not be able to reach "predominance" within fifteen years.[61] Assuming that the private sectors do not stagnate, the choice is more dramatic: either there is fairly massive conversion of existing firms, or predominance of the new sector within the foreseeable future is a pipe dream.

Within the present Peruvian regime, strong military support is crucial if a policy is to be implemented. It is not clear that a

[61] Some calculations under a variety of assumptions may be found in Roberto Abusada, "Propiedad Social."

commitment to the new sector is shared by all sections of the military, and it will be remembered that the principal civilian proponents of social property do not represent organizations with any substantial popular base. During implementation—in which institutional and class interests will come into play more strongly —lack of enthusiasm for the new sector in the central bureaucracies and influential interest groups will make progress toward the goal of predominance dependent both on continued impulse from the top of the system and the generation of political support for the new sector at the grass-roots level. Velasco appeared to be attacking potential bureaucratic sluggishness in his July 28, 1974, message to the nation calling for "immediate" reorientation of those parts of the state apparatus responsible for the creation and strengthening of the new sector. It is too soon to say how effective this pressure from the top has been.

The social-property issue and, in general, the "deepening of the revolution" appear to have been important issues in the first major political crisis of the regime, precipitated by the illness of President Velasco (beginning in February 1973). A second crisis in May and June 1974, which forced the resignation of two conservative naval officers of ministerial rank (including a member of the ruling junta itself) appears to have been more related to the upcoming expropriation of the remaining opposition press and the issue of President Velasco's personal leadership. But on both occasions, the more radical forces within the government were able to mobilize popular support in the streets from among the Peruvian labor unions (except for those dominated by APRA), beneficiaries of the agrarian reform, the Confederation of Industrial Communities, and representatives of urban squatter settlements (*pueblos jóvenes*). Although it is difficult to judge to what extent mass demonstrations influence power calculations of contending factions within the military government, these crises have appeared to strengthen the resolve of Velasco and his inner circle to push on with additional structural reforms.

Yet the government has not created a political party, nor has it openly welcomed the support it has received from the Communist party and unions. APRA, which remains the party with the largest mass base, is opposed to social property in its present form. Very few entrepreneurs and managers have broken ranks with the Society of Industries and support the creation of the social-property sector as a real opportunity for true entrepreneurs.[62] A basic issue in the Peruvian process, then, is whether the aspirations of all those groups which have benefited from the regime's reforms, or hope to do so in the future, can join together to neutralize the traditional conservative groups and provide pressure from below to implement the social-property sector.

Paradoxically, the same reforms that were instrumental in moving the government toward social property now stand as potential obstacles to its full implementation via the conversion route. The sugar cooperatives have lobbied strongly against conversion and even effusively thanked President Velasco for indicating that the government was studying the recognition of a fifth sector (cooperatives), in which they might be included.[63] Conversion, of course, would diminish their control over income arising from rich natural endowments. Whereas the obvious base of support for conversion would be the labor movement, as of April 1975 the strongest unions were still controlled by the Communists and APRA, and in any case the provisions of the Social-Property Law regarding unions are not likely to be well received.

The workers of reformed private firms can bargain with their employers over wages and are relatively well off compared to the bulk of the Peruvian population. In addition they are acquiring individualizable wealth as their labor communities accumulate shares in their firms. These workers may not relish the thought that should conversion occur, wage negotiations would ultimately be with the government-dominated National Social-Property Commission. Furthermore, a reform of the labor-community laws may eliminate a number of abuses by which employers siphon off net income. If this and other possible modifications take place, it may be even harder to organize support for conversion among workers of the reformed private sector.

If economic pluralism is maintained and a start made in creating the social-property sector, "peaceful competition" between the different sectors is likely to prove an illusion. The rules of the

[62] See, for example, the interview with Jaime Newel in *Oiga*, Sept. 9, 1973, and Ismael Frías, "Un Documento 'Secreto' de CADE 71," *La Nueva Crónica*, Nov. 23, 1972, and Ruben Lisigursky, *La Revolución Peruana: Que Es y Donde Va* (Lima: Editorial Santa Isabel, 1973).

[63] See the large advertisement by central cooperative linking twelve sugar cooperatives, CECOAAP, in *La Prensa*, Aug. 15, 1974, and full page advertisements in *La Crónica* and *Expreso*, Oct. 2, 1974. For Velasco's statement, see *El Peruano*, Aug. 9, 1974.

game are simply not the same for capitalist, state, and social-property firms, and any competition between them is analogous to that between three teams on a football field, one playing soccer, another rugby, and the third North American football, each with its own ball: collisions are likely to occur, and confusion may be widespread. One or more of the teams may abandon the field, but it will be hard to say which has won. The form of taxation applied, differential access to investment funds, and many other discriminatory devices are built into the Social-Property Law in addition to the fundamentally different form of internal organization.

The presence of the social-property sector may spur the private sectors to greater efforts in order to justify their continued existence. But it seems more likely that the effect will be to further depress private investment as uncertainty regarding the future of the reformed private sector is heightened despite repeated declarations by government spokesmen that economic pluralism will be maintained. Although the Social Property Law provides for agencies of the central government and state enterprises to provide priority support for the implementation of the new sector, no sanctions are specified if this does not occur in practice. All of these factors will affect the rate of expansion of the different forms of firm and may confine social property to a minor role.

Growth versus Distribution

Reconciling the objectives of increased production and capital formation with those of greater equality in income distribution and employment opportunities was one of the most difficult problems facing Peruvian policy makers. The Social-Property Law attempts such a reconciliation, at the cost of sacrificing some ground in the realm of participation. The monitoring powers of CNPS, FNPS, COFIDE, and ultimately the Council of Social Property are strong, especially regarding wage setting and what amounts to taxes on income unrelated to labor effort. Whether this sacrifice of autonomy at the firm level is justified by the achievement of greater equality in income distribution and faster self-sustained growth of the social-property sector remains to be seen.

It is likely to prove technically difficult to distinguish nonlabor income from that due to superior effort or entrepreneurial activity. So long as material incentives are relied upon to stimulate hard work, care must be taken not to regulate or tax away excessive amounts of these kinds of labor income. On the other hand, the reliance on market forces and material incentives to guide the new sector may make it difficult to achieve the aim of solidarity. In certain conditions worker solidarity within the firms may degenerate into group egoism as has been the case in the CAPs.

Financing by *accio-bonos* may pose a threat to more equitable income distribution. The *accio-bonos* scheme was designed to permit faster growth of the social-property sector by tapping private capital markets. But if *accio-bonos* are widely resorted to as a source of finance, income inequalities based upon capital ownership will be perpetuated by permitting a rentier class to receive tax-free income at the expense of workers in the social-property sector.

Degree of Decentralization

The Western liberal and the anarcho-syndicalist traditions have been hostile toward centralized bureaucratic power—seen as profoundly dangerous for human freedom—and Marxist-Leninist thought is strongly opposed to decentralization, which may permit enemies of the revolutionary party to capture power within decentralized units while permitting excessive influence of market forces on product mix and income distribution decisions. Elements of this ideological struggle are present in the Peruvian process. In a decentralized system, capitalism is likely to swamp socialistlike initiatives or at best reduce them to offshoots of capitalism which serve as barriers to propagating socialist values. A highly decentralized system of self-managed firms operating in a pluralistic economy is likely to mean that the distribution of income, and thus "voting power" in the market for goods and services, will be very inequitably distributed in Peru for some years to come.

This fact may justify the decision to maintain considerable elements of central planning and control as well as strong economic support by the state, at least in the early stages of implementation. But when a market is permitted to develop, the existing distribution of income becomes a factor influencing how much and what is produced and who consumes how much of what. Direct government measures beyond the creation of social-property firms are likely to be necessary if production and consumption are to be in accord with social necessities and a market economy retained.

The problem here, of course, is avoiding the creation of an all-powerful centralized bureaucracy that might develop its own class interests and in turn stand as a barrier to a greater degree of autonomy or a more just distribution of income in the future. Peruvian policy makers may eventually decide to decentralize some of the financial decisions within the social-property sector by creating regional social-property funds receiving a percentage of the resources flowing to the FNPS. Investments approved at the regional level could be required to be consistent with national and regional development plans. Such a scheme might have the political advantage of securing greater popular support at the grass roots, since most provincial Peruvians distrust Lima bureaucracies. At the same time it would guard against the more purely economic pitfalls of bureaucratic myopia at the center.

SUMMARY AND CONCLUSIONS

The concept of workers' self-management has deep roots in the cooperativist, anarcho-syndicalist, and social Christian traditions, which originated in Europe. The first modern political movement to make the promotion of cooperatives an integral part of its scheme for organizing the Peruvian economy was APRA. In the early 1960s the PDC and MSP each proposed a form of self-managed enterprise which might be arrived at via intermediate stages of comanagement and co-ownership. But the most complete Peruvian formulation of a system of self-managed firms prior to the present military regime was the PDC draft law of *empresas comunitarias* of February 1968.

Not until the military took power under Velasco, however, was a Peruvian government prepared to accept and implement the concept of workers' self-management on a national scale. The new social-property sector approximates the Vanekian ideal of a self-managed market economy, albeit within a larger and pluralistic national economic system and subject to significant restraints on the freedom of a firm's workers to make decisions regarding investments, wages, and salaries. For the Velasco regime, the social-property sector is one of a series of structural reforms designed to create a participatory social democracy in which future Peruvian generations can achieve justice and liberty.

The CAP, the SAIS, and the industrial firm as reformed via the labor community may be interpreted as early moves by the military government in the direction of workers' self-management. Almost five years before the Social-Property Law was decreed, however, civilian intellectuals and technicians were already designing an integrated sector of cooperatives and self-managed firms which was eventually to become the social-property sector. These civilians, many of whom worked in government agencies, lacked an independent mass power base. In COAP military legislators studied this and other civilian initiatives as well as the experience of other countries with systems of worker-managed firms. In mid-1972, as it became increasingly clear that the Velasco regime's earlier reforms were incapable of achieving the multiple goals set for them, civilian creativity was harnessed by Peru's military rulers, who decided to draft a law to implement a Peruvian definition of social property on which they had been working sporadically since October 1968.

Almost two years later, following an important public debate, the completed law was decreed. The opinions of political parties, labor unions, other organized groups, and private individuals (including foreign experts), as well as those of civilian government officials, were carefully studied by COAP and some of these contributions appear to have influenced the text of the Social-Property Law. Nevertheless, the final decisions were taken by the all-military Council of Ministers advised by COAP and reportedly prodded by President Velasco himself.

The social-property sector is supposed to give concrete expression in the economic sphere to the regime's "neither capitalist nor communist" self-definition. Government spokesmen have repeatedly declared that the social-property sector is to play a central role in creating a new moral order emphasizing solidarity rather than individualism. But this must be accomplished within a pluralistic market economy with two private sectors, which may be expected to continue promoting capitalistic values, and a dynamic state sector. All three of these sectors plus the SAISs and cooperatives of various sorts will compete with the nascent social-property sector for scarce financial and human resources. And the market within which the social-property sector must operate is strongly influenced by both a highly unequal distribution of income and consumption values originating in rich industrialized countries. Furthermore, the social-property sector is also supposed to take the lead in solving Peru's severe employment problem, train manpower outside the formal educational system, upgrade worker housing, and provide common health, education, and recreational services to workers and their families.

It may legitimately be asked whether these multiple goals are not overly ambitious, given the severe constraints imposed on the social-property sector, particularly regarding conversion to the new sector of existing firms, and the virtual absence of a strong political base for the new sector. Indeed, many of these goals in principle could be achieved more efficiently using the national taxation and expenditure system rather than relying upon resources to be generated within an untried sector which will have to compete in the marketplace with existing firms not expected to achieve so much. But the notorious centralization of the state bureaucracy may argue in favor of using the social-property enterprises as decentralized sources of managerial skill, thus by passing existing bureaucratic bottlenecks and allowing many decisions to be made at the base of the system.

The strongest potential support for the social-property sector would be the Peruvian labor movement and the members of production cooperatives, assuming the conversion of existing firms to the social-property sector appeared to them as an attractive alternative to their present status. However, these groups did not have an important role in designing the social-property sector. Their purely economic interests may not be favored in the short run by some provisions of the Social-Property Law intended to increase social accumulation and income equality at the cost of sacrificing autonomy at the firm and even the regional level. Meanwhile they are acquiring vested interests through earlier reforms, and for the most part they are already among the upper quartile of the Peruvian income distribution. Thus it appears that the regime, in seeking to socialize accumulation by virtually legislating major economic decisions of each social-property firm at the level of the CNPS, FNPS, and COFIDE, has allowed theoretical considerations to prevail over practical politics in the design of the new sector, at least if the regime maintains its commitment to economic pluralism.

But official declarations and the Social-Property Law itself have indicated that the social-property sector will receive strong financial and technical support from government agencies and operate in alliance with state enterprises in basic industry which will often be suppliers or customers of social-property firms, sometimes on preferential terms. No doubt such state assistance could give an important economic boost to the social-property sector, but again it must be asked where the pressure to do so will come from. Already there are signs that the response of government agencies and state enterprises to presidential demands for action have been less than enthusiastic. And if recent trends continue, it appears that the state sector rather than the social-property sector may become predominant within the Peruvian economy.

It therefore appears that the promoters of the social-property sector face many obstacles as they enter the implementation phase. It is still too early to predict the outcome of this ambitious attempt to move toward workers' self-management within a pluralistic economy. If the prospects appear somber on the basis of the analysis presented here, the reader must remember that the creation of the social-property sector is not taking place in a vacuum, but rather as part of a much broader series of structural transformations unleashing new forces which may have unforeseen consequences. And Peru's military leaders have shown themselves to be both pragmatic and creative in responding to changing circumstances while gradually "deepening the revolution."

Belaúnde and Velasco:
On the Limits of Ideological Politics

Jane S. Jaquette

The study of politics in Latin America has recently experienced a resurgence of interest in the question of ideology as part of what Kalman Silvert has described as the rejection of the positivist, neoutilitarian view dominant for twenty years. A return to institutionalism is now seen, not to the sterile institutionalism of the past with its dry totting up of legal documents and its inability to deal with extraconstitutional political arrangements, but to a broader definition of institutions as, in Silvert's words, "historically developed clusters of routinized behavior patterns with their appropriate sets of sanctions."[1] This definition invites examination of such phenomena as dependency, clientele networks, coercion, and ideology itself.

Although this new direction in research serves to reemphasize the centrality of ideology in Latin American politics in contrast to the North American experience (where ideological content, although it is possibly just as central, goes unrecognized as such), there remains the problem of choosing a suitable methodology to deal with the subject. In the context of this debate, it should be noted that the purpose of this chapter is quite limited indeed. The purpose of comparing ideology and practice under Belaúnde and Velasco is to discuss parallels—not to discover the sources of Velasco's "revolution" in the *Manual Ideológico* of Belaúnde's Acción Popular (AP), but rather to plot the intent and path of Peruvian ideological developments through the identification of key similarities between Belaúnde's ideology and that of the Velasco regime. These similarities rest on shared middle-class and technocratic values, including a deep fear of violent revolution.

However, the task of prediction based on an assessment of the

[1] Kalman Silvert, "Politics and the Study of Latin America," paper delivered at the 1973 APSA convention, New Orleans, Sept. 4–8, 1973.

underlying values represented by the regime is further complicated by the issue of legitimacy. In baldest terms, as elections are not now held in Peru, the dominant political currency in the political system today is military force. Despite evidence of deportations and press control, however, the "Revolutionary Government" is attempting to construct a broad basis of support through the credibility of its ideology and by its promises to restructure society and redistribute power. Due in part to the lag between policy invention and policy implementation, in part to the revolutionary and anti-imperialist image Peru has created for itself internationally, and in part to competition among elites at the top, the process of legitimization has come to rest heavily on the continuing development of "advanced" ideological principles which can claim to be both revolutionary and uniquely derived from the Peruvian case, and on their conversion into legislation to create new institutions. It is this process which I have labeled "ideological politics."

Although modern ideologies, including that of the military regime in Peru, have not only metaphysical but material components, their impact is still difficult to measure. One result of the coup is that certain kinds of economic data which were formerly made public are now difficult to acquire and may be altered by the government to more closely approximate stated goals. Thus answers to simple comparative questions—such as What is the rate of growth of the GNP now as compared to that in the Belaúnde period?—are of doubtful reliability. On a more complex level, it is nearly impossible to measure whether a given ideological principle has been implemented by the creation of a new set of institutions. Can one say, for example, that the "pluralist" economic institutions created by the military have measurably increased levels of participation or national solidarity?

The answer is, of course, that one cannot say this. Yet, the regime and those who would analyze it do use certain measures to estimate the impact of new policies. The military argues that its approach is different from that of its predecessors, hence truly revolutionary. In this context, all comparisons between Velasco and Belaúnde can be interpreted as detracting from the legitimacy of the regime and as questioning its success. Similarly, any discovery of historical antecedents casts doubt upon the regime's claims to be original and unique. Thus there is a tension between the scholar's desire to describe and predict and the regime's view of its needs. And while the lag between ideology and implementation may increase legitimacy by reducing the pressure that can realistically be put on the military to produce concrete successes, it also works to the regime's disadvantage by creating expectations which can never be proven to have been fulfilled. Thus ideological politics has built-in limitations which should be kept in mind in the discussion which follows.

IDEOLOGY IN PERU: BACKGROUND

Throughout the twentieth century, the contrasts to be found in Peru—the wealth of the oligarchs and the poverty of the peasants, the power of the "white" ruling class and the submission of the Indian, and, more recently, the wretchedness of the squatter settlements and the elegance of Lima's rich suburbs—have generated ideological demands for revolution and the drastic reordering of society. Víctor Raúl Haya de la Torre's Alianza Popular Revolucionaria Americana (APRA), the party and its program, are widely considered as the most advanced attempt to create an indigenous ideology of continent-wide revolution. José Carlos Mariátegui's analysis of the Peruvian "reality" is a much-acclaimed Marxist analysis of Latin American underdevelopment. Despite this strong ideological tradition and aside from the brief period of APRA's partial access to power between 1945 and 1948 (under the presidency of José Luis Bustamante y Rivero), the post–World War II era in Peru has been a markedly anti-ideological period. This is commonly attributed to the influence of the foreign-investment sector in collusion with the exporting oligarchy of Peru, both of whom benefited from the open economy, absence of controls, and low taxes which were guaranteed both by the military regime of Manuel Odría (1948–1956) and by the constitutional presidency of Manuel Prado (1956–1962).

An analysis of newspapers and weekly magazines during this period reveals that with the exception of *La Prensa*'s editorial justification of the *status quo* and *El Comercio*'s mild efforts toward promoting more nationalism, economic and social policies were not the subject of general public debate. Even the elections of 1956 and 1962 (which pitted Fernando Belaúnde Terry and Acción Popular against Haya de la Torre and APRA) centered on the procedural issue of whether APRA would be allowed to take power and what role the military would play in elections rather than on ideology *per se*. The real growth of public interest in these issues, as gauged by newspaper coverage, did not occur until well into Belaúnde's administration, that is, after 1965 when his agrarian reform had lost its momentum and guerrilla *focos* began operating in the jungle. During this period Belaúnde's economic policies also came under heavy attack, which raised the issues of devaluation, new taxes, and the imposition of controls. As the scheduled elections of June 1969 approached, ideological divisions became more salient. The Acción Popular–Christian Democratic alliance collapsed, the left wing of Acción Popular itself became restive and eventually broke openly with Belaúnde in the late summer of 1968, and the Unión Nacional Odriísta (UNO), the right-wing bloc in Congress which had joined in coalition with APRA throughout the Belaúnde period, split into two groups. In addition to the party splinter groups, a number of interest groups from businessmen to lawyers made public their programs for future economic and social policy. In this atmosphere of intense ideological debate the military took power in October 1968.[2] By this time the simplistic view of a good but suppressed majority arrayed against a bad but powerful oligarchy had given way to more complicated ideological positions. The 1968 coup ensured that the debate would not occur within the open arena of party competition but rather within a "revolutionary process" channeled and dominated by the military.

Those who would place the military's Revolutionary Government in its historical context often cite parallels between its radical positions and those held by Apristas: (1) the battle against imperialism and its allies in the oligarchy; (2) the emphasis on nationalization and industrialization to counterbalance U.S. power and create a national state; (3) the nationalization of land and the establishment of cooperatives; and (4) Latin American unity. Further analysis reveals, I believe, some shared nonradical biases as well.[3] First is the tendency toward economic rather than political definitions of Peruvian problems; this leads in turn to a

[2] See Jane Jaquette, "The Politics of Development in Peru," Cornell University Dissertation Series no. 33 (Ithaca, N.Y., 1971).

[3] For an analysis of the military government as a "liberal" revolution, see my "Liberalism and the Peruvian Revolution," paper presented to the Conference on Ideology and Inter-American Politics, sponsored by the Center for Inter-American Relations, Feb. 1974.

view of revolution that is largely administrative rather than value-oriented, a view in which changes in the structures are justified not as ends in themselves but by the degree they can contribute to increased economic productivity. An administrative focus also legitimizes the existence of an administrative class. These tendencies can be traced through the ideology of APRA,[4] Acción Popular, and now the military Revolution, where they provide a rationale against democratization.

Finally, APRA's views on the role of the middle class during the period of transition to socialism are strikingly similar to the military's early belief, which it shared with AP, that a national bourgeoisie does exist and that a policy must be developed to free it from suppression by the oligarchy. In one sense, all of the reforms which have since been decreed in the area of worker participation have clung to one principle: that the basic motor force for development and investment lies outside the bureaucracy. Thus the goal is to expand access to capital not only to the middle class but to the workers and beyond, if necessary, in the search for entrepreneurs. Similarly APRA would, in the period of transition to socialism,

utilize the anti-imperialist forces, without excluding the middle classes, which, pushed to the wall by imperialism, look to the State to defend them; and the State, by the progressive and socialized nationalization of the means of production, will orient itself definitively toward *State capitalism*, thus redirecting the tendency of the middle classes toward *gran capitalismo privado*, which would mean the return to imperialism.[5]

These tendencies—(the acceptance of economic definitions, the administrative viewpoint, the emphasis on productivity, and the role of the national bourgeoisie)—may be contrasted in spirit, if not in practice, with the antibureaucratic, value-based, egalitarian and antimaterial ideologies of Cuba and China, countries

[4] See, for example, Manuel Seoane, *Nuestros fines*, quoted in Harry Kantor, *The Peruvian Aprista Movement*, University of California Publications in Political Science no. 4 (Berkeley, 1953), p. 312.

[5] Víctor Raúl Haya de la Torre, *Teoría y táctica del aprismo* (Lima: 1931), p. 31.

with which the Revolutionary Government compares itself. Despite pressure from the left and the right, this essentially middle-class view of the Revolution is, in my view, a fundamental orientation of the military regime, an orientation that will change only if there is a major realignment of power within the elite.

Agrarian Reform

For Acción Popular, agrarian reform (along with the necessary legal changes to make it feasible and credit reform to make it productive) was the first principle, the *sine qua non* of their program. Whereas APRA had emphasized small holdings and the establishment of cooperatives, in latter years exempting the productive coastal estates (those whose workers had been successfully unionized by APRA), AP sought application of the law in principle to all landholdings (thus attacking the coastal oligarchy and APRA). The issue of worker participation in the agro-industrial complex was raised. However, the AP bill was substantially modified in Congress by the coalition of APRA and UNO (the conservative party headed by exdictator Manuel Odría), so that the 1964 law represented a compromise for AP.[6] The productive coastal haciendas were exempted, and the issue of worker participation was postponed for a "future industrial law." The first article of the bill suggests the priorities which ultimately emerged: agrarian reform is an "integral, nonviolent, and democratic process" (thus peasant uprisings and land take-overs were not condoned, and the political power of the oligarchy could be brought to bear on the "democratic" process) intended to create "a just system of property, tenure and land use" in order to "raise the output and productivity of the land . . ." (thus tying the issue of redistribution to agricultural productivity).

The reform was further compromised in its implementation. To expropriate a hacienda, a zone of agrarian reform had to be declared for the area, and the power to declare such zones rested

[6] For contrasting interpretations of the relative positions of APRA and AP on agrarian reform, see Grant Hilliker, *The Politics of Reform in Peru* (Baltimore: The Johns Hopkins Press, 1971), pp. 138ff., and Carlos Astiz, *Pressure Groups and Power Elites in Peruvian Politics* (Ithaca, N.Y.: Cornell University Press, 1969). See also Edgardo Seoane, *Ni tiranos ni caudillos: cartas y hechos del proceso político 1962–1968* (Lima: Editorial Italperú, 1969).

in the hands of a commission on which landowners (and APRA) had representation. The budget for the reform, which had to cover cash and bond payments, technical support for farmers, and the operating costs of the Office of Agrarian Reform, was never met by congressional appropriations.

The process of compromise and frustration within the ranks of Acción Popular and its ally, the Christian Democrats, set the political parameters of the Belaúnde period. Many of Belaúnde's AP backers urged him to "observe the law" (a process similar to but less powerful than a veto), or to hold a plebiscite (for which there was a weak but serviceable constitutional precedent). Belaúnde did neither, thus dividing his party support and permanently losing his legislative initiative. With the exception of the Marginal Highway, which was intended to alleviate the agrarian problem through colonization of the potentially productive High Jungle, Belaúnde's political efforts in Congress were concentrated on gaining support for existing programs. The political energies of his ministers were put into gaining congressional approval for the annual budget. The opposition coalition of APRA and UNO retained an effective veto and opposed new taxes but did not themselves push for basic reforms. The result was stagnation and disillusionment on the part of the radical reformers in AP and among their Christian Democratic allies, and a noticeable restiveness among certain groups in the military. When guerrilla groups denounced the agrarian reform and began operations in the Sierra in 1965, the conviction grew among those who were later to lead the 1968 coup that radical structural reforms would be necessary to offset the potential for rural revolutionary violence.[7]

After the Velasco government was established in 1968, its immediate priority was the nationalization of Peru's economic and foreign policy. International Petroleum's complex at Talara was taken over in a dramatic military occupation of the site. Subsequent U.S. threats to activate the Hickenlooper Amendment and cut Peru's sugar quota were resisted; the cutoff of public and private investment funds and U.S. opposition to Peru's two-

---

[7] The role of the guerrilla threat in solidifying military opinion is argued in Luigi Einaudi, *Peruvian Military Relations with the United States*, Rand paper P-4389 (Santa Monica, Calif., 1970), and in Victor Villanueva, *¿Nueva mentalidad militar en el Perú?* (Lima: Editorial Juan Mejía Baca, 1969).

hundred-mile limit became nationalist issues which contributed to the regime's legitimacy. The government began to develop a coherent set of policies to control the impact of foreign investment.

At the same time, however, domestic policy was not totally neglected. The process of creating an "authentic" agrarian reform was begun through the circulation of a draft law. After the resignation of the first minister of agriculture (who opposed the more radical aspects of the draft), the new Agrarian Reform Law was announced on June 24, 1969.

In keeping with the original AP bill, the new statute included expropriation of coastal haciendas. Implementation was rapid, and the government announced its intent to "break the back" of the oligarchy. The dramatic occupation of haciendas when owners resisted gave the initial impression that the military was more concerned with eliminating the oligarchy than with facing the difficult problem of agrarian reform in the Sierra. However, the process of expropriation was soon extended to the highlands, cooperatives were established (to avoid dividing haciendas into unproductive *minifundia*), and water rights made subject to state regulation, all of which enhanced the government's claim of authentic reform.

In line with the position of CEPAL (UN Economic Commission for Latin America) and the intent of the AP bill, the military sees the social and economic aspects of the nonviolent reform as fully compatible with one another. The peasant is viewed not as a revolutionary or cultural force, as suggested by early APRA doctrine or by today's Third World cultural nationalism, but as a better producer and consumer in a rationalized economy. Thus President Velasco stated in his speech of June 24th:

The social inspiration of the new law is entirely compatible with the necessity of guaranteeing the maintenance of high levels of production which agricultural technology has made possible [on the coastal haciendas].

With the rationalization of the use and the ownership of land and with the creation of new incentives derived from broader access to land, the agrarian reform will tend to produce more and better agricultural landholders.

Further:

The new responsibilities for Peru which arise out of the policy of Regional and Subregional integration demand of our country a vigorous industrial effort. . . . For this reason the Law is also a law of impulsion for Peruvian industry whose future depends on the creation of an ever-growing internal market of high, diversified consumption. . . .[8]

Although the military's intent to implement an effective agrarian reform is clear from the process of expropriation and its unprecedented commitment of personnel and funds, certain organizational questions (such as the optimal size of the basic agrarian unit, relationships among cooperatives, and links between cooperatives and urban distribution systems), and the fundamental issue of participation have not yet been resolved. The government's efforts to restrict Aprista influence, particularly on the coastal haciendas formerly unionized by APRA, led to charges that the military was reverting to its prerevolutionary pattern of trying to destroy APRA, one of the few groups in the Peruvian political system which could compete with the military in terms of organization, doctrine, and a legitimate claim to popular support. Further, it was suggested that the government's policy in the Sierra was not revolutionary at all, that the old *patrón* had merely been replaced by government officials who were managing the haciendas (now "cooperatives") under a paternalistic system of rewards and sanctions similar to that which had existed under the old regime.[9]

In response to such criticisms and to pressures to acknowledge the issue of participation, the National System of Support for Social Mobilization (SINAMOS) was set up in 1971 to develop participatory mechanisms in all sectors.[10] Originally created by

[8] Reprinted in *El Peruano*, June 25, 1969.

[9] See Julio Cotler, *El populismo militar como modelo de desarrollo moderno* (Lima: Instituto de Estudios Peruanos, 1969); Norman Gall, "The Master Is Dead," in *Dissent*, July 1971; and David Scott Palmer, "Revolution from Above: Military Government and Popular Participation in Peru," Cornell University Dissertation Series no. 47 (Ithaca, N.Y., 1973).

[10] But there has been a battle with the Ministry of Industry and Commerce over who will control the "capacitation" of the workers in the industrial

combining a number of preexisting "popular" state-financed organizations (such as Cooperación Popular and the federation of
barriada organizations), SINAMOS attracted a number of radical
young *técnicos* who were committed to the ideal of mass mobilization and favored the creation of national institutions to
foment and channel it. As a result of its size and activism,
SINAMOS has become a focus of conflict, with other ministries
and existing participatory organizations (particularly unions) attempting to limit its influence. Its first definitive test was its decision in April 1972 to hold "universal" elections (that is, with
APRA participation) in the north coast haciendas, risking the
possibility that Apristas would gain control of the cooperatives
and embarrass the government. The elections were held, and although Apristas were elected, the cooperatives did not strike,
and the government's position was not threatened. In his *28 de
julio* speech, Velasco took full credit for having faced the specter
of "opposition" participation:

Now that this transcendent social conquest has been made, the
false criticism of those who maintain that the Revolutionary
Government was trying to replace the *patrón* with the State
is definitively disproven. Faithful to our profound confidence
and our faith in the capacity of the workers, we men of the
Revolution decided upon this transcendent measure,
convinced that the people would be worthy of the great
challenge of becoming the directors of their economic and
social destinies, in the enterprises which represent the very
heart of the agrarian economy in Peru.[11]

Despite this successful effort, the debate over the legitimacy
of SINAMOS is far from over. In October 1972 it was argued in an
opposition journal that "in effect, the national teachers' strike, the
mobilization of the miners, and finally that of the sugar workers,
made it necessary to create organizations which serve to *mediate*
between the state and the popular masses. These will serve as a
channel of persuasion and 'assistance' [*asistencialismo*] on the
one hand, and will absorb the immediate demands of the popular

---

communities, and both agencies were involved in the National Congress of
Industrial Communities (see section 5, Enterprise Reform). (Interviews in
SINAMOS, July 1972.)

[11] Reprinted in *El Peruano*, July 29, 1972.

sectors."[12] The elimination or reorganization of existing interest groups such as the National Agrarian Society and the National Industrial Society,[13] the creation of vertical organizations combining representatives of workers and employers under the guidance of government agencies, and the attempt to weaken the labor movement through formation of industrial communities and through the creation of a government-sponsored union are taken as evidence of the government's intent to co-opt and ultimately control popular demands by means of corporatist organization:

> In this way the institutional mechanisms that the military government has created to favor "full participation" of the population are to be viewed as attempts to clientelize the segmented popular classes through the formation of vertical, hierarchical organizations, with the consequent depoliticization of the dominated population at the moment when the antioligarchic reforms have reduced the differences that separate them [*procurán su homogenización*].[14]

Whether or not the quality of participation the government is seeking in Peru can legitimately be characterized as corporatist, this ideological debate has had practical consequences. SINAMOS began publication of a journal which it called *Participación* to counter the arguments of its leftist critics in *Sociedad y Política*. The minister of finance, whose official responsibilities are far distant from the issue, made a point of distinguishing publicly between "organized" participation, as fomented by the government, and "manipulated" participation. He specifically denied that the government was limiting the mechanisms of participation to its own creations, the cooperatives and the industrial communities, and stated that the government would not adopt the *partido único*, or single party, as a vehicle of support.[15]

The issue of participation is clearly a basic question the gov-

---

[12] Julio Cotler, "Bases del Corporativismo en el Perú," *Sociedad y Política,* vol. 1, no. 2 (Oct. 1972), p. 9.

[13] See discussion in text; for an interpretation of the military's intent, see Cotler, *Bases*, p. 11.

[14] Ibid., p. 10.

[15] Reprinted in *Oiga*, Nov. 17, 1972.

ernment must face, with ramifications in the Sierra very different from those on the coast. It is perhaps a sign of weakness that the military has responded to criticism by engaging in ideological debate with left-wing intellectuals rather than by mobilizing direct popular support. The way in which this issue is resolved and the degree of participation that is achieved will certainly have a major impact on the legitimacy of the government and the future structure of Peruvian society.

Nationalism

In the course of its history, Peru's economic growth has been largely export-derived, from the guano boom of the last century to the development of copper and fishmeal exports in the 1960s.[16] APRA's program emphasized a long-term plan for the nationalization of land and industry, with emphasis on the mining industry, and inter-American cooperation with joint ownership of the Panama Canal. Although this program was softened considerably during World War II, it provides a bench mark against which to measure Peruvian policy and the positions of competing parties and groups.

The year 1948 marked the end of a brief (1945–1948) experiment with controlist policies under APRA-backed president José Bustamante y Rivero.[17] Since then, under military dictator Manuel Odría and elected president Manuel Prado, Peru's economic system has been remarkably open—that is, market-oriented and hospitable to foreign investment.[18] The maintenance of a free enterprise economy can be attributed in part to the ideological convictions of one individual, newspaper editor and sometime finance minister Pedro Beltrán, and to the fact that the open economy favors exporters and foreign investors, two of the most powerful groups in pre–1968 Peru. *Laissez faire* policies were also consistent with a respectably high growth rate, which in turn made possible the rapid expansion of the urban sector and the

[16] See Jonathan V. Levin, *The Export Economics* (Cambridge: Harvard University Press, 1960).

[17] See José Luis Bustamante y Rivero, *Tres años de lucha por la democracia en el Perú* (Buenos Aires: Bartolome U. Chiesino, 1949).

[18] Rosemary Thorp, "Inflation and Orthodox Economic Policy in Peru," *Bulletin of the Oxford University Institute of Economics and Statistics*, vol. 29, no. 3 (Aug. 1967), pp. 185–210.

creation of a new, professional sector of the middle class.[19] The success of the Peruvian economy relative to other Latin American economies in the late fifties and early sixties made *"criollo liberalism"* appear as economic law, to be violated at the risk of inflation and loss of economic momentum.[20]

Thus it is not surprising that Belaúnde and Acción Popular took an accommodating stance toward foreign investment. The official AP position was that "rejection of foreign assistance on the basis of a fanatic doctrine or a misunderstood nationalism can have fatal consequences for the revolutionary movement."[21] The attempt to eliminate foreign capital inflows is doomed to failure, "as the Cuban example reveals." Besides, "the imperialistic attitude of the great powers is declining rapidly," and as a result of this change of heart the underdeveloped countries can obtain better prices for their products and better contracts with foreign enterprise.[22] Belaúnde's only nationalist position was a promise, in his inaugural address, to resolve "within ninety days" the old controversy between Peru and International Petroleum Company (a special case because of IPC's unconstitutional claim to subsoil rights). Despite congressional pressure, the controversy was not settled for five more years. Although Belaúnde showed both an ideological and a pragmatic willingness to continue the open economy for the benefit of foreign private investment, the dynamics of Peruvian-U.S. relations during this period made it impossible even for Belaúnde to sustain this optimistic approach. As a result of his declared intent to resolve the IPC issue, the American government cut nearly all aid to Peru, and the U.S. Embassy became deeply involved in a campaign to force a settlement on IPC's terms.[23] Although congressional initiatives at one point put IPC up for international bids, a serious effort was not made by the Executive to resolve the issue until Manuel Ulloa became minister of finance in June 1968.

At this time the Congress, which had previously opposed

[19] See Magali S. Larson and Arlene E. Bergman, *Social Stratification in Peru* (Berkeley, Calif.: Institute of International Studies, 1969), and François Bourricaud, "Los militares: ¿por que y para que?" *Aportes*, vol. 16 (Apr. 1970).

[20] See Jaquette, "The Politics of Development in Peru," chap. 2.

[21] Acción Popular [Francisco Miró-Quesada], *Manual Ideológico* (Lima: 1964), p. 200.

[22] Ibid., p. 201.

[23] Richard Goodwin, "Letter from Peru," *New Yorker* (May 17, 1969), pp. 41–46.

Belaúnde's policies by joint action of the opposition parties, granted Ulloa and the cabinet "extraordinary powers" to act for sixty days without congressional review. Under the extraordinary powers, which were the result of a political compromise between Belaúnde and APRA (and were negotiated by Ulloa with the prospect of a *belaundista*-APRA alliance for the June 1969 elections) an agreement between IPC and the government was finally signed in August 1968. It was part of a broader package of economic policies which were nationalist for their time, among them a policy which granted special privileges to and limited foreign shares in "national" banks, and a decree (340 HC) which introduced the principle of Peruvianization of basic industries by reserving the future development of the petrochemical industry to mixed corporations with 30 percent of their shares in Peruvian hands and 66 percent of their boards of directors controlled by Peruvian nationals.

Gone was the apparent acceptance of the compatibility of foreign investment and Peruvian sovereignty, and in its place appeared the concept of the "State" as guarantor of the independence of the Peruvian private sector:

Foreign private capital is badly needed, but it must be administered with care and firmness to keep it from dominating and colonizing our productive activity. . . . The State must do everything in its power, through its organs of credit, to facilitate the formation of Peruvian capital so that it may . . . put itself above the inevitable temptations which may exist for the great foreign powers to reduce our independence.[24]

The future of mining investment and petrochemical development were dependent on a settlement of the IPC issue. Projected contracts for copper exploitation, worth over $300 million, had been postponed as part of the general campaign to put pressure on the government, and plans for a Peruvian petrochemical industry awaited the settlement of the issue of petroleum supply. As a result of stepped-up negotiations and concessions on both sides, agreement was reached by August. IPC gave up its claim

[24] Manuel Ulloa, "La estratégia del desarrollo vista por un peruano," in *Acción Para el Desarrollo, El Perú en la próxima década* (Lima: Cahuide, 1968), pp. 140–141.

to the subsoil rights and its demand for an operating contract for the fields of La Brea and Pariñas in return for the formal cancellation of alleged debts (back taxes and illegal profits) claimed by Peru. Later decrees involved additional concessions: IPC was granted the right to expand its refinery and distribution network (the largest in the country) and given an exploration concession in the Amazon region, where oil exploration contracts were being negotiated with other major petroleum companies. Although the contract came under some fire from nationalist critics, it probably would have held had the "page 11 scandal" (in which government ministers 'were accused of removing a key page of the contract in order to convince the IPC representative to sign it) never broken. But the television *exposé* of the existence of a missing page doomed the contract and Ulloa's political future, and it set off a series of events that culminated in the October coup.[25]

Within a week of the coup, the Velasco junta nationalized IPC's oil fields and the refinery at Talara; later the distribution network and other assets were seized. However, the government argued that IPC was a special case and that foreign investment would continue to be welcomed, "subject to the laws"—that is, without special privileges. Since 1968, however, the military has moved much closer to the ideological position of the dependency theorists. In Velasco's words, "foreign investment creates focal points of development," but it "also serves as a means of sucking up the wealth of Latin American countries."[26] At various times foreign investment has been accused of depriving Peru of the power to make its own economic decisions and of increasing cultural dependency.[27]

The military's response has been to strengthen its bargaining position by: (1) control of the terms on which investment enters through contracts themselves and through sectoral laws which establish the standard terms of contracts; (2) adoption of the principle of fade-out joint ventures, which guarantees foreign

[25] The above discussion of the Ulloa period is taken from Jaquette, "The Politics of Development in Peru," chap. 5.

[26] Speech before "Los 77," Oct. 28, 1971 (reprinted by the National Office of Information).

[27] For example, the regime attempted to remove "Americanisms" (like Santa Claus) from the celebration of Christmas in 1971. Numerous speeches by Velasco and others have emphasized this attempt. Hippies in Lima are attacked in the press for being decadent and antinationalist.

capital a reasonable rate of return for a set period of time, with the stipulation that the company must turn over an increasing percentage of its shares to Peruvian nationals so that Peruvians hold a majority of shares within a maximum of fifteen years;[28] (3) the search for new sources of foreign capital in Western Europe, Japan, and in Communist countries with which the government opened diplomatic relations; (4) the attempt to create a united front of Latin American countries with coordinated policies toward investment, aid, and international lending agencies; (5) the promotion of the Andean Group as a regional force and a means to insure a wider market for Peruvian goods; and (6) state control of basic industries (energy, steel, utilities) including state control of export marketing. In this way the negative effects of foreign investment (tendency to form enclaves, to employ financial leverage, and to use the political power of the country in which the parent company is located to further its economic interests) will be reduced while—in theory—needed investment will still enter as the rules are established and reasonable profits "guaranteed."

The government has achieved some notable successes in attracting different types of foreign investment under these conditions: the Cuajone contract for development of a large copper mine, contracts with major oil companies for exploration and production, its mixed enterprise arrangement with Massey-Ferguson, Volvo, and Perkins Engines to set up tractor and diesel engine factories, and a $40 million loan from Poland (which will conform to fade-out stipulations)—to name a few key examples. However, the total inflow of new capital has been limited. Credit lines, cut off after the nationalization of IPC, were reopened twelve to eighteen months later, but often went unused because the private sector was holding back and the government did not have its projects sufficiently well developed to make use of the capital.[29]

Nonetheless, the government has taken a series of steps which have increased uncertainty in the foreign-investment sector. IPC was to be a special case, but it was followed by the expropriation of lands held by American firms under the Agrarian Reform Law; ITT's telephone company and the Chase Manhattan–owned

[28] The fade-out policy was later restricted to companies producing goods for export to Andean Group countries. See the *Peruvian Times*, Oct. 29, 1971.

[29] See *Caretas*, Mar. 15–Apr. 8, 1970.

bank were bought out by the government, and, although the terms were favorable to the companies, most private-sector long-term investment plans were negatively affected. Negotiations with Cerro de Pasco mining interests were accompanied by threats to take the mines "by force if necessary,"[30] the state has nationalized the fishing industry,[31] and state participation as well as controls have been extended to pharmaceuticals. The pattern of expansion into existing industries has increased uncertainty about the future role of foreign investment and of the private sector in general.

On the positive side, the World Bank granted its first loan to Peru since the expropriation of IPC in August 1973, and Peruvian and U.S. officials began a series of what Peruvian sources labeled very secret discussions on the question of future U.S. investment in Peru,[32] which resulted in an agreement in February 1974 on the compensation Peru would pay to the U.S. government for nationalized firms.[33] In the face of continued uncertainty, the government reiterates the official position—that the "rules of the game have been established" and that foreign investments are welcomed "insofar as they contribute to greater social justice among Peruvians"; they are "guaranteed a profit" in addition to the tax and other incentives available to Peruvian industry. Indeed, some sources within the government have argued privately that foreign investment is the essential basis on which future development and distribution possibilities rest,[34] and that the government is favoring foreign investment—particularly large-scale investment—over internal privately or publicly financed development.

Administrative Reform

On the surface, the issue of administrative reform appears to be a rather technical matter focused on such questions as merit

[30] This is according to Cerro. See *Latin American Report*, vol. 2, no. 1 (Aug. 1973), p. 6. The government claims it was "misquoted"; see extensive report in the *Peruvian Times*, Sept. 28, 1973.

[31] In May 1973. For reactions by the private sector, see *Oiga* for May and June 1973.

[32] Reported in *Oiga*, July 20, 1973, and in *Latin American Report*, vol. 2, no. 1 (Aug. 1973).

[33] *Latin American Report*, vol. 2, no. 7 (Feb. 1974), p. 5.

[34] Confidential interview, Oct. 1973.

systems of hiring, training programs, and reorganization of the bureaucracy to increase effective performance. It has often been equated with the elimination of graft and corruption. In the Peruvian context, however, the issue has deeper significance: how powerful should the state be vis-à-vis other institutions in Peruvian society?

In the past, the state has been weak, and one assumption shared by APRA, AP, and the military is that the state is little more than an agent of the oligarchy, which has subverted the legal and administrative power of the government to serve its own ends. As a result, a truly national state has never existed in Peru. A justification for the restructuring, not the elimination, of the state can be found in the Aprista ideal of the state as a guarantor of the "life, health, moral and material well-being, education, liberty, and economic emancipation of the working classes,"[35] and as an anti-imperialist force. The state as an instrument of class domination was to be replaced by a functional democracy with rights and obligations to be derived from the individual's role in the economy as well as from his role as citizen.[36]

Acción Popular adopted a similar philosophy: although the existing state is an instrument of class control, the goal of elimination of the state was "utopian." The AP ideal was the "service state" with the following functions: economic planning, the implementation of "distributive justice," national integration, and the promotion of a "social concept of property." In form it would be both democratic (through "democratic elections of those who govern") and decentralized.[37]

In practice, Belaúnde's regime showed some fidelity to these principles. Agrarian reform and Cooperación Popular reflected concern for distributive justice, the oppression of the peasant masses, and the goal of national integration; democracy and decentralization were pursued by allowing municipalities to elect their own local officials rather than appointing them in Lima (although the issue of whether illiterates could vote was not raised), and the work of the National Planning Institute (set up during the military interregnum of 1962–1963) was officially recognized and expanded. State investment was stepped up and directed into infrastructure and education.

[35] From *Plan de acción*, quoted in Kantor, *The Peruvian Aprista Movement*, p. 68.

[36] Ibid., pp. 69–70.   [37] *Manual Ideológico*, pp. 60–64.

However, these measures were neither strong enough nor implemented with sufficient thoroughness to achieve progress toward the goals for which they were designed. The agrarian reform was compromised, Cooperación Popular lost the president's support when party members tried to turn it into an instrument of politicization,[38] the Planning Institute collected data and created "plans" which were never instruments or guides to economic policy,[39] and the projected reorganization of the bureaucracy itself was never carried out.

One of the main weaknesses of Belaúnde's vision of the state was his failure to adopt a clear economic policy. In light of the Velasco regime's promotion of "pluralism" it is significant that the AP *Manual Ideológico* envisioned a pluralist economy of sectors: a cooperative sector, to preserve capital assets and economies of scale in agriculture; private property on a small scale (to "satisfy the normal desire for gain which is present in most human beings");[40] and a nationalized state or "socialist" sector. The state would have a role in "harmonizing" these sectors according to "purely technical" criteria.[41] Implementation of this scheme was never promoted by Belaúnde. The cooperatives that came into existence under the agrarian reform were producer co-ops, geared to operation within the market economy. The state did not expand the very limited economic role it had inherited from Odría and Prado, except for the emphasis on infrastructure investments.

As a result of a number of circumstances including the aftereffects of the 1967 devaluation, continuing balance-of-payments problems, rising levels of inflation, and foreign pressures on the banking sector, the end of Belaúnde's administration was a period of new emphasis on economic policy, with the state taking a more direct role. In a series of actions that began with an administrative decree setting new tariffs and import controls in March 1968 and culminated in the promulgation of a number of long-postponed policies under the "extraordinary powers," the state increasingly took on new regulatory functions vis-à-vis the private sector. But as the implementation period was so brief,

[38] See *Oiga*, Dec. 6, 1968.

[39] For comparisons of the INP under Belaúnde and the military, see Robert Klitgaard, "Observations on the Peruvian National Plan of Development, 1971–75," *Inter-American Economic Affairs*, vol. 25, no. 3 (Winter 1971).

[40] *Manual Ideológico*, p. 55.   [41] Ibid., p. 197.

only the intent and not the long-run effects of this shift can be observed.

When the military took over in October, one of its basic principles was to reject the orthodox "liberal" view of the limited state. The Manifesto of the Revolutionary Government declared that the coup was "inspired by the necessity of transforming the structure of the State . . . to permit efficient action by the Government, to transform the social, economic, and cultural structures, and to maintain a definite nationalist position. . . ."[42] The result has been a series of measures to enhance the government role, ranging from a direct attack on the oligarchy (accused of subverting the state to its own ends) to a functional reorganization of ministries according to economic sectors and the creation of a powerful planning group to advise the president (the COAP). The National Planning Institute has been revitalized, and ministry budgets must be coordinated with planning priorities.[43] New attention has been given to training programs, and a large number of trained *técnicos* (who were not always able to find work in the private sector in the Belaúnde period) have been sought out and hired to fill new slots.[44]

On the economic front, the change has been even more marked. The government has (1) created new laws, sector by sector, to regulate and promote economic activity; (2) provided for direct investment in totally state-owned or mixed enterprises in critical areas of the economy; (3) made the state's share the predominant share of the banking sector through the purchase of private banks, the expansion of state banks, and exclusive state control of foreign exchange; and (4) established a state development corporation (COFIDE) to capitalize high priority projects (and to help finance the development of the projected social-property sector). From this expanded economic capacity, the government finds itself in a much stronger position to compete

[42] Manifesto of the Revolutionary Government, Oct. 3, 1968, reprinted in *El Peruano*, Oct. 4, 1968.

[43] See Klitgaard, "Observations."

[44] Thus fulfilling one of Belaúnde's promises—to hire the professionals graduating from Peru's universities with very little prospect of employment in the private sector. The role of this class in determining the technical and elitist biases of the Belaúnde and Velasco governments deserves more study, particularly in the light of reported civil-military conflict within the bureaucracy and the economy in general; civilian professional employees often refer to themselves as second-class citizens.

with, nationalize, or regulate private investment and to determine the optimal use of foreign aid.

Yet there is a definite limit to state expansion at present in that the government is unwilling, and perhaps unable, to establish a "command" economy. From the beginning, the military's position has been that private investment is essential to Peruvian growth, providing it can function within the general parameters set by the government, and reassurances have often been given that state expansion will be limited. Motivating the military's attempt to calm private investor fears while setting the new rules of the game under which they will operate is the view that the private sector is a dynamic force, capable of being harnessed, a source of economic energy. Without this belief—and the tension that continues to exist between the government and investors, combined with continued low rates of private investment and economic stagnation, indicates that it is a matter of faith—the government would be faced with the prospect of indefinite expansion into the private sector, an outcome it associates with totalitarian control.[45] Instead, it has attempted to create incentives for investors, to increase available credit, to encourage the more cooperative entrepreneurs, and to maintain a dialogue with even the more recalcitrant representatives of the private sector.

Tax and Credit Reform

Acción Popular's original vision of credit reform was dramatically populist: without credit reform there could be no effective agrarian reform; thus the intended beneficiaries of the credit revolution were the peasants, and the major goal of credit reform the increase of agricultural production. Under Ulloa, the emphasis shifted to the question of how to channel savings and wealth toward the sources of production,[46] that is, toward productive entrepreneurs. On the one hand, it is agreed that financial resources are dominated by a very small group (the oligarchy), hence there is need for state intervention in the credit sector to loosen up the system. Financial resources misused by the oli-

[45] The classic presentation of this position is Velasco's speech at CADE-70, in *La Crónica*, Nov. 16, 1970.

[46] From a Deltec study (headed by Ulloa), *El mercado de capitales en el Perú* (Mexico City: Grafica Panamericana, 1968), from which some of his policies as finance minister were adapted.

garchy should be subject to taxation, and capital flight should be brought under control. Second, it is assumed that if credit is more widely available, and if the state provides the necessary support through incentives, infrastructure, and rational planning, there will be a group of individuals—a national bourgeoisie—capable of utilizing the newly available capital in productive investments.

On the basis of these principles, Ulloa established a property tax in Peru (oligarchs are landowners; speculation in urban land is not a productive use of capital), made the income tax somewhat more progressive, and abolished unregistered stocks (thought to be an important means of tax evasion for the wealthy as well as a deterrent to the formation of a stock market). He further sought to reorganize the banking system by taking power away from the commercial-bank-dominated regulatory agency, the Superintendencia de Bancos, by giving the Central Bank new planning functions, and by restricting the operation of foreign banks, as noted earlier.

When the military took over shortly after these decrees were issued, they continued or extended many of Ulloa's policies. Tax policy went almost unchanged,[47] and radical redistributive measures which might have threatened the middle classes and potential entrepreneurs have not been adopted, although there have been periodic threats of major tax reform. The banking sector was further brought under national (and government) control. On paper, at least, a policy of "directed credit" to meet investment priorities on a sector-by-sector basis was adopted. In spite of these measures ostensibly favoring the growth of a national entrepreneurial class, relations between the private sector and the government have been marked by conflict and frustration. The result has been economic stagnation.[48] While government response has ranged from tolerance to threats, its official position is that it has been consistent with regard to its expectations:

[47] An increase in taxes on the middle classes has been discussed but not implemented. (Interview with John Strasma, July 1972.)

[48] Government figures show a growth rate of 5 to 6 percent in 1972, with projected government investments up 47 percent (to 20 percent to total budget for 1973–1974), according to the *Peruvian Times*, Feb. 23, 1973. Foreign credits were said to have increased from $230 million in 1971 to $800 million in 1972 (*Peruvian Times*, Dec. 29, 1972). Government figures are not fully reliable, however, and the *Peruvian Times* of Oct. 5, 1973, reported that the growth rate would not exceed 5 percent in 1973 with 11 percent inflation.

Within the new conditions created by the revolutionary
changes, modern investors and entrepreneurs have all the
guarantees and all the incentives to which they can legitimately
hope to aspire. And this is the way many businessmen, whom
the government supports and encourages, see it. But despite
the support of other governments and of national and foreign
companies, a lack of confidence persists on the part of
oligarchs, who refuse to collaborate in the effort of bringing
the economy forward. This is the employment of economic
withdrawal as a counterrevolutionary instrument.[49]

Yet economic policy seems to follow a cyclical pattern. In 1970
several laws were passed intended to set the rules by which private enterprise would operate. In May, the government converted all foreign currency holdings held by Peruvian nationals
into *soles* and made foreign currency accounts illegal. A new Industrial Law was passed, and although it was primarily promo-
tional in intent, with incentives for investments outside of Lima
and in priority areas, the concept of worker participation in
management and profits was introduced. This was implemented
shortly thereafter by the Law of Industrial Communities. November 1970 marks the beginning of a dialogue between industrialists and the government, and through 1971 there were relatively few changes in policy. In 1972, however, the government
presented a new plan to establish a sector of "social property"
with firms organized on the principle of worker self-management. In 1973 state enterprise expanded into areas which had
formerly been private-sector preserves. As noted above, the take-
over of the fishing industry, the establishment of a state pharmaceutical firm in competition with private firms,[50] and the successful negotiation of a new joint enterprise project (combining state
and foreign capital) to manufacture tractors, combined with continued pressure on foreign investors, increased private-sector
uncertainty.

Such policy cycles have been cited by the private sector as reasons for its inability to meet government expectations. In addition, many industrialists feel that they have been barred from
participation in the formulation of basic economic policy. The

---

[49] Velasco's speech to the armed forces, Mar. 20, 1969. This theme is still
repeated. See, for example, the *28 de julio* speeches of the president for 1971
and 1972.

case of the National Society of Industries (SNI), the peak association of industrial entrepreneurs, indicates the degree of tension that exists between the government and a substantial proportion of the private sector. In 1972, the SNI was named the official representative of private industry; by July, however, the government was calling for a total reorganization of the association in order to guarantee "authentic representativeness." In December, the government withdrew its official designation and announced a new and artificial association, the National Association of Industrial Enterprises (ANEI), to involve all types of industrial enterprises including those in the state sector and in the new sector of social property (still undefined in practice), as well as worker representatives from the private sector.[51]

Finally, efforts on the part of the SNI to have the minister of industries and commerce (Alberto Jiménez de Lucio) removed in 1973 met with failure and were labeled by the regime a rightist counterrevolutionary tactic.[52] This evidence would indicate that the rules of the game are not yet clearly established, that a healthy pattern of communication between the private sector and the regime (which might counterbalance the negative effects of policy shifts) does not exist, and that there is considerable debate within the government on what concessions, if any, can be made to the private investors.

However, even if relations between the government and the private sector improved dramatically, the problem of poor economic performance would not necessarily be resolved. Eric Hobsbawm has analyzed the government's dilemma as follows:

The generals' policies are not intended to be anti-business, in spite of putting all the basic industries into the public sector. They are certainly in favor of indigenous capitalist development, doubtless under the control of a commanding state sector, but also benefitting from its activities. Such a symbiosis is today normal, and in Latin America even the dynamic local capitalisms of Brazil and Mexico rely largely on it. But Peru is not Brazil or Mexico. There is no effective national bourgeoisie, and military decisions are unlikely to create what several centuries of history have denied the country.

[50] *Peruvian Times*, June 22, 1973.   [51] *Oiga*, Dec. 7, 1972.
[52] *Oiga*, July 20, 1973.

He concludes:

> What is most likely to happen is that the extreme weakness of
> domestic private enterprise and the restrictions on the
> participation in it of foreign capital will make the public sector
> grow far beyond the original intentions of the government. It
> will have to, unless Peru is to relapse into its old pattern of
> dependence. This will raise acute questions, analogous to those
> in Eastern Europe, about the suitability of large state
> bureaucracies in backward countries as economic
> entrepreneurs, about the role of incentives, technocrats, etc.[53]

Nor are the penetration of the private sector by state enterprise and projected increases in government investment any
guarantee of economic growth. The government bureaucracy in
Peru has not yet adjusted to its role as entrepreneur, and there
is no necessary connection between the development of bureaucratic power and the creation of viable economic projects. One
indicator of bureaucratic weakness in this sector is that despite
access to domestic and foreign capital assets, the government has
been unable to utilize these resources productively—its problem
has not been overextension but too much liquidity.[54]

Although there are practical as well as ideological reasons for
avoiding a command economy, it is difficult to create alternatives.
The government's response to continued stagnation has been to
expand the number of state enterprises and to search for a new
ideological solution. That search has increasingly focused on the
social-property sector, discussed at length by Peter Knight in
Chapter 9 of this volume. Politically the development of the social-property sector to resolve the twin problems of growth and
participation is the most obvious case of the government's ten-

---

[53] E. J. Hobsbawm, "Peru: The 'Peculiar' Revolution," *New York Review
of Books* (Dec. 16, 1971), pp. 33–34.

[54] Interviews in the Banco Central de Reserva and the Ministry of Industry
and Commerce, July 1972. *Caretas* argued the same case throughout 1970. To
this must be added evidence of interministerial conflicts over power, civil-military hostility, and serious splits at the cabinet level among the generals themselves. For an interesting case study of the battle between the INP and the
ministries over foreign aid, see Robert E. Klitgaard, "On Assessing a Gift
Horse: The Evaluation of Foreign Aid by Recipients," Rand paper no. 5040
(Santa Monica, Calif.: July 1973). Civil-military problems are aggravated by
rumors and some evidence of military corruption.

dency to resort to ideological politics and will be discussed below.

Enterprise Reform

The rationale for enterprise reform, or worker participation, is the ideal of the elimination of class conflict, which is condemned as both socially destructive and economically costly. This position was most fully developed in Peru by the Christian Democrats. As Héctor Cornejo Chávez, the party's leader and theoretician, describes it, enterprise reform would "bring the workers and capitalists to the same table to manage the enterprise, to divide profits, and to make every employee an owner. . . ." The result would be the establishment of "a fraternity between capitalists and workers . . . as a result of their common interest in the prosperity of a common enterprise."[55]

The goal of enterprise reform was one of the basic points of the AP-DC program. But as the focus of Belaúnde's policy and the thrust of the Agrarian Reform Law of 1964 were toward a solution of the agrarian problem in the Sierra, the issue of enterprise reform (which might have been relevant had the coastal agro-industrial enterprises been included) was never seriously raised. The Ulloa reforms, which represented in other ways a return to the original AP program, did not touch on this issue. This is perfectly consistent with Ulloa's responsiveness to the interests of a nascent—even hypothetical—national bourgeoisie whose attitude toward worker participation was hardly favorable. Yet in late 1968, Belaúnde's failure to move toward enterprise reform was one of the major criticisms made by his own party, which also emphasized the weakness of his agrarian reform and his capitulation to foreign interests.

Under the Velasco regime, worker participation has developed into an issue with ramifications extending far beyond the original intent of the 1970 Law of Industrial Communities. The conflicts between ideology and practice and the regime's response to this provide a bellwether case study of the government's approach to structural change in an area where its potentially contradictory goals—productivity and participation—are at stake.

The 1970 law established a new entity within all industrial

[55] Héctor Cornejo Chávez, *Que se Propone la Democracia Cristiana* (Lima: Ediciones del Sol, 1962), p. 56.

firms having more than six employees, the industrial community (IC). Each IC was to receive 15 percent of the net profits of the firm each year, which it would in turn reinvest in the firm, thus acquiring ownership shares up to 50 percent of the company's assets. Workers were to accumulate their portion of the total IC assets as individuals, the amount to be calculated in terms of days worked. Each IC has a general assembly which would elect a council to oversee IC assets and to send representatives to the company's board of directors, with the IC representation on the board increasing as their percentage ownership increases. An additional 10 percent of net profits were to be distributed directly.

The law came under considerable criticism from both sides. Those favoring more radical worker participation pointed out that the councils would be dominated by skilled workers and technicians, since representation was to be split among categories (unskilled worker, skilled worker, etc.) within the IC, and this would favor the technicians and underrepresent the more numerous unskilled workers. Further, it was argued that at 15 percent of current net profit rates, it would take an estimated fifty years or more for workers to achieve 50 percent ownership and thus equal representation on the managing board. So-called temporary workers (*contratados*) were ineligible to receive shares, and it was pointed out that the radical future goal of accumulation of assets in the hands of the industrial community would be bought at the price of lower wages in the present. Finally, it was argued that the ICs were in direct competition with the labor unions, and that the military was criticized for its presumed intent to destroy APRA. The law as written would encourage private firms to join with the state in mixed enterprises, since the latter were exempt from the requirement to form such communities.[56]

Individual entrepreneurs and the SNI objected strenuously to worker participation in management decisions, arguing that the workers were not sufficiently educated or properly motivated to cooperate with management and that the owner would lose the power to make necessary economic decisions. Some argued that, because their workers would rather have the 15 percent of the

[56] See reports in *Oiga, Caretas,* and *Sociedad y Política,* Sept. 1970 through 1971; this was reconfirmed by interviews in INP and DESCO, July 1972.

profits distributed as hard cash than as shares, there would be an increase in worker cynicism and a tendency for workers to leave their jobs in order to redeem their shares upon termination, as provided by the law.[57] Further, it was objected that the law was drawn up without consultation.

Negative response on the part of industrialists and continued strikes and union agitation led to government warnings in October that "existing legal order in the field of labor" would be maintained and that the government would be inflexible in sanctioning all who continued to "create situations—workers, union leaders, or *empresarios*."[58] The annual meeting of executives held in November of that year marked the first sign of dialogue between the government and the industrial sector. President Velasco, although he attempted to persuade the industrialists that their true interests lay in accepting the new program (since workers would be more productive and more inclined to view the company's interest as their own)[59] nonetheless stated emphatically that there would be no compulsory cooperativization.[60] The resignation of the Minister of Industry and Commerce, who had promoted worker participation, and his replacement by a "technician" were thought to be favorable signs. A number of formal and informal meetings between government officials and businessmen as a result of the conference were taken as evidence that cooperative relations between the private sector and the military government might be restored.

However, the cycle reversed itself again in 1972 with the announcement that the government would promote the social-property sector. A major reason for the announcement was government frustration with low levels of investment. However, a second factor, and a very significant one in light of subsequent developments, was the view that the industrial communities did not take a sufficiently advanced view of worker participation. ICs are based on the principle of private property (with shares in the firm held by individuals, and the individual profit motive central to worker-management cooperation), rather than on a "social" or communal view of property; further, the elimination of "owners"

[57] Interview with Raymundo Duharte, president of the SNI, July 1972.
[58] *Caretas*, Sept. 30–Oct. 14, 1970.
[59] *La Crónica*, Nov. 16, 1970.
[60] *Caretas*, Nov. 20–Dec. 1, 1970.

makes *cogestión* (comanagement) unnecessary and substitutes the more radical principle of *autogestión* (self-management).[61] The changing concept of worker participation is thus as much a result of the government's frustration with labor as with the private sector.

The government's policy in the labor field did not produce the intended results of harmony between management and the workers or between labor and the government. Instead, there was a continuation of the previous pattern of frequent strikes involving major sectors of the economy, with the mining *sindicatos* exerting the most pressure. Continued independent activity on the part of the unions and some indications of industrial sabotage (in the state-owned steel mill),[62] suggest that the intent to co-opt worker activism with a "radical" worker participation program was not fully successful. The government has made repeated warnings that incidents fomented by union leaders will be "sanctioned with all the force of the law," and the APRA union federation (the CTP) has been undermined by government support of the Communist CGTP and by the creation of a new federation, the Central de Trabajadores de la Revolución Peruana (CTRP).

Although some strikes have been repressed, the government has not declared all strikes illegal. If we can apply James Payne's analysis of labor violence in *Labor and Politics in Peru,* strikes are a legitimate and recurring form of interest articulation in the Peruvian system.[63] The military appears to have adjusted itself to this reality, despite its ideological view that class conflict should be eliminated and despite what might be hypothesized as a strong motivation for any military government—its desire to impose order. It has also been successful in winning the cooperation of the Communist CGTP in support of controversial strike settlements and for its labor policy in general, although the CGTP has openly opposed the government for its brutality in dealing with "illegal" strikes. Strikes have not diminished in number and intensity, however, and there have been violent out-

[61] Interview, July 1972. See also interview with Jaroslav Vanek, consultant to the Peruvian government and chief promoter of the Yugoslav model of a worker-managed economy, in *Caretas,* Aug. 31–Sept. 11, 1970.

[62] *Oiga,* June 1, 1970.

[63] James Payne, *Labor and Politics in Peru: The System of Political Bargaining* (New Haven: Yale University Press, 1965).

breaks in support of the striking teachers' union, particularly in the Sierra.[64]

One of the more interesting facets of government-labor relations is the government's seeming inability to control the institutions it has set up to channel participation. In February 1973 it sponsored the National Congress of Industrial Communities, with seven hundred delegates "carefully prepared" by SINAMOS and the Ministry of Industries. The congress was billed as an open forum, one in which support for the program could be expressed and constructive criticisms solicited. The result was a surprising show of independence and a series of attacks on key government policies. The worker delegates asked for more representation and a veto power in management, and there were complaints that of the 10 percent net profits distributed each year, a disproportionate share went to the higher-paid employees. Motions were presented calling for "acceleration of the land distribution program, without compensation for expropriated landowners," a "complete nationalization of national resources,"[65] and conversion of the ICs to social property.

As a result, the congress became something of an embarrassment to the government. Its official position was that the workers' demands would result in the conversion of the "reformed private sector" (with comanagement through the industrial communities) into the equivalent of the self-managing social-property sector, and thus deny the ideological principle of a pluralist economy, a patently weak, formalistic defense. Further, unofficial statements indicate that the government opposed the congress on the grounds that it would become "a powerful political instrument superior to the parties themselves and to the union confederations." This was to be resisted because "such a national entity, unforeseen in the law of industrial communities, could come to represent a virtual time bomb against the pluralist, humanist, and libertarian revolutionary process itself, and prematurely accelerate its rhythm."[66]

In spite of government opposition, however, the National Con-

[64] See *Latin America*, Mar. 16, 1973, for a report on CGTP, and *Los Angeles Times*, Nov. 30, 1973, for an account of government repression and continued unrest. Resistance in Cuzco and Puno has been marked throughout the regime and has been largely student-led.

[65] *Latin America*, Mar. 9 (pp. 77–78) and Mar. 16 (pp. 85–90), 1973.

[66] *Oiga*, Mar. 2, 1973.

federation of Industrial Communities (CONACI) was formed and continues to raise the issues discussed by the congress and to seek an advisory relationship to the Ministry of Industry and Commerce. It has requested the right to collect dues from the two hundred thousand workers who are members of industrial communities.[67] Neither SINAMOS nor the ministry had any part in the creation of CONACI, and its formation is attributed to ultra-left-wing efforts to infiltrate the labor movement.[68] Nonetheless, President Velasco, Premier Mercado Jarrín, and others have met with representatives of CONACI, and Mercado Jarrín has agreed to consider changes in the rules governing the industrial communities, calling this National Congress "the most important mobilization of workers in the history of Peru."[69]

Although it seems that a *de facto* pattern of mutual adjustment has worked thus far, there is always the possibility that the government's view of what is desirable for the future of the revolution will narrow, or its tolerance be put to too strong a test— which could easily happen if the unions struck in opposition to the regime itself rather than pressing for changes within the general guidelines the military has set. There are very high stakes on both sides. At this point it can only be said that ideologically-motivated institutional "solutions" to labor-management problems have not worked as planned and that this has led both to a flexible policy and to a search for new approaches that will bring about the desired pattern of worker-management cooperation. Again, the social-property sector is being viewed as the most promising means to create a radically new form of participation while hopes decline for the success of the industrial communities as they were originally conceived.

REGIME LEGITIMACY AND IDEOLOGICAL POLITICS

The two patterns under comparison, that of the Belaúnde regime and that of the military regime headed by Velasco, could hardly provide a greater contrast. Belaúnde developed a *pro forma* ideology—one taken seriously by many of his supporters in AP and the military, perhaps, but intended by Belaúnde himself to serve more as propaganda. As a candidate, Belaúnde avoided the hard economic issues and presented much of his program as a re-

[67] *Oiga*, June 15, 1973.   [68] *Oiga*, June 28, 1973.
[69] *Oiga*, June 15, 1973.

turn to the inspiration of the Inca past, a tradition based on co-operative labor. He relied on his reformist image, government spending, and large doses of idealism to resolve conflicts.

Despite his weaknesses, however, Belaúnde lost the presidency in a military coup that seems difficult to account for using the traditional explanations of military intervention. The economy was showing clear signs of recovery and a new direction under the guidance of finance minister Ulloa, and Belaúnde's electoral alliance with APRA, if consolidated, would have guaranteed the AP-APRA coalition a solid popular victory at the polls the following June. Thus, there was neither an economic nor a political crisis to legitimize a military take-over. Further, the coup required an unusual degree of unanimity and decisiveness on the part of a particular group of military men who felt they had the ability, the program, and the potential popular support to restructure the Peruvian economy and society, conditions that seemed improbable in mid-1968.

In contrast to Belaúnde, the military has neither personal nor collective charisma. Its ideology is intended as a blueprint for a new society, not mere propaganda, and the Revolutionary Government has made a determined effort to destroy the old power structure rather than accommodate itself to the existing elites. Yet those strengths are also weaknesses. The military government is trying to build a new society on the basis of an unprecedented and perhaps fatally weak political combination. It can count on few resources: an ideology that is complex and difficult to implement effectively, a resourceful but divided group of administrators, and the unity of the military itself, which must be preserved at all costs if the ultimate threat of force is to remain credible. With the exception of the church, the old elites—exporters, landowners, industrialists—are under attack and in opposition to the government. The intellectuals are split, the press demoralized, and the government is under pressure from both the far Left and the conservative Right. Despite agrarian reform and worker participation, the Revolutionary Government has not been able to create a popular mass base. Nor has it resorted to a consistent strategy of utilizing nationalism to draw attention from the two internal challenges which, by its own ideology, must be met: the challenge of increased investment and production, and the challenge of authentic participation.

The military government has created a new pattern of policy

formulation and implementation. It begins by positing an ideological goal, then decrees a general law and a detailed set of regulations designed to implement the ideological objective. This is
followed by some awkward, even hostile, confrontations with
"reality" (e.g., persistent low levels of investment, continued
strikes), which inevitably result in official frustration and the
search for a new institutional arrangement that will more closely
approximate the original goal. The result is often a dizzying
spiral of rhetoric and policy which has the effect of destroying
the very institutions that were so recently created; this is clearly
the case with the industrial communities, but it may also be seen
in agrarian cooperatives and in the nationalization of the fishmeal
industry. As a result, it is unable to consolidate support on the
basis of one set of institutions or even establish a stable constel-
lation of ideological goals.

Within this revolutionary process—as the regime itself has
labeled it—there are three negative tendencies which could have
long-term consequences for the Peruvian experiment. First, as
specific institutional inventions fail to achieve desired goals, rhetoric escalates, and the ideology itself becomes more abstract. The
military is presently relying heavily on two slogans to describe
its philosophy; neither seems to have concrete meaning, nor do
they generate visible popular support. The first is that the Peruvian system is "neither communist nor capitalist," which refers
to the regime's intent to avoid the twin evils of individual ownership and state control of the economy. The alternative (or "third
solution") has been defined by a second slogan: the "pluralist
economy." This phrase has recently been used in such diverse
contexts that it has lost its specificity, and perhaps its credibility.[70] Broadly speaking, however, Peruvian pluralism retains
some of its North American connotations in the military's usage—
it suggests openness, a nonviolent and gradual progress toward
the goals of the revolution, and the existence of multiple, competing organizations (i.e., the absence of the vertical, hierarchical
organizations characteristic of corporatism). Like the phrase
"neither communism nor capitalism," however, it is more specific
about what is to be avoided than about the manner in which

[70] For a particularly revealing use of the term *pluralist economy* to avoid
discussing specifics of the social-property sector (Q: What will the social-property sector be like? A: It will be a part of the pluralist economy.), see the
interview with Arturo Valdez in *Oiga*, July 6, 1973.

plural institutions will operate in a traditional society undergoing revolution from above. As rhetoric escalates, the regime becomes more guarded on the issue of who can legitimately represent it. As of May 1974, only the prime minister and Velasco himself were "authorized" to make "general political statements"; other government ministers who did so would be forced to resign.[71]

Second, as the military's ideology becomes more abstract, it also tends to become more "radical" in the sense that it feeds on itself, moving further away from real confrontation with the institutions it is attempting to restructure. One example of this tendency is the idealized view of the workers that has emerged in the process of changing the officially favored model of worker participation from industrial communities to the social-property sector. In theory, workers in this sector will no longer work primarily for private gain, but for the increasing benefits available to the community and for the rewards of solidarity. In the words of a high government official:

It must be understood that the notion of profit, of personal gain, loses its human and historical importance next to solidarity, to the generous offer (of oneself), to social participation. To work intensely, with faith, with enthusiasm, with conviction, with a just wage . . . is incomparably more important and more worthy than working for oneself. . . .[72]

In this highly charged ideological atmosphere, the regime may be forming institutions that have little relation to the needs of the workers themselves. It is not clear, for example, whether workers would choose participation—much less solidarity—over increases in salary and benefits.[73] Recently, rightist opponents of

71 *Latin American Report*, vol. 1, no. 10 (May 1972), p. 7.

72 This is from a speech by Jorge Fernández Maldonado, minister of energy and mines, reprinted in *Oiga*, June 1, 1973. Fernández Maldonado has been developing this approach to worker participation over a period of time. See *Oiga*, Feb. 9, 1973. This position is not unrelated to the AP promotion of the "cult of work" (*Manual Ideológico*, p. 57), with the significant difference that the military regime will attempt to devise an institutional means of implementing it rather than declaring it a principle and then returning to business as usual.

73 See an interesting discussion of this question in Charles W. Anderson,

the regime have publicized demands by *campesinos* in the north that the agrarian reform be stopped: employees of SINAMOS were accused of promoting "forced collectivization" of small holdings.[74] And while in practice the military has avoided measures that would redistribute the wealth and advantages of the middle classes, its ideological pronouncements have moved further toward erasing the distinctions between the middle classes and the "workers." Should this tendency be carried to its farthest extreme, there is the possibility of a Chilean-type polarization which could jeopardize consensus within the military, an institution composed of a majority of individuals committed to the pursuit of upward mobility and competitive consumerism.

The traditional isolation of the military from the rest of the society[75] creates a third tendency: the proclivity to decree political solutions in a social vacuum. Closer networks of personal ties and clientele obligations might act as a restraining influence or facilitate policy implementation. Yet for many reasons, including the historic distance between the military and the upper classes, the rapid expansion of the state bureaucracy since 1968, and the military's commitment to "moralistic" values which are in conflict with clientelism, such an informal network appears weak or almost nonexistent. Peru's leaders do not control the levers of a corporatist or authoritarian society,[76] nor have they yet established chains of clientele linkages on the basis of patronage and public expenditures. Further, since the requirements of institutional unity inhibit the development of charismatic leadership

---

"Public Policy, Pluralism, and the Further Evolution of Advanced Industrial Society," paper presented to the 1973 APSA convention, New Orleans, Sept. 4–8, 1973.

[74] See *Oiga*, July 20 and July 6, 1973.

[75] See Einaudi, *Peruvian Military Relations*, Villanueva, *Nueva mentalidad*, and Bourricaud, "Los militares."

[76] See Susan Kaufman Purcell, "Decision-Making in an Authoritarian Regime: Theoretical Implications from a Mexican Case Study," *World Politics*, vol. 26, no. 1 (Oct. 1973), pp. 28–54; R. Rogowski and L. Wasserspring, "Does Political Development Exist? Corporatism in Old and New Societies" (Beverly Hills, Calif.: Sage Publications, 1971); and various articles by Juan Linz and Philippe Schmitter. For applications of the concept to Peru, see Julio Cotler, *Bases*; David Collier, "Squatter Settlement Formation and the Politics of Co-optation in Peru" (Ph.D. dissertation, University of Chicago, 1971); and Scott Palmer, "Revolution from Above," chap. 1; and James M. Malloy, "Populismo militar en el Perú y Bolivia: Antecedentes y posibilidades futuras," *Estudios Andinos*, vol. 2, no. 2 (1971–1972), pp. 113–134.

and the creation of a party of the revolution, the issue of participation is defined in economic terms, a view which, ironically, recalls APRA's goal of functional democracy.

The military fears political mobilization because it cannot control it. When economic mobilization, deemed necessary for integration and growth, proved to have political side effects, the regime's response was pluralism. In the Peruvian ideal of a pluralist economy, individuals are mobilized, but there are no large-scale concentrations of power which might compete with the state, hence the Revolutionary Government's opposition to the National Congress of Industrial Communities as a threat to pluralism. And ideally, competition among groups reduces the need for direct state intervention, costly from both a political and economic standpoint.

However, the absence of the prerequisites for a truly pluralist society in a country with little experience with popular organizations or grass roots political initiative is an issue the regime refuses to confront. Existing organizations which might become true interest groups and make demands on the government are declared illegitimate by virtue of their pre-Revolutionary origins. New groups may function only within the limits set by the government under the watchful eye of SINAMOS, and independent groups which oppose the regime risk sanctions or outright proscription. The development of a number of competing participant units is a goal, but one that is reserved for an ideal future when the Revolution is firmly established.

The three tendencies outlined above will have their effects in the long run. For the present the military government will remain in power because it has a monopoly of force and because it has not yet reached the limits of ideological politics. It is aided by the fact that its opponents are divided and have been unable to offer better solutions with greater appeal to the "masses," the middle classes, or to those within the military itself who might ally themselves with civilian opposition. This regime may well survive; it has already made significant advances in changing the structure of Peruvian society, and has developed ideological alternatives that will be copied elsewhere. It is not yet clear, however, whether it will be able to create a sound institutional base to give substance to the Revolution in Peru.

Appendix

Guide to the Study of Contemporary Peru

Abraham F. Lowenthal

This appendix is intended to help those who wish to pursue further research on Peru. It is by no means an exhaustive bibliography: the footnotes to the individual chapters are often more complete on particular points, and even those references are selective. My aim has been simply to provide some guidance regarding where to turn first for useful material. I gratefully acknowledge the suggestions colleagues have provided, and particularly the many entries on economic matters furnished by Shane Hunt.

I. GENERAL INTRODUCTION TO PERU

I know of no satisfactory general introduction to modern Peru in any language. Probably the best book is François Bourricaud, *Power and Society in Contemporary Peru*, New York: Praeger, 1970; but Bourricaud presumes considerable familiarity with Peru. Other general works in English include Carlos A. Astiz, *Pressure Groups and Power Elites in Peruvian Politics*, Ithaca, N.Y.: Cornell University Press, 1969, and Fredrick Pike, *The Modern History of Peru*, New York: Praeger, 1967, but each book may be severely criticized for shortcomings in interpretation; Pike's work is overwhelmingly anti-Aprista, and Astiz strongly exaggerates the supposedly immutable character of Peru's social order.

Additional general sources on Peru's history and society are:

American University, Foreign Area Studies Division. *Area Handbook for Peru*. Washington, D.C.: Government Printing Office, 1972.
Basadre, Jorge. *Historia de la República del Perú*, 5th ed. Lima: Historia, 1961.

Basadre, Jorge. *Perú, problema y posibilidad: ensayo de una sín-tesis de la evolución histórica del Perú*. Lima: Editorial Rosay, 1931.

Bergman, Arlene, and Larson, Magali. *Social Stratification in Peru*. Berkeley: University of California, Institute of Interna-tional Studies, 1969.

Chaplin, David (ed.). *Peruvian Nationalism: A Corporatist Rev-olution*. New Brunswick, N.J.: Transaction Books, forthcom-ing.

Delgado, Carlos. *Problemas sociales en el Perú contemporáneo*. (Perú Problema no. 6) Lima: Instituto de Estudios Peruanos, 1971.

Martínez de la Torre, Ricardo. *Apuntes para una interpretación marxista de historia social del Perú*. Lima: Empresa Editorial Peruana, 1947.

Matos Mar, José, et al. *Perú, hoy*. Mexico City: Siglo XXI, 1971.
———. *Perú problema no. 1: 5 ensayos*. Lima: Instituto de Estudios Peruanos, 1968.

Peru has been the subject of an extensive and excellent anthro-pological literature. Among the main sources are:

Adams, Richard N. *A Community in the Andes: Problems and Progress in Muquiyauyo*. Seattle: University of Washington Press, 1959.

Doughty, Paul L. *Huaylas: An Andean District in Search of Prog-ress*. Ithaca, N.Y.: Cornell University Press, 1968.

Holmberg, Allan R., et al. *Vicos: método y práctica de antropo-logía aplicada*. Lima: Editorial Estudios Andinos, 1966.

Patch, Richard. Periodic reports on Peru in American University Field Staff, *West Coast South America Series*. New York: 1960–1971.

II. PERU'S POLITICAL SYSTEM

A. General

Alberti, Giorgio. "Inter-Village Systems and Development: A Study of Social Change in Highland Peru" (Latin American Studies Program, Dissertation Series; mimeo). Ithaca, N.Y.: Cornell University, 1970.

Chaplin, David. "Peru's Postponed Revolution," *World Poli-tics*, vol. 20 (Apr. 1968), pp. 393–420.

————. "Peruvian Social Mobility: Revolution and Development Potential," *Journal of Inter-American Studies*, vol. 10, no. 4 (Oct. 1968), pp. 547–570.

Cotler, Julio. "Crisis política y populismo militar en el Perú," *Revista Mexicana de Sociología*, vol. 32, no. 3 (Apr.–June 1970), pp. 737–784.

————. "The Mechanics of Internal Domination and Social Change in Peru," *Studies in Comparative International Development*, vol. 3, no. 12 (1968), pp. 229–246.

Dew, Edward. *Politics in the Altiplano: The Dynamics of Change in Rural Peru*. Austin: University of Texas Press, 1969.

Dobyns, Henry F., and Vásquez, Mario C. (eds.). *Migración e integración en el Perú*. Lima: Editorial Estudios Andinos, Monografías Andinas, no. 2, 1963.

Epstein, Erwin H. "Education and *Peruanidad:* 'Internal' Colonialism in the Peruvian Highlands," *Comparative Education Review*, vol. 15 (June 1971), pp. 188–201.

Fishel, John T. "Politics and Progress in the Peruvian Sierra: A Comparative Study of Development in Two Districts." Unpublished doctoral dissertation, Indiana University, 1971.

Jaquette, Jane S. "The Politics of Development in Peru" (Latin American Studies Program, Dissertation Series; mimeo). Ithaca, N.Y.: Cornell University, 1971.

McCoy, Terry L. "Congress, the President, and Political Instability in Peru," in Weston H. Agor (ed.), *Latin American Legislatures: Their Role and Influence*. New York: Praeger, 1971.

Matos Mar, José, et al. *Dominación y cambio en el Perú rural*. Lima: Instituto de Estudios Peruanos, 1969.

Quijano Obregón, Aníbal. "Tendencies in Peruvian Development and in the Class Structure," in James Petras and Maurice Zeitlin (eds.), *Latin America: Reform or Revolution?* Greenwich, Conn.: Fawcett Publications, 1968.

Vandendries, René. "An Appraisal of the Reformist Development Strategy of Peru," in Robert E. Scott (ed.), *Latin American Modernization Problems*. Urbana: University of Illinois Press, 1973.

Yepes del Castillo, Ernesto. *Perú 1820–1920: un siglo de desarrollo capitalista*. Lima: Instituto de Estudios Peruanos, Campodónico Ed., 1972.

Zuzunaga Florez, Carlos. "La situación del Perú en 1967: ensayo de hipótesis causales y de proyecciones pasivas," in *El Perú en la próxima década*. Lima: Acción para el Desarrollo, 1968.

B. *Main Actors in Peruvian Politics*

1. PEASANTS

Alberti, Giorgio. "The Breakdown of Provincial Urban Power Structure and the Rise of Peasant Movements," *Sociologia Ruralis*, vol. 12, no. 3/4 (1972), pp. 315–333.

Ani Castillo, Gonzalo. *Historia secreta de las guerrillas*. Lima: Ediciones Más Allá, 1967.

Blanco, Hugo. *Land or Death: The Peasant Struggle in Peru*. New York: Pathfinder Press, 1972.

Bourque, Susan C. "Cholification and the Campesino: A Study of Three Peruvian Peasant Organizations in the Process of Social Change" (Latin American Studies Program, Dissertation Series; mimeo). Ithaca, N.Y.: Cornell University, 1971.

Campbell, Leon G. "The Historiography of the Peruvian Guerrilla Movement," *Latin American Research Review*, vol. 8, no. 1 (Spring 1973), pp. 45–70.

Cotler, Julio, and Portocarrero, Felipe. "Peru: Peasant Organizations," in Henry Landsberger (ed.), *Latin American Peasant Movements*. Ithaca, N.Y.: Cornell University Press. 1969.

Craig, Wesley. "The Peasant Movement of La Convención," in Henry Landsberger (ed.), *Latin American Peasant Movements*. Ithaca, N.Y.: Cornell University Press, 1969.

Gott, Richard. *Guerrilla Movements in Latin America*. New York: Doubleday, 1971, pp. 307–394.

Handelman, Howard. "Struggle in the Andes: Peasant Political Mobilization in Peru." Unpublished doctoral dissertation, University of Wisconsin, 1971.

Mercado, Rogger. *Las guerrillas del Perú*. Lima: Fondo de Cultura Popular, 1967.

Neira, Hugo. *Cuzco, tierra y muerte*. Lima: Ediciones Populares, 1963.

———. "Sindicalismo campesino y complejos regionales agricolas (Peru: 1960–1970)," *Aportes*, no. 18 (Oct. 1970), pp. 27–67.

Quijano Obregón, Aníbal. "Contemporary Peasant Movements," in Seymour Martin Lipset and Aldo Solasi (eds.), *Elites in Latin America*. New York: Oxford University Press, 1967.

Tullis, F. LaMond. *Lord and Peasant in Peru: A Paradigm of Political and Social Change*. Cambridge, Mass.: Harvard University Press, 1970.

2. "OLIGARCHY"

Bourricaud, François, et al. *La oligarquía en el Perú*. (Perú Problema no. 2). Lima: Instituto de Estudios Peruanos, Moncloa-Campodónico Ed., 1969.

Malpica, Carlos. *Los dueños del Perú*, 3d ed. Lima: Ediciones Ensayos Sociales, 1968.

Spaey, Phillipe. *L'élite politique péruvienne*. Paris: Editions Universitaires, 1972.

Stephens, Richard H. *Wealth and Power in Peru*. Metuchen, N.J.: The Scarecrow Press, 1971.

3. LABOR

Mejía Valera, J., "El comportamiento del obrero peruano," *Aportes*, no. 24 (Apr. 1972), pp. 101–115.

Payne, James L. *Labor and Politics in Peru*. New Haven: Yale University Press, 1965.

4. URBAN MIGRANTS

Andrews, Frank M., and Phillips, George W. "The Squatters of Lima: Who They Are and What They Want," *Journal of Developing Areas*, vol. 4, no. 2 (Jan. 1970), pp. 211–224.

Collier, David. *Squatters and Oligarchs: Modernization and Public Policy in Peru*. Baltimore: Johns Hopkins Press, forthcoming.

———. "Squatter Settlements and Migrant Adaptation in Lima," *Monograph Series on Migration and Development*, Massachusetts Institute of Technology, Cambridge, Mass., 1975.

Dietz, Henry A. "The Office and the Poblador: Perceptions and Manipulations of Housing Authorities by the Lima

Urban Poor." Unpublished paper presented at the meeting of the American Society for Public Administration, Los Angeles, Apr. 1973.

―――. "Urban Squatter Settlements in Peru: A Case History and Analysis," *Journal of Inter-American Studies*, vol. 2, no. 3 (July 1969), pp. 353–370.

Goldrich, Daniel, et al. "The Political Integration of Lower-Class Urban Settlements in Chile and Peru," *Studies in Comparative International Development*, vol. 3, no. 1 (1967–1968), pp. 1–22.

Mangin, William. "Squatter Settlements," *Scientific American*, vol. 217, no. 4 (Oct. 1967), pp. 21–29.

Matos Mar, José. "Migration and Urbanization—The 'Barriadas' of Lima: An Example of Integration into Urban Life," in P. M. Hauser (ed.), *Urbanization in Latin America*. New York: Columbia University Press, 1961, pp. 170–190.

Powell, Sandra. "Political Participation in the Barriadas: A Case Study," *Comparative Political Studies*, vol. 2 (July 1969), pp. 195–215.

5. MILITARY

Astiz, Carlos A. "The Military Establishment as a Political Elite: The Peruvian Case," in David H. Pollock and Arch R. M. Ritter (eds.), *Latin American Prospects for the 1970's: What Kinds of Revolutions?* New York: Praeger, 1973, pp. 203–229.

―――, and García, José Z. "The Peruvian Military: Achievement Orientation, Training, and Political Tendencies," *Western Political Quarterly*, vol. 25, no. 4 (Dec. 1972), pp. 667–685.

Bourricaud, François. "Voluntarismo y experimentación. Los militares peruanos: manos a la obra." *Mundo Nuevo* no. 54 (Dec. 1970), pp. 4–16.

Einaudi, Luigi R. "The Military and Government in Peru," in Clarence E. Thurber and Lawrence S. Graham (eds.), *Development Administration in Latin America*. Durham, N.C.: Duke University Press, 1973.

―――. *The Peruvian Military: A Summary Political Analysis*. Santa Monica, Calif.: Rand Corporation, May, 1969.

————. "Revolution from Within—Military Rule in Peru Since 1968," *Studies in Comparative International Development*, vol. 8, no. 1 (Spring 1973), pp. 71–87.

Gerlach, Allen. "Civil-Military Relations in Peru: 1914–1945." Unpublished doctoral dissertation, University of New Mexico, 1973.

Johnson, Charles W. "Perú: los militares como un agente de cambio económico," *Revista Mexicana de Sociología*, vol. 34, no. 2 (Apr.–June 1972), pp. 293–316.

Malloy, James M. "Dissecting the Peruvian Military: A Review Essay," *Journal of Inter-American Studies and World Affairs*, vol. 15, no. 3 (Aug. 1973), pp. 375–382.

Mercado Jarrín, Edgardo. "Insurgency in Latin America," *Military Review*, vol. 49, no. 3 (Mar. 1969), pp. 10–20.

Rozman, Stephen L. "The Evolution of the Political Role of the Peruvian Military," *Journal of Inter-American Studies*, vol. 12, no. 4 (Oct. 1970), pp. 539–564.

Suárez, M. D. "Militares y oligarquía en el Perú,"*Mundo Nuevo*, no. 43 (Jan. 1970), pp. 19–24.

Valdéz Pallete, Luis. "Antecedentes de la nueva orientación de las fuerzas armadas en el Perú," *Aportes*, no. 19 (Jan. 1971), pp. 163–181.

Villanueva, Víctor. *El CAEM y la revolución de la Fuerza Armada.* Lima: Instituto de Estudios Peruanos, 1973.

————. *100 años del ejército peruano: frustraciones y cambios.* Lima: Editorial Juan Mejía Baca, 1972.

————. *El militarismo en el Perú.* Lima: Scheuch, 1962.

————. *¿Nueva mentalidad militar en el Perú?* Lima: Editorial Juan Mejía Baca, 1968.

6. CHURCH

Astiz, Carlos A. "The Catholic Church in Latin America Politics: A Case Study of Peru," in David H. Pollock and Arch R. M. Ritter (eds.), *Latin American Prospects for the 1970's: What Kinds of Revolutions?* New York: Praeger, 1973.

Comisión Episcopal del Perú. *Documento del episcopado peruano sobre "La justicia en el mundo."* Lima: Comisión Episcopal, 1969.

Drury, John (trans.). *Between Honesty and Hope: Documents about the Church in Latin America. Issued at Lima*

by the Peruvian Bishops' Commission for Social Action.
Maryknoll, N.Y.: Maryknoll Publications, 1970.

Macaulay, Michael G. "Ideological Change and Internal
Cleavages in the Peruvian Church: Change, Status Quo,
and the Priest; The Case of Onis." Unpublished doctoral
dissertation, Notre Dame University, 1972.

Pike, Fredrick B. "The Catholic Church and Modernization
in Peru and Chile," *Journal of International Affairs,* vol.
20 (1966), pp. 272–288.

7. PARTIES

Clinton, Richard L. "APRA: An Appraisal," *Journal of Inter-American Studies,* vol. 12, no. 2 (Apr. 1970), pp. 280–
297.

Epstein, Edward. "Multinational Bases for Loyalty in the
Peruvian Aprista Party." Unpublished doctoral dissertation, University of Illinois, 1972.

Forrester, Virginia O'Grady. "Christian Democracy in Peru."
Unpublished doctoral dissertation, Columbia University,
1970.

Hilliker, Grant. *The Politics of Reform in Peru: The Aprista
and Other Mass Parties of Latin America.* Baltimore: Johns
Hopkins Press, 1971.

Kantor, Harry. *The Ideology and Program of the Peruvian
Aprista Movement.* Washington, D.C.: Savile Books, 1966.

Klarén, Peter F. *Modernization, Dislocation, and Aprismo:
Origins of the Peruvian Aprista Party, 1870–1932.* Austin:
University of Texas Press, 1973.

North, Liisa. "The Origins and Development of the Peruvian
Aprista Party." Unpublished doctoral dissertation, University of California, Berkeley, 1973.

Villanueva, Víctor. *La tragedia de un pueblo y de un
partido: páginas para la historia del Apra.* Lima: 3d Edición popular, 1957.

8. FOREIGN INFLUENCES

Bollinger, William S. "The Rise of United States Influence
in the Peruvian Economy, 1869–1921." Unpublished master's thesis, University of California at Los Angeles, 1971.

Brundenius, Claes. "The Anatomy of Imperialism: The Case

of the Multinational Mining Corporations in Peru," *Journal of Peace Research*, 1972 series, no. 3, pp. 189–208.

Carey, James C. *Peru and the United States: 1900–1962.* Notre Dame, Ind.: University of Notre Dame Press, 1964.

Dye, Richard W. "Peru, the United States, and Hemispheric Relations," *Inter-American Economic Affairs*, vol. 26, no. 2 (Autumn 1972), pp. 69–88.

Goodwin, Richard. "Letter from Peru," *New Yorker* (May 17, 1969), pp. 41–109.

Peeler, John. "Foreign Aid, Influence, and Tax Administration in Peru," *Inter-American Economic Affairs*, vol. 22, no. 4 (Spring 1969), pp. 19–29.

Sharp, Daniel A. (ed.). *U.S. Foreign Policy and Peru.* Austin: University of Texas Press, 1972.

U.S., Congress., Senate, Committee on Foreign Relations. *United States Relations with Peru.* Hearings before the Subcommittee on Western Hemisphere Affairs of the Committee on Foreign Relations. 91st Cong., 1st sess., Apr. 14, 16, and 17, 1969.

III. PERUVIAN POLITICAL HISTORY

Alianza Acción Popular–Demócrata Cristiano. *Bases para el Plan de Gobierno.* Lima, 1963.

Bejar Rivera, Héctor. *Perú 1965: una experiencia libertadora en América.* Mexico City: Siglo Veintiuno Ed., 1969.

Chirinos Soto, Enrique. *Cuenta y balance de las elecciones de 1962.* Lima: Ediciones Perú, 1962.

Cornejo Chávez, Héctor. *Nuevos principios para un nuevo Perú.* Lima, 1960.

———. Ediciones del Sol, *Qué se propone la Democracia Cristiana,* Lima, 1962.

De la Puente Uceda, Luis F. "The Peruvian Revolution," *Monthly Review*, vol. 17, no. 6 (Nov. 1965), pp. 12–28.

Karno, Howard. "Augusto B. Leguía: The Oligarchy and the Modernization of Peru, 1870–1930." Unpublished doctoral dissertation, University of California at Los Angeles, 1970.

Martínez G., S. *Ideario y plan de gobierno de los partidos políticos.* Lima: Industrial Gráfica, 1962.

Payne, Arnold. *The Peruvian Coup d'Etat of 1962: The Over-*

throw of Manuel Prado. Washington, D.C., Institute for the Comparative Study of Political Systems, 1968.

Pike, Fredrick B. "Peru and the Quest for Reform by Compromise," *Inter-American Economic Affairs,* vol. 20, no. 4 (Spring 1967), pp. 23–38.

Salazar Bondy, Augusto. *Entre Escila y Caribdis.* Lima: Instituto Nacional de Cultura, 1973.

Villanueva, Víctor. *Un año bajo el sable.* Lima: Scheuch, 1963.

IV. Main Issues in Peruvian Politics

Alexander, Robert J. (ed.). *Aprismo: The Ideas and Doctrines of Victor Raúl Haya de la Torre.* Kent, Ohio: Kent State University Press, 1973.

Baines, John M. *Revolution in Peru: Mariátegui and the Myth.* University, University of Alabama Press, 1972.

Belaúnde, Victor Andrés. *La realidad nacional.* 3d ed. Lima: Ediciones Mercurio Peruano, 1963.

Belaúnde Terry, Fernando. *Peru's Own Conquest.* Lima: American Studies Press, 1965.

Chavarría, Jesús. "The Intellectuals and the Crisis of Modern Peruvian Nationalism: 1870–1919," *Hispanic American Historical Review,* vol. 50, no. 2 (May 1970), pp. 257–278.

Davies, Thomas M., Jr. *Indian Integration in Peru: A Half Century of Experience, 1900–1948.* Lincoln: University of Nebraska Press, 1974.

———. "The Indigenismo of the Peruvian Aprista Party: A Reinterpretation," *Hispanic American Historical Review,* vol. 51 (Nov. 1971), pp. 626–645.

González Prada, Manuel. *Horas de lucha.* Buenos Aires: Americalee, 1946.

Haya de la Torre, Víctor Raúl. *El antiimperialismo y el Apra.* 2d ed., Santiago: Ediciones Ercilla, 1936.

———. *Pensamiento político.* 5 vols. Lima: Ediciones Pueblos, 1961.

Mariátegui, José Carlos. *Seven Interpretive Essays on Peruvian Reality.* Austin: University of Texas Press, 1971.

Paulston, Rolland G. *Society, Schools, and Progress in Peru.* New York: Pergamon Press, 1971.

Plank, John N. "Peru: A Study in the Problems of Nation-Forming." Unpublished doctoral dissertation, Harvard University, 1958.

V. THE PERUVIAN "REVOLUTION"

A. General

Aguirre Gamio, Hernando. "El proceso revolucionario peruano," *Cuadernos Americanos*, vol. 187, no. 2 (Mar.–Apr. 1973), pp. 17–45.

Bourricaud, François. "Los militares: ¿Por qué y para qué?" *Aportes*, no. 16 (April 1970), pp. 13–55.

Comité de Asesoramiento de la Presidencia de la República. *La revolución nacional peruana: 1968–1972*. Lima, 1972.

Cornejo, Raúl-Estuardo. *Velasco, o el proceso de una revolución*. Lima: CEPEID, 1969.

Delgado Olivera, Carlos. *Testimonio de lucha*. Lima: Editorial Peisa, 1973.

Frías, Ismael. *La revolución peruana y la vía socialista*. Lima: Editorial Horizonte, 1970.

García, José Z. "Military Government in Peru, 1968–1971." Unpublished doctoral dissertation, University of New Mexico, Albuquerque, 1973.

Graham Hurtado, José. *Filosofía de la revolución peruana*. Lima: Oficina Nacional de Información, 1971.

Hobsbawm, E. J. "Peru: The 'Peculiar' Revolution," *New York Review of Books*, Dec. 16, 1971, pp. 33–34ff.

Jaquette, Jane S. "Revolution by Fiat: The Context of Policy-Making in Peru," *Western Political Quarterly*, vol. 25, no. 4 (Dec. 1972), pp. 648–666.

Klitgaard, Robert. "Observations on the Peruvian National Plan of Development 1971–1975," *Inter-American Economic Affairs*, vol. 25, no. 3 (Winter 1971), pp. 3–22.

Letts, Ricardo [Pumaruna]. *Perú: mito de la revolución militar*. Caracas: Ediciones Barbara, 1971.

Malloy, James M. "Authoritarianism, Corporatism, and Mobilization in Peru," *Review of Politics*, vol. 36, no. 1 (Jan. 1974), pp. 52–84.

———. "Populismo militar en el Perú y Bolivia: antecedentes

y posibilidades futuras," *Estudios Andinos*, vol. 2, no. 2 (1971–1972), pp. 113–136.

Palmer, David Scott. "Revolution from Above: Military Government and Popular Participation in Peru, 1968–1972," (Latin American Studies Program, Dissertation Series; mimeo). Ithaca, N.Y.: Cornell University, 1971.

————, and Rodríguez Beruff, Jorge. "The Peruvian Military Government: The Problems of Popular Participation," *Bulletin of the Institute of Development Studies* (University of Sussex), vol. 4, no. 4 (Sept. 1972), pp. 4–15.

Petras, James, and Laporte, R. *Perú: ¿transformación revolucionaria o modernización?* Buenos Aires: Amorrortu Editores, 1971.

Quijano Obregón, Aníbal. *Nacionalismo, neoimperialismo, y militarismo en el Perú*. Buenos Aires: Ediciones Periferia, 1971.

Velasco Alvarado, Juan. *Velasco: La voz de la revolución*. Lima: Editorial Ausonia, 1972.

B. *Reforms and Policies*

1. AGRARIAN REFORM

Aguirre Gamio, Hernando. "El proceso de la reforma agraria en el Perú," *Mundo Nuevo*, no. 43 (Jan. 1970), pp. 24–35.

Alberti, Giorgio, and Cotler, Julio. "La reforma agraria en las haciendas azucareras del Perú" (mimeo). Lima: Instituto de Estudios Peruanos, 1971.

Alderson-Smith, Gavin. "Peasant Response to Cooperativization under Agrarian Reform in the Communities of the Peruvian Sierra." Paper presented at the Ninth International Congress of Anthropological and Ethnological Sciences, Chicago, Aug. 28–31, 1973.

Carroll, Thomas F. "Land Reform in Peru," *AID Spring Review of Land Reform*, June 1970, 2d ed., vol. 6 (Land Reform in Bolivia, Ecuador, and Peru), country papers.

DeProspro, Ernest R., Jr. "The Administration of the Peruvian Land Reform." Unpublished doctoral dissertation, Pennsylvania State University, 1967.

Gall, Norman. "Peru: The Master Is Dead," *Dissent*, vol. 18, no. 3 (June 1971), pp. 281–320.

Gitlitz, John S. "Impressions of the Peruvian Agrarian Reform," *Journal of Inter-American Studies*, vol. 13, nos. 3–4 (July–Oct. 1971), pp. 456–474.

———. "Opposition to the Peruvian Agrarian Reform." Unpublished paper, University of North Carolina, May 1974.

Horton, Douglas E. "Haciendas and Cooperatives: A Preliminary Study of Latifundist Agriculture and Agrarian Reform in Northern Peru." Land Tenure Center, University of Wisconsin, Madison, Research Paper no. 53, Sept. 1973, mimeo.

LaFosse de Vega-Centeno, Violeta Sara. "La ley de reforma agraria (No. 17716) y sus implicaciones en la estructura familiar" (mimeo). Lima: CISEPA, 1969.

MacDonald, Alfonse (ed.). *La reforma agraria en dos complejos agro-industriales, Cayaltí y Tumán*. Lima: Pontificia Universidad Católica del Perú, 1970.

MacLean y Estenos, Roberto. "La reforma agraria en el Perú," *Derecho y Reforma Agraria*, vol. 4, no. 4 (Mar. 1973), pp. 11–199.

Mann, Fred (ed.). *Preliminary Analysis: Agrarian Reform Law No. 17716*. USAID, 1969.

McClintock, Cynthia. "The Impact of Agrarian Reform Organizations on Members' Attitudes and Behavior in Peru." Unpublished paper, Massachusetts Institute of Technology, May 1974.

Middlebrook, Kevin. "Land for the Tiller: Political Participation in the Peruvian Military's Agrarian Reform." Unpublished B.A. thesis, Harvard University, 1972.

Pásara, Luis. "El primer año de vigencia de la ley de reforma agraria," mimeo. Lima: DESCO, 1970.

Strasma, John. "The United States and Agrarian Reform in Peru," in Daniel A. Sharp (ed.), *U.S. Foreign Policy and Peru*. Austin: University of Texas Press, 1973.

Van de Wetering, Hylke. "The Current State of Land Reform in Peru," *LTC Newsletter*, no. 40 (Apr.–June 1973), pp. 5–9.

2. INDUSTRIAL REFORM

De Las Casas, Pedro; De Las Casas, Angel; and Llosa, Augusto. *Análisis de la participación de la comunidad in-*

dustrial en el capital social de la empresa. Lima: Universidad del Pacifico, 1970.

DESCO. Centro de Estudios y Promoción del Desarrollo. *Manual del comunero industrial.* Lima: Campodónico, 1972.

Gouverneur, Jacques. "La reforme de l'entreprise au Pérou," *Cultures et Développement,* no. 9 (1972) pp. 707–730.

Pásara, Luis, and Santistevan, Jorge. " 'Industrial Communities' and Trade Unions in Peru: A Preliminary Analysis," *International Labor Review,* vol. 108, no. 2–3 (Aug.–Sept. 1973), pp. 127–142.

Pearson, Donald. "The Comunidad Industrial: Peru's Experiment in Worker Management," *Inter-American Economic Affairs,* vol. 27, no. 1 (Summer 1973), pp. 15–29.

3. ECONOMIC POLICY

Ballantyne, Janet. "The Political Economy of Peruvian *Gran Minería.*" Unpublished doctoral dissertation, Cornell University Business School, 1974.

Ferrer, Esteban, "Peru: The General as Revolutionary," *Columbia Journal of World Business,* vol. 5, no. 6 (Nov.–Dec. 1970).

Figueroa, Adolfo. "El impacto de las reformas actuales sobre la distribución de ingresos en el Perú," *Apuntes,* vol. 1, no. 1 (1973), pp. 67–82.

Mallon, Richard D. "Reform of Property Ownership and Income Distribution in Peru." Unpublished paper, Harvard University, Dec. 1973.

Mesa-Lago, Carmelo. "Social Security Stratification and Inequality in Latin America: The Case of Peru." Unpublished paper, University of Pittsburgh, 1973.

Strasma, John. "Some Economic Aspects of Non-Violent Revolution in Chile and Peru, with Emphasis on the Mining and Manufacturing Sectors." Unpublished paper, University of Wisconsin, 1971.

Utley, Jon. "Doing Business with Latin Nationalists," *Harvard Business Review,* vol. 51, no. 1 (Jan.–Feb. 1973), pp. 77–86.

4. EDUCATIONAL REFORM

Carpio Becerra, Alfredo. "La reforma educativa en marcha," *Ministerio de Educación Pública* (March 1973).

Escobar, Alberto. "Reforma o contrareforma: las paradojas de la ley universitaria," *Aportes*, no. 15 (Jan. 1970), pp. 6–12.

Molina, Guillermo et al. *Detrás del mito de la educación peruana*. Lima: DESCO, 1972.

Perú. Ministerio de Educación. Comisión de Reforma de la Educación. *Reforma de la educación peruana: informe general*. Lima, 1970.

5. SOCIAL PROPERTY

Abusada Salah, Roberto. "Propiedad social: algunas consideraciones económicas." CISEPA Serie de Documento de Trabajo no. 12, Oct. 1973.

Pásara, Luis. "Propiedad social: la utopia y el proyecto." CISEPA Serie de Documento de Trabajo no. 13, Oct. 1973.

Vanek, Jaroslav. "The Economics of the Peruvian Law Defining the Self-Managed Sector of Social Property." Cornell University, Department of Economics, Working Paper no. 62 (mimeo). Ithaca, N.Y., 1973.

VI. PERU'S ECONOMY

A. Macroeconomic Policy, Money, and Finance

Baker, Arnold, and Falero, Frank. "Money, Exports, Government Spending and Income in Peru, 1951–1966," *Journal of Development Studies*, vol. 7 (July 1971), pp. 353–364.

Ferrero, Rómulo. "Economic Development of Peru," in Committee for Economic Development, *Economic Development Issues: Latin America* (CED Supplementary Paper no. 21). New York, 1967, pp. 211–259.

Grieve, Jorge. "Análisis de la economía peruana, 1950–1962," *Revista de la Facultad de Ciencias Económicas y Comerciales*, UNMSM, no. 68 (Jan.–June 1964), pp. 86–135.

Hayn, Rolf. "Peruvian Exchange Controls, 1945–1948," *Inter-American Economic Affairs*, vol. 10 (Spring 1957), pp. 47–70.

O'Mara, G. T., and Garrido-Lecca, Guillermo. "The Urban Informal Credit Market in a Developing Country under Financial Repression: The Peruvian Case" (mimeo). 1972.

Taylor, Milton. "Problems of Development in Peru," *Journal of Inter-American Studies*, vol. 10 (Jan. 1967), pp. 85–94.

Thorp, Rosemary. "Inflation and Orthodox Economic Policy in Peru," *Bulletin of the Oxford University Institute of Economics and Statistics*, vol. 29 (Aug. 1967), pp. 185–210.

Tsiang, S. C. "An Experiment with a Flexible Exchange Rate System: The Case of Peru, 1950–1954," International Monetary Fund, staff papers, vol. 5 (Feb. 1957), pp. 449–476.

B. *Planning*

Reinafarje, Walter. "Un modelo de simulación para la economía del Perú," *Comercio Exterior* (Mexico City), vol. 23, no. 7 (1973), pp. 645–649.

Thorbecke, Eric. "Determination of Aggregate and Sectoral Growth Rates for Peru 1960–1970," *International Studies in Economics* (Iowa Peru Monograph no. 1), 1966.

———, and Condos, Apostolos. "Macroeconomic Growth and Development Models of the Peruvian Economy," in Irma Adelman and Eric Thorbecke (eds.), *The Theory and Design of Economic Development*. Baltimore: Johns Hopkins, 1966, pp. 181–208, with comment by Arthur Goldberger, pp. 208–209.

C. *Industry*

Chaplin, David. *The Peruvian Industrial Labor Force*. Princeton University Press, 1967.

Clague, Christopher. "An International Comparison of Industrial Efficiency: Peru and the United States," *Review of Economics and Statistics*, vol. 49 (Nov. 1967), pp. 487–493.

Roemer, Michael. *Fishing for Growth. Export-Led Development in Peru, 1950–1967*. Harvard University Press, 1967.

UN Economic Commission for Latin America. *The Industrial Development of Peru*. Mexico City: United Nations, 1959.

Vega-Centeno, Máximo. "El financiamento de la pequeña industria" (mimeo). Lima: CISEPA Serie de Documento de Trabajo no. 9.

Wils, Fritz. "La industria y los industriales en el área metropolitana de Lima-Callao" (mimeo). Lima: CISEPA, 1972.

D. *Agriculture*

Coutu, Arthur, and King, Richard. *The Agricultural Development of Peru*. New York: Praeger, 1969.

Fitchett, Delbert. "Agricultural Land Tenure Arrangements on the Northern Coast of Peru," *Inter-American Economic Affairs*, vol. 20 (Summer 1965), pp. 65–86.

Inter-American Committee for Agricultural Development (CIDA) *Tenencia de la tierra y desarrollo socio-económico del sector agrícola: Perú*. Washington: Pan American Union, 1966.

Van de Wetering, Hylke. "Agricultural Planning: The Peruvian Experience," in Eric Thorbecke, (ed.). *The Role of Agriculture in Economic Development*. New York: National Bureau for Economic Research, 1969.

E. Employment and Income Distribution

Hunt, Shane. "Distribution, Growth, and Government Economic Behavior in Peru," in Gustav Ranis (ed.), *Government and Economic Development*. Yale University Press, 1971, pp. 375–416, with comment by Daniel Schydlowsky, pp. 416–428.

Lewis, Robert A. "Employment, Income, and the Growth of the Barriadas in Lima, Peru," Cornell University Dissertation Series no. 46, May 1973.

Thorp, Rosemary. "A Note on Food Supplies, the Distribution of Income and National Income Accounting in Peru," *Bulletin of the Oxford University Institute of Economics and Statistics*, vol. 31 (Nov. 1969), pp. 229–241.

Webb, Richard. "The Distribution of Income in Peru," Princeton University Research Program in Economic Development, Discussion Paper no. 26, Sept. 1972 (mimeo).

———. "Tax Policy and the Incidence of Taxation in Peru," Princeton University Research Program in Economic Development. Discussion Paper no. 27, Sept. 1972 (mimeo).

———. "Trends in Real Income in Peru, 1950–1966," Princeton University, Research Program in Economic Development, Discussion Paper no. 41, Feb. 1974 (mimeo).

F. Sources

Key continuing publications for analyzing Peru's economy include:

Banco Central de Reserva del Perú, *Cuentas Nacionales del Perú*.

Perú. Oficina Nacional de Estadística y Censos [formerly Dirección Nacional de Estadística], *Anuario Estadístico del Perú*.

Perú. Superintendencia General de Aduanas, *Comercio Exterior del Perú*.

Perú. Ministerio de Agricultura, *Estadística Agraria Anual*.

Perú. Ministerio de Industria, *Evolución de la Industria Manufacturera Peruana*.

Other major sources include the quarterly *Report on the Economic Situation of Peru*, published by the Banco Continental; the periodic reports issued by the Ministerio de Economía y Finanzas, including the biennial budgets and the semiannual evaluation thereof, and also the frequent speeches the minister delivers; and the various documents released by the Instituto Nacional de Planificación. The reports on Peru by various international organizations are usually restricted, but one major source available to the public is José Guerra et al., *Current Economic Position and Prospects of Peru*, a report of the World Bank's 1973 mission to Peru (Washington, D.C., International Bank for Reconstruction and Development, 1973).

The annual volumes published by the Conferencia Anual de Ejecutivos (CADE) provide a quick introduction to the changing perspectives of Peru's business community.

VII. Bibliographic Studies

Three excellent bibliographic guides are available to facilitate further inquiry:

Herbold, Carl, Jr., and Stein, Steve. *Guía bibliográfica para la historia social y política del Perú en el siglo XX (1895–1960)*. Lima: Instituto de Estudios Peruanos, 1971, provides valuable annotations on salient sources for the study of twentieth-century Peru, up to 1960.

Matos Mar, José, and Ravines, Rogger. *Bibliografía peruana de ciencias sociales (1957–1969)*. Lima: Instituto de Estudios Peruanos, 1971, is fairly complete for the 1960s.

Martínez, Héctor; Cameo C., Miguel; and Ramírez, Jesús. *Bibliografía indígena andina peruana (1900–1968)*. Lima: Centro de Estudios de Población y Desarrollo, 1969, provides an excellent guide to Peru's anthropological literature.

There is no good bibliographic guide to Peru's economic history, but professors Shane Hunt (of Boston University) and

Pablo Macera (of San Marcos in Lima) are collaborating on one which will eventually be published by the Committee on Economic History of the Joint Committee on Latin American Studies (Social Science Research Council/American Council of Learned Societies).

VIII. KEEPING UP ON PERU

The quality of international press coverage, and of the Peruvian press, has always made it difficult to keep up with Peru from a distance. The following sources are suggested for those who wish to do research on Peru since 1968, but the difficulty of doing so is underlined by the fact that the first three publications listed have all been closed by the Peruvian regime since mid-1974.

Oiga. A weekly magazine, often opinionated, that provides a weekly overview of the news ("De viernes a viernes") and publishes many key speeches and documents.

Caretas. A biweekly magazine, often critical of the military regime (which has closed it from time to time). Publishes well-informed commentary in its "Mar de fondo" section, plus fairly frequent extensive interviews.

Andean Times (formerly the *Peruvian Times and Andean Mail*). A weekly English-language publication geared to the interests of the international business community. Excellent on the economy and includes frequent features on rural Peru.

Información Político-Mensual (DESCO). A monthly mimeographed summary of major news items, as reported in the Lima press.

Latin America. A weekly British journal which provides frequent, perceptive, but insufficiently sustained and not always accurate coverage of Peru.

Sociedad y Política, until it was closed by the military regime late in September, 1973, provided intelligent criticism from a Marxist perspective.

Participación, the regime's answer to *Sociedad y Política,* is a journal worth consulting.

The books, anthologies, and occasional papers published by the Instituto de Estudios Peruanos are almost uniformly worthwhile. Other Peruvian sources of social science literature are CISEPA (the social science research center of Pontifical Catholic

University of Peru) and DESCO, a Christian Democrat–oriented research and social action center.

Lima's leading daily newspapers—*El Comercio, La Prensa, Correo, Expreso,* and *La Nueva Crónica*—are useful, though not always illuminating or complete.

Index

Other Works in the Social Sciences Sponsored by the Center for Inter-American Relations

Latin America: The Search for a New International Role, ed. R. G. Hellman and H. Jon Rosenbaum, *Latin American International Affairs* series, volume I, Sages/Halsted, New York and Beverly Hills, California, 1975 (297 pp.)

Americas in a Changing World, Commission on U.S.-Latin American Relations, Quadrangle, New York, 1975 (248 pp.)

Ideology in Inter-American Politics, ed. Morris J. Blachman and R. G. Hellman, ISHI Press, Philadelphia, Pa., forthcoming Spring 1976 (300 pp.)

Coalition Government in Latin America: Essay on Political Economy in Colombia, ed. R. Albert Berry, R. G. Hellman, and Mauricio Solaun, Cyrco Press, Inc., New York, forthcoming Spring 1976 (320 pp.)

Library of Congress Cataloging in Publication Data
Main entry under title:

The Peruvian experiment.

Includes index.
1. Peru—Economic conditions—1918-   —Ad-
dresses, essays, lectures. 2. Peru—Economic
policy—Addresses, essays, lectures. 3. Peru—
Social conditions—Addresses, essays, lectures.
I. Lowenthal, Abraham F.
HC227.P42   338.985   75-2998
ISBN 0-691-07572-7